Panic in the Loop

Panic in the Loop

Chicago's Banking Crisis of 1932

Raymond B. Vickers

LEXINGTON BOOKS
Lanham • Boulder • New York • Toronto • Plymouth, UK

Published by Lexington Books
A wholly owned subsidary of Rowman & Littlefield
4501 Forbes Boulevard, Suite 200, Lanham, Maryland 20706
www.rowman.com

10 Thornbury Road, Plymouth PL6 7PP, United Kingdom

The hardback edition of this book was previously
cataloged by the Library of Congress as follows:

ISBN: 978-0-7391-6640-6 (cloth : alk.paper)
ISBN: 978-0-7391-6641-3 (pbk. : alk. paper)
ISBN: 978-0-7391-6642-0 (electronic)

British Library Cataloguing in Publication Information Available

Library of Congress Cataloging-in-Publication Data
Vickers, Raymond B., 1949-
  Panic in the loop : Chicago's banking crisis of 1932 / Raymond B. Vickers.
    p. cm.
  Includes bibliographical references and index.
  1. Bank failures—Illinois—Chicago—History—20th century. 2. Banks and banking—
Corrupt Practices—Illinois—Chicago—History—20th century. 3. Financial crises—
Illinois—Chicago—History—20th century. 4. Depressions—1929—Illinois—Chicago. I.
Title.
HG2613.C4V53 2011
322.1'223097731109043—dc23
                                                                        2011030551

⊖™ The paper used in this publication meets the minimum requirements of American
National Standard for Information Sciences—Permanence of Paper for Printed Library
Materials, ANSI/NISO Z39.48-1992.

Printed in the United States of America

For Sandee, Jane, Vic, and Chris

Contents

Introduction ix

Chapter 1 Insiders of Business and Banking:
Samuel Insull and Charles Dawes 1

Chapter 2 The Fall of Insull 47

Chapter 3 Insiders at the Reconstruction Finance Corporation 87

Chapter 4 Insider Abuse at the Dawes Bank 139

Chapter 5 Dawes Plays His Hand 181

Chapter 6 Playing the Young Card 213

Chapter 7 The Winners and Losers 239

Conclusion 267

Bibliographical Essay 285

Abbreviations Used in the Notes 303

Select Bibliography 307

Index 329

About the Author 347

Introduction

The time is coming when all business will have to be done with glass pockets.

—J. P. Morgan, 1913[1]

Chicago roared through the 1920s, while Prohibition made Scarface Al Capone the city's most colorful citizen. Still, during this period of lawlessness, the machine guns of Capone's gang proved less of a threat to society than the fountain pens of elite businessmen and bankers.[2]

Operating quietly in their wood-paneled boardrooms, the financial leaders wildly speculated with money unsuspecting stockholders, bondholders, and depositors entrusted to them. Because of the chicanery in the boardrooms, Chicago experienced a banking panic of historic proportions in the last two and a half weeks of June 1932. It resulted in the failure of forty-two banks. In each and every case, fraud and insider abuse crippled the banks that failed. Their officers and directors had engaged in illegal and unsound practices that encumbered every one of these banks with reckless loans and unsafe securities investments, which no prudent management should have made.

Significantly benefiting from the recklessness and deception of these bankers was Samuel Insull who was often the banks' largest customer and borrower. When his utility empire disintegrated, many of Chicago's most prominent banks also collapsed. Under such circumstances, these banks were not strong enough to withstand the downturns of the Depression. And the panic their collapse engendered dampened the business and household spending in the Chicago region, thereby exacerbating already depressed conditions.[3]

ix

Yet the collapse of major banks in Chicago was not a matter solely of mismanagement and fraud inside the financial institutions. Closely tied to this debacle were the cozy relationships that the bankers enjoyed with politicians and top regulators who benefited financially from the misconduct of the bankers. The bankers formed alliances and financed the public officials who promoted favorable government treatment of their interests. And the political interference compromised the work of state bank examiners who were appointees beholden to the leaders of the party in power.

On the federal level, the situation was much the same. No better example exists of the workings of "crony banking" than the behavior of officials of the Reconstruction Finance Corporation, which enormously benefited the interests of Charles G. Dawes. In the midst of the Chicago panic, the RFC authorized $90 million in government loans to bail out the Central Republic Bank and Trust Company of Chicago, a bank deeply enmeshed with Insull and his interests. The Central Republic Bank, which also received an additional $5 million in loans from the other four major banks in Chicago as part of the bailout package, was known as the Dawes bank. It was controlled by Dawes, the former vice president of the United States under Calvin Coolidge and a formidable insider in Illinois and national politics. What prompted criticism and controversy at the time was that Dawes had only resigned as president of the RFC less than two weeks before his former colleagues approved the unprecedented bailout package, which was worth about $1.5 billion in today's money. (Generally, dollar amounts from the early 1930s can be multiplied by 15 to get a sense of current value.)[4]

As the account that follows will demonstrate, the Hoover administration's $90 million in loans to the Dawes bank, which was hopelessly insolvent at the time, resulted from fraudulent behavior by Charles Dawes; self-interest on the part of his former colleagues on the RFC board; and political expediency by President Herbert Hoover. If the $90 million in government loans had been designed to stimulate the economy, they could have helped to salvage Hoover's presidency. Instead, the bailout became an embarrassment to the president because it was an unparalleled squandering of the government's limited resources. As it turned out, the bailout was among the largest ever authorized by the RFC in over two decades of operations (Congress abolished the corporation in 1953). To place the loan in context of the federal government's budget in 1929: only about $200 million was spent on construction projects.[5]

This book is more than a fresh look at three of the most prominent men in the first third of the twentieth century, Charles Dawes, Samuel Insull, and Jesse H. Jones. The study of these three men prompts a consideration of a profound issue of public policy in the United States at both the state and federal levels. In the Dawes bailout, the bailout of the Jones real estate and financial empire, and the attempted rescue of Insull's far-flung utility entities, there were complex schemes of self-dealing among private sector executives and public officials. The case studies presented here are not anomalies. Similar patterns of toxic behavior can be found in recent financial crises—the S&L crisis of the 1980s; the Enron fiasco and other comparable business failures during the late 1990s and early 2000s; and finally the financial meltdown of 2008. How then to cope with this troubling aspect of American public life—the capture of financial institutions and regulatory agencies for the primary benefit of high-paid executives? How does society trump the pattern of private sector executives, like Dawes and Jones, moving into public positions because of their supposed "expertise," and then, because of official secrecy, promoting their private interests over those of the public?

Over the years, Congress has passed legislation to slow the revolving door but to no effect. The Barack Obama administration issued rules limiting the hiring of former lobbyists to top policy positions. But exceptions were immediately made to the strictures. They were quickly superseded—on the day the rules on former lobbyists were announced—to allow the appointment of Mark Patterson as chief of staff of the Treasury Department. He was a former lobbyist for Goldman Sachs, one of the firms that brought about the Wall Street failure in the first place. Indeed, the U.S. Senate Permanent Subcommittee on Investigations, in April 2011, issued a bipartisan report declaring that "conflicts of interest" were at the "heart of the Wall Street crisis." The report revealed that "investment banks such as Goldman Sachs assembled toxic securities, misled the clients they sold them to, and then profited by betting against the very same investments they had sold to their clients."[6]

In January 2011, as he focused on his reelection campaign, Barack Obama named a new chief of staff of the White House: William M. Daley, the ultimate insider who was a senior executive for J. P. Morgan Chase & Co., which paid billions of dollars in fines and settlements to resolve criminal investigations and litigation resulting from the Enron and WorldCom scandals, and then taxpayers bailed it out after the 2008 fiasco. As part of the most powerful family of Chicago (his father and brother were longtime mayors of the city), Daley, a former Secretary of Commerce under Bill Clinton, was the co-chair of a lobbying group sponsored by the U.S. Chamber of Commerce which opposed real transparency and meaningful reform of the financial industry. As Obama's chief of staff, he will be in a key position to raise campaign contributions from Wall Street. During the 2008 campaign, Obama, whose wife Michelle was an assistant to Daley's brother, Mayor Richard M. Daley, raised more than \$24.6 million from the banking, finance, investment, and securities industries, not counting the contributions from lawyers and lobbyists representing those industries.[7]

Regulatory transparency would have a chilling effect on wily public officials who would breach their fiduciary duty to the public to favor the interests of the financial industry where they have made their careers and plan to return. To significantly lessen the impact of this powerful special interest, the actions of the regulators and policy makers must be revealed while they are still in public office. As a routine matter, state and federal banking regulators produce detailed reports about the financial health of banks and the behavior of their officials. State and federal laws prohibit public access to the invaluable information in the examination reports, letters, e-mails, and other regulatory records. Regulatory officials and executives in the financial industry strongly support the secret regulatory system, which continues behind closed doors despite the recently enacted "reforms," which reorganized the regulators and consolidated the consumer regulatory authority in the new Consumer Financial Protection Bureau.

But I have believed for four decades that regulatory transparency is the most effective way to rid the banking industry of insider abuse and fraud. During the 1970s, I witnessed at close range the power of the banking lobby when I served as Assistant Comptroller of Florida, the state's top appointed banking and securities regulator. In 1975, we ran into the wall of secrecy surrounding the banking industry when we tried to convince the Florida Legislature to pass the "Banking-in-the-Sunshine" bill which would have opened the state's regulatory system to public scrutiny. Then in the 1980s, when I represented, as an attorney, more than a hundred banks and S&Ls, I understood the need to release the secrets contained in the examination reports and other regulatory records. The wide-ranging research I conducted for *Panic in Paradise* and this book only strengthened my conviction of the need for transparency in the bank regulatory system.

Using a broad array of records not examined in previous studies, I was able to uncover why bank failures in Chicago reached epidemic proportions during June 1932 and to determine the complex political and financial maneuvering that led to the Dawes bailout. What is clear from the available public records is that the bankers, including the top officials of Chicago's three largest banks in the Loop (the downtown business district), verified, under oath, reports of conditions that were false and then published them in local newspapers. Fraudulent call reports listed the nonperforming and worthless loans at their full book values, thus avoiding the appearance of devastating decreases in the banks' capital. Hence, the depositors were deceived into leaving their savings in the custody of reckless and dishonest bankers.[8]

Regulators were far more interested in maintaining confidentiality about the troubled institutions than in forcing the resignations of their rogue officials, demanding the restoration of impaired capital, or appointing receivers for insolvent banks. So, while the regulators took little or no enforcement action, insiders quietly withdrew their own cash, as well as other depositors' money, in the form of unsecured loans or loans secured with worthless or severely deflated collateral, causing a liquidity crisis. Certainly the Depression significantly affected the banks of Chicago and Cook County. But the question has always remained: Why did forty-two Chicago and Cook County banks fail during the last two-and-a-half weeks of June 1932 while many others did not?[9]

My approach in researching this book was to review every aspect of the banks of Chicago and Cook County, along with the business and political activities of the men who controlled them in the 1930s. This is the first work to analyze federal banking records in conjunction with the receivership records of state banks, the records of the RFC, the bankruptcy and litigation records, both civil and criminal, and the probate records and private papers of the delinquent borrowers, stockholders, and officials of both the failed banks and the RFC. The federal bank examination reports expose extensive transactions between the national banks of Chicago and Cook County and their affiliated state banks, along with the insider abuses of the interlocking directors and their companies, many of which were forced to file for bankruptcy protection. The insights of the federal bank examiners illuminate the state liquidation records on file at the Cook County Courthouse.

Given that this is the first study to analyze the inextricably entwined records to determine why each national and state bank that failed in Chicago and Cook County during June 1932 did so, it is no surprise that my conclusions differ from those of previous studies, which proposed various theories to explain the bank failures based on incomplete or incorrect information. In a bibliographic essay at the end of the book, I discuss the relevant works about the banking crises of the 1930s.

Researching and writing a book about bank failures is difficult because as long as a bank survives, its regulatory records are permanently sealed and their confidentiality enforced with criminal penalties. Even *after* a bank fails, the secrecy continues for decades. The federal government's regulatory and liquidation records of a failed national bank remain confidential for fifty years after it closes. Thus, the federal records of a national bank that failed in 2010 will be sealed until the year 2060.[10]

State banking records are even less transparent. In forty-four states, the regulatory records of failed state banks have either been destroyed or permanently sealed. State archivists who have fought to preserve this "wealth of

economic history" have been no match for the powerful banking lobby. The
state of Washington, for example, suffered "a terrific loss" when its banking
regulators destroyed all of the state regulatory records from the 1920s and
1930s. After losing the disclosure and preservation fight, Sidney McAlpin,
the state archivist of Washington for three decades, said he had "never seen
such a successful lobbying effort to deny public access." After a careful review
of the examination reports and other regulatory records, he discovered that
"the only impact of disclosure would be to embarrass a lot of bank officials
regarding their loan policies and bank management." Failing to persuade state
regulators to release the records after "50 or 100 years," McAlpin concluded
that they are "scared of the industry they are regulating."[11]

Researchers can now gain access to the examination reports, correspondence, and other regulatory records of national banks that failed in the 1930s.
Rarely used, these records are a national treasure. Without using these primary source materials to analyze the assets of failed national banks, including their loans and securities portfolios and other investments, it is literally
impossible to determine why a particular national bank failed or the cause of
an affiliated state bank failure.[12]

Commercial bankers embraced secrecy during the New Deal, convincing
Congress that revealing the true condition of the nation's banks would cause
violent bank runs. Nonetheless, the Roosevelt administration adopted Louis
D. Brandeis's "money trust" argument about disclosure relating to the investment banking industry. Three weeks after having to proclaim a national banking holiday, President Roosevelt proposed that Congress pass the Securities
Act of 1933, which would open the investment banking industry to public
scrutiny. In making his case for the new law, he told Congress that since
the public had suffered significant losses "through practices neither ethical
nor honest," the federal government would have to mandate that the sale of
securities be "accompanied by full publicity and information, and that no
essentially important element attending the issue shall be concealed from the
buying public." The legislation he proposed would, he said, put "the burden of
telling the whole truth on the seller. It should give impetus to honest dealing
in securities and thereby bring back public confidence." Roosevelt emphasized that the law's purpose would be "to protect the public with the least
possible interference with honest business." Roosevelt went on to say, "What
we seek is a return to a clearer understanding of the ancient truth that those
who manage banks, corporations, and other agencies handling or using other
people's money are trustees acting for others."[13]

The president had asked his close friend, Felix Frankfurter, a professor
at Harvard Law School, for help in drafting the securities legislation, which
Congress subsequently passed. A few months later, Frankfurter wrote that the

new law was intended to operate "on the principle that when a corporation seeks funds from the public it becomes in every true sense a public corporation. Its affairs cease to be the private perquisite of its bankers and managers; its bankers and managers themselves become public functionaries."[14]

Despite the bank failures of the 1930s, secrecy about how commercial bankers managed their financial affairs and invested depositors' money had many advocates. One of the most ardent was Herbert Hoover. He blamed his Democratic opponents for forcing the publication of the names of the banks and the amounts of the loans they received from the RFC—the agency he heralded as the centerpiece of his economic recovery program—for causing runs on hundreds of banks and the subsequent failure of many of them. Hoover wrote in his memoirs that the limited disclosure of the RFC loans was "terribly dangerous . . . which was ultimately to contribute to more disaster." Since that time, Hoover's rationale for bank secrecy has become so embedded in our regulatory system that it could be regarded as one of his most enduring legacies.[15]

Although Hoover lost the 1932 election, the secrecy he supported continued unabated. Commercial bankers escaped disclosure during the 1930s, arguing to Congress and to the press, as Hoover had, that the publicity surrounding the RFC loans caused irrational depositor runs and bank failures. But this study will disprove that argument. Actually, the Dawes bank, where publicity stopped its depositor run, disavowed Hoover's theory that publication of the RFC loans "probably increased the number of bank failures" by spreading fear among depositors. Nevertheless, scholars, regulators, and bankers have agreed with Hoover's theory without credible evidence for the last eight decades. No doubt this theory of the virtues of secrecy has influenced Congress and state legislatures to erect a wall of secrecy around the federal and state bank regulatory systems, which are as confidential today as they were in 1932.

But the assumed relationship between transparency and bank runs is a false one. As Jesse Jones, the longtime head of the RFC, wrote in 1951 about his thirteen years at the agency, "Yes, the truth can hurt, but not as badly as uncertainty and fear." This study demonstrates that the banks in Chicago and Cook County in June 1932 did not fail because of transparency but rather because of the fraud and insider abuse that thrived in an atmosphere of secrecy.[16]

Undermining the secrecy theory is that the publication of the RFC's loans to thirty-five of the state and national banks of Chicago and Cook County that failed during the panic of June 1932 occurred on January 25, 1933, some seven months after the banks had closed. Since the RFC's loans remained a secret until after the banks closed, it cannot be argued with any credibility that adverse publicity about the receipt of government loans caused their failures.[17]

This study makes several contributions to ongoing scholarly and policy debates. It examines in detail one of the major bank panics of the early part of the 1930s, adding to our understanding of the origins and persistence of the Great Depression. It demonstrates the consequences of secrecy in regulation, revealing the tangled relationships between bankers, politicians, and regulators, many of whom had career paths that moved them through a revolving door that took them from the private to the public sectors and back again. In raising such questions about secrecy and the entwined interests of private and public sector officials, this study contributes to the ongoing debates about banking regulation and the policy discussions of what needs to be done to prevent the recurrence of the policy mistakes of the early 1930s, the S&L fiasco of the 1980s, the business failures of the Enron era, and the near collapse of the economy in 2008.

My research on the behavior of bankers, business leaders, and their political allies in Chicago shows the importance of the historian's attention to the way in which insiders behaved and the role that such behavior had on institutions, such as banks and systems of regulation. Economists and economic historians who have studied the banking crises of the early 1930s have not dealt in depth with the individuals and the banks they presided over. As a result, they have missed the issues of serious maladministration and fraud on the part of bankers and the failure of regulators to do their jobs, behavior abetted by secrecy and revolving doors.[18]

Another contribution of this study is to enhance our understanding of systemic flaws in banking regulation. The great regulatory failure was then, and remains today, a commitment to secrecy by state and national regulatory agencies about the performance of banks and the behavior of their officials. On the one hand, secrecy keeps from depositors, bondholders, and stockholders in banks a clear understanding of their operations. On the other, secrecy also keeps the public from grasping the failure of regulators in doing their jobs. Promoting transparency should be one of the most important aspects of the American regulatory tradition. Fundamentally, transparency reflects a belief in markets and the importance of accurate information for informed decisions by depositors, investors, and borrowers.[19]

In Chicago in the decades before the 1932 panic, there were exceedingly cozy relations among bankers, corporate executives, regulators, and politicians. Many of these men were responsible for the "panic in the Loop." Despite their standing in the community—in the case of Samuel Insull and Charles Dawes, their national celebrity—these men, at best, had questionable ethical standards, and, at worst, they engaged in fraud and other criminal behavior. What made "crony banking" possible in Chicago was the ineffectiveness of public oversight based on secrecy in banking regulation. Kept from the public were illuminating reports of federal and state regulators detailing the insolvent condition of banks and the imprudent and often illegal behavior of their officials who had raided the vaults of the banks in a desperate effort to save their own personal fortunes.

Insider abuse and fraud, regulatory failure, official secrecy, and a regular rotation of officials between the public and private sectors are still with us. These are the same ills that caused the epidemic of S&L failures during the 1980s and the collapse of Enron and WorldCom in the early 2000s. The two corporate failures led to the largest bankruptcies in American history up to that time and to monumental losses to stockholders, as well as loss of employment and pensions for a large number of employees. In the case of Enron, the frauds perpetrated by its management were facilitated by officials at two of the nation's major banks, Citicorp and Chase Manhattan. By assets, these two banks were part of the largest (Citigroup) and the second largest (J. P. Morgan Chase) financial institutions in the country. Had secret bank examiners reports—with their detailed analyses of the sham transactions and phony loans—been available to the public, such corporate catastrophes could have been avoided.

These banking and corporate scandals have led to lively, and lengthy, debates about what kind of policies government should follow to prevent such debacles in the future. In the case of the S&Ls, taxpayers bailed out the industry, and some of the worst offenders in the S&L scandal were prosecuted, with mixed results, as was the case in the 1930s.[20]

Much of the policy discussions prompted by the Enron collapse have been focused on issues of corporate governance. Because of the 2002 Sarbanes-Oxley legislation, chief executive officers and chief financial officers now must attest to the truth and accuracy of corporate financial reports, a requirement similar to the reporting requirements of state and national banks during the 1930s. In analyzing what went wrong at Enron, one leading legal scholar, John C. Coffee, has argued that the company's spectacular collapse resulted from what he calls the failure of corporate "gatekeepers," that is, auditors, attorneys, security analysts, and rating agencies. Coffee focuses on those who should help police corporate behavior from the perspective of the expertise of their professions. But the work of security analysts and rating agencies has been greatly diminished because they lack access to regulatory records.[21]

Clearly, many of the gatekeepers failed in their professional responsibilities in monitoring activities at Enron. The most well-known failure was that of the once distinguished accounting firm of Arthur Andersen, which ultimately went out of business because of the Enron fiasco. Merely improving the performance of the accountants and lawyers—without putting a spotlight on their clients—will not prevent future crises. They are paid far too much in fees by those they are supposed to be watching.

Regulators and other professionals fulfilling their fiduciary duties should have been forced to disclose the insider abuse that they saw recently and in the past. Had the Illinois and federal bank regulators not been compromised in the 1920s and 1930s, the panic in Chicago could have been averted. And had the gatekeepers not been compromised in the 1990s, the abuses at Enron could have been prevented. But we now know that in both periods of wildcat speculation, far too many unscrupulous bankers and corporate executives unduly influenced their regulators and gatekeepers. Unfortunately, the rewards of remaining silent and the competition among the gatekeepers are far too great to expect lawyers and auditors to blow the whistle on their clients.

The Wall Street fiasco of 2008 was yet again the failure of the public and private regulatory systems. Regulators, accountants, attorneys, and ratings agencies failed to live up to their responsibilities to investors as "crony banking" played a major part in the current crisis. There were cozy, mutually beneficial relationships among bankers, politicians, lobbyists, regulators, and academics that led to public policies that weakened existing regulation and kept off limits to regulators some aspects of "innovative" finance—mortgage-based derivatives and credit default swaps. The regulation that existed suffered from the same fate of regulation in other periods: secrecy that kept vital information about the behavior of management and the performance of institutions from investors.

Aggravating the secrecy in the run-up to the 2008 crisis was the failure to regulate entire aspects of investment banking. Wall Street financed key members of Congress and then enjoyed immunity from regulation of the marketing of derivatives based on sub-prime mortgages. Complicit in limiting and preventing regulation were prominent academics extolling the notion that markets were self-regulating in what they called the "efficient market theory."[22]

If, as they argued, markets assessed risks accurately and established prices reflecting risk, there was no need for regulation. But without regulation, there was no chance of public access to information about the behavior of the top officials of the institutions at the heart of American finance. From the perspective of the irresponsible and reckless investment bankers, their academic apologists provided cover for their activities, which were sealed from public scrutiny.[23]

Preventing regulation was in large part a result of the persistent problem of the revolving door between the public and private sectors in the years leading up to September 2008. Wall Street executives occupied central positions at the top level of economic policy-making in the administrations of Bill Clinton, George Bush, and Barack Obama. Two secretaries of the Treasury (Robert E. Rubin under Clinton and Henry M. Paulson under Bush) headed Goldman Sachs before taking their cabinet positions. When Rubin left the Treasury, he became a board member, consultant, and eventually chairman for a brief stint at Citigroup, which was one of the two most troubled banks following the 2008 meltdown. Many other officials of those three administrations had strong ties to Wall Street firms before they rotated into government and then back to the private sector.

According to the majority report of the Financial Crisis Inquiry Commission, Rubin and his successor at the Treasury, the economist Lawrence H. Summers, joined hands, along with Alan Greenspan and SEC Chairman Arthur Levitt, who later became an advisor to Goldman Sachs, to prevent the regulation of derivatives, a lucrative business for Goldman Sachs and other investment banks. But the widespread use of derivatives, unregulated and left to the reckless behavior of investment and commercial bankers, was a major cause of the 2008 debacle that crippled the international financial system and brought about the worst recession since the 1930s.[24]

The majority report of the financial crisis commission concluded, in January 2011, after an in depth investigation of the "financial upheaval":

> The crisis reached seismic proportions in September 2008 with the failure of Lehman Brothers and the impending collapse of the insurance giant American International Group (AIG). Panic fanned by a lack of transparency of the balance sheets of major financial institutions, coupled with a tangle of interconnections among institutions perceived to be "too big to fail," caused the credit markets to seize up. Trading ground to a halt. The stock market plummeted. The economy plunged into a deep recession.[25]

To oppose the need for regulation altogether and transparency in the regulatory agencies ignores a well-established tradition. Louis Brandeis, whom historian Thomas McCraw described as a "prophet of regulation," was way ahead of his time when he called for full disclosure in his 1914 book, *Other People's Money and How the Bankers Use It*: "Sunlight is said to be the best of disinfectants; electric light the most efficient policeman." Any regulatory system would fail, Brandeis argued, if it denied public access to financial information and relied solely on the government to process and interpret what its regulators found about the behavior of those regulated. He called for "real disclosure" to reveal banking activities to the public. The publicity would create an informed consent similar to the labeling requirements of the Pure

Food Law. But nearly a century has passed, and the federal and state bank regulatory systems are still in desperate need of a complete overhaul, with transparency, not secrecy, as their basis.[26]

OVERVIEW OF THE BOOK

Chapter 1 looks in detail at the two Chicago business and banking leaders (Insull and Dawes) who were at the center of the Chicago banking panic in 1932, which led to the Dawes loans from the RFC. Chapter 2 focuses on the decisions and actions of Samuel Insull that led to the collapse of his companies, contributing greatly to the Chicago banking panic. In chapter 3, I examine the cozy relationships among Charles Dawes, Jesse Jones, and the other top officials at the RFC who were also powerful insiders in the nation's banking community and political establishment during the 1930s. Chapter 4 details the insider abuse at the Dawes bank and how that triggered the panic and the RFC's bailout of the bank. In chapter 5, I reveal the machinations at the RFC that cleared the way for the unprecedented loans that saved the fortune of Dawes, the recent head of the RFC. Chapter 6 is a detailed account of the role Owen Young of General Electric played in helping Dawes achieve his audacious objectives at the RFC. Chapter 7 examines how Insull failed and how, in contrast, Dawes and his associates triumphed because of the massive government bailout. The conclusion discusses the entire account and suggests its importance to understanding the Great Depression and the still unmet need to open the banking and financial regulatory system.

Notes

1. J. P. Morgan made the comment just before his death in 1913, after being grilled publicly by Samuel Untermyer during the Pujo Committee investigation of the investment banking industry. See Vincent P. Carosso, *Investment Banking in America: A History* (Cambridge, Mass.: Harvard University Press, 1970), 137–55.

2. Josephine Young Case and Everett Needham Case, *Owen D. Young and American Enterprise: A Biography* (Boston: David R. Godine, 1982), 612–14; *Stock Exchange Practices: Hearings before a Subcommittee of the Committee on Banking and Currency, United States Senate, Seventy-Second Congress, Second Session, on S. Res. 84 and S. Res. 239, Resolutions to Thoroughly Investigate Practices of Stock Exchanges with Respect to the Buying and Selling and the Borrowing and Lending of Listed Securities the Values of Such Securities and the Effects of Such Practices. Part 5 (Insull), February 15, 16, and 17, 1933* (Washington, D.C.: Government Printing Office, 1933), 1698–1703.

3. See the bank examination reports, correspondence, and other regulatory records of failed Chicago national banks in USOCC/WNRC. Also see the receivership records of the failed state banks in the Cook County Courthouse. "The Loss of Owen D. Young," *Nation*, January 4, 1933, 4. For discussions of Prohibition and politics in Chicago during the 1920s, see Alex Gottfried, *Boss Cermak of Chicago: A Study of Political Leadership* (Seattle: University of Washington Press, 1962), 102, 115–16, 140–42, 319; Dennis E. Hoffman, *Scarface Al and the Crime Crusaders: Chicago's Private War against Capone* (Carbondale: Southern Illinois University Press, 1993), xi, 2, 3, 5, 7–33; Finis Farr, *Chicago: A Personal History of America's Most American City* (New Rochelle, N.Y.: Arlington House, 1973), 345–55.

4. The bank loans of $5 million that the Dawes bank received as part of the bailout package would be worth about $78.5 million today. The value of the RFC loans and bank loans to the Dawes bank in today's dollars was computed by using the consumer price index. See Samuel H. Williamson, "What Is the Relative Value? Seven Ways to Compute the Relative Value of a U.S. Dollar Amount, 1774 to Present," Measuring Worth, April 2010.

5. For a good discussion of the federal government's role in the economy in the Hoover years, see Maury Klein, *Rainbow's End: The Crash of 1929* (New York: Oxford University Press, 2001), 245–46. Klein points out that overall the federal government was much smaller then than now. Federal expenditures represented a mere 2.5 percent of the Gross National Product; in 1990 it was 22 percent. Also see Susan Estabrook Kennedy, *The Banking Crisis of 1933* (Lexington: University Press of Kentucky, 1973), 40–42.

6. "Mark Patterson," WhoRunsGov.com, *Washington Post*; "Geithner Names Ex-lobbyist as Treasury Chief of Staff," *USA Today,* January 27, 2009. For a discussion of Goldman Sachs alumni working at federal financial and banking policy posts, see "The Guys from Government Sachs," Business Section, *New York Times,* October 17, 2008; *Wall Street and the Financial Crisis: Anatomy of a Financial Collapse*, Majority and Minority Staff Report, Permanent Subcommittee on Investigations, U.S. Senate, April 13, 2011, www.hsgac.senate.gov.; "Bipartisan Report Reveals Conflicts of Interest at Heart of Wall Street Crisis," Press Release, U.S. Senator Carl Levin, April 15, 2011.

7. See presidential campaign contributions to Barack Obama from industries in 2008 at the Center for Responsive Politics, OpenSecrets.org; *Restoring Confidence in the U.S. Capital Markets: A Call for Financial Services Regulatory Modernization*, Center for Capital Markets Competitiveness, U.S. Chamber of Commerce, Washington, D.C., March 11, 2009; "William Daley," WhoRunsGov.com, *Washington Post*; Carrie Johnson, "Settlement in Enron Lawsuit for Chase, *Washington Post*, June 15, 2005.

8. See the requirement in the Illinois banking law that each bank file call reports with the state auditor of public accounts detailing their assets and liabilities, which were verified by the president or cashier of the bank and were published in the local newspaper where the bank was located. *Banking Law State of Illinois*, Section 7; Oscar Nelson, Auditor of Public Accounts, comp., *Statement Showing Total Resources*

and Liabilities of Illinois State Banks, June 30, 1932 (Springfield, Ill.: Journal Printing Company, 1932); Elmus Wicker, *The Banking Panics of the Great Depression* (New York: Cambridge University Press, 2000), 110–16; Joseph Russell Mason, "The Determinants and Effects of Reconstruction Finance Corporation Assistance to Banks during the Great Depression" (Ph.D. diss., University of Illinois, Urbana-Champaign, 1996), 76–83; Milton Esbitt, "Bank Portfolios and Bank Failures during the Great Depression: Chicago," *Journal of Economic History* 46 (June 1986): 455–62; Lee J. Alston, Wayne A. Grove, and David C. Wheelock, "Why Do Banks Fail? Evidence from the 1920s," *Explorations in Economic History* 31 (1994): 409–31.

9. Esbitt, "Bank Portfolios and Bank Failures during the Great Depression," 455–56.

10. Raymond B. Vickers, *Panic in Paradise: Florida's Banking Crash of 1926* (Tuscaloosa: University of Alabama Press, 1994), xi–xiv. See *Guide to the National Archives of the United States* (Washington, D.C.: National Archives and Records Administration, 1987), 161.

11. R. D. Jones, Assistant Supervisor of Banking of Washington, to author, July 9, 1991; Tom Ruller, Alabama Department of Archives and History, to Sidney F. McAlpin, Washington State Archivist, April 30, 1987; Zack Thompson, Alabama Superintendent of Banks, to author, July 10, 1991.

12. In 1966, the historian Joel A. Tarr acknowledged that the examiner's reports of national banks "formed an indispensable source for [his] article. They include lists of bank officers, stockholders, bank holdings, and outstanding loans." But Tarr complained about the secrecy surrounding the government records: "Unfortunately, while the writer was engaged in his research, the comptroller increased the restriction on the use of his records from fifty to seventy-five years." Joel A. Tarr, "J. R. Walsh of Chicago: A Case Study in Banking and Politics, 1881–1905," *Business History Review* 40, no. 4 (Winter 1966): 452–53.

13. Franklin D. Roosevelt, *The Public Papers and Addresses of Franklin D. Roosevelt*, edited by Samuel Rosenman (New York: Random House, 1938), 2:24–29, 48, 93–94; Thomas K. McCraw, *The Prophets of Regulation* (Cambridge, Mass.: Harvard University Press, 1984), 1–25, 112–14; Louis D. Brandeis, *Other People's Money and How the Bankers Use It* (New York: Frederick A. Stokes Company, 1932), 92–108; Louis D. Brandeis, *Other People's Money and How the Bankers Use It*, edited by Melvin I. Urofsky (Boston: Bedford Books of St. Martin's Press, 1995), iii, v, vi, 1–35, 150–56; Vincent P. Carosso, *The Morgans: Private International Bankers, 1854–1913* (Cambridge, Mass.: Harvard University Press, 1987), 639–40; Carosso, *Investment Banking in America*, 137–55; Charles H. Hession and Hyman Sardy, *Ascent to Affluence: A History of American Economic Development* (Boston: Allyn and Bacon, 1969), 717; James J. White, *Teaching Materials on Banking Law* (St. Paul, Minn.: West Publishing, 1976), 80–82.

14. Orange County Trust Company, Middletown, New York, to Franklin D. Roosevelt, n.d. (telegram); C. H. Plenty to Roosevelt, April 18, 1933 (telegram); J. A. Broderick to Marguerite Le Hand, May 1, 1933 (telegram); William H. Kelly to Roosevelt, April 25, 1933 (telegram); William S. Irish to Roosevelt, May 1, 1933;

R. H. Barber to Roosevelt, May 9, 1933; Elmer F. Seabury to Roosevelt, May 18, 1933; Adolph Rado to Roosevelt, March 16, 1933, all in RFC Collection, FDRP/ FDRL; Carosso, *Investment Banking in America*, 353.

15. Herbert Hoover, *The Memoirs of Herbert Hoover: The Great Depression 1929–1941* (New York: Macmillan, 1952), 110–11; Roosevelt, *Public Papers and Addresses*, 24–29, 48, 93–94; James Ring Adams, *The Big Fix* (New York: John Wiley & Sons, 1990), 6.

16. Cyril B. Upham and Edwin Lamke, *Closed and Distressed Banks: A Study in Public Administration* (Washington, D.C.: Brookings Institution Press, 1934), 155–56; Jesse H. Jones, with Edward Angly, *Fifty Billion Dollars: My Thirteen Years with the RFC (1932–1945)* (New York: Macmillan, 1951), 87; Paul M. Horvitz, "Financial Disclosure: Is More Always Better?" *Journal of Retail Banking Services* 18, no. 4 (1996): 58.

17. Richard H. Keehn and Gene Smiley, "U.S. Bank Failures, 1932–1933: A Provisional Analysis," *Essays in Economic and Business History* 6 (1988): 136–56; Richard H. Keehn and Gene Smiley, "U.S. Bank Failures, 1932–1933: Additional Evidence on Regional Patterns, Timing, and the Role of the Reconstruction Finance Corporation," *Essays in Economic and Business History* 11 (1993): 131–42; Milton Friedman and Anna Jacobson Schwartz, *A Monetary History of the United States: 1867–1960* (Princeton, N.J.: Princeton University Press, 1963), 325; Jones, *Fifty Billion Dollars*, 82; James L. Butkiewicz, "The Impact of a Lender of Last Resort during the Great Depression: The Case of the Reconstruction Finance Corporation," *Explorations in Economic History* 32, no. 2 (1995): 197–201, 207–10, 214; Vickers, *Panic in Paradise*, xi–xiv; Mark Anthony Guglielmo, "Illinois State Bank Failures in the Great Depression" (Ph.D. diss., University of Chicago, 1998), 44–62.

18. For a broad cultural approach to the collapse in 1929 and the subsequent depression, see Maury Klein's *Rainbow's End*. In the introduction to his book, Klein sees the crash as part of an optimism born of unprecedented prosperity created in part by the material comforts brought about for many by new technologies and by an enchantment with the idea that the 1920s were a "new era" where many of the old rules of personal, financial, and business behavior did not seem to apply. This is not the whole of Klein's analysis because his work spends much time on the misbehavior of leading figures on Wall Street and in corporate America, men responsible for the stock market boom and bust. They were the individuals who profited because they offered the margin loans that stoked stock market speculation. Their investment trusts and holding companies produced the new stocks that stimulated the appetite for new investors to plunge into the market. The stock market collapse over the last week of October 1929 brought an end to the optimistic world view of much of the public. Some of those responsible for the stock market debacle were themselves ruined financially and personally. But many remained unbowed, exhibiting little understanding or acceptance of their role in the collapse. Few of those responsible for the worst behavior of the time showed any remorse. My account has similar findings for those most responsible for the banking panic in Chicago in June 1932.

19. For reviews of the American regulatory tradition, see Thomas McCraw's *Prophets of Regulation*, and Richard H. K. Vietor, *Contrived Competition: Regulation and Deregulation in America* (Cambridge, Mass: Belknap Press of Harvard University Press, 1994).

20. Lawrence J. White, *The S&L Debacle: Public Policy Lessons for Bank and Thrift Regulation* (New York: Oxford University Press, 1991), 193–96.

21. John C. Coffee, *Gatekeepers: The Role of the Professions in Corporate Governance*, Clarendon Lectures in Management Studies (New York: Oxford University Press, 2006).

22. For a good discussion of what the author calls "the efficient market fallacy," see George Cooper, *The Origin of Financial Crises: Central Banks, Credit Bubbles, and the Efficient Market Fallacy* (New York: Vintage Books, 2008); "Financial Crisis Inquiry Commission Releases Report on the Causes of the Financial Crisis," January 27, 2011, www.fcic.gov; *The Financial Crisis Inquiry Report*, Financial Crisis Inquiry Commission (Washington, D.C.: Government Printing Office, January 2011), xv–xxviii.

23. Roger Thompson, "'Too Big to Fail': Reining in Large Financial Firms," Harvard Business School Working Knowledge, June 22, 2009, http:/hbswk.hbs.edu/item/6230.html.

24. Rick Schmitt, "Prophet and Loss," *Stanford Magazine,* March/April 2009, on the failed effort of Brooksley Born, the head of the Commodities Futures Trading Commission, to regulate derivatives; *The Financial Crisis Inquiry Report*, xv–xxviii, 47–49; "Levitt to Advise Goldman Sachs," *New York Times*, June 2, 2009.

25. *The Financial Crisis Inquiry Report*, xv, xvi.

26. McCraw, *Prophets of Regulation*, 1–25; Brandeis, *Other People's Money and How the Bankers Use It*, 89–96.

Chapter 1

Insiders of Business and Banking: Samuel Insull and Charles Dawes

Owen Young: I believe Mr. Samuel Insull was very largely the victim of that complicated structure, which got even beyond his power, competent as he was, to understand it.
Senator Smith W. Brookhart: Although he created it himself?[1]

"Charles G. Dawes's part in the Lorimer bank swindle makes it impossible for honest citizens to vote for him as the Republican vice presidential nominee."

—Moses E. Clapp, former Republican senator, 1924[2]

Electricity transformed the United States in the early decades of the twentieth century. While it changed the way industry worked and people lived, it also made many of those associated with electricity's "magic" into the wealthiest men in the country. None who brought electricity into factories, transportation, offices, and homes profited more handsomely than Samuel Insull. Beginning in the late nineteenth century, Insull's strategy utilized vast amounts of capital to create large holding companies. In doing so, Insull put together regional companies to produce and distribute electricity and natural gas. Because of the antitrust laws, holding companies were the device of choice for those wishing to gain market share and monopoly positions.

In addition to amassing a significant fortune, Insull became a leading figure in Chicago as, among other things, a supporter of the arts, especially opera. He was the driving force behind the building of Chicago's Civic Opera House. His fame, wealth, and connections to business, banking, and political leaders made him one of the most influential people in the city.

1

Image 1.1. Samuel Insull, the "emperor" of Chicago, controlled a utility empire with assets of $3 billion in depression-era dollars. (Courtesy, Loyola University Chicago Archives)

Charles Dawes was an equally important figure in Chicago and on the national scene. Early in his career, at the age of 31, he served as comptroller of the currency, who had overall responsibility for chartering and regulating national banks. He distinguished himself during World War I as head of the General Purchasing Board, representing the U.S. Army on the Military Board of Allied Supply in Paris, where he exhibited strong organizational skills and an ability to work with foreign officials. Following the war, President Warren G. Harding appointed Dawes as the first director of the budget. He then gained an international reputation as head of the American delegation to an international reparations committee of experts to resolve the dispute that erupted when Germany failed to pay reparations at the end of World War I. Because Germany had defaulted on its payments, France occupied the Ruhr, the center of the German coal, iron, and steel industries. The plan that bore Dawes's name led to the removal of French troops from the Ruhr, along with

Image 1.2. Charles Dawes (right), the U.S. Vice-President under Calvin Coolidge (left), abused his position as president of the Reconstruction Finance Corporation and committed fraud to survive the Chicago banking panic of 1932. (Courtesy, Library of Congress)

a new schedule of reparations payments, so Dawes was awarded a share of the Nobel Peace Prize. He was then invited to be Calvin Coolidge's vice-presidential running mate in 1924. After serving in that post, he later became U.S. Ambassador to Great Britain under President Hoover. And then in 1932, Hoover appointed him as the head of the Reconstruction Finance Corporation, the centerpiece of the administration's effort to cope with the deepening consequences of the 1929 stock market collapse.

Dawes became a celebrity following a more traditional political and public-service path. He was not an original thinker nor particularly self-reflective. As with many professional politicians, he could be counted on to espouse the conventional wisdom of his party at the time. Nor was he unusual in that as he gained political fame and occupied important government positions, he also amassed a personal fortune. Without apparent qualms, he used political party contacts and official appointments to build his wealth through banking and investments in utilities. Dawes and Insull found the other useful for their own purposes, forming a strategic alliance between the utility empire builder and the political banker.

SAMUEL INSULL

During the 1920s and early 1930s, the press dubbed Samuel Insull as "the emperor" of Chicago for good reason. He was the head of a public utility monopoly providing gas and electricity to 4,500,000 customers. His empire was financed by 600,000 stockholders and 500,000 bondholders whose savings had purchased utility assets valued at approximately $3 billion in Depression-era dollars ($47.1 billion in today's dollars), all of which Insull personally controlled. Before the stock market crashed in 1929, his personal fortune had reached $150 million on paper (a net worth about $1.88 billion today). By 1932, Insull was a dapper, white-haired man with a full mustache and pince-nez glasses. He smoked a dozen cigars a day and was fond of telling people that "the first million was the hardest. After I got that the rest was easy."[3]

After the stock market crash of 1929, Insull's fortune and reputation suffered. Insull's larger-than-life persona was all-important when he was selling the stocks and bonds of his companies, but as the prices of the publicly traded securities plummeted, so did his public image. When condemnation replaced praise, Insull began receiving so many death threats that he feared assassination and hired armed bodyguards to protect him and his family. He drove through the streets of Chicago in a heavily armored Cadillac, complete with one-inch-thick bullet-proof windows.[4]

Insull, who had begun his career modestly enough on the ground floor of the electrical business, could not have imagined how fierce the wind would be blowing at the top when he was the most influential leader in the industry. Born in London in 1859, he immigrated to America in 1881 at the age of 21. Having worked for a couple of years as secretary to Thomas A. Edison's agent in London, Insull was hired as Edison's private secretary in New York City. Edison's biographer and confidant, Alfred O. Tate, depicted Insull during this period as a handsome young man with a "winning smile" and "graceful manner," which would facilitate his dealings with the financial leaders of New York. Standing only five feet three inches and weighing 117 pounds, Insull possessed a steel-trap mind and boundless energy, both of which would serve him well as he worked alongside the already famous inventor, who was only thirty-four years old.

For the dozen or so years when Edison was developing the nascent electric lighting industry, Insull was his right-hand man. When the time came,

Edison put him in charge of marketing electric plants throughout the United States and Canada. To arrange franchises from city governments, Insull often engaged in illegal forms of influence peddling to persuade corrupt local officials of the wisdom of issuing an electric utility franchise. However arrived at, it was his success on the road that brought him increasing influence in the Edison organization. And the crude lessons Insull learned as he arranged "personal, extralegal" deals for corrupt politicians would later be used to expand his Chicago empire.[5]

When Edison's various companies merged into the Edison General Electric Company in 1889, Insull's role expanded as he became a vice president and a member of its board of directors. In 1892, Drexel, Morgan and Company—Edison's banker, whose partners were minority stockholders in his company—financed the organization of the General Electric Company (GE). This fifty-million-dollar transaction was the result of combining Edison's company with the Thomson-Houston Electric Company of Lynn, Massachusetts, each by then a major manufacturer of electrical equipment. But it was the Edison Company's rapid expansion that led to $3.5 million of short-term debt, forcing it to merge into GE. Insull had arranged the financing, which was a foreshadowing of what would happen to his own companies forty years later when they collapsed under the weight of colossal debt.

After Edison lost control of his company, Insull, who had supported the merger, became the second vice president of the newly consolidated company, with a significant salary of thirty-six thousand dollars a year. Yet the ambitious thirty-two-year-old soon decided to resign his post—even though he was the third-ranking officer of a major manufacturing concern—to accept the presidency of the Chicago Edison Company. This was a relatively small electric generating company, which had been operating for five years as one of thirty central station companies providing Chicago with electricity. His annual salary was only twelve thousand dollars, but as part of his compensation package Marshall Field, the founder of the department stores and a director of Chicago Edison, loaned him $250,000 to purchase stock in the company, an enticement that made his new position much more attractive.[6]

Adding to the allure of the small but powerful company was the involvement of Robert Todd Lincoln, the son of Abraham Lincoln, whose law firm represented Chicago Edison. Lincoln was serving as Benjamin Harrison's Minister to the Court of St. James in London, but he would become the vice president of Chicago Edison and an active member of its board of directors upon his return to Chicago in 1893. Lincoln, whose law firm also represented Marshall Field, had served as Secretary of War in the administrations of James Garfield and Chester Arthur.[7]

Insull had clearly given this move considerable thought, in part because Edison had once told him that Chicago had the potential to become a major electric market. Its population (including that of suburban Cook County) of more than 1.2 million had at that time fewer than five thousand consumers of electricity. Insull's goal was to monopolize the electric generating business in the region. Insull saw a monopolistic position as necessary to rationalize and make more efficient the production of electricity. He planned to expand and construct new central stations, acquire competitors and their franchises, and aggressively market his product with the goal of having his company supply every home in the Chicago metropolitan area with electricity. Implementing his strategic plan, Insull built an empire acquiring twenty-four entities for a total cost of $5,330,000—about $142 million today—during the depression years of 1893 to 1898, the year Insull was elected president of the National Electric Light Association. Following the Panic of 1893, Insull's audacious expansion loaded his utility business with debt, along with the intangible but worthless asset of goodwill, during the difficult economic period, thus making it more challenging to raise equity, which was already difficult because of the depressed conditions. In a capital-intensive business, more than half of the acquisition cost, a sum of $2,812,500, was attributable to goodwill, representing the premiums that Insull paid above the book values of the companies. So eager was Insull to expand market share that he paid exorbitant prices even for small companies with obsolete equipment.[8]

Insull was prepared to do whatever it took to realize his goal, so he paid a thinly disguised bribe of between $50,000 and $170,000 to a bipartisan faction of aldermen on the Chicago City Council for a shell corporation they had created named the Commonwealth Electric Company. The "Gray Wolves," as these wily and corrupt aldermen were known, had formed this company only on paper and granted it a fifty-year franchise to provide electric service for the city of Chicago specifically as a way to shake down Insull. Though Insull was holding the exclusive rights to buy electrical equipment in Chicago, he paid the Gray Wolves an amount worth today between $1.2 million and $4.1 million. After the more than significant payoff, Insull's Chicago Edison was operating in the downtown Loop, and his Commonwealth Electric was operating in the other areas of Chicago. With the rest of his recently acquired companies operating in the surrounding residential areas, Insull was determined to control the electrical services throughout the metropolis.[9]

By the turn of the century, Insull was positioned to become the most powerful utility executive in Chicago. But it took him another decade to gain the upper hand over the gas companies, which still dominated the artificial lighting market with an 80 percent share. He preached the "gospel of consumption," which consisted of an innovative rate-making structure that reduced rates by one-third for residential users. Insull also instructed his salesmen to offer free wiring of lighting outlets and discounts to new customers. To finance the expansion, he created long-term bonds secured with open-ended mortgages on his plant facilities. By 1932, he had issued $500 million worth of these mortgage-backed bonds.[10]

Between 1902 and 1911, Insull aggressively expanded his energy operations in suburban Cook County and along the North Shore of Lake Michigan into Lake County, both of which were experiencing rapid increases in their populations. Using the North Shore Electric Company as his corporate entity, he acquired fourteen electric and gas companies. It was a shrewd move since gas companies were providing more and more of their product for household cooking and heating.

In 1907, Insull combined the Chicago Edison Company with the Commonwealth Electric Company to form the Commonwealth Edison Company. The franchise of the new company would expire in 1947, so it issued long-term utility bonds maturing over the next four decades. Insull's empire building attracted competitors, and he proved that he was a fierce competitor. In 1909, Charles A. Coffin, then the president of GE, informed Insull that the Westinghouse Electric and Manufacturing Company, a large manufacturer of electrical equipment, was trying to make inroads into the Chicago market. Westinghouse planned to sell electrical equipment to the Chicago Railways Company. Insull became agitated at the prospect of Westinghouse "butting in" on his territory. He had learned from another source that Westinghouse was "intent on raiding our property," constructing its own electrical generating plant and cutting prices to below its costs until it got the business. He told Coffin that "the proper thing for me to do is to serve the Westinghouse Company with notice that they should keep their hands off our business. I am inclined to think that it has got beyond the diplomatic stage. It has got to a place where we are suffering from the disadvantage of a kind of guerilla warfare without the advantage of a plainspoken actual declaration of hostilities."

Insull was threatening to warn the membership of the National Electric Light Convention that Westinghouse was going to raid their territories. Coffin questioned whether it was in Insull's best interests to threaten Westinghouse directly. He suggested that Insull should tell his colleagues about notorious Westinghouse acts of "treachery" such as its selling generating equipment to the competitors of its existing customers. Since Insull bought most of his equipment from GE and none from Westinghouse, Coffin assured him that "the General Electric Company would go to any reasonable length and do everything possible to prevent the encroachment of the Westinghouse

Company upon your field in any way. You may depend upon our doing every-thing we can to strengthen your hands."[11]

While holding Westinghouse at bay, Insull doubled electrical consumption in the Chicago area. He quickly negotiated contracts with the Chicago City Railway Company and the other solvent transit companies. These contracts provided collateral for bank loans and facilitated his expansion program. During each of his first five years as head of Chicago Edison, Insull had increased the capacity of his central generating stations by an average of 49,000 light bulbs. That number would accelerate to an average of 200,000 incandescent lights added to his system during each of the following five years.

Though electric lighting remained a luxury for most people, Insull's rate-cutting and marketing tactics had nonetheless resulted in the wiring of almost 80,000 homes by 1912, when the combined population of Chicago and Cook County had grown to more than 2.4 million people, and his utilities system was servicing a total of 239,000 consumers, a number that would grow to more than 500,000 by 1917. Still unsatisfied, Insull began acquiring gas and water concerns and transportation companies. He merged the North Shore Electric Company and four other utility groups, comprising thirty-nine enti-ties, into the Public Service Company of Northern Illinois, a holding com-pany that combined ownership and management control of the five operating entities. This new company provided gas, water, and railway services to 96 communities with a total population of 302,409, including 36,040 electric customers.[12]

In 1912, Insull formed the Middle West Utilities Company—a Delaware holding company—to purchase utility properties, particularly in smaller com-munities. By the time it went into receivership on April 15, 1932, Middle West owned more than a hundred companies operating in 5,321 communities. To support its extensive operations, by 1932 the company had raised equity of $596 million from nearly 100,000 stockholders. But it also had outstanding bonds of $653 million and tens of millions of dollars of bank debt.[13]

Insull's constantly expanding system required heretofore unimaginable amounts of debt. His financing skills were tested in the summer and fall of 1914 after the collapse of the LaSalle Street Trust and Savings Bank and its affiliated banks, which sparked a panic and caused a regional depression in Chicago. William Lorimer, the boss of Cook County and the Illinois Repub-lican Party, controlled the banking chain. During the ensuing crisis, the Chicago stock exchanges closed and the surviving banks—unlike Lorimer's banks—received regulatory scrutiny, making commercial loans difficult to obtain. Even if a company was able to secure a bank loan, the interest rates were high, 7 to 8 percent, and sometimes even higher. The bond houses also stopped issuing commercial bonds or any other debt instruments. Insull's response was to cut expenses at all of his entities. On September 15, 1914, he confidentially reported on the "tense business situation" to William G. Beale, who was Robert Lincoln's partner and Insull's confidant. Beale was vacationing in Europe, but Insull asked him to return to Chicago as soon as possible:

> I have been engaged for the last six weeks in cutting the expenses of all the concerns that I run, and I am just as drastic in my treatment in running the affairs of the Commonwealth Edison Company as I am in some little company in Oklahoma. I have laid off in the Commonwealth Edison Company alone, around 1,000 employees in the last six weeks. . . . The fact is, we are passing through the most tremendous crisis in business that I have known since I first went into business, therefore, it seems the proper thing for everybody, whether they are conducting the business themselves or advising the people who do conduct such business, to be home and on the job.[14]

Insull and his companies survived the banking crisis of 1914, and by the time America declared war on Germany on April 6, 1917, Insull controlled four major utility companies and had a powerful friend in Springfield. He and his entities had contributed heavily to the gubernatorial campaign of Frank O. Lowden, who had been a founding director of the Dawes bank in 1902. After the successful campaign, the newly elected governor appointed Insull to the high-profile chairmanship of the State Council of Defense of Illinois, which made Insull the state's top salesman of war bonds.

The mobilization efforts for World War I spawned a land boom for Chicago and its environs. This came on top of Chicago's early twentieth-century population boom, fostered by its central location and strategic railway system. At the same time, the city's population swelled with the influx of European immigrants. By the 1920s, there were 400,000 German-Americans and 250,000 Italian-Americans living in Chicago. Flourishing manufacturing and industrial sectors provided jobs for the new residents, and they, in turn, provided an expanded consumer market. As economic activity increased, the city's real estate market experienced a corresponding rise in values. Banks were among the major beneficiaries of the soaring economy, as local businesses needed capital to expand.[15]

Throughout the 1920s, Chicago's landscape constantly changed as construction crews erected skyscrapers along the shores of Lake Michigan. Office buildings and high-rise luxury apartments rose along Lake Shore Drive and other streets in the lakefront area, which became known as the "Gold Coast." Joining in the frenzy, Insull took control of the Chicago Civic Opera

Company and built the opulent Civic Opera House, a forty-five-story monument encompassing an entire block at 20 North Wacker Drive. To produce more income, it was designed as an office building, but it ended up costing the staggering sum of $23,385,000. When construction costs overran the budget, George Reynolds and his brother Arthur—entwined in the folly—arranged for their Continental Illinois Bank and Trust Company to provide a second mortgage of $3.4 million, which Insull personally guaranteed.

Insull's personal office occupied the penthouse floor of the building, complete with an adjoining apartment and private elevator. On its opening day, Insull's "favorite plaything" landed him on the cover of *Time* magazine, which described the opera house as "second to none for luxury." But his critics described the building as "Insull's Throne." And the timing of its completion was unfortunate in that the opera's first performance was held on November 4, 1929, shortly after the crash on Wall Street, when patrons' thoughts had turned to matters more pressing than opera.[16]

Insull had developed an appreciation for music and the opera as a young man working in London. But he also viewed his support of the arts as a way to advance his influence in society and the business community, which overlapped in Chicago as in other urban centers. And his actress wife, Gladys, gave him a personal reason for becoming the leading patron of the Chicago opera. They first met in 1897 when Gladys was twenty-eight years old, a decade younger than he was. She was performing on stage in a starring role at a theater near Insull's office. The petite beauty, who stood not quite five feet tall and weighed something less than ninety pounds, swept the powerful millionaire off his feet. They were married in 1899, and she gave birth to their only child, Samuel Insull Jr., in 1900.

They did not live happily ever after. Though they remained married until he died in 1938, according to Forrest McDonald, Insull's biographer, Gladys "closed the bedroom door" in 1912 when she was forty-three years old and he was fifty-three. McDonald relied on a conversation with Insull Jr., who in turn had received his information from his mother after his father's death when a Chicago newspaper reported that he had kept a mistress. Since there is no way of confirming what went on in Insull's bedroom, we don't know if Insull took a mistress before or after Gladys "cut him off." Nevertheless, McDonald asserts that her rejection had so damaged his ego that it drove him to excessively expand his empire in an unrelenting effort to insulate himself from a future rejection. Insull's control of the opera company apparently impressed his wife, who in 1925—at the age of fifty-six—played Lady Teazle in her own production of Richard Sheridan's *The School for Scandal*. One thing seems certain: Insull's championing the opera house gained him standing in Chicago's polite society.[17]

Insull understood early on the importance of creating a positive public image for an industry that depended on politicians to sanction rate increases. His public relations experience as head of the State Council of Defense led to his formation, in 1919, of the Committee on Public Utility Information, which was specifically designed to disseminate his message to the public. The propaganda arm of his system served a dual purpose: spreading goodwill in the communities his companies served while creating a public market for their securities. Insull's most effective public relations tool was his encouragement of widespread customer ownership of his companies' stock. He realized that customers who had a personal financial stake in the company were likely to be reasonable about utility rates. Insull also sold corporate bonds to his customers—nearly $200 million worth in one year. But unlike common stock, which required no interest payments, the bonds expanded his companies' debt burden and contributed to their collapse during the Depression year of 1932.[18]

Insull realized that good publicity was not enough to operate his public utilities on a grand scale. He knew that he had to dominate the politics of Chicago. So as he was building his domain, he was quick to respond to requests from Charles Dawes for substantial contributions to Republican candidates running for local, state, or national offices. He soon became an expert at accumulating political power. Refusing to discriminate between party affiliation and ideology, he cannily poured money into the coffers of both political parties. His influence peddling ranged from the subtle to the crude, as he contributed to politicians of all stripes and kept at least one U.S. senator— Lawrence Y. Sherman—on retainer.

Insull valued Sherman's influence in Washington and his friendship with Charles Dawes, who was critical to Insull's expansion plans. While Sherman received his monthly retainer, the Dawes bank flagrantly violated the Illinois banking code, making excessive loans to Insull's companies. Insull continued to pay Sherman a monthly retainer—as a "personal matter"—throughout the 1920s, even though Sherman left the Senate in 1921. Putting distance between him and the payments, Insull arranged for them to be made through Robert Lincoln's former law firm: Isham, Lincoln and Beale.

For three decades, Insull relied on the influence of Lincoln and the discretion of his former law firm. Lincoln, who was the president and then chairman of the Pullman Company, made a fortune and traveled throughout the nation in his private railroad car, which he used to entertain politicians and business leaders including Charles Dawes when he was comptroller of the currency. In 1905, Lincoln completed Hildene, his mansion located on 412 acres in Manchester, Vermont, where he lived in grand style and comfort "with a permanent domestic staff of three maids, a butler, valet, chef, chauffeur,

Image 1.3. U.S. Senator Lawrence Sherman of Illinois received a monthly retainer from Samuel Insull, who made the secret payments through Robert Todd Lincoln's law firm. (Courtesy, Library of Congress)

groomsman, coachman, and private secretary." While living at Hildene, Lincoln enjoyed playing golf at Ekwanok Country Club, where he was president for twenty-two years, and riding around the countryside in his chauffeured automobile, which was a Rolls-Royce late in his life.

In 1911, Lincoln purchased a "magnificent three-story brick mansion" in the Georgetown section of Washington, which was originally built around 1800. The former minister to Great Britain remained influential by entertaining members of both political parties much like a member of the British nobility. Meanwhile, he traveled with his entourage in his private railroad car, complete with a separate freight car for their luggage, between his residences in Vermont and Washington.

During this period of expansion, Lincoln served Insull well as the first vice president of the Commonwealth Edison Company through 1914, and

Image 1.4. Robert Todd Lincoln (right) at the dedication of his father's memorial in 1922, along with Chief Justice and former President William Howard Taft (left) and President Warren Harding (center). (Courtesy, Library of Congress)

as one of its directors until his death in 1926. Insull's cozy banking relationships were also enhanced because Lincoln served as a director of Insull's two largest bank creditors: Continental and Commercial Trust and Savings Bank and the Continental and Commercial National Bank of Chicago, in which he remained a director until his death. The two banks, controlled by George and Arthur Reynolds, later merged to become the Continental Illinois Bank and Trust Company, the largest bank in Chicago which issued loans of $59,857,135 to Insull's group of companies. After the death of William Beale in 1923, Isham, Lincoln and Beale remained Insull's law firm. And the law firm continued to make the payments to Sherman, who had become dependent on them.[19]

By 1926, Insull had become powerful enough to mount an effective challenge to an incumbent U.S. senator, but his hyperactive fund-raising practices generated negative publicity. During the 1926 Illinois senatorial campaign, Insull and his entities contributed heavily to Frank L. Smith, chairman of the Illinois Commerce Commission, which regulated the rates and service of public utilities. Smith raised a total of $285,452 for his campaign; Insull and his companies contributed $125,000 of that amount. Insull also supported Smith indirectly, contributing $33,735 to fund a campaign against the World Court, which was a major campaign issue. Insull's total contribution of $158,735 would be worth more than $1.9 million in today's dollars. But his practice of writing "political insurance" where he deemed it necessary prompted him to also contribute $15,000 to the Democratic candidate for the same seat, George E. Brennen.

This time, however, Insull's extravagant contributions to a campaign backfired. After the election, a Senate committee investigated the money that flowed to Smith from Insull and other members of the utility industry when Smith was the chairman of the Illinois Commerce Commission and a candidate for the Senate. In an unusual move, a majority of the United States Senate voted to refuse to seat Smith because of his corrupt fund-raising practices. Insull's blatant influence peddling was exposed during the controversy, which besmirched his reputation and made him a target.[20]

Insull would recover and go on to amass far more power, assets, and debt, but the controversy followed him into the Depression and would surface again when he was most vulnerable. Ultimately, Insull's empire would collapse, and his career would end with him on the run. By then, his powerful friends in banking and business would not be able to save him. None of his friends were more powerful than Charles Dawes. He and his brothers gained wealth and political clout knowing that the banking business was closely tied to politics and, in particular, to the politicians who controlled the regulation of banks at the state and federal levels. But Dawes used a velvet glove, having his bank make secret loans to politicians, while Insull continued to seek the limelight, a far more dangerous place to occupy.[21]

CHARLES DAWES

While Samuel Insull was expanding his empire and political influence during the early decades of the twentieth century, he shrewdly developed close ties to Charles Dawes. He and his brothers mixed banking and politics to their own benefit and that of their closest associates. Dawes, as the former top regulator of national banks and the founder of a state-chartered Loop bank, was a solid member of the Chicago financial community and had entrée to bankers throughout the national system, including the money-center banks of New York.

Charles and his brothers had been raised in a political and business environment. Their father, Rufus R. Dawes, was brevetted the rank of brigadier general during the Civil War. Upon returning home, he achieved equal success as a civilian building the Dawes Lumber Company in Marietta, Ohio, into a thriving enterprise and serving one term in congress, from 1881 to 1883. His sons followed in their father's footsteps. Charles entered national politics in 1896 as the Illinois campaign manager of his father's friend, Governor William McKinley of Ohio. McKinley had served in Congress alongside Charles's father. Soon after he was elected president, McKinley appointed Dawes as his comptroller of the currency in Washington. A young man in a hurry, Dawes promptly abused this high public position in order to advance his own political career.[22]

Dawes never had any qualms about using depositors' money to subsidize his political aspirations. He raised eyebrows when he appointed Lawrence Sherman, an ambitious lawyer and the speaker of the Illinois House of Representatives from 1899 to 1903 and later a U.S. senator, as his special liquidation attorney, even though he had already hired local lawyers to represent the same receiverships. Sherman's two-man firm thus found itself representing some of the nation's largest insolvent national banks in the states of Washington, Colorado, Montana, Oregon, and Maryland.[23]

A lawyer himself, Dawes guaranteed that the up-and-coming Sherman had more than enough work by "holding open a lot of matters" for him. In letters marked "personal," he assured Sherman that "there is always enough" legal work in the comptroller's office, which was certainly true, given that national bank assets of $40 million were in the hands of Dawes's receivers, an amount worth about $1.04 billion in today's dollars. Dawes added that it would be "a great pleasure . . . to cooperate in [Sherman's business] plans" by sending legal work of "the highest class" to his Macomb, Illinois, law firm. And Dawes made sure that Sherman was always fully and quickly paid for his legal services.

Like Dawes, Sherman was moving rapidly up the political ladder. It was not long before the two had become powerful allies. So, naturally, when Dawes decided to run for the U.S. Senate, he turned to a willing and by now useful Sherman for support. Dawes announced his candidacy in July 1901, but his campaign was short-lived. Almost immediately, his rival politicians began charging, accurately, that he had squandered depositors' money as comptroller of the currency when he hired political attorneys, including Sherman, to represent insolvent national banks. Then, two months after his announcement, Dawes's patron and strongest political asset, President McKinley, was assassinated. This sudden loss of influence in Washington, combined with the continuing and effective opposition from the political machine of William Lorimer, became the deciding factors in Dawes's abrupt withdrawal from the Senate race.[24]

Dawes had first met Lorimer when the two were rising politicians. Dawes had already learned to live by the maxim: "Keep your friends close but your enemies closer." So when Lorimer's political machine defeated his Senate run, Dawes worked on forming an intimate working relationship with his former opponent. They had a lot in common. Primarily, they shared an innate grasp of the close relationship between banking and politics, both freely utilizing their banks as their political headquarters and enhancing their political operations by selling bank stock to their political allies. Major depositors and borrowers became fertile sources of campaign funds and political support. Dawes and Lorimer also made sure that friendly regulators—ones who could be counted on to turn a blind eye to their chicanery—were ensconced in state and federal regulatory offices. These two promoter-bankers also made bogus loans to the regulators of their banks, enabling them to operate without fear of prosecution inside the secret bank regulatory system. During the so-called Progressive Era, Dawes and Lorimer engaged in the same pattern of self-dealing between corresponding bankers, fraud, and insider abuse—all concealed by bribery and secrecy—that would become standard in Chicago's promoter banks during the 1920s, resulting in their collapse during the banking panic of 1932. As a result, their banks ignored state and federal regulations with impunity. But of the two, Dawes was the master of influence peddling, so his bank would survive Lorimer's by two decades.[25]

Lorimer, who never had a formal education, had started out selling newspapers and shining shoes but rapidly rose to become the boss of the West Side of Chicago after he won a series of bare-knuckle political fights. By 1895, he had managed to wrest control of the state Republican Party, which rewarded him with a seat in Congress. His career reached its pinnacle in 1909 when the Illinois General Assembly elected him to the United States Senate. Though a cloud of suspicion followed him to Washington, his political machine in Illinois, reinforced by the strength of his charismatic personality, made him a powerful force within the administration of William Howard Taft.

On arriving in Washington, Lorimer, like Dawes, lost no time in using his public office to augment his personal patrimony. He soon filed an application with the comptroller of the currency's office to charter the LaSalle Street National Bank. Thus Lorimer, a political boss but never a banker, became president of a newly chartered bank while he was still a senator. It took only three years for him to be ousted from the Senate on a vote of 55 to 28, for "flagrant bribery in the solicitation of votes" during his election in 1909. And by then—July 1912—he had already wrecked his bank, which would fail two years later.[26]

The inherent conflict of interest between Lorimer's responsibilities to his depositors and his political commitments would have condemned the bank to an early demise even without the rampant insider abuse and fraud. But from the institution's inception on May 9, 1910, Lorimer abused his fiduciary position at the bank with reckless abandon until worthless loans dominated

Image 1.5. U.S. Senator William Lorimer of Illinois, a Chicago political boss who engaged in an elaborate bank fraud conspiracy with Charles Dawes in 1912. (Courtesy, Library of Congress)

its assets, leading its clearinghouse bank to cancel its privileges a scant year after the ribbon-cutting ceremony. Nonetheless, Lorimer continued to utilize the savings of depositors to solidify his political base, making bribes disguised as loans to prominent politicians. While Lorimer's bank made loans to local politicians, his bank and its affiliates collected more than $1 million in deposits from the city of Chicago. Lorimer then circulated the city's deposits in the form of loans to members of his organization, operating what amounted to a pyramid scheme with taxpayers' money. Lorimer was running a political machine, not a bank. Meanwhile, the extent of the corruption was hidden in secret federal, and then state, examination reports.

When it closed, Lorimer's bank showed loans of $5,426,657 on its books, most of which were non-performing and worthless. No more than $1,793,931 of its assets was performing. And more than half of its loans were to companies controlled by Lorimer and his partner, Charles B. Munday, the bank's vice president. The Lorimer-Munday bank also purchased bonds, many of which were issued by companies controlled by Lorimer's friends. The bonds were carried on the books as assets valued at $917,600, when in reality they were worth only $255,385, according to state bank examiners. Missing entirely from the bank's vault was $105,137 in cash.[27]

Lorimer's political and business ambitions quickly extended far beyond the founding of just one bank. He found a willing collaborator in Charles Dawes. Never one to deny a request from Lorimer, Dawes, then the president of the Central Trust Company of Illinois, was only too willing to participate in an elaborate bank fraud conspiracy designed by the recently disgraced but still powerful political boss. In 1912, Theodore Roosevelt split the Republican Party in two when he ran for president on the Progressive Party ticket, challenging William Howard Taft, the incumbent president who was supported by the "old guard" Republicans, including Lorimer and Dawes. Just before the election, in October 1912, when it was all but certain that Woodrow Wilson would be elected, Lorimer, with Dawes's help, converted his national bank into a state bank. As a state bank, it would be subject to the regulation of the friendly offices of James J. Brady, the elected Illinois auditor of public accounts and banking commissioner.

Already during its existence, according to the Supreme Court of Illinois, Lorimer's bank had been "examined at various times by a national bank examiner and its method of doing business had been severely criticized by him." But the examiner's supervisor, Lawrence O. Murray, the comptroller of the currency under Taft, was a close friend of Dawes. Instead of seizing Lorimer's insolvent bank, he approved its conversion into a state institution. The timing of the conversion prompted allegations of favoritism, since the delegates that Lorimer had delivered to the besieged president during the tumultuous Chicago Republican Convention of 1912 had not gone unnoticed. But for the time being, Lorimer—whose fraudulent conduct was shielded from depositors by bank secrecy—remained undeterred.[28]

There was just one problem: the struggling bank lacked the cash needed to meet the capital requirements for a state bank. This problem was solved by Dawes whose bank issued a phony loan of $1.25 million to Lorimer's bank, thereby allowing the state examiner to declare that the bank had the necessary cash. By honoring a bogus cashier's check for $1.25 million (about $28.5 million today), Dawes enabled Lorimer to create a fictitious net worth for the bank in an instant.

During the same October afternoon, immediately after the bank examiner had certified that Lorimer's bank now had sufficient capital to operate as a state bank, Lorimer handed the money back to the Dawes bank, completing the sham transaction. Lorimer's bank thus began operating as a state bank with a negative net worth. Though Dawes clearly had known at the time that Lorimer's bank was "hopelessly insolvent" prior to its conversion, one of Dawes's attorneys later attempted to explain the fraudulent transaction as merely a "courtesy" to Lorimer.[29]

To perpetuate the illegal scheme, Lorimer persuaded his good friend James Brady, the state's elected auditor and banking commissioner, to name one of his confederates, L. L. Bacchus, as the state's top appointed bank regulator. Brady could be expected to cooperate since he had received abundant campaign contributions from Lorimer plus a $5,000 personal loan from his bank. Lorimer was therefore able to implement his larger scheme of forming a statewide banking organization when he received charters from Brady for banks throughout Illinois. The vast majority of their capital accounts were comprised of phony loans from Lorimer's parent bank, the LaSalle Street Trust and Savings Bank, until the state examiner certified that their capital was adequate. Once that was obtained, the fictitious capital was returned to Lorimer's parent bank. And after these affiliated banks opened, Lorimer used them as dumping grounds for the LaSalle Street Trust and Savings Bank's bad loans.

Thus the likelihood of a catastrophe increased with the opening of each new bank, and Brady approved twenty of these affiliated bank charters for Lorimer. Half of the banking chain was concentrated in the Chicago area, with the other affiliates located in southern Illinois. And five of Lorimer's defunct banks were holding $1,070,000 of the city of Chicago's deposits. Ignoring the negative reports from his own examiners, Brady, in his capacity as state auditor, also deposited state funds into Lorimer's fledgling banks. These public deposits, which were bolstered with deposits of $200,000 in federal funds, spoke volumes about Lorimer's political clout, especially since they lacked competitive bidding and collateral to secure the deposits.

To cover up his insider abuse and outright fraud, Lorimer hired state regulators as officials of his banks and then issued loans to them. The revolving door between Brady's office and Lorimer's banks, as well as "the policy loans," made a mockery of the regulatory system. Bank examination reports would suddenly disappear after bank failures, obstructing criminal prosecutions. Prosecutors clashed with the ever loyal Brady, who owed his election as public auditor in large part to Lorimer, when he refused to release the examination reports of Lorimer's banks, claiming that they were secret documents.

All of this amounted to a formula for disaster, and when Lorimer's banking chain inevitably crashed, it caused bank runs similar to those in the Panic of 1873 when Chicago's largest bank, the Union National, and other major banks suspended operations. On June 12, 1914, the day that the LaSalle Street Trust and Savings Bank locked its tellers' cages, mounted policemen had to quell the riot. The panic quickly spread to affiliated banks, which failed one

Image 1.6.   Depositors run on William Lorimer's LaSalle Street Trust and Savings Bank, which collapsed in 1914 because of insider abuse and fraud. (Courtesy, Chicago History Museum)

by one in a domino effect because their liquid cash had previously been trans-ferred to Lorimer's headquarters on LaSalle Street.[30]

After a postmortem examination of the bank identified worthless assets of more than $3.6 million, Illinois Attorney General Patrick J. Lucey filed a peti-tion of receivership for the LaSalle Street bank. It charged that Lorimer and his partner, Charles Munday, had operated the bank in an "illegal, fraudulent, and unsafe manner." At that point, Brady had no choice but to declare that the bank was "hopelessly insolvent."[31]

Dawes became publicly associated with this scandal when the receiver of Lorimer's bank sued Dawes's bank, demanding the return of the original

$1.25 million that had represented the entire capital and surplus of Lorimer's flagship bank. The receiver charged that the Dawes bank had "manipulated" the phony loan "in an improper manner." In an effort to avoid liability for his bank, Dawes's lawyers advanced a disingenuous argument, which was rejected by each tribunal along the way in a series of legal actions. It went as follows: "The entire transaction in question was done and carried out by William R. Dawes, the cashier of the [Dawes bank], under the authority of Charles G. Dawes, its president, without the knowledge or authority of the board of directors or executive committee . . . and . . . any acts done by them of that character were beyond their authority and not binding on the [bank]."

It was William R. Dawes, Charles Dawes's cousin and cashier of the Dawes bank since its opening in 1902, who had been given Lorimer's worthless check for $1.25 million, drawn on a fictitious account, and in return had handed Lorimer $1.25 million in cash through the teller's window. The fictitious account was comprised of ten promissory notes of $125,000 each, which were from ten of Lorimer's friends, "one of whom was worth $2,000 and none of them worth very much." Lorimer presented the cash to John H. Rife, the state bank examiner responsible for ensuring the validity of the bank's capital, who merely counted the money he had been given. Lorimer then returned the cash to William Dawes, who in turn gave back Lorimer's check, which Lorimer promptly destroyed. No case of fraud could have been clearer, and as a result Rife was later indicted as part of the conspiracy. Soon after the transaction, Lorimer hired Rife as a senior officer at one of his banks. Rife's supervisor, L. L. Bacchus, who had approved the conversion of Lorimer's national bank to a state-chartered institution, was also rewarded for his cooperation; Lorimer hired him as a vice president and director of the new state bank. In addition, he was made the treasurer of the Illinois Louisiana Land Company, which had sold $205,200 of its bonds to Lorimer's bank and had procured loans from it. Rife and Bacchus jointly borrowed $9,317 from Lorimer's bank and then defaulted on the loan.[32]

Dawes lost his case at the trial level, and his bank, which was serving as the receiver for one of Lorimer's bankrupt companies, was held liable for $1,487,854, a sum worth $32.8 million in today's dollars. Unwilling to concede defeat or settle the matter, Dawes began a series of appeals through every level of the Illinois court system, a process that would take a decade to play out and involve two separate appeals to the state supreme court. After Dawes lost the first appeal in 1917, he corresponded with his ally and friend Lawrence Sherman in the U.S. Senate about the defeat. Sherman was worried that the "harsh judgment" would have an adverse effect on Dawes and his bank, and he criticized former senator Lorimer for "his misdeeds." Dawes maintained that he would win the next appeal, and that, in any event, the judgment would "not interfere even with [the Central Trust Company's] dividends." Dawes calculated that he would be able to get the judgment further reduced to about $300,000, an amount "of no material consequence" to his $60 million bank. Expressing no regrets, Dawes thanked Sherman for his concern and his "loyal friendship throughout all the years."[33]

Dawes continued his financial support of Sherman during his Senate tenure, and Sherman repaid him many times over as Dawes frequently lobbied about issues and appointments and especially banking matters. So helpful was his loyal friend that Dawes felt compelled to tell him at one point that his responsiveness was "really embarrassing at times." Nonetheless, in the very same letter, he asked Sherman for yet another favor. Nor were Dawes's brothers, Henry and Rufus, timid about using their influence with Sherman whenever the Senate was considering legislation that affected the family's business interests. Charles Dawes's alliance with Sherman, established when he hired the ambitious lawyer early in his career, paid off handsomely in the long run.[34]

Despite setbacks in the Lorimer case and the attendant bad press, Dawes remained active in state and national politics. His audacity and his ever-expanding circle of friends allowed him to play a prominent role on the world's center stage. When the United States entered World War I in 1917, he joined the staff of his close friend, General John J. Pershing, who was commander-in-chief of the American Expeditionary Forces. Dawes's relationship with Pershing had been forged from 1887 to 1894 when they lived in Lincoln, Nebraska. Dawes was a young lawyer, and Pershing, also a lawyer, was a second lieutenant in the U.S. Army and commandant of cadets at the University of Nebraska. Because of his friendship with Pershing, Dawes was appointed as chairman of the General Purchasing Board, representing the U.S. Army on the Military Board of Allied Supply in Paris. Dawes had a talent for managing high-ranking people well, so he was able to work cooperatively with the French, English, and American officers. His work resulted in him being brevetted the rank of brigadier general by the end of the war. Moreover, he was awarded the Distinguished Service Medal for "exceptionally meritorious and distinguished service."

After the war, President Warren Harding named Dawes the nation's first budget director in 1921. To help him prepare the first federal budget, Dawes appointed his brothers Rufus and Henry to the executive budget committee. Sherman had resigned from the Senate, citing the financial hardship of serving, so Dawes appointed him to the executive budget committee. Sherman accepted with alacrity, well aware that the success of the law firm he was planning to form in Daytona Beach would depend heavily on Dawes, who was on his way to becoming a titan in the Republican Party.

In thanking Sherman for the work he had done on the budget, Harding assured him that the White House would always be open to him, adding, "I want to make an expression at this time of my gratitude for the very great help you have given to the administration. . . . I hope an abundance of compensation will come to you."[35]

Secretary of State Charles Evans Hughes named Charles Dawes, whose military service during World War I had brought him prestige in Europe, to join the international reparations committee of experts that had been formed to resolve the postwar reparations dispute between France and Germany. Dawes and Owen Young, the Democratic member of the committee, named Rufus Dawes as the chief of staff of the American delegation. Rufus helped his brother and Young develop the Dawes Plan, which became effective in September 1924 and would temporarily ease Germany's payments of war reparations and stabilize its currency. Dawes was not an expert on the complicated details of the plan that had his name, but he was gregarious and seemingly always available for the press, something that could not be said of the others on the commission. Rufus then became the assistant to Young, who was named as the agent to implement the plan. Because the Dawes Plan would result in France's peaceful withdrawal of troops from Germany, Charles Dawes shared the Nobel Peace Prize in 1925 with Sir Austen Chamberlain, the British foreign secretary. This gained him an international reputation and fame that greatly enhanced his political career and business opportunities.[36]

While Charles and Rufus were in Paris, Henry, the youngest Dawes brother, was working in Washington as comptroller of the currency. President Harding's appointment, in 1923, made Henry the second member of the family to serve as the nation's chief banking regulator. Following Harding's death, Calvin Coolidge reappointed him to the powerful post.[37]

After widespread press coverage and favorable international reaction to the Dawes Plan, Coolidge asked Charles Dawes to run as his vice president in 1924. Dawes accepted but was immediately deluged with negative publicity surrounding the Lorimer scandal. On the very day that Dawes was formally selected as the Republican vice presidential nominee, the supreme court of Illinois ruled that he had been a central figure in the demise of Lorimer's bank. And despite the earlier attempt to hold his bank separate from his misconduct, the court also ruled that the bank was liable even though no profit from the transaction appeared on its books. Dawes had colluded with a state bank examiner when he made a fictitious loan to Lorimer's bank in order to provide enough capital temporarily for it to pass an audit. Dawes then facilitated Lorimer's fraudulent conversion of his insolvent shell to a state charter. Unfortunately for depositors—the victims of the shenanigans—the

Dawes "loan" enabled Lorimer to plunder his bank for another two years, until 1914.[38]

Consequently, Senator Smith W. Brookhart, a progressive Republican from Iowa, accused Dawes of being "unfit for public service." Brookhart argued that since Dawes was an active participant in the bogus transaction, he should either resign or be dropped as the vice presidential candidate. Burton K. Wheeler, a Democratic senator from Montana and running mate of Senator Robert M. La Follette of Wisconsin on the Progressive Party ticket, who was viewed as a radical by conservatives in both major parties, also attacked "the crooked bank deal of banker Dawes." He condemned Dawes for being involved in "a fraudulent banking transaction that robbed 4,000 Chicago citizens of their savings."[39]

During the campaign, Dawes refused to discuss the case. But a leading Chicago Democrat, John Barton Payne, who was then Dawes's attorney and chairman of the American Red Cross but formerly Woodrow Wilson's secretary of the Interior, categorically responded that "no possible basis exists for criticism of General Dawes." Unknown to the public was that Payne owned 762 shares of the Dawes bank. (The RFC would later be forced to sue Payne to collect his stockholder's liability of $76,200.) Payne quoted from a decision of a lower state appellate court that the Supreme Court of Illinois had reversed. The decision of the lower court held that Dawes's "act was a mere courtesy extended to a neighbor without charge or hope of reward." Payne chose to overlook the political favors Dawes could reasonably expect as a subsequent quid pro quo from Lorimer, the Republican boss. Furthermore, Payne asserted that "what was done by the Central Trust Company and General Dawes in providing the cash, and by the auditor of the State of Illinois in counting it, knowing that it had been provided for that purpose, had been the practice in Illinois for generations."[40]

Payne's remarkable statements did not go unanswered. They brought Moses E. Clapp out of retirement. Formerly Minnesota's attorney general and a progressive Republican U.S. senator, he had once been a leader in opposition to the Republican old guard. Retorting that Dawes was "a proven cheat" who was "unworthy of his party and of the votes of the American people," Clapp compared the Dawes defense to one "offered by pickpockets when they are caught." Mincing no words, Clapp went on to say, "No one except [Dawes's] attorney at that time, John Barton Payne, has attempted to excuse him. . . . The only excuse offered for Dawes's action, namely, that it is a common practice between bankers in Illinois, I regard as a slander upon reputable banks. If it is true that any banks in Illinois or elsewhere resort to such methods, it is a condition dangerous to the Republic's welfare."[41]

Coolidge and Dawes won in a landslide against John W. Davis, the Democrat, and Senator Robert M. La Follette, a Republican running on the Progressive Party ticket. The Dawes scandal did not affect the campaign because of the known rectitude of Coolidge, who had restored confidence in the White House after the death of President Harding, whose cronies had tarnished his administration. Coolidge's popularity allowed Dawes to survive the attacks and become vice president, but the Lorimer scandal would not be the last time he would be embroiled in a banking controversy. Nor would it be the last time he would manipulate the books of an insolvent bank. His business dealings with the Mizner Development Corporation, then in possession of what was arguably Florida's most valuable real estate, in Boca Raton, again demonstrated his propensity to cross the line to advance his economic interests. These questionable dealings would take place in the midst of the Florida banking panic of 1926, while Dawes was serving as vice president of the United States.

Through a complex series of moves, Vice President Dawes and his brothers secured for themselves $10.5 million worth of purchase contracts, along with all of the unencumbered assets, of the Mizner Development Corporation, amounting to about $127 million in today's dollars. In so doing, they left nothing for the stockholders and unsecured creditors of the Mizner company except its debts and other liabilities.[42]

THE INSULL AND DAWES CONNECTIONS

Charles Dawes and his brothers, ambitious businessmen who were making their fortune in the emerging utilities industry, watched Insull's activities at the end of the nineteenth century. In 1895, the Dawes brothers acquired the Northwestern Gas Light and Coke Company, which was located in Evanston. It had found a growing market in the suburbs and in servicing Northwestern University. When Charles Dawes became the nation's comptroller of the currency in 1897, his brother Rufus, two years his junior, managed the Dawes family's gas interests. The Dawes brothers proceeded to expand along Chicago's North Shore, purchasing gas companies in Wilmette, Kenilworth, Gross Point, and Waukegan.

They received much of the financing for these acquisitions from the Chicago National Bank. John R. Walsh, the bank's controlling stockholder and president, was Dawes's partner in the Northwestern Gas Light and Coke Company and in the Akron Gas Light Company of Akron, Ohio, and Walsh was Insull's partner and a director at the North Shore Electric Company, which had arranged loans and sold its bonds to Chicago National and its affiliated banks.

Dawes and Walsh had begun their relationship in 1893 when Dawes, a director of the American Exchange National Bank of Lincoln, Nebraska, arranged a $50,000 emergency loan for his bank from Walsh's bank. They became partners in 1895 when they acquired the Northwestern Gas Light and Coke Company together. Then they formed another partnership to acquire the Akron Gas Light Company in 1896, the same year that they joined forces in William McKinley's presidential campaign along with Insull, whose Chicago Edison gave $5,000 to the McKinley campaign. Walsh was a powerful Democrat whose bank nevertheless provided the funds that also made him a major player in the Illinois Republican Party. He had close ties to Congressman William Lorimer of Chicago and helped raise a significant war chest for McKinley's campaign in the all-out effort to stop the crusading William Jennings Bryan and his gospel of free silver. When McKinley became president and appointed Dawes as the comptroller of the currency, Dawes became the regulator of Walsh's national bank. Before the creation of the Federal Reserve System and the Federal Deposit Insurance Corporation, the comptroller of the currency was the most powerful bank regulator in the nation. Dawes, just thirty-one years old, suddenly had the power to charter new national banks in every state in the Union, as well as the authority to seize insolvent national banks and appoint receivers to operate them and lawyers to represent them.[43]

Despite the obvious conflict of interest, Walsh's Chicago National Bank continued to finance his and Dawes's Northwestern Gas Light and Coke Company during the four-and-a-half years that Dawes was the chief regulator of the Walsh bank. Beyond the questionable financing schemes, Walsh and Dawes crossed the line when the banker bought his regulator's interest in the Akron Gas Light Company soon after Dawes was appointed the comptroller of the currency. After the assassination of McKinley in September 1901, Dawes returned to Chicago and formed a new partnership with Walsh and Insull. This was a cozy arrangement, in that Walsh's bank was also providing financing for Insull's acquisitions.

With these resources and his partnership with the well-connected Dawes, Insull had formed a strategic alliance at a propitious time. It was a dynamic period for gas companies as they moved away from lighting to become a niche industry for household cooking and heating. The partnership with Insull was also beneficial for the Dawes brothers, who negotiated an agreement to merge their Chickasha Light, Heat and Power Company of Chickasha, Oklahoma, into the Chickasha Gas and Electric Company, a subsidiary of Middle

West Utilities Company, in 1914. The Dawes brothers exchanged shares of stock with Insull's company, so they continued as Insull's partners in the Chickasha Gas and Electric Company.[44]

Business deals flowed easily among the partners who had become friends. On a cold night in January 1902, Insull and his wife, Gladys, enjoyed a pleasant dinner with Dawes and his wife, Caro, at the Dawes home in Evanston. The purpose of the dinner was to discuss the forming of a partnership with Walsh in order to purchase the South Cook County Gas and Electric Company, which was operating properties in the Chicago suburbs of Blue Island, Harvey, and Chicago Heights. But the purpose of the entertaining evening must have seemed secondary to the feeling of fellowship engendered by the presence of the delicate but strong-willed wives of the two men with such big plans. Nevertheless, during the course of the dinner, Insull and Dawes talked about the role that Walsh and his bank might play, eventually agreeing to invite Walsh into the venture and to finance it with loans from Walsh's bank.[45]

Walsh's bank remained an important source of funding for Dawes and Insull until it and its two affiliated banks collapsed in 1905 because of illegal loans to Walsh, Insull, and their entities. Dawes's successor as comptroller of the currency from 1901 to 1908, William Barret Ridgely, observed immediately after the bank's closing: "There is seldom a failure which is not due to excessive loans, either directly to the officers or to various concerns in which they are in some way interested." But Ridgely, the son-in-law of U.S. Senator Shelby M. Cullom (R-Illinois) and a partner of Dawes in several gas deals, had known about the illegal loans to Walsh and Insull since 1903; nonetheless, he downplayed the misconduct, even though Walsh had willfully misapplied fourteen million dollars from his three banks, which had combined deposits of twenty-five million dollars. A federal grand jury indicted Walsh, and he was convicted in 1908. He was then sentenced to five years at the federal prison at Fort Leavenworth, Kansas, for issuing fraudulent call reports, which concealed the massive insider abuse.[46]

John Walsh died on October 23, 1911, just eight days after being released from Leavenworth prison. Despite the scandal, Dawes had remained loyal to Walsh for many reasons. The Dawes bank, then known as the Central Trust Company of Illinois, which was formed in 1902 and was a correspondent bank of Walsh's Chicago National, held lucrative deposits of public funds from the Chicago South Park Board, which Walsh and his political allies controlled. And Lyman A. Walton, a partner of Dawes in the gas enterprises, was a senior official in the Home Savings Bank and the Equitable Trust Company, which were also part of Walsh's failed banking chain. There were other

Image 1.7.   Depositor run on John Walsh's Chicago National Bank in 1905. Walsh, who was the partner of Charles Dawes and Samuel Insull in several gas deals, served three years in the federal prison at Fort Leavenworth for issuing fraudulent call reports, which concealed the massive insider abuse at his failed bank. (Courtesy, Chicago History Museum)

connections, too. Dawes continued to invest in Walsh's companies, and the Dawes bank made personal loans to Walsh prior to his incarceration. Dawes invested in Walsh's Southern Indiana Railway Company, the financing of which became part of the indictment against Walsh, and he put twenty-five thousand dollars in Walsh's Chicago Southern Railway Company. Finally, Dawes turned his friend's adversity into an opportunity when he bought the magnificent Chicago National Bank building, making it the new home of the Dawes bank.

During the next three decades after the demise of the Walsh banks, Dawes would have extensive business, political, charitable, and social dealings with Insull, who had been a director of one of Walsh's banks. Insull also had been a stockholder of Walsh's Illinois Southern Railway Company, which had been a beneficiary of the ill-gotten gains procured from the bank fraud. Drawing repeated criticisms from federal bank examiners, Insull had procured loans totaling $157,000 from the Chicago National Bank, which were far in excess of its statutory limit of $100,000 in loans to a single borrower. Despite having intimate knowledge of the insider abuse, Comptroller Ridgely, the partner of Insull and Dawes, took no enforcement action to stop the plunder.[47]

Dawes and Insull also organized and acquired other energy companies, including the Metropolitan Gas and Electric Company and the Union Gas and Electric Company. Although Dawes was the controlling stockholder in both, he was not a director of either. Instead, he installed his younger brothers as officers and directors, making Rufus president, treasurer, and a director; Henry Dawes a vice president; and Beman G. Dawes a director. Charles Dawes also named Insull and Comptroller Ridgely as directors of his companies. The Dawes brothers would continue to control the Metropolitan Gas and Electric Company and the Union Gas and Electric Company throughout the 1920s and 1930s. Rufus remained president of the gas companies and Dawes Brothers, Inc., the holding company set up in 1908, which controlled the gas companies and the Central Trust Company.[48]

OWEN YOUNG

Always eager to maintain alliances with funding sources, Samuel Insull had been careful to stay close to Dawes and officials of the Dawes bank throughout the 1920s. He also rewarded those at other banks and businesses essential to his operations and the funds he always seemed to need. Among the most important was Owen Young, chairman of the board of GE.

In the summer of 1929, there was a breach in the cozy relationship between Insull and Dawes after Dawes criticized Insull for failing to underwrite the Chicago World's Fair of 1933. Young played a decisive role in bridging the gap. The success of the project, known as "A Century of Progress" and created to celebrate the city's hundredth birthday, was important to the Dawes brothers because Rufus was president of the Chicago World's Fair organization, and Charles was chairman of its finance committee. When the World's Fair opened, *Time* magazine featured Rufus on its cover.[49]

Far more than the credibility of the Dawes name was on the line because the Dawes brothers had personally guaranteed the colossal project. So it was a crucial development for the success of the project when Herbert Hoover appointed Charles Dawes as the ambassador to Great Britain, where Insull had purchased a country estate. As soon as Dawes settled into the ambassador's residence in London, in May 1929, he prodded Insull to become an underwriter for the Chicago extravaganza, but to no effect. Dawes then upped the ante, asking Insull to head the fund-raising efforts for the project. When Insull refused to take on this assignment, Dawes promptly wrote to him, saying that it was critical that Insull and his entities guarantee the project, a step that would have significantly reduced the financial exposure of Dawes and his brothers. Dawes noted that he had persuaded Melvin A. Traylor, president of the First National Bank of Chicago, and other bankers to assist in issuing $10 million in bonds to construct the exhibitions. He divulged that his own companies were guaranteeing $1 million to the project, of which he and his brother Rufus were personally responsible for $100,000 each. Dawes pointed out none too subtly that his longtime friend should participate because he was "under great obligations" to Dawes. Dawes's presumption offended Insull, who responded that the ambassador was "under just as much of an obligation" to him.[50]

Insull had previously taken offense when Dawes lost his temper—he was known for his irascibility—and berated Harold L. Stuart, Insull's investment banker, angrily reminding Stuart that the Insull companies had huge loans at Dawes's Central Trust Company. At that, R. Floyd Clinch, a director of the Dawes bank, had stepped forward to caution the mercurial Dawes that Insull's companies also had more than $6 million in deposits at the Dawes bank.[51]

Nearly a year passed in which Insull was still not legally committed to the project, although by then he had visited Dawes in London and indicated a willingness to participate. To close the deal with Insull, Dawes enlisted the help of his business partner, Owen Young, the chairman of GE, who was arguably even closer to the curmudgeonly tycoon than Dawes was. (At the time, Dawes and Young owned jointly controlling interest in the New York and Richmond Gas Company, which serviced Staten Island. Rufus Dawes managed the company for his brother and Young.) Insull and Young had enjoyed mutually beneficial dealings: Young as an insider in Insull's stock offerings and Insull from GE's generous financing arrangements to one of its premier customers. From the American embassy in London, on April 11, 1930, Dawes cabled Young, advising him that Insull had finally agreed to participate in the electrical industry exhibit, but only if Young's GE would assume the lead role. (Later, when it was apparent that the fair would generate a surplus, Dawes told Young that the success of the project meant that its bonds would be repaid with interest. By 1934, Dawes and his companies would be committed to $2 million of the bonds of the highly risky venture, an amount worth about $32 million in today's dollars.)[52]

Since Young was now responsible for the fair's electricity and radio exhibits, which by the spring of 1930 represented 50 percent of the exhibits committed to the project, the endeavor was assured success. At first blush it appeared that the combination of Dawes's persistence and Young's gentle persuasion finally brought Insull to the table. But a closer look revealed that Insull could not turn down his banker, who also happened to be the ambassador to the Court of St. James, and Young, who was his largest and most accommodating vendor. Both men were in daily communication with influential leaders of the Hoover administration, Congress, and the financial community. As a result, Insull and his son, Samuel Insull Jr., became, with the Dawes brothers, founding members and directors of the board of trustees of A Century of Progress, the Chicago World's Fair organization. By October 1931, Rufus reported to his relieved brother Charles: "Nothing could be finer than the cooperation [Insull] has extended through all of his companies. Not only do we feel the effects of his great influence and the active support of many of his managers, but several of them have practically devoted the greater part of their time to advancing our cause." In fact, Insull had committed the following companies, all of which were borrowers of the Dawes bank, to become guarantors: Commonwealth Edison Company; Peoples Gas, Light, and Coke Company; Chicago Rapid Transit Company; Public Service Company of Northern Illinois; Chicago, North Shore and Milwaukee Railroad Company; Western United Gas and Electric Company; Middle West Utilities Company; and Midland Utilities Company. [53]

In one of his many telegrams to Rufus, Dawes worried that "I am at a distance and [I realize] that my reputation as well as yours is at stake in an enterprise the magnitude and difficulties of which it is easy to underestimate." While Charles was focused on raising $10 million for the project, the condition of his bank was rapidly deteriorating. Rufus, too, was concentrating on fund-raising to the detriment of his own investments, as well as the business of the family bank. He was relying on his brother Henry, the youngest of the four Dawes brothers, who also served on the bank's board, but Henry was primarily involved in the business of the Pure Oil Company. So Charles was relieved after Owen Young, "that Prince of Friends," as Dawes referred to him, sent him a telegram saying that he would shoulder the burden of closing the World's Fair deal with Insull: "Don't worry about it—you have enough to do without that."[54]

There were many ways in which Young could be helpful, not only to Charles Dawes, but also to Samuel Insull, who was always in need of large loans and flexible terms from Young's company and for credit facilities from New York bankers who worked with Young on a daily basis. Young was, after all, deputy chairman and a member of the executive committee of the Federal Reserve Bank of New York, which gave him clout with the financial and business leaders of the Northeast. He was also chairman of the Banking and Industrial Committee of the Second Federal Reserve District, which was responsible for encouraging private lending activity in the business community. It should be no surprise that Insull had secretly allowed this consummate insider in business and government to buy stock in a number of insider syndicates at below-market prices during 1929 and 1930.[55]

Late in 1928, Insull had asked Young "to join as one of the underwriters [of Insull Utility Investments, Inc.] and thereby aid him in the perpetuation of his organization." The Insull family would control the holding company "to insure security to the management." Management included his son, Samuel Insull Jr., who, Insull said, needed more time "to demonstrate his usefulness" as president of the Midland Utilities Company, and his brother Martin, president of the Middle West Utilities Company.[56]

On January 22, 1929, Young signed a contract with Insull, as president of Insull Utility Investments (IUI), agreeing to purchase 4,000 shares of the common stock of IUI at $12 a share for a total of $48,000. His friendship and loyalty were soon rewarded. By August of the same year, Young's stock position in IUI was worth $597,000, representing a paper profit of $549,000 in just eight months, a profit worth about $6.88 million in today's dollars. But Young would have had to sell his stock to realize the profit, which he did not do.[57]

During the same month, August 1929, Young was "invited" to purchase an additional 500 shares of IUI preferred stock at $100 a share, for a total purchase price of $50,000. A few weeks later, in September, Young exercised his right to subscribe to 908 shares of common stock of IUI at $50 a share, for a total of $45,400. Also in September, Insull gave Young a participation commitment of $500,000 in the Middle West Utilities syndicate. As it happened, the syndicate manager had only called upon 6 percent of the commitment, or $30,000, before the company went into a receivership in 1932, but had the securities risen in value as expected, Young could have made a huge profit. In October 1929, Young speculated in the securities of Insull's Corporation Securities Company when he bought 300 units at $75 a unit, equaling one share of common stock and one share of preferred stock, for a total purchase price of $22,500. Once again, in April 1930, Young was given "an allotment," this time consisting of 1,000 common shares of Corporation Securities at $27.50 a share, which he exercised for $27,500. Insull also invited Young to join the controversial IUI syndicate. Insull allotted Young a $75,000 commitment in the syndicate, and Young received calls requiring him to put up $15,194 of that amount.

For all of the preferential insider treatment he received, Young's investments with Insull turned into a disaster. Riding the roller coaster to its height in 1929, he hung on to ride it into the ground in 1932, when Insull's companies filed for bankruptcy. By March 1932, Young's investments in Insull's entities totaled $238,601, an amount worth about $3.75 million in today's dollars.[58]

Young was not the only one favored at GE. The company's president, Gerard Swope, maintained a lower profile than Young, but he was as important as anyone on Insull's insider list. GE, Young, and Swope were entwined with Insull and his companies. After all, Insull had engaged in transactions exceeding $100 million with GE during the four decades that he headed the Chicago Edison Company and then its successor, the Commonwealth Edison Company. Swope had served on Woodrow Wilson's War Industries Board when Bernard M. Baruch, Young's good friend and a Democratic powerhouse, was its chairman. And Swope's recommendations, along with those of the U.S. Chamber of Commerce, would lead to the creation of the National Industrial Recovery Act in June 1933. Herbert Hoover condemned the recovery act as "sheer fascism" that would result in "a remaking of Mussolini's 'corporate state.'" But historian David M. Kennedy described Swope as a "progressive businessman." Still, he was not too progressive to participate in a number of Insull's insider syndicates.[59]

In January 1929, Insull had invited Swope to purchase 2,000 shares of IUI stock at the same below-market price of $12 a share that Young was offered. Swope accepted Insull's offer and invested a total of $24,000, which was allowed to be paid in four installments. And as he did for Young, in August 1929, Insull made "an allotment" for Swope to subscribe to 500 shares of IUI's preferred stock at $100 a share. Swope took advantage of the entire allotment and invested $50,000. Additionally, in October 1929, Insull, Son & Company carved out for Swope a $250,000 share of the Middle West syndicate of preferred and common stock, half of what Young was allotted in the syndicate, which had a significant upside but no real downside. Swope was required to pay only $15,000 of the allotment and made a profit of $3,760 by January 1930, when the syndicate was terminated because of adverse market conditions—a 25 percent profit in three months. In the same three months, Young made a profit of $7,521 on his $30,000 investment in the Middle West syndicate.[60]

When Insull was forming the Insull Utility Investments, Inc. Syndicate in August 1930, in the midst of the Depression, he urgently needed all of the financial and political muscle he could muster to fend off a hostile takeover attempt of his utility properties. Thus he granted influential insiders, including Swope and Young, the privilege of purchasing a grand total of $5,750,000 of IUI stock at $50 a share. (Swope invested a total of $113,738 in the securities of IUI.) This was $9.25 below the market price and represented an immediate profit on paper of $1,063,750 to members of the syndicate.

Disclosure of the list of insiders, in the fall of 1932 after the collapse of Insull's companies, caused a furor because of the high-profile names it contained: Chicago's Democratic mayor, Anton J. Cermak; Melvin Traylor of the First National Bank of Chicago, whose solvency was in jeopardy because of its concentration in Insull loans; and William Lorimer, the Republican boss who had participated with Dawes in the 1912 bank fraud conspiracy and who, as yet unchastened, remained ready to participate in any profitable insider deal. All in all, the list of insiders included 250 high-ranking state officials—including Joseph P. Tumulty, once the powerful personal secretary of Woodrow Wilson, the lieutenant governor of Illinois, the speaker of the Illinois House of Representatives, and state and federal judges—and bankers who had lent millions of dollars to Insull and his companies. It also included the name of the chief investigator for John A. Swanson, the Republican prosecuting attorney for Cook County and a stockholder of the Dawes bank, who was later to bring criminal charges against Insull but not Dawes or any other official of the Dawes bank. (Swanson also maintained a "special" account of the state attorney's office in the amount of $40,623 at the National Bank of the Republic, which was merged into the Dawes bank in July 1931.)[61]

Insull also selected George and his brother, Arthur Reynolds, the controlling stockholders of the Continental Illinois Bank, which was Insull's largest creditor by far, for insider treatment. According to examiners of the Federal Trade Commission, Arthur Reynolds, chairman of the board of Continental Illinois Bank, admitted that he had been "tipped off" that "something big was doing" in the common stock of Middle West Utilities Company. Consequently, between June 17 and July 17, 1929, Arthur Reynolds purchased 8,600 shares of Middle West's common stock for $1,938,831 as its share price rose from $181.50 to $306. And during the same time period, his brother George purchased 1,050 shares for $193,675. Both brothers also took profits and reduced their exposure when they sold about half of their stock positions while the price of the stock was rising. Each of the Reynolds brothers also received an insiders' allocation of $500,000 of the Middle West Preferred and Common Stock Syndicate, which generated a profit of 25 percent between September 1929 and January 1930 on the $30,000 that they had paid. Insull made sure that the money continued to gush from Continental Illinois Bank, which had lent his group $59,857,135 by April 16, 1932. He granted preferred insider status to a total of thirteen officers and directors of the bank, including the Reynolds brothers.[62]

Owen Young and Melvin Traylor, two of the most prominent names on Insull's list of insiders, had been at the height of their prestige and influence in 1931. By then Traylor had been the president of both the Illinois Bankers

Association and the American Bankers Association, as well as the vice president of the Federal Advisory Council of the Federal Reserve Board, which gave him access to the nation's financial leaders. Both were considered dark-horse candidates for the Democratic presidential nomination, representing conservative elements of the party. But within months, their political aspirations were subordinated to their struggle to bolster the crumbling Insull utility system, given that they had both directed their companies to lend millions of dollars to it.[63]

By the end of 1931, Traylor's First National Bank had lent more than $24.2 million, nearly 100 percent of its capital, to the Insull group, at a time when the bank's capital was $25 million. Three of Insull's companies—IUI, Corporation Securities Company of Chicago, and Middle West Utilities Company—had each borrowed $5 million from Traylor's bank. Insull's Utility Securities Company had borrowed another $1.5 million, and the bank had purchased $480,000 of bonds from Insull entities. Insull's brother Martin had also borrowed $600,843, and numerous other borrowers had used the stocks and bonds of Insull's companies as collateral for their loans at the First National Bank.[64]

Facilitating the financing of all of Insull's entities at the bank was Bernard E. Sunny. Once the Chicago manager of the Thomson-Houston Electric Company, he had become a director of GE after its formation in 1892. In typical insider fashion, by the 1930s, Sunny, still on the board of GE, was a director of Insull's Middle West Utilities Company and a director and member of the powerful executive committee of the First National Bank and a director of its subsidiary, the First Union Trust and Savings Bank of Chicago. He had also personally borrowed $240,462 from the First National Bank, whose president, Melvin Traylor, was also a director of Owen Young's GE. Besides being a formidable business leader, Bernard Sunny also wielded significant political clout, serving as a commissioner on the South Park Board and working with Insull to support governors and other politicians friendly to the utilities industry.[65]

And so it went. Eventually, the self-dealing of these inveterate insiders brought down their fragile house of cards, along with tens of thousands of innocent victims. Revealing the extent of the looming Insull crisis, in December 1931, a federal bank examiner warned Comptroller John Pole about the forthcoming "crash of Insull":

INSULL CONCENTRATION: Unquestionably the most dangerous and the most undue credit advance in [First National Bank]. A thorough understanding of the ramifications of this group would require months of exhaustive study. However right at this time it is apparent that "Insull" has reached the end of his rope and from now on it is a question of working out of the matter in the best way possible. The Insull Utility Investment Co., the Corporation Securities Co. and A. B. Leach and Company are admittedly insolvent and it will be noted [First National Bank] holds large lines on all of them. Just what the crash of "Insull" will mean to the country is problematical. That it will work much hardship is a foregone conclusion, considering the terrific amounts various large city banks have advanced, plus the thousands and thousands of innocent citizens who purchased stocks and bonds of the "Insull Group."[66]

The examiner had sounded the death knell for Insull and his bankers, but his politically appointed boss did nothing to avert the crisis. Comptroller Pole stood silent when Traylor and other Loop bankers published fraudulent statements of condition, which counted the Insull loans as being worth 100 percent of their outstanding balances. Though the federal government would prosecute Insull for his indiscretions, it would still use $165 million of taxpayer funds through the Reconstruction Finance Corporation to bail out his bankers, a sum worth about $2.59 billion today.[67]

Notes

1. *Stock Exchange Practices, Insull,* 1516.

2. *New York Times*, October 4, 1924.

3. "The Crime Hunt in Insull's Shattered Empire," *Literary Digest,* October 15, 1932, 12–13.

4. Richard D. Cudahy and William D. Henderson, "From Insull to Enron: Corporate (Re)Regulation after the Rise and Fall of Two Energy Icons," *Energy Law Journal* 26, no. 1 (2005): 36; Edward F. Dunne, *Illinois: The Heart of the Nation* (Chicago: Lewis Publishing, 1933), 2:509–11; Richard Garrett Sherman, "Charles G. Dawes: An Entrepreneurial Biography, 1865–1951" (Ph.D. diss., University of Iowa, 1960), 117; Laurence Bergreen, *Capone: The Man and the Era* (New York: Simon & Schuster, 1994), 225–26; John F. Wasik, *The Merchant of Power: Samuel Insull, Thomas Edison, and the Creation of the Modern Metropolis* (New York: Palgrave Macmillan, 2006), 3, 151, 162–63, 220; "The Crime Hunt in Insull's Shattered Empire," 12; "Insull: Prodigal in Jails and Courts of Former 'Empire,'" *Newsweek* 3, no. 20 (May 19, 1934): 15; "Insull Lives in Athens, Greece," *New Outlook* 162, no. 4 (October 1933): 56–60; Harold L. Platt, *The Electric City: Energy and the Growth of the Chicago Area, 1880–1930* (Chicago: University of Chicago Press, 1991), 271–73; Thomas P. Hughes, *Networks of Power: Electrification in Western Society, 1880–1930* (Baltimore: Johns Hopkins University Press, 1983), 225–26; Forrest McDonald, *Insull* (Chicago: University of Chicago Press, 1962), 275; Francis X. Busch, *Guilty or Not*

Guilty? (Indianapolis: Bobbs-Merrill, 1952), 139–41; William H. Stuart, *The Twenty Incredible Years* (Chicago: M. A. Donohue, 1935), 228; Farr, *Chicago*, 348–51; John R. Schmidt, *"The Mayor Who Cleaned Up Chicago": A Political Biography of William E. Dever* (Dekalb: Northern Illinois University Press, 1989), 115–20; Edgar Lee Masters, *The Tale of Chicago* (New York: G. P. Putnam's Sons, 1933), 307–8; Dorsha B. Hayes, *Chicago: Crossroads of American Enterprise* (New York: Julian Messner, 1944), 272; George P. Stone, "Samuel Insull Is Chicago's Biggest Boss," *New York Times Magazine*, August 15, 1926; *Sunday Oregonian*, July 1, 1934; Williamson, "What Is the Relative Value?"

5. Samuel Insull to Thomas A. Edison, March 21, April 11, 1887; Transcript of Conversations between Insull and Burton Berry, 6, SIP/LU; "58 Years of Business Life," outline of testimony for the federal mail fraud trial, SIP/LU; Samuel Insull, *The Memoirs of Samuel Insull* (Polo, Ill.: Transportation Trails, 1992), v–ix, 17–64; Wasik, *The Merchant of Power*, 5–10; McDonald, *Insull*, 3, 21–24, 29, 30, 33, 82; Platt, *Electric City*, 59–60, 66–67, 76–79; *Chicago Tribune*, April 16, 1932; Alfred O. Tate, *Edison's Open Door* (New York: E. P. Dutton, 1938), 49–50, 52, 139, 141, 147, 249, 256, 261–66, 293; Matthew Josephson, *Edison* (New York: McGraw-Hill, 1959), 150, 249, 253, 254, 273; "Samuel Insull: The Rise to Power," *New Republic*, September 21, 1932, 142–44; Edward Wagenknecht, *Chicago* (Norman: University of Oklahoma Press, 1964), 78–81.

6. "58 Years of Business Life," outline of testimony for the federal mail fraud trial; Thomas A. Edison to Samuel Insull, December 22, 1925, December 22, 1926, SIP/LU; Carosso, *The Morgans*, 390–91; McDonald, *Insull*, 39–54; Platt, *Electric City*, 67–68; Tate, *Edison's Open Door*, 147, 249; Hughes, *Networks of Power*, 202–4; Thomas P. Hughes, "The Electrification of America: The System Builders," *Technology and Culture* 20 (January 1979): 139–41; Insull, *Memoirs*, 37–64; Josephson, *Edison*, 352, 353, 362–65.

7. John S. Goff, *Robert Todd Lincoln: A Man in his Own Right* (Manchester, Vermont: Friends of Hildene, Inc., 2005), vii, 98, 171–176, 216, 217, 226; Insull, *Memoirs*, 163; McDonald, *Insull*, 90; Platt, "Cost of Energy," 32; Doug Wead, *All the Presidents' Children: Triumph and Tragedy in the Lives of America's First Families* (New York: Atria Books, 2003), 175–83.

8. Platt, *Electric City*, 74–79, 98, 108, 171; McDonald, *Insull*, 58–59, 62–63; Williamson, "What Is the Relative Value?"

9. Platt, *Electric City*, 81–82, 132–35, 313; McDonald, *Insull*, 81–89; Wasik, *The Merchant of Power*, 77–78; Hughes, *Networks of Power*, 206; Marvin N. Olasky, "Hornswoggled!" *Reason* 17 (February 1986): 29; Forrest McDonald, "Samuel Insull and the Movement for State Utility Regulatory Commissions," *Business History Review* 32, no. 3 (Autumn 1958): 244, 245; *Moody's Manual of Investments, American and Foreign: Public Utility Securities, 1932* (New York: Moody's Investors Service, 1932), 826; Josephson, *Edison*, 363.

10. Platt, *Electric City*, 82–92, 98–101, 127–30, 143, 159–60; McDonald, *Insull*, 91–93; Harold L. Platt, "The Cost of Energy: Technological Change, Rate Structures,

and Public Policy in Chicago, 1880–1920," *Urban Studies* 26 (February 1989): 35; McDonald, "Samuel Insull and the Movement for State Utility Regulatory Commissions," 245–46.

11. In 1917, Owen D. Young, the future head of General Electric, described Charles Coffin as one of the pioneers of the electric utility industry along with Insull and Edison. Owen D. Young to Samuel Insull, June 22, 1917; C. A. Coffin to Insull, May 19, 22, 24, 25, 1909; Insull to Coffin, May 21, 22, 24, 27, 1909, SIP/LU; "Receiver's Report of Transfer to Reconstruction Finance Corporation of Certain Securities," May 25, 1944, People of the State of Illinois ex rel Edward J. Barrett, Auditor of Public Accounts v. Central Republic Trust Company, CCCC; Platt, *Electric City*, 173–74.

12. Platt, *Electric City*, 98, 120–21, 127, 160; McDonald, *Insull*, 122, 142–44.

13. Frederick Sargent to Samuel Insull, April 6, 1914, SIP/LU; *Moody's Manual of Investments: Public Utilities Securities, 1932*, 586–92; *Chicago Tribune*, April 16, 1932.

14. "Grand Jury Indictment for Conspiracy," The People of the State of Illinois v. William Lorimer, Sr., et al., October 22, 1914, CrCCC; Samuel Insull to William G. Beale, September 15, 1914, SIP/LU.

15. Hughes, *Networks of Power*, 201–2; Sherman, "Dawes," 64, 65; Platt, *Electric City*, 98; McDonald, *Insull*, 243.

16. Insull, *Memoirs*, 105–9; Wasik, *The Merchant of Power*, 183–84; "Samuel Insull," *Time*, November 4, 1929, 54; McDonald, *Insull*, 242–44; Sherman, "Dawes," 107–9; Platt, *Electric City*, 236; Gottfried, *Boss Cermak of Chicago*, 353; Farr, *Chicago*, 342, 365, 370–72; Frederick L. Collins, "A Woman Whose Dream Came True," *Delineator* 3 (October 1927): 12, 131–33.

17. Gladys Insull was born in 1869 with the name Margaret Anna Bird. Before her marriage to Samuel Insull, she had been known as Gladys Wallis. Wasik, *The Merchant of Power*, 75, 76; McDonald, *Insull*, 74, 75, 147–49, 233–35; Insull, *Memoirs*, 94, 99; Forrest McDonald, *Recovering the Past: A Historian's Memoir* (Lawrence: University Press of Kansas, 2004), 14, 15.

18. Platt, *Electric City*, 231; Arthur M. Schlesinger Jr., *The Crisis of the Old Order, 1919–1933*, Vol. 1, *The Age of Roosevelt* (Boston: Houghton Mifflin, 1957), 120; McDonald, *Insull*, 182–85, 203–5.

19. Samuel Insull to L. Y. Sherman, May 12, 1916; Sherman to Insull, May 13, 1916; Sherman to Isham, Lincoln and Beale, January 13, 1930; and Isham, Lincoln and Beale to Sherman, January 17, 1930; Charles G. Dawes to Samuel Insull, February 11, 1903 (telegram); Insull to Dawes, February 12, 1903, LYSP/ALPL; Goff, *Robert Todd Lincoln*, 98, 222–224, 226, 238, 239, 258, 262; Charles Lachman, *The Last Lincolns: The Rise and Fall of a Great American Family* (New York: Sterling Publishing, 2008), 338, 343, 348; *Records of the Examining Division, Comptroller of the Currency's Office, USOCC/WNRC; In re: Insull Utility Investments, Inc., Bankrupt, U.S. District Court of New York,, SIP/LU;* Insull, *Memoirs*, 163; McDonald, *Insull*, 90; Platt, "Cost of Energy," 32; *Who's Who in Finance, Banking and Insurance: A Biographical Dictionary of Contemporary Bankers, Capitalists and Others*

Engaged in Financial Activities in the United States and Canada, vol. 1, edited by John William Leonard (New York: Joseph & Sefton, 1911), 143; *Biographical Directory of the United States Executive Branch, 1774–1989*, Ed. Robert Sobel (Westport, CT: Greenwood, 1990), 234; *Moody's Analyses of Investments, Part II, Public Utilities and Industrials. New York: Moody's Investors Service, 1914, 308, and 1915, 817*; James, *The Growth of Chicago Banks*, 2:786, 787, 948, 949, 951, 1169, 1170, 1210, 1211, 1214; *Stock Exchange Practices*, 1698.

20. Stuart, *Twenty Incredible Years*, 253, 257–58; Wasik, *The Merchant of Power*, 146–48, 150; McDonald, *Insull*, 255–67; Douglas Bukowski, *Big Bill Thompson, Chicago, and the Politics of Image* (Urbana: University of Illinois Press, 1998), 167–69; John D. Hicks, *Republican Ascendancy, 1921–1933* (New York: Harper & Row, 1960), 129, 145; Williamson, "What Is the Relative Value?"

21. *Utility Corporations, Letter from the Chairman of the Federal Trade Commission Transmitting, in Response to Senate Resolution No. 83, 70th Congress, a Monthly Report on the Electric Power and Gas Utilities Inquiry, Middle West Utilities Co. and Subsidiaries, December 16, 1931*, Washington, D.C.: Government Printing Office, 1932, 194–200; Carl D. Thompson, *Confessions of the Power Trust* (New York: E. P. Dutton, 1932), 244–46.

22. John E. Pixton Jr., "The Early Career of Charles G. Dawes" (Ph.D. diss., University of Chicago, 1952), 20–21, 26–27, 87–133; *Biographical Directory of the American Congress: 1774–1961* (Washington, D.C.: Government Printing Office, 1961), 788–89; Sherman, "Dawes," 7–14; Bascom N. Timmons, *Portrait of an American: Charles G. Dawes* (New York: Henry Holt, 1953), 9–11, 68–69.

23. Pixton, "The Early Career of Charles G. Dawes," 192–95; *Biographical Directory of the American Congress*, 1593; Charles G. Dawes, *Journal of the McKinley Years* (Chicago: Lakeside Press, R. R. Donnelley & Sons, 1950), 260; Timmons, *Portrait of an American*, 107–9.

24. Charles G. Dawes to L. Y. Sherman, February 13, 18, 19, 23, March 23, April 20, May 4, June 11, 30, August 2, 31, 1901, August 11, 1904; Dawes to D. G. Tunnicliff, February 13, 1901; Tunnicliff to Sherman, July 13, 1901; Tunnicliff to Dawes, March 22, 1901, LYSP/ALPL; Dawes, *Journal of the McKinley Years*, 287, 295–96, 308–11; Pixton, "The Early Career of Charles G. Dawes," 204–38; Williamson, "What Is the Relative Value?"

25. Petition of Bernard Horwich, as receiver of the Ashland-Twelfth State Bank, March 31, 1915, People of the State of Illinois, Ex Rel James J. Brady, Auditor of Public Accounts of the State of Illinois v. LaSalle Street Trust and Savings Bank, et al., In Chancery No. B3379, CCCC; F. Cyril James, *The Growth of Chicago Banks* (New York: Harper and Brothers, 1938), 2:834, 836; Bruce Bliven, "Charles G. Dawes, Super-Salesman," *New Republic*, January 25, 1928, 263–64; *Chicago Tribune*, March 21, 1916.

26. James, *The Growth of Chicago Banks*, 2:831–32; *Chicago Tribune*, June 24, 1914, April 14, 1916; Stuart, *Twenty Incredible Years*, 3, 10, 203–5.

27. Petition of Bernard Horwich, as receiver of the Ashland-Twelfth State Bank, March 31, 1915, People of the State of Illinois, Ex Rel James J. Brady, Auditor of

Public Accounts of the State of Illinois v. LaSalle Street Trust and Savings Bank, et al, In Chancery No. B3379, CCCC; James, *The Growth of Chicago Banks*, 2:832, 834–37; *New York Times*, June 20, 1914; *Chicago Tribune*, June 13, 19, July 14, 1914, November 20, 1915; Joel A. Tarr, *A Study in Boss Politics: William Lorimer of Chicago* (Urbana: University of Illinois Press, 1971), 308–12.

28. The Central Trust Company of Illinois was the predecessor to the Central Republic Bank and Trust Company, which was the Dawes bank that Hoover's RFC bailed out in 1932. Donald R. Richberg, "De-Bunking Mr. Dawes," *New Republic*, July 9, 1924, 180–81; *Chicago Tribune*, June 24, 1914, September 25, 1915; John Barton Payne to the editor of the *Independent*, August 20, 1924, *Independent* 113 (September 13, 1924): 146; "A Stab in the Dark," *Independent* 113 (September 13, 1924): 145–46; Paul F. Boller Jr., *Presidential Campaigns* (New York: Oxford University Press, 1985), 191–201.

29. John F. Golden et al., Appellants, v. John A. Cervenka et al., Appellees; William C. Niblack, Appellant v. John F. Golden et al., Appellees, *Reports of Cases at Law and in Chancery Argued and Determined in the Supreme Court of Illinois*, vol. 278, 1917, 409–64; Petition of Bernard Horwich, as receiver of the Ashland-Twelfth State Bank, March 31, 1915, People of the State of Illinois, Ex Rel James J. Brady, Auditor of Public Accounts of the State of Illinois v. LaSalle Street Trust and Savings Bank, et al., In Chancery No. B3379, CCCC; James, *The Growth of Chicago Banks*, 2:832–33; Sherman, "Dawes," 97–98; *Chicago Tribune*, September 25, 1915; Williamson, "What Is the Relative Value?"

30. Claim of Illinois Surety Company, June 17, 1914; Claim of Southern Surety Company, March 31, 1915; Petition of Bernard Horwich, as receiver of the Ashland-Twelfth State Bank, March 31, 1915, People of the State of Illinois, Ex Rel James J. Brady, Auditor of Public Accounts of the State of Illinois v. LaSalle Street Trust and Savings Bank, et al, In Chancery No. B3379, CCCC; James, *The Growth of Chicago Banks*, 2:830–37; *New York Times*, June 13, 26, 28, October 2, 1914; *Chicago Tribune*, June 13, 16, 19, 20, 22, 23, 25, July 5, 1914.

31. Receiver's First Report and Account Current, June 2, 1915, People of the State of Illinois, Ex Rel James J. Brady, Auditor of Public Accounts of the State of Illinois v. LaSalle Street Trust and Savings Bank, et al., In Chancery No. B3379, CCCC; *Chicago Tribune*, June 14, 15, 20, 21, 1914, July 23, 1915.

32. The People of the State of Illinois, Defendant in Error v. Charles B. Munday, Plaintiff in Error, *Reports of Cases at Law and in Chancery Argued and Determined in the Supreme Court of Illinois*, vol. 293, June 1920, 191–210; Receiver's First Report and Account Current, June 2, 1915; Answer of William C. Niblack, as receiver of the LaSalle Street Trust and Savings Bank . . . May Term 1915; Petition of Bernard Horwich, as receiver of the Ashland-Twelfth State Bank, March 31, 1915; Promissory Note $9,317.70 of L. L. Bacchus and John H. Rife, May 28, 1914; Collateral Note of $5,500 of Illinois Louisiana Land Company by L. L. Bacchus, Treasurer, December 24, 1913, People of the State of Illinois, Ex Rel James J. Brady, Auditor of Public Accounts of the State of Illinois v. LaSalle Street Trust and Savings Bank,

et al., In Chancery No. B3379, CCCC; Sherman, "Dawes," 91, 96; *Chicago Tribune*, September 25, November 20, 1915, April 6, 1922; *New York Times*, June 18, 19, 1914, July 23, September 25, 1915, Richberg, "De-Bunking Mr. Dawes," 181–82; Bliven, "Charles G. Dawes, Super-Salesman," 263–67.

33. John F. Golden et al. Appellants, v. John A. Cervenka et al. Appellees; William C. Niblack, Appellant v. John F. Golden et al. Appellees, *Reports of Cases . . . in the Supreme Court of Illinois*, vol. 278, 1917, 409–64; The Chicago Title and Trust Company, Receiver of LaSalle Street Trust and Savings Bank, Cross-complainant and Appellant v. Central Trust Company of Illinois, Cross-defendant and Appellee, *Reports of Cases Determined in the Appellate Courts of Illinois*, vol. 224, 1922, 475–505; The Chicago Title and Trust Company, Receiver, Appellant, v. The Central Trust Company of Illinois, Appellee—The Chicago Title and Trust Company, Appellee, v. The Central Trust Company, Appellant, *Reports of Cases at Law and in Chancery Argued and Determined in the Supreme Court of Illinois*, vol. 312, 1924, 396–519; James, *The Growth of Chicago Banks*, 2:833; Sherman, "Dawes," 97–98; *Chicago Tribune*, September 25, 1915, November 20, 1915, April 6, 1922; *New York Times*, September 25, 1915, April 6, 1922, September 19, 21, 1924; C. G. Dawes to L. Y. Sherman, August 1, 1916, April 30, 1917; Sherman to Dawes, April 28, 1917, LYSP/ALPL.

34. C. G. Dawes to L. Y. Sherman, July 2, 15, 1913, January 8, 1915, February 1, 26, 1916, May 22, August 1, 1916, February 21, 1917; Sherman to Dawes, February 19, 1912, June 3, 1914, February 4, 27, May 27, 1916; H. M. Dawes to Sherman, December 3, 1916; R. C. Dawes to Sherman, February 1, October 24, 1918; Sherman to R. C. Dawes, November 6, 1918, LYSP/ALPL; *New York Times*, February 2, March 27, 1913; Stuart, *Twenty Incredible Years*, 11, 15, 162, 163.

35. Charles G. Dawes, *The First Year of the Budget of the United States* (New York: Harper and Brothers, 1923), 84; Warren G. Harding to L. Y. Sherman, October 11, 1921, LYSP/ALPL; Dunne, *Illinois: The Heart of the Nation*, 3:11–12; Timmons, *Portrait of an American*, 22, 28.

36. Sherman, "Dawes," 63; Edward Adolph Goedeken, "Charles G. Dawes in War and Peace, 1917–1922" (Ph.D. diss., University of Kansas, 1984), 28–30, 155–56, 215–26; Timmons, *Portrait of an American*, 164–69, 174–86; Ida M. Tarbell, *Owen D. Young: A New Type of Industrial Leader* (New York: Macmillan, 1932), 159–82; *New York Times*, April 8, 1923, December 10, 11, 1926; Dunne, *Illinois: The Heart of the Nation*, 3:19. Also see, Liaquat Ahamed, *Lords of Finance: The Bankers Who Broke the World* (New York: Penguin Press, 2008), 192–216.

37. *New York Times*, March 30, 1923, December 3, 19, 1924; *Annual Report of the Comptroller of the Currency* (Washington, D.C.: Government Printing Office, 1968), 189.

38. C. G. Dawes to L. Y. Sherman, August 1, 1916, April 30, 1917; L. Y. Sherman to C. G. Dawes, April 28, 1917, LYSP/ALPL; Richberg, "De-Bunking Mr. Dawes," 180; Goedeken, "Charles G. Dawes in War and Peace," 290–91.

39. *New York Times*, September 21, 26, 27, October 1, 1924; *Chicago Tribune*, September 21, 26, 1924; Schlesinger, *The Crisis of the Old Order*, 101.

40. Complaint, RFC v. Central Republic Trust Company, et al., In Equity No. 34-C-24606, CCCC; Bliven, "Charles G. Dawes, Super-Salesman," 263–64; *Chicago Tribune*, September 19, 1924, January 24, 1935; *New York Times*, September 19, 1924, January 24, 1935; Richberg, "De-Bunking Mr. Dawes," 182; E. A. Nicolaysen to Donald R. Richberg, July 18, 1924; Richberg to *New Republic*, July 18, 1924; Henry Spindler to Richberg, August 22, September 1, 1924; Myron McLaren to Richberg, August 24, 1924; Richberg to John M. Nelson, September 4, 1924; Harry Bergson to Editor, *New Republic*, September 15, 1924; Bruce Bliven to Richberg, September 16, 1924 (telegram), September 17, 1924, all in Box 3, DRRP/CHM.

41. *New York Times*, October 4, 1924; Dan and Inez Morris, *Who Was Who in American Politics* (New York: Hawthorn Books, 1974), 149; G. Theodore Mitau, *Politics in Minnesota* (Minneapolis: University of Minnesota Press, 1960), 105; Theodore C. Blegen, *Minnesota: A History of the State* (Minneapolis: University of Minnesota Press, 1975), 466–68; William E. Lass, *Minnesota: A History* (New York: W. W. Norton, 1998), 211–13.

42. See details of the fraudulent and predatory practices of the Dawes brothers during the Florida land boom and bust in my previous book, *Panic in Paradise*.

43. Samuel Insull to Charles G. Dawes, January 18, 1902; Dawes to Insull, April 29, 1902, CGDP/NUL; Pixton, "The Early Career of Charles G. Dawes," 122–23; *Chicago Tribune*, December 18, 19, 24, 1905; Platt, *Electric City*, 170–71, 185, 190; Sherman, "Dawes," 46–47, 50–53, 58–60, 83, 86, 117; Timmons, *Portrait of an American*, 35, 38–39, 132–34; James, *The Growth of Chicago Banks*, 1:644, 2:715; Tarr, "J. R. Walsh of Chicago," 451–66; Tarr, *A Study in Boss Politics*, 9, 75.

44. Samuel Insull to Charles G. Dawes, October 5, 1904, December 15, 1905, January 10, May 2, September 14, December 24, December 27, 1906, June 8, 1917; Martin Insull to Charles G. Dawes, April 26, June 5, July 21, August 26, September 26, December 22, 1916, May 15, 1917; Dawes to Samuel Insull, February 4, 1905, June 12, 1917 (telegram), CGDP/NUL; Minutes of Board of Directors of Middle West Utilities Company, October 7, December 12, 1912; June 13, 1913; January 13, 1914, SIP/LU.

45. Samuel Insull to Charles G. Dawes, January 18, March 25, April 30, December 8, 10, 1902, December 29, 1916; Dawes to Insull, January 20, March 15, April 29, 1902, CGDP/NUL; Wasik, *The Merchant of Power*, 75, 76; McDonald, *Insull*, 74, 75.

46. *Chicago Tribune*, December 19, 21, 24, 1905, January 19, November 14, 1907, January 5, 7, 9, 10, 11, 14, 15, 16, 17, 18, 19, 20, March 12, 13, 14, 1908, October 1, 1909, January 19, 21, 1910, October 24, 1911, June 16, 18, 1914; James, *The Growth of Chicago Banks*, 2:714–21; Tarr, "J. R. Walsh," 461–64.

47. Tarr, "J. R. Walsh," 453–54, 458–60.

48. *Chicago Tribune*, December 21, 1905, December 12, 15, 19, 1907, October 1, 1909, October 24, 1911; Pixton, "The Early Career of Charles G. Dawes," 290;

Samuel Insull to Charles G. Dawes, January 18, 1902, July 22, August 4, December 3, 1903, November 26, 1904, May 28, October 22, 1908, January 6, 1915; Dawes to Insull, April 29, 1902; Charles Fairchild and Company to Samuel Insull, October 20, 1908; Charles G. Dawes to Owen D. Young, August 7, 1935, CGDP/NUL; Receiver's Petition, January 29, 1938, People of the State of Illinois ex rel Edward J. Barrett, Auditor of Public Accounts v. Central Republic Trust Company, CCCC; Dawes, *A Journal of the McKinley Years*, 269, 293, 306–7; Platt, *Electric City*, 170–71, 185, 190; Sherman, "Dawes," 46–47, 50–53, 58–60, 117.

49. R. F. Clinch to C. G. Dawes, June 22, 1929; J. E. Otis to Dawes, July 24, 1929; C. G. Dawes to R. C. Dawes, November 10, 1930, CGDP/NUL; *Time*, May 22, 1933; *Moody's Manual of Investments: Public Utility Securities, 1932*, 586–92, 826–29, 981–85, 1007–13, 1270–74; and *1933*, 337–43, 508–14, 1110–23, 2138–55, *Rufus Cutler Dawes, 1867–1940* (Chicago: A Century of Progress, 1940); *Who's Who in America*, edited by Albert Nelson Marquis (Chicago: A. N. Marquis Company, 1932), 671; *Poor's Register of Directors of the United States and Canada, 1929* (New York: Poor's Publishing Company, 1929), 422–23; Stuart, *Twenty Incredible Years*, 228, 529, 530.

50. C. G. Dawes to Samuel Insull, May 25, 1929; R. C. Dawes to C. G. Dawes, June 20, 1929, CGDP/NUL.

51. R. F. Clinch to C. G. Dawes, June 22, 1929; C. G. Dawes to Clinch, July 5, 1929; J. E. Otis to Dawes, July 24, 1929, CGDP/NUL.

52. C. G. Dawes to O. D. Young, April 11, 17, 1930 (telegrams); Young to Dawes, April 16, 1930, CGDP/NUL; Case and Case, *Owen D. Young*, 361–62, 464; C. G. Dawes to O. D. Young, October 24, 1934, CGDP/NUL; Williamson, "What Is the Relative Value?"

53. "Report of the President of A Century of Progress to the Board of Trustees," March 14, 1936, Library of Congress, Washington, D.C.; R. C. Dawes to C. G. Dawes, October 30, 1931, CGDP/NUL.

54. See the list of guarantors of "A Century of Progress"; R. C. Dawes to C. G. Dawes, July 10, 1929; C. G. Dawes to R. C. Dawes, April 16, 1930 (two telegrams), CGDP/NUL.

55. R. F. Clinch to C. G. Dawes, June 22, 1929; J. E. Otis to Dawes, July 24, 1929, CGDP/NUL; Everett Case to Eugene Meyer, July 20, 1932; "Manning the Credit Pump"; "Bringing Up Reinforcements"; "Young Committee Will Meet Monday"; "Hoover Is Gratified by N.Y. Move to Put Money Back at Work"; "Harrison Organizes Committee to Push Expansion of Credit," n.d.s, clippings in Meyer's scrapbook, EMP/LC; *New York Times*, September 30, 1932; "The Loss of Owen D. Young," *Nation*, January 4, 1933, 4; McDonald, *Insull*, 289, 310; Schlesinger, *The Crisis of the Old Order*, 72, 73, 120; Roy V. Peel and Thomas C. Donnelly, *The 1932 Campaign: An Analysis* (New York: Farrar and Rinehart, 1935) 41.

56. "Mr. Young's Investments in Insull Companies"; Owen D. Young, "To the Board of Directors of the General Electric Company," December 2, 1932; "Mr. P. D. Reed's Memorandum of Mr. Young's Investments in Insull Companies," ODYP/SLU.

57. "Mr. Young's Investments in Insull Companies"; Owen D. Young, "To the Board of Directors of the General Electric Company," December 2, 1932; Agreement between Insull Utility Investments, Inc. and Owen D. Young, January 22, 1929; "Mr. P. D. Reed's Memorandum of Mr. Young's Investments in Insull Companies," ODYP/SLU; Williamson, "What Is the Relative Value?"

58. Owen D. Young, "To the Board of Directors of the General Electric Company," December 2, 1932; "Mr. Young's Investments in Insull Companies," and "Mr. P. D. Reed's Memorandum of Mr. Young's Investments in Insull Companies"; Insull Utility Investments Syndicate Agreement; 60,000 Shares of Insull Utility Investments, Inc., January 16, 1929; Insull, Son & Co., Inc. to Owen D. Young, October 7, 1929, February 25, March 21, May 11, 1932; Middle West Preferred and Common Stock Syndicate Agreement, September 17, 1929; "History of Insull Utility Investments Syndicate," and "History of Middle West Preferred and Common Stock Syndicate," and "History of Insull Utility Investments, Inc., 6% Preferred," and "History of Insull Utility Investments, Inc., Common," and "History of Corporation Securities Company of Chicago," September 28, 1932, ODYP/SLU; Williamson, "What Is the Relative Value?"

59. Hoover, *The Memoirs of Herbert Hoover*, 334–35, 420–21; Insull, *Memoirs*, 203; David M. Kennedy, *Freedom from Fear: The American People in Depression and War, 1929–1945* (New York: Oxford University Press, 1999), 292; Schlesinger, *The Crisis of the Old Order*, 37; Bernard M. Baruch, *Baruch: The Public Years* (New York: Holt, Rinehart and Winston, 1960), 238.

60. Owen D. Young, "To the Board of Directors of the General Electric Company," December 2, 1932; "Insull Matter," memorandum, n.d.; "Mr. Swope's Statement," September 23, 1932; "Mr. Young's Investments in Insull Companies," ODYP/SLU; Deposition of Gerard Swope, January 4, 1933, In re: Insull Utility Investments, Inc., Bankrupt, U. S. District Court of New York, 379–84, SIP/LU.

61. Debtor's Petition of Insull, Son & Co., Inc., April 18, 1933; Trustee's Report and Account of Collections Made from the Subscribers to the Insull Utility Investments Syndicate Agreement of August 15, 1930, December 19, 1939; Petition of Rosenthal, Hamill, Eldridge and King for Final Allowance of Compensation for Services as Attorneys and Counsel for Trustee and for Reimbursement of Expenses, June 29, 1940, In the Matter of Insull, Son & Co., Inc., Bankrupt, In Bankruptcy No. 52930; and Decree of Judge James H. Wilkerson, May 1, 1937, RFC v. Central Republic Trust Company, et al., Equity No. 14189, USDC/NDI; Deposition of Gerard Swope, January 4, 1933, In re: Insull Utility Investments, Inc., Bankrupt, U. S. District Court of New York, 383–84; *New York Times*, September 30, 1932; *Chicago Tribune*, November 21, 1934; "Examiner's Report of the Condition of National Bank of the Republic," April 18, 1931, USOCC/WNRC; McDonald, *Insull*, 308–12.

62. *Utility Corporations . . . Federal Trade Commission . . . Monthly Report . . . Middle West . . .* , July 18, 1934, 718–19; *Stock Exchange Practices*, 1698.

63. *Stock Exchange Practices*, 1698; Dunne, *Illinois: The Heart of the Nation*, 3:7, 8.

64. E. Ogden Ketting to W. H. Dadd, February 8, 1932, EOKP/LU; Alfred P. Leyburn to Comptroller of the Currency, February 6, 15, 1932; "Insull Trust Assets Shrink 333 Millions," n.d., USOCC/WNRC; *Stock Exchange Practices*, 1698.

65. Alfred P. Leyburn to Comptroller of the Currency, February 6, 15, 1932, USOCC/WNRC; "Memorandum to Mr. Stewart, Subject: Insull Properties," August 17, 1932, ISEP/NA; *Moody's Manual of Investments, American and Foreign: Industrial Securities, 1931* (New York: Moody's Investors Service, 1931), 972; *1932*, 2346; Platt, *Electric City*, 171. Stuart, *Twenty Incredible Years*, 214–15.

66. "INSULL CONCENTRATION," December 30, 1931, USOCC/WNRC.

67. Williamson, "What Is the Relative Value?"

Chapter 2

The Fall of Insull

"The most you can say of that old man is that he had too much confidence in this country and his own companies."

—Owen Young, January 1933

"I cannot tell you how pleased I am that you spoke out so strongly. I congratulate you on your courage in taking this open stand, and I congratulate Mr. Insull on having such a true and powerful friend."—In a letter to Owen Young from T. B. Macaulay, the president of Sun Life Assurance Company of Canada, a large stockholder in Insull's Middle West Utilities Company, January 1933[1]

The collapse of Samuel Insull's empire in April 1932 was one of the most dramatic indicators of the seriousness of the economic crisis that gripped the United States in the years following the October 1929 stock market crash. If Insull's failure stopped talk of him as a "genius" and robbed him of public adulation, it also created fear and apprehension among those closely tied to him, including no less a figure than Charles Dawes, then the president of the Reconstruction Finance Corporation.[2]

PRELUDE TO PANIC

Samuel Insull, one of the key figures in the unfolding crisis, had been under unrelenting pressure from many of his bankers to reduce his loans—the same bankers who had been so eager to make those very loans. Watching his pledged securities continue to suffer a dramatic shrinkage in their values,

Insull was reaching the point of desperation by the end of 1931. So he scheduled a meeting with his old friend, Owen Young, at a time when his New York bankers, those outside of his sphere of influence, were reluctant to throw good money after bad.[3]

On December 10, 1931, Insull met privately with Young in his New York office to request a loan package of $2 million from General Electric. After a confidential discussion, Young invited Gerard Swope, GE's president, to join them, and Insull repeated that he was seeking the significant advance "without specifying which of his companies were to be the borrowers" or indicating "what collateral would be put against the note." Nevertheless, Young and Swope, "with very little discussion, all taking place in the presence of Mr. Insull," agreed to make the loans, "subject to approval of the executive committee."[4]

Four days later, Swope received a letter from Insull, which included schedules listing bank loans to Insull Utility Investments (IUI) of $53,257,145, and showing that Corporation Securities owed another $27,269,851 to various banks in Chicago and New York on a short-term basis. Insull, however, did not include any financial information about Middle West Utilities Company, which would receive $500,000 of the loan proceeds. Swope, who had personally invested $113,738 in the securities of IUI, immediately telephoned Insull to say that Melvin Traylor, who was a director of GE as well as being Insull's banker, would be handling the terms and interest rate of the loans. Insull was delighted, knowing that he could count on Traylor. Swope then telephoned Traylor to discuss Insull's extraordinary request. Swope later testified that during that conversation with Traylor, he told him: "We were approving the making of [these] loan[s]." Traylor had responded that "he thought it was all right" to make the loans, and he recommended that GE issue three loans with six-month terms and 5 percent interest rates.

The staff of the investigating subcommittee of the Senate Committee on Banking and Currency considered Swope's telephone call to Traylor "particularly important because of its date, and because it shows that the various parties both in New York and in Chicago were not, at any time, acting wholly independently, but were in constant touch with each other." More to the point, it indicated that Young, Swope, and Traylor, representing the management of GE, were fully informed about the hopelessly insolvent condition of the three Insull entities seeking the emergency loans from GE, a publicly owned company.

That same day, December 14, 1931, Insull's son met with Traylor and the other Insull bankers in Chicago. The next day, he traveled to New York and met with all of the New York banks that were holding short-term Insull loans. Traylor then telephoned Young to discuss the Insull crisis. During this period,

Traylor and Young were having many conversations about the urgent need for Congress to create the Reconstruction Finance Corporation, which, although not designed to make loans to utilities, would be allowed to make emergency loans to banks holding Insull securities.

Insull was under intense pressure from officers of the Central Hanover Bank and Trust Company of New York to make significant payments on his loans, which totaled $20 million at the bank, including loans of $5 million each to IUI and Corporation Securities, and a $10 million loan to National Public Service Corporation, one of Insull's eastern subsidiaries. The timing of the loan disbursements from GE was crucial because the IUI loan, which had a balance of $4 million, was due on December 24, 1931. (The Corporation Securities loan of $5 million was due on December 30, so Insull was facing maturities of $9 million by the end of the month at just one New York bank.) So urgent was the need for the $2 million from GE that it was arranged that Insull's companies would receive the GE checks on December 22, eight days *before* GE's executive committee was able to meet and approve the transactions on December 30, which would have been too late to satisfy the demands of the Central Hanover Bank to make a significant reduction of the IUI loan by December 24.

Young and Swope had demonstrated their loyalty to Insull—in violation of their duty to GE—when they expedited the $2 million in loan closings to such an extent that Insull received the funds, which would be worth about $28.2 million today, only twelve days after their initial meeting, leaving GE's staff insufficient time to conduct a due diligence investigation of the troubled companies. Indeed, Insull waited until he returned to New York, on December 21, before mentioning that Middle West Utilities Company would be one of the companies receiving the proceeds of the loans. The credit facility turned out to be three loans: $1 million to the Corporation Securities Company, $500,000 to IUI, and $500,000 to Middle West. But IUI, Corporation Securities, Middle West, and Insull, in his individual capacity, would all be seeking bankruptcy protection from their creditors, including GE, in short order.[5]

When Young was deposed during the IUI bankruptcy proceedings, he testified that "as a matter of fact, [Insull] had asked for no financial aid from the General Electric Company since 1915." However, when the creditors of IUI deposed Swope, who proved to be a more credible witness than Young, he contradicted Young. Swope testified that GE had made a loan of $2,250,000 to Insull's American Power and Light Company in 1926, a loan that would be worth about $27.3 million today. The loan certainly seemed large enough to be remembered.

Several months later, after Insull had fled the country becoming a fugitive from justice, Young sent a memorandum to GE's board of directors explaining his "personal relationship with the so-called Insull companies." He admitted that he should have revealed the facts to GE's board earlier, but blamed the delay on his busy schedule. He disclaimed any knowledge of the other people on Insull's insider lists, which by then was quite notorious. He said that Insull did not tell him about any of the others who would also be invited to join the special "underwriting," except for Gerard Swope. He also did not reveal that Samuel Insull Jr., who spent most of his time financing deals instead of operating the companies, had telephoned him on September 15, 1931, to inform him that the Insull family was forming "a syndicate of some of their friends" to purchase Middle West Utilities stock at a below-market price. Insull Jr. asked Young if he would be interested in five hundred thousand dollars of the syndicate. Young, without consulting Swope or his board of directors, immediately agreed to the purchase. Despite Insull offering and Young accepting many sweetheart deals, Young had lost so much money speculating in the stock market that by the end of 1932 he had "a negative net worth of $2 million." Yet Young did not forget Insull's generosity.[6]

Young expressed strong support for Insull before the Senate in February 1933, when Ferdinand Pecora, the Senate subcommittee's special counsel, questioned him. Young described Insull as a competent utility executive who had become a "victim" of his own "complicated structure." Young was forceful but not candid about one of the primary reasons behind the complicated structure of the Insull system. In addition to perpetuating his control over the far-flung utilities system and avoiding unfriendly state regulatory commissions, Insull created multiple companies as a way to circumvent the loans-to-one-borrower prohibitions in the various state and federal banking codes. Under the Illinois banking code, state banks were prohibited from lending more than 15 percent of their unimpaired capital and surplus to one borrower.[7]

Insull made special efforts to reward Young and Traylor, considering that both men had the financial and political connections Insull needed to expand his sprawling organization. Traylor, the "banker-political boss" of Chicago, was said to have had the most influence with Mayor Cermak and other local officials, and both Traylor and Young were considered dark horse presidential candidates for the Democrats. But the presidential aspirations of both men would suffer irreparable damage when Insull's empire collapsed. As the presidential bid of Franklin Roosevelt surged forward, the two GE colleagues had to focus their attention on their own financial survival.

By late 1931 and early 1932, Insull needed Traylor's bank to continue making loans to his entities so they could make payments on previous loans. By the middle of April 1932, when IUI, Corporation Securities, and Middle

Image 2.1. Owen Young (right), chairman of General Electric and partner of Charles Dawes, used his considerable influence to ensure the bailout of the Dawes bank. Young and Dawes (left), formerly the chairman of Central Republic Bank and Trust Company of Chicago, waiting to testify before the Senate committee investigating the Samuel Insull fiasco. (Courtesy, St. Lawrence University Special Collections)

West were filing for bankruptcy protection from their banks and other creditors, Traylor's bank had made loans totaling $20,080,267 to Insull's group. But the pyramiding loans continued to increase until August 1932, when they reached a total of $26,439,001, representing more than 100 percent of the paid-in capital of the First National Bank, an amount worth about $415 million today.[8]

Insull also stayed close to Dawes and his bank's officials throughout the 1920s. During the formation of his investment trusts, IUI and Corporation Securities, Insull rewarded officials of the Dawes bank, who would continue to provide loans for his escalating financing needs. The executives of the Dawes bank were among the Insull insiders who bought 250,000 shares of the common stock in IUI at less than half the price the public was offered, in what John Kenneth Galbraith described as a "new and exciting issue" on the Chicago Stock Exchange. Insull's insider syndicate included Joseph Edward Otis, formerly the vice president of Dawes's Central Trust Company from 1911 to 1922, whom Dawes had put in charge of the daily operations of the bank as its chairman and president before he left for Paris to head the reparations committee. Otis remained at the head of the bank while Dawes was in

Washington, and then he became co-chairman after the Dawes bank merged with National Bank of the Republic in 1931. After the merger, Otis's son, Joseph E. Otis Jr., joined the board of directors of the Dawes bank.

Insull's syndicate also included R. Floyd Clinch, a director of Dawes's Central Trust Company, who died in the fall of 1930 after suffering heavy losses in the stock market. Clinch's estate was salvaged when Insull purchased its holdings of coal properties, but it failed to pay the Dawes bank a $33,000 demand loan of the Clinch Mitchell Construction Company that Clinch had personally guaranteed. The worthless loan and the Clinch guarantee were pledged to the RFC to secure the Dawes bailout loans.[9]

Insull gave both Otis, who was also a director of Insull's Chicago, North Shore and Milwaukee Railroad Company, and Clinch the opportunity to purchase one thousand shares of IUI stock at $12 a share. The IUI stock that they purchased at $12 in January 1929 was trading at $127.50 on July 31. It reached a high of $149.25 on August 4, 1929, making each of their stock positions worth $149,250. Had they sold at the August price, each would have made a profit of $137,250 in eight months. Obviously, they had an irresistible reason to approve Insull's loan requests.[10]

Insull also sold additional stock in his companies and issued major bond offerings to banks, insurance companies, and the general public. Earnings of his companies kept increasing throughout the 1920s, and dividends to his stockholders fueled the hysteria as stock prices rose dramatically. The stock market boom of the 1920s was tailor-made for Insull, as he issued more and more shares in his many companies. Until the autumn of 1929, it seemed that the bull market would never end as prices in Insull's companies rose to $100, then $200, then $300, then $400, and then more than $500 a share. The trading of the shares of Middle West provides a good example of the speculative frenzy. On September 21, 1928, Middle West closed at $110 a share, but a year later, on September 21, 1929, it closed at $529 a share. When his net worth reached nearly $150 million (about $1.88 billion today), Insull felt so rich that he told an associate, only half in jest, that he was going to purchase an ocean liner. But then the stock market crashed, and the shares of his companies continued to decline throughout 1930 and 1931 until the Insull securities pledged to the New York and Chicago banks were significantly less than the outstanding loans.[11]

Yet Insull's acute financial problems did not constrain the Dawes bank or the Reynolds brothers' Continental Illinois Bank from funding the Insull family and their companies during the last few months leading up to the major Insull bankruptcies in April 1932 and even beyond that time. On December 31, 1931, shortly after Insull closed the $2 million in loans from GE, he arranged a loan from the Dawes bank for $2,821,577 in the name of IUI, a company in which investors would suffer "real value" losses of $180,187,499, excluding the losses of the banks on their loans.[12]

Then on the eve of the bankruptcy filings, on April 1, 1932, the Dawes bank issued a loan in the amount of $550,000 to Insull's Chicago, North Shore and Milwaukee Railroad Company, which was insolvent, while Otis sat on its board of directors. The railroad company secured the loan with one of its bonds in the amount of $666,000, so the Dawes bank was facing a total loss on what was an insider loan because Otis was a director of the bank and the borrower.

The Dawes bank also made three loans totaling $262,200, at a preferential interest rate of 4.5 percent, to Martin Insull between September 29 and November 16, 1931. Earlier in the year, the Dawes brothers approved and their bank made a $500,000 loan to Samuel Insull, secured with shares of IUI and Insull's Corporation Securities Company, and a loan of $1,787,014 to Insull's Utility Securities Corporation. Dawes' bank continued to accept as collateral the securities of IUI and Corporation Securities even after they had filed for bankruptcy.

In addition, the Dawes bank made loans totaling $269,418 to Martin Insull and his partner, Washington Flexner, between May 16 and June 6, 1932, the day that Martin's brother, Samuel, resigned as the head of his empire. The public held securities worth about $250 million in the two Insull investment trusts, IUI and Corporation Securities, when Samuel Insull's son, Junior, was president of both companies. The Insull family and other investors would lose $245.7 million in these companies when the proceedings were completed, and again, that amount does not include the losses incurred on bank loans. Nevertheless, the Dawes bank pledged its worthless loans to secure the RFC's bailout loans.

The Reynolds brothers, who controlled the Continental Illinois Bank, a much larger bank, were just as reckless as the Dawes brothers when they approved a personal loan of $2,775,000 to Insull on January 6, 1932, giving him a preferential interest rate of 4.5 percent and taking as the primary collateral IUI common and preferred stock and shares of the Corporation Securities Company. Then, two days later, the Reynolds bank issued loans of $18,987,500 to IUI, $7,035,356 to Insull Son and Company, Inc., and $5.75 million to the Corporation Securities Company. Investors in the latter company's securities would lose 99 percent of their investments, a real value loss of $65,589,797. As Insull continued to borrow at a frantic pace during this desperate time, on January 25, 1932, the Reynolds brothers made a loan of $2.5 million to the Midland Utilities Company, whose president was Insull's son, Junior, who was thirty-one years old. Investors would lose $30,595,162 in real investment value in the securities of Midland Utilities. Next, the Reynolds bank issued a $3,125,000 loan to Insull's Midland United Company, whose bankruptcy would cost its investors $43,874,459. And by the middle of February 1932, the bank had made two more loans, for a total of $5 million, to Insull's Middle West Utilities Company, in which investors would lose $135,255,400, or 91 percent of the real value of their holdings.

When the inevitable crash came, the Continental Illinois Bank was also holding promissory notes of $3,385,000 from Insull's 20 Wacker Drive Building Corporation, the holding company for the Civic Opera House building, which Samuel Insull personally guaranteed in 1931. By then Samuel Insull would sign any loan guarantee placed before him. The bank also issued loans to Insull's Public Service Company for $1,790,000; Insull's Utility Securities Company for $5,430,698; and numerous other entities and individuals considered as part of the Insull group. The total borrowing of Insull's entities, affiliates, and associates from the Continental Illinois Bank was $59,857,135 on April 16, 1932, representing 80 percent of its capital and 43 percent of its combined capital and purported surplus. Even so, the Reynolds brothers continued to publish fraudulent financial statements on behalf of their bank, certifying that its Insull loans were worth 100 percent of the amounts carried on its books.[13]

It took thirty months for Insull's system to collapse after the stock market crash in October 1929. On the day after Black Thursday, Hoover had reassuringly declared, "The fundamental business of the country, that is, production and distribution of commodities, is on a sound and prosperous basis." Projecting hopefulness and optimism was Hoover's way of dealing with growing public apprehension about the consequences of the 1929 crash. Unlike previous presidents faced with major economic downturns, Hoover determined to be an activist, at least as compared to his predecessors. His goal was to discourage the private sector from its traditional response to economic collapse, which was to lay off employees and cut expenses, and then wait for an upturn in economic activity. The administration's "activism" included support of Secretary of the Treasury Andrew Mellon's income tax cut proposal and plans to accelerate public works projects, which had been long-talked about and deferred. In the December State of the Union message, he also advocated Congressional action on consolidating railroads, revising the tariff, and dealing with the troubled banks.[14]

Hoover's most visible response was to convene a series of conferences with leaders from industry, railroads, and utilities. The president wanted to encourage these leaders not to cut back from planned expenditures but instead to expand their companies. Insull was invited to the session devoted to the utilities industries. During a late November 1929 meeting of one of these "business-as-usual" conferences, Hoover secured a promise from Insull and other utility executives "to continue and expand their construction activities."[15]

Convinced that the Depression was only temporary and, as usual, in an expansion mode, Insull claimed that expanding his utilities conglomerate was merely keeping his promise to Hoover. Though the times and his level of debt should have dictated otherwise, Insull spurred his companies into a spending spree. In 1930, Insull's companies borrowed $197 million. After the stock market crash and into the spring of 1932, the bankers of Chicago kept supplying Insull with tens of millions of dollars in loans.[16]

Insull had tossed caution to the wind, seemingly forgetting the difficult times that his companies had gone through in 1914 after the collapse of Lorimer's banking chain caused a regional depression in Chicago. The bankers also remained in a delusional state after the stock market crash of 1929, as Traylor described later when he testified before Congress. Traylor conceded that he and the other bankers and businessmen of Chicago were operating with "a watered state of mind in which we all thought we were richer than we were, and were living beyond our means." Forrest McDonald, in his biography of Insull, reported that the president of Continental Illinois Bank told Samuel Insull Jr.: "Say, I just want you to know that if you fellows ever want to borrow more than the legal limit, all you have to do is organize a new corporation, and we'll be happy to lend you another $21,000,000."[17]

And the money kept rolling in. Eager to speculate with Insull, officials of the three major Loop banks published false financial statements, violating state and federal banking laws because they counted the Insull loans as being worth the full amounts of their outstanding balances. The bankers also evaded the loans-to-one-borrower regulations designed specifically to prevent excessive concentration. Thus, by August 1932, Insull and his companies had borrowed from just the Dawes bank, the Reynolds' bank, and Traylor's bank a total of nearly $98.4 million, which would be more than $1.55 billion today.[18]

An examination of the loan portfolios of the three banks reveal why the public lost confidence in these institutions. Despite warnings from federal regulators to Traylor and the other officers of the First National Bank that the Insull loans represented a "treacherous" concentration, in eight months those loans rose $2,229,583, to a total of $26,439,001 by August 1932. The total exposure of the bank increased significantly when Insull's Public Service Company of Northern Illinois borrowed $4,043,208 from Traylor's bank. By July, IUI, the Corporation Securities Company of Chicago, and the Middle

Image 2.2. The Dawes brothers controlled the hopelessly insolvent Dawes bank, which was bailed out by the Reconstruction Finance Corporation. (Courtesy, Library of Congress)

West Utilities Company were all in receiverships, freezing $14,438,606 of the assets of the First National Bank.[19]

Dawes's Central Republic Bank and Trust Company had used 80 percent of its capital to finance Insull's expansion. The Dawes brothers had controlled the bank for thirty years, from its inception in 1902 to its demise in 1932. Through entities including Dawes Brothers, Incorporated, the Central Illinois Company, the Central Illinois Securities Corporation, the Central Republic Company, and Hinshaw and Company, the Dawes brothers had absolute control of the bank. As already noted, it was because of the influence of Charles Dawes and his brothers over the policies and daily operations of the bank that it became commonly known as the "Dawes Bank."

On April 16, 1932, when the Illinois banking code prohibited a single customer from borrowing more than 15 percent of a bank's unimpaired capital and surplus, Insull's companies and affiliates and the officers, directors, and employees of his entities owed the Central Republic Bank $11,977,400 in forty-one loans, representing almost 50 percent of its capital and surplus.

Because the Central Republic Bank had purported capital and surplus of $24,000,000, its loans to Insull and his entities of more than $3,600,000 violated the state's policy against the excessive concentration of loans to one group of borrowers. State law established an unambiguous yardstick for determining what a prudent banker, operating a bank in a safe manner, should have done when one man who controlled numerous companies applied for loans greatly exceeding the 15 percent rule.[20]

Ferdinand Pecora and the U.S. Senate subcommittee's investigators focused their attention on the improper loans of the Dawes bank but missed its reckless speculation in the stocks and bonds of Insull's companies. As of June 30, 1932, the Dawes bank gambled away several millions of dollars of its nearly $19 million securities portfolio speculating in the stocks of Insull's investment trusts, the Corporation Securities Company and IUI, as well as in the stocks of the following Insull companies: the Commonwealth Edison Company, the Middle West Utilities Company, the Peoples Gas Light and Coke Company, the Public Service Company of Northern Illinois, the Midland Utilities Company, the Midland United Company, the Chicago, North Shore and Milwaukee Railroad Company, the Chicago Rapid Transit Company, the Central and South West Utilities Company, the Southwestern Light and Power Company, the United Public Service Corporation, the Western United Gas and Electric Company, the Seaboard Public Service Company, the Northeastern Public Service Company, the Northwest Utilities Company, the North American Light and Power Company, the New England Public Service Company, and the Michigan Public Service Company. The Dawes bank further concentrated its securities portfolio in the corporate bonds of Insull's companies such as the Chicago Aurora and Elgin Railroad Company, the Chicago, North Shore and Milwaukee Railroad Company, the Chicago Rapid Transit Company, the Missouri Gas and Electric Service Company, and the Pecos Valley Power and Light Company.[21]

When Charles Dawes testified before the Senate subcommittee investigating the Insull debacle on February 15, 1933, he admitted that the Insull loans, which were more than three times the loans-to-one-borrower restriction in the Illinois banking code, violated the public policy principle that a bank should not concentrate its assets in one customer. Dawes also admitted that the worthless or severely deflated Insull loans had been used as collateral to secure his ninety-million-dollar RFC loan.[22]

Insull violated the loans-to-one-borrower law for years, procuring bank loans in his own name or personally guaranteeing corporate loans and then getting his companies to indemnify him and hold him harmless from any loan payments. Beyond the question of illegality, the Insull loans were so excessive as to evidence gross negligence on the part of Henry, Rufus, and William Dawes, who were members of the bank's board of directors when the loans were made to Insull's entities, along with other officials of the Dawes bank, including Charles Dawes—who remained a voting member of the board despite his absence while he was in Washington and London.[23]

The Illinois banking code mandated a clear standard of care for the prudent banker to operate a state bank:

> every director, officer, of any such [bank], who shall violate, or participate in, or assent to such violation, or who shall permit any of the officers, agents or servants of the [bank] to violate the provisions hereof, shall be held liable in his personal and individual capacity for all damages which the [bank], its sharehold-ers or any other person shall have sustained in consequence of such violation.

At a minimum, the officers and directors of the Dawes bank that violated the principle of the loans-to-one-borrower restriction should have been held personally liable for their gross negligence.[24]

If the directors of the RFC had properly performed their fiduciary duty to the taxpayers who owned their agency, then they would have forced the Dawes brothers and the bank's other negligent directors to resign before any funds were disbursed. Since the bailout loans were tens of millions of dollars more than the value of the pledged assets, the RFC directors were also guilty of gross negligence when they authorized the loans.

THE INSULL COLLAPSE

Why had Insull taken on such crushing debt? It was in large part to keep at bay Cyrus S. Eaton of Otis and Company, an investment banking company based in Cleveland, Ohio. By the mid-1920s, Eaton, a former Baptist min-ister, had become an aggressive stock speculator, making his fortune in the steel, railroad, and utilities industries and then developing a keen interest in Insull's entities. He was chairman of Continental Shares, Inc., whose advisory committee consisted of "several men of broad experience in the public utility field." In 1927, the officers of Continental Shares quietly began accumulat-ing major blocks of common stocks in Insull's operating companies: Com-monwealth Edison Company, the Peoples Gas Light and Coke Company, the Public Service Company of Northern Illinois, and Middle West Utilities Company. Somewhat disingenuously, Eaton claimed that the purchases were "solely for investment" and not a hostile takeover attempt or greenmail scheme.[25]

Nevertheless, Insull, who viewed Eaton's actions with suspicion, over-reacted in a series of complicated maneuvers pyramiding his utility companies through holding companies created to maintain control of his empire. Insull's numerous entities became so complex that his friend, Owen Young, as we have seen, argued that Insull had become a victim of his own corporate structure. But after carefully reviewing Insull's machinations, Judge Evan Alfred Evans concluded that Insull's reorganized utility system, controlled through his giant holding companies, was "nothing but a glorified gambling institution."[26]

On the eve of the public hearings into Insull's business practices, the Senate's lead investigator, J. B. McDonough, advised Ferdinand Pecora, the Senate's chief counsel:

> The main motive which can be traced throughout the so-called Insull picture is the desire for personal power, personal wealth and all that goes with it. This is true, not only of Samuel Insull, but of his associates and of the other members of his family. There is another motive which is manifested as an insistent undertone. This motive is fear. This fear fixed itself in the fear of loss of control of the three main operating companies. Accompanying both is an undercurrent of disregard, if not contempt, for the rights of the investing public whose money made possible the development of these schemes.[27]

With the Eaton threat looming, Insull converted his utilities system into a virtual casino, gambling with the savings of tens of thousands of investors who believed his utility companies to be a safe investment. He concentrated a huge amount of short-term bank debt in his holding companies to secure control of the operating companies, which was reckless in the extreme after the stock market crashed. Insull was far more interested in maintaining control of Commonwealth Edison, Middle West Utilities, People's Gas, and Public Service than in fulfilling his fiduciary duties to his stockholders.

Insull's madcap borrowing would extend to the operating companies when he bought out Eaton at an exorbitant price, so when the inevitable bankruptcy filings came, stockholders at both levels of his complicated system would have to stand in line behind the creditors. But the stockholders of the operating companies owned shares representing the ownership of income-producing properties while the stockholders of the holding companies were merely holding worthless pieces of paper.

In addition, Insull was playing with depositors' money when he borrowed their savings from the big three banks in the Loop. Forming IUI in December 1928 to buy shares of his major operating companies, he used it to issue more and more stocks and bonds until it had invested some $250 million in the operating utility companies. His other super-holding company, the Corporation Securities Company of Chicago, formed in September 1929, raised $150 million from investors. It was used to purchase about $150 million in the operating companies. Between them, IUI and Corporate Securities invested some $400 million, which diluted the voting power of the shares that Eaton controlled but would fall short of securing Insull's control of his kingdom.[28]

Insull had gambled all of his chips on one game of poker. Between December 1928 and September 1929, he exchanged all of his own stock in the operating companies, which had substantial assets and relatively secure cash flows from utility properties, for shares of IUI and Corporation Securities, whose only assets were the securities of the operating companies. When the values of the shares held through the holding companies precipitously dropped in 1930, and the dividends from the operating companies were drastically reduced because of the deepening Depression, the holding companies were overwhelmed with principal and interest payments while facing a cash-flow crisis. Selling the securities—owned through the holding companies but pledged to the banks—to relieve the demands of the short-term debt was no longer an option, and Insull's bankers knew that basic fact all too well. Because the servicing of the gargantuan bank debt was dependent on the dwindling dividends and rapidly shrinking share prices, IUI and Corporation Securities were suddenly insolvent and forced into bankruptcy court. As a result, Insull lost his fortune, which he had accumulated over fifty years.

During the exhilarating ride, Insull; his wife, Gladys; his son, Samuel Insull Jr.; and his brother, Martin, all exchanged shares in Commonwealth Edison, Peoples Gas, Public Service, Middle West, and related entities with a market value of $9,765,908 for 764,000 common shares of IUI at $7.54 a share, and 40,000 preferred shares of IUI at $100 a share. The preferred shares included a two-year option to buy 200,000 common shares of IUI at $15 a share. When the option was exercised, the Insull family held a total of 964,000 shares of its common stock.[29]

With the formation of IUI and Corporation Securities, the fight for control of the Insull system began in earnest. As Insull's entities and Eaton's group bought blocks of stock, share prices of Insull's utilities companies rose to record heights during 1929. In August of that year, a few months before the crash, Commonwealth Edison reached $450 a share and Middle West reached $529. Meanwhile, Peoples Gas rose to $404; and Public Service hit $425. The dramatic increase in the share prices forced Insull to borrow incessantly in his effort, as his press release announced, "to perpetuate the existing management of the Insull group of public utilities." Insull, who was sixty-nine years old when IUI was formed, also was attempting to guarantee control of the company from the grave to ensure that Junior, his only son, who was then twenty-eight years old, would name the officers and directors of his companies after Insull Sr. died. This obsession with control would soon bankrupt him and his estate.[30]

The battle for control between Insull and Eaton ran up the stock price of Insull's entities and created a bubble. Eaton, the wily raider, was only interested in making large amounts of money, so he unloaded his stock before the bubble burst. Relying on Insull's burning desire to maintain control of his life's work, Eaton and his group were richly rewarded in June 1930. Eaton sold his group's holdings for $56 million, which would have a relative value of about $719 million today. The transactions reflected a price of $350 for each share of Insull stock that the Eaton group owned, consisting of 85,800 shares of Commonwealth Edison, which Eaton bought for an average of $207 a share; 60,600 shares of Peoples Gas, bought for an average of $188 a share; and 13,600 shares Public Service, bought for an average of $190 a share. In the first closing with Insull, Eaton's group received $48 million in cash and $8 million in common shares of IUI and Corporation Securities. And then in March 1931, Eaton sold his remaining shares of IUI and Corporation Securities to Insull. At the end of the transactions, Eaton's group realized a profit of $22,784,421.[31]

To finance the acquisition of Eaton's holdings, the Insulls and their entities had to borrow more than $30 million from Traylor's First National Bank, George Reynolds's Continental Illinois Bank, and the Dawes bank. Donald R. McLennan, a director of the Continental Illinois Bank and a director of Insull's Commonwealth Edison, facilitated the transactions. Eventually, Insull's investment trusts—IUI and Corporation Securities—would pledge their entire portfolios to banks in Chicago and New York in order to secure their loans. This increased the need for Insull to maintain friendly relations with his Chicago bankers.[32]

Adding to the intolerable level of debt at all of Insull's entities, Middle West Utilities Company, a major holding company that owned operating companies in a number of states, borrowed $50 million in 1930. The five-year debt issue created a significant financial strain on the company because $10 million of the bonds matured during each of the five years. Insull's other entities had borrowed more than $150 million during 1930 through the issuance of bonds, debentures, and notes. But it was the Eaton-related transactions that forced Insull and his holding and operating companies to borrow heavily from the all-too-willing banks in the middle of the bear market, with no time for, or hope of, issuing general corporate obligations.

In fact, the bankers mistakenly saw Insull's plight as an opportunity. Otis told Dawes on May 1, 1931: "There is much financing to be done in order to relieve floating indebtedness of utility and other corporations as there has been no bond market, as you know, for more than a year." The bankers on La Salle Street in downtown Chicago found it was much easier and more profitable to lend money to one man's organization than to evaluate loan applications from hundreds of firms. In their zeal, the bankers engaged in unsafe and unsound practices, violating state and federal banking laws and recklessly concentrating in loans to Insull's various enterprises. By the end of 1931, the banks of Chicago had made loans of more than $150 million to Insull and his entities, as well as other Insull-related loans to individuals, who pledged the paper of Insull's companies as security.[33]

In addition to beguiling bankers, Insull was so successful at selling his companies to the public through his program of "customer ownership" that he raised public awareness to a level uncomfortable for a man who ran his empire much like an Old World potentate. He felt the double-edged sword at the annual stockholders' meetings of IUI and Corporation Securities Company, both held on February 16, 1932, in the opera building that Insull had so proudly inaugurated a little more than two years earlier. As angry stockholders voiced concern about the solvency of his companies, it became clear that times had changed dramatically. Many stockholders were understandably alarmed because the financial statements of his companies disclosed that they had lost four hundred million dollars in value. But Insull still had more supporters than detractors and he was able to walk away from the meeting feeling "gratified."[34]

Samuel Insull's humiliation, however, was just beginning. Two weeks later, he presided over the annual stockholders' meeting of the Commonwealth Edison Company, which he had founded in 1907 and which now had about forty thousand stockholders. The meeting, held in Customer's Hall at the Edison Building in downtown Chicago, ran according to its script until a disgruntled stockholder raised his hand. The following exchange revealed that the emperor was losing his clothes.

Mr. Keil: Well, Mr. Chairman, I bought this stock a year ago at 235.
Chairman Insull: Yes.
Mr. Keil: And now it is 105.
Chairman Insull: Yes.
Mr. Keil: I would like to have that explained.
Chairman Insull: Well, you can only explain that by studying the economic conditions in this country and everywhere else. I did the same thing. I did exactly what you did.

Mr. Keil: I wouldn't do it over again.

Chairman Insull: What?

Mr. Keil: I wouldn't do it over again.

Chairman Insull: Well, there are lots of us whose hindsight is much better than our foresight. There are a great many things I have done in the last year or two that I wouldn't do over again, and I think that applies to most of us.

Insull, one of the best at reacting on his feet, was flustered for a brief moment and then he put the meeting back on track, but the point had been made.[35]

As his financial problems, both personal and corporate, intensified, Insull approached Charles Mitchell, the president of the National City Bank of New York, for a personal loan of $5 million sometime before September 1, 1931. This transaction indicates a much different situation than Forrest McDonald's conspiracy theory advanced in his biography of Insull, in which he relied heavily on self-interested and off-the-record interviews. McDonald blamed Insull's downfall on the New York bankers, vividly portraying them as greedy robber barons whose motives were tainted because they planned to destroy Insull so that they could control his utility network. But the loan from Mitchell's National City Bank to Insull was more an act of friendship than a hard-nosed business transaction.[36]

Owen Young's sworn testimony before the Senate and before the special master in the IUI bankruptcy proceedings contradicted McDonald's theory. Feeling increasingly insecure about the value of the Insull securities they were holding as collateral, the New York bankers began searching for "independent avenues of information" along with a procedure for safeguarding against intercompany transactions between Insull's entities and other extraordinary expenses that were adverse to their interests.

Insull asked Owen Young to intervene and use his influence with the New York bankers in an effort to stall the impending receiverships. Young testified that in February 1932, "Insull came to me and said that he and his associates had been arranging for a standstill agreement by the bank creditors of their companies, explaining that by standstill he meant that all banks would extend their loans to a definite date in the future." Two New York banks, Central Hanover Bank and the Irving Trust Company, would not agree to the standstill agreement. Therefore it was not binding, because "each bank had undertaken to enter the standstill only on condition that all agree." Young determined that the New York banks "felt they had no adequate information as to the current activities of the Insull companies, and that they did not feel at liberty to rely on the reports of the Chicago banks." Young also discovered that "all the New York banks had that same apprehension about the Insull situation. The structure was very complicated, the movement of funds between those companies was difficult to follow, and the New York banks felt that if they were to agree to a standstill they should have better sources of information." The fact that Insull's companies owed New York banks more than $50 million made acquiring sound information imperative to the banks.[37]

After meeting with the New York bankers, Young went to Chicago to try to reach a standstill agreement among all of Insull's bankers to forbear on selling their collateral as the loans slid into default. Young held a meeting in Insull's office on Saturday, February 27, 1932, which Insull and his son attended, along with James L. Leavell, Herman Waldeck, and Stanley Field, who was representing the Continental Illinois Bank but was also a director of Commonwealth Edison and Peoples Gas, Melvin Traylor and Edward Brown of the First National Bank, Joseph Otis, chairman of the Dawes bank, Solomon A. Smith, chairman of Northern Trust Company, and a representative from Harris Trust and Savings Bank.

Young opined that the New York bankers had raised "a reasonable objection" and had made "a reasonable point" about their need for reliable information about the precarious condition of the Insull companies. Later that year, when he testified about the meeting with the Insulls and their Chicago bankers, Young said:

> I stated to them quite frankly what the position of the New York banks was, and said that it seemed to me that their position was reasonable; that if they were to be asked to go along with the standstill agreement, they should have their independent avenue of information; and that if the reports showed that things were taking place which were prejudicial to the banks, that they ought to have some understanding with Mr. Insull that nothing would take place which was not assented to by their representative. There was no objection to that on the part of either Mr. Insull or of the Chicago banks.

So it was agreed that Insull would retain Arthur Andersen, a well-known Chicago accountant, and his firm, Arthur Andersen and Company, to conduct the due diligence on behalf of the New York banks, assuming they agreed on the man that Insull and his personal bankers in Chicago had selected. Young immediately returned to New York and convinced the New York banks that Andersen should be retained to monitor all transactions and approve extraordinary expenses. Young would also testify that Andersen and members of his firm were independent professionals that Insull hired to convince the bankers to extend the maturity dates on his loans.[38]

Arthur Andersen was well known to Insull. In fact, he was a member of the board of trustees of A Century of Progress (the official name of the 1933

Chicago World's Fair), along with Insull, his son Junior, and Charles and Rufus Dawes. Andersen had long had a close relationship with the Dawes brothers for many years. When Charles Dawes was ambassador to Great Britain, Andersen traveled to London on business, and Rufus Dawes asked his brother to "do whatever you can to make his visit to London successful." Rufus described Andersen "as one of the most patient, loyal and devoted friends that I have ever known." Rufus was president of A Century of Progress when Andersen was its comptroller, and Rufus relied heavily on Andersen for the project. Andersen was also the auditor for the Dawes brothers' Pure Oil Company, and Rufus told Charles that their brother Henry had "repeatedly spoken in the highest appreciation of the work that he has done for them." Perhaps more important, Arthur Andersen and Company had made an unsecured loan of $7,177 to Charles Cutler Dawes, Rufus's son, which became a matter of public record in 1935 when young Charles filed for bankruptcy.[39]

Despite these connections, Andersen unearthed extensive insider abuse by the Insull family and transactions that appeared to be fraudulent. Beginning in April 1932, the Chicago newspapers reported the "revelations" on a daily basis. It soon became apparent that Insull's IUI, Corporation Securities, and Middle West were not only hopelessly insolvent but had suffered significant losses due to the misconduct of the Insull family.[40]

Unsubstantiated rumors had been flying that J. P. Morgan and Company, through its control of the United Gas Improvement Company of Philadelphia, and the Public Service Corporation of New Jersey, was interested in buying Insull's eastern subsidiaries. United Gas already owned a minority position of 577,696 shares of common stock in Insull's Midland United Company, which was confronted with losses of more than $43.8 million. The theory was that the Morgan interests planned to assert their banking power to facilitate the sale of Insull's eastern units to their utility holding companies, forcing Insull to retreat from the East Coast.

Charles Dawes did not view the New York bankers as villains. He knew them to be an easy and sometimes cheap source of capital for his speculative ventures. In the fall of 1931—before the difficulties of Insull and Dawes were well known in banking circles—Dawes borrowed $75,000 from J. P. Morgan and Company (which would be worth about $1,060,000 today). Even after the collapse of Insull and the Dawes bailout, in November 1933, Dawes received a $90,000 demand loan with a 3 percent interest rate from Central Hanover Bank and Trust Company of New York to purchase 4,300 shares of publicly traded stock. Less than a month earlier, he had arranged a demand loan of $81,275 from the Harris Trust and Savings Bank of Chicago to speculate in the stock market, but it carried an interest rate of 5 percent.[41]

Fears of Insull's demise were realized when significant parts of his organization sought the protection of the federal court system. Heading into bankruptcy were some of his more high-profile companies, including IUI and the Corporation Securities Company, where the wealth of the Insull family was concentrated; the Middle West Utilities Company, which was burdened with its holdings of worthless IUI securities; the National Electric Power Company, a subsidiary of Middle West that operated utilities in fourteen eastern states; and the Midland United Company, a holding company that owned twenty-three companies, including the Midland Utilities Company, operating in Indiana, Ohio, Michigan, and Illinois, but it was also facing gigantic losses in its portfolio of IUI securities.[42]

By March 1932, the difficulties of the Middle West Utilities Company, at the core of the Insull system with subsidiaries in thirty-two states, were being described on a daily basis in the *Chicago Tribune*. Stockholders and bondholders of the Insull company, who were also depositors of Chicago banks, which had outstanding loans of more than $150 million to Insull's entities, making their survival dependent on the survival of Insull's companies, must have read each article with increasing alarm.[43]

Public officials and bankers described the depositors of Chicago's banks as hysterical during this period, so it is illuminating to examine what they were reading in their local newspapers on a daily basis. Doing so indicates that, under the circumstances, the withdrawal of one's savings from a Chicago bank that had funded Insull's reckless expansion and his takeover fight with Eaton should have been viewed as complying with the prudent man investment rule. For example, in 1932, the public held a "real value" of $2.64 billion of common and preferred stocks, bonds, and other Insull securities. By 1946, the public would suffer losses of $638 million from that amount, excluding loss of interest and dividend payments, following the reorganizations of forty-one of Insull's companies. After fourteen years of bankruptcy proceedings, the public lost the equivalent of about $7 billion in today's dollars. Amid the rubble, major Insull operating entities survived: the Commonwealth Edison Company; the Peoples Gas Light and Coke Company, the provider of gas to Chicago; and the Public Service Company of Northern Illinois, servicing the greater Chicago metropolitan area with electricity and gas. Commonwealth Edison was the backbone of the operating companies, providing electricity to almost all of Chicago. In 1932, the "real value" of the public's holdings of Commonwealth Edison's securities was about $305.4 million, of which the long-term amount of public investment was about the same in 1949. But speculators who bought common shares of Commonwealth Edison in 1929 at $449 a share watched their price plummet to $30.50 a share by 1933, when

60,000 investors still owned its stock. By 1946, the common stock of Commonwealth Edison was selling on the open market for a value, after taking into consideration a four-for-one stock split, of $136 a share. The holders of its first mortgage bonds fared much better; in fact, on only three occasions did the value of the bonds drop below $90. By 1939, all of its bonds had been redeemed at an average retirement price of $107.[44]

On March 29, 1932, Joseph Otis, the chairman of Dawes's Central Republic Bank and a director of Electric Household Utilities Corporation, whose largest stockholder was Owen Young's GE and which was a major customer of the Dawes bank, forwarded a memorandum to Young. Young was heading the effort to salvage Insull's system. The memorandum suggested that five large life insurance companies should be approached to provide loans totaling $65 million to Insull's struggling companies as a way to "dispel the fears that possess the public mind."

B. A. Mattingly, the vice president of the Dawes bank who prepared the memorandum, viewed the insurance companies as lenders of last resort because the RFC was prohibited from making loans to public utility companies. He said the securities market was not an option for refinancing because "rumors concerning the Insull companies have been so vicious and widespread that, in my opinion, it will be impossible for even the large operating companies to successfully market refunding securities before their present obligations mature." Mattingly acknowledged that Insull's banks, including the Dawes bank, had such high concentrations of Insull loans that they were not willing "to materially increase their risks." Mattingly recognized the difficulty of arranging such a loan package but suggested that President Hoover could pressure the insurance companies, which were "the only reservoirs of large cash and/or credit from which relief might be sought." He urgently wrote: "I do not believe that such a loan as is suggested would be made by the insurance companies unless the President of the United States should interest himself in the situation and bring pressure to bear but I do believe that Mr. Hoover is sufficiently conversant with the seriousness of the situation to be agreeable to use his influence." The insurance companies did not make the loan, but Hoover did use his influence three months later to bail out the Dawes bank, which was insolvent in large part because of its nearly $12 million in Insull loans.[45]

Then on March 31, below an article in the *Chicago Tribune* about a wishful report that Insull had issued, was a story titled "RECEIVERSHIP ASKED FOR INSULL UTILITY INVESTMENTS, INC." Helen Samuels, who owned four $1,000 debenture notes of IUI, had filed a petition alleging the insolvency of IUI and seeking its receivership and distribution of its assets to creditors. The action alleged that the rapid decline of the market had caused IUI's assets, consisting of listed securities of other Insull companies, to plummet to a value of only $27 million, compared to its liabilities of $121 million. (As a result, the company had a negative net worth of $94 million.) According to the petition, the assets of IUI were purchased at the height of the bull market in 1929 for $232 million. But the company's assets had declined to $120 million by the end of 1931 and had lost an additional $90 million plus in value during the first three months of 1932. The petition also alleged that Insull and other company officials had "manipulate[d] the sale and distribution of the capital stocks" of Insull's affiliated entities.[46]

Insull did not immediately respond to the receivership petition against IUI, and his lack of action had a negative effect on the stock exchanges, where his companies continued to lose ground. His refusal to present a realistic refinancing plan to solve the Middle West crisis, or even to comment on it, was driving the market values of the various Insull securities into the ground. That, in turn, compounded the problem with the New York bankers, who were watching their collateral evaporate while quietly reading Insull's unadorned financial statements, which revealed the fragility of his world. The bankers, who had viewed Insull as one of the nation's premier customers just nine months earlier, now had cold feet.[47]

On April 6, 1932, the *Chicago Tribune* declared that the fate of Middle West "rested in the balance" as Insull met with his bankers in Chicago to work out a reorganization. Officials of the Loop banks—including Edward Brown, the executive vice president of the First National Bank of Chicago, and Abner J. Stilwell, a confidant of the Insull family who was a vice president of the Continental Illinois Bank and Trust Company of Chicago—huddled with Insull to discuss the debt-laden company's fate when one of its $10 million notes matured on June 1. Middle West also needed to refinance nearly $30 million in bank loans, but the uncertainty of the company was causing "violent price fluctuations" in its securities on the New York and Chicago exchanges. While Insull met with his bankers, the company's securities hit new lows when its common stock sold for less than a dollar for the first time.[48]

Young's involvement in the Insull negotiations made news the next day. Because Insull's companies had been major customers of GE for years, under normal circumstances Young's role at the Federal Reserve Bank would have given Insull leverage with the New York bankers. Insull had prepared for this day with all those insider deals offered to Young in 1929 and 1930. Now Young's private interest was in direct conflict with his public position.[49]

Even Young's considerable influence could not solve Insull's cascading problems this time, especially since he refused to recognize that his back was finally against the wall. For even a part of his fortune to have survived the crisis, Insull would have had to focus on the preservation of share value, not on who controlled his empire. Insull's obsession with control, in large part because of his concern for Junior's future but also to perpetuate his legacy, was what had placed his family in harm's way in the first place. At this critical moment, Insull desperately needed to relinquish control of his utility system to attract a large equity injection. If he had sold his interests in the holding companies for even one dollar per share, he would still have walked away from the table a millionaire (and one million Depression-era dollars would be worth $15.7 million in today's money). To buy more time, at the very least he needed to sell some of his cherished assets. For example, he could have sold the eastern properties of Middle West that had been purchased in 1930 and 1931 during his last great expansion program. Despite the stock market crash of 1929, Insull continued to expand, financing his acquisitions with short-term bank debt. And the bond market's deterioration meant that his companies were now facing balloon maturities without the prospect of long-term public financing. Insull's reckless expansion and paralysis of action were more reminiscent of a second generation executive of a family business than a man with fifty years of major corporate experience behind him.[50]

While the negotiations dragged on in New York, Insull securities showed "conspicuous weakness" on the exchanges. They continued to experience "severe strain" throughout the next week, and then, on April 14, 1932, news broke that Middle West was headed for bankruptcy court. A "receivership for a corporation the size of Middle West [had] never been known in industrial history." The company's stock plummeted to 25 cents a share. Insull had failed to attract fresh equity or sell any of his major assets, so his bankers had refused to continue to fund the madness.[51]

Unable to obtain the necessary financial commitments, Insull arranged a friendly receivership. The receivership resulted when the Lincoln Printing Company, which was owed $8,000 from Middle West, filed a bankruptcy petition against Insull's company. The president of Lincoln Printing Company, Washington Flexner, was the partner of Samuel Insull's brother, Martin, the president of Middle West, who was also a large stockholder of Lincoln Printing.[52]

The next day the *Chicago Tribune* was filled with news of the historic receivership, with the organizational chart of Insull's company displayed in bold print. At the time, the receivership was regarded as "the most important in the history of finance." Middle West's assets were estimated to be worth more than $2.5 billion dollars (more than $39.3 billion today). The holding company owned 119 companies, including electrical, bus, and railway systems, pipelines, and investment companies. Insull blamed the holders of his securities for his woes: "The extent to which the market price of these securities has declined can only be explained by the existence of confusion, misunderstanding, and misapprehension in the public mind." In his statement, he differentiated Middle West from his three major operating companies— Commonwealth Edison, Peoples Gas, and Public Service—and, as a result, their shares climbed precipitously. They had suffered from the speculation centered on Middle West, but its receivership seemed to calm fears about the other companies, at least temporarily.[53]

The selection of Washington Flexner's company as the moving party in the prearranged receivership was not without controversy. Flexner had maintained a personal brokerage account in his own name for the benefit of Martin Insull. Congressional investigators determined that Flexner's account was fraudulently used for "the unloading upon Middle West Utilities Co. by Martin J. Insull, president of the company," of securities—that Martin Insull personally owned—which had suffered significant losses. Investigators also found a fraudulent transaction involving Insull's Public Service Company. Insull's company purchased 2,500 shares of the Peoples Trust and Savings Bank from Earle H. Reynolds, the president of the bank, in July 1930. Earle Reynolds was the son of George Reynolds, the head of affiliated Continental Illinois Bank, which had invested 80 percent of its capital in Insull loans.

In addition, Flexner and Martin Insull defaulted on a loan of $172,500 from the Dawes bank in the name of their partnership, Flexner and Insull, and their partnership defaulted on another loan in the amount of $301,843 at Traylor's First National Bank. And Flexner individually defaulted on a $115,000 loan from the Dawes bank, while Martin defaulted on another $263,000 loan from the same bank. Martin had also defaulted on loans totaling $299,000 from Traylor's bank, where the Middle West Utilities Company had defaulted on a $5 million loan.[54]

Insull's law firm, Isham, Lincoln and Beale, drafted the petition of the Lincoln Printing Company and filed it on April 14, 1932, before Judge James H. Wilkerson, who was assigned to the bankruptcy section of the Chicago federal district court. Judge Wilkerson issued an order continuing the proceeding until the next day. Without giving an explanation, Wilkerson was then absent from the court for the next several days. On April 15, he was replaced by Judge Walter C. Lindley—a federal judge with ties to Insull— from Danville, Illinois, about 150 miles from Chicago, even though two other federal judges from Chicago were present on the same floor of the federal building. Judge Lindley appointed three receivers: Samuel Insull; Edward N. Hurley, the chairman of the executive committee of Electrical Household Utilities Company, an affiliate of Owen Young's GE, and a director of

Dawes's Central Republic Bank; and Charles A. McCulloch, the chairman of John R. Thompson Company and a director and stockholder of Traylor's First National Bank.

Defensive about the Insull appointment, Judge Lindley said in response to objections from an attorney representing a stockholder of Middle West: "The court is under no obligation to anybody for making these appointments. . . . The court must be free from any ties. The court is free. I am of the opinion that the appointments are not improper. Mr. Insull has had long and intimate familiarity with this company since its organization. In a sense, it may be said that it is his child."[55]

A subcommittee of the U.S. House Judiciary Committee charged that Insull handpicked Judge Lindley to handle the receiverships of his entities. The subcommittee's probe of Lindley determined that during his previous ten years holding court in Chicago he had never appointed a receiver or law firms to represent a company in a receivership. Indeed, the appointment of Insull and the other receivers and their lawyers for Insull's Middle West was the first time he had made such appointments in Chicago. The House subcommittee subpoenaed the telephone records of Judge Lindley and Insull's lawyers, and, according to those records, on April 14, the day before the appointments, Insull's personal lawyers in Chicago—Schuyler, Dunbar and Weinfeld— called Lawrence Allen, a lawyer in Danville who had been a close friend of Judge Lindley's for thirty years. Allen then called Judge Lindley "asking him when he was coming to Chicago." Two days later, Judge Lindley appointed Lawrence Allen's small law firm from Danville—Allen and Dalby—to represent Insull's immense Chicago-based IUI when it filed for the federal court's protection. According to the subcommittee's report, Lawrence Allen "had his name placed on the door of Schuyler & Weinfeld, who were the personal attorneys for Mr. Insull, and established his office there."

Lindley also appointed Daniel J. Schuyler, who had been Insull's "political lawyer" for twenty years, and his law firm—Schuyler, Dunbar and Weinfeld—to represent the receivership. In addition, to represent the receivers of IUI, Lindley appointed Judge Wilkerson's former law firm, then known as Cassels, Potter and Bentley, which may partially explain Wilkerson's sudden absence.[56]

Schuyler, Dunbar and Weinfeld was also the law firm for Insull's Corporation Securities, Commonwealth Edison, and Peoples Gas. Daniel Schuyler's successor firm, Schuyler, Weinfeld and Hennessy, ran into controversy after collecting $300,000 in fees (more than $4.7 million in today's dollars) representing the receivers of nine closed banks, when the depositors of the banks had received only between fifteen and thirty cents on each dollar of savings.[57]

Dawes's Central Republic Bank was also well represented in the receiverships. Samuel W. White, a vice president of the Central Republic Company, the investment affiliate of the Central Republic Bank, was appointed receiver for three Middle West subsidiaries: the United Public Service Company of New Jersey, the United Public Utilities Company, and the Southern United Gas Company. Then White, acting in his capacity as the federal receiver of United Public Service Company, stalled a receivership petition filed in New Jersey. The New Jersey action occurred after the affiliated United Public Utilities Company defaulted on the interest payments of its bonds. On White's motion, the federal court in Chicago enjoined the New Jersey action.[58]

It was expected that the bankruptcy of Middle West would trigger the receiverships for IUI—which was facing an unfriendly petition in federal court—and the Corporation Securities Company of Chicago. Both companies owned major positions in Middle West, Commonwealth Edison, Peoples Gas, and Public Service of Illinois. Middle West had more than one hundred thousand stockholders, many of whom were also depositors in Chicago's major banks, which held tens of millions of dollars of nonproducing loans. So the receivership of Middle West clearly was a prelude to widespread panic.[59]

Fearing a panic, Melvin Traylor and his colleagues at the First National Bank of Chicago, which held $26,439,001 of worthless and questionable Insull loans, continued to publish fraudulent financial statements in the *Chicago Tribune*. They certified to the comptroller's office and the public that the Insull loans were fully performing assets and that 100 percent of their outstanding balances would be collected in the normal course of business. Middle West had loans totaling $4,942,903 at Traylor's bank, and the bank had purchased $147,255 of the company's bonds. IUI, the company in which Traylor had personally purchased discounted shares, had also borrowed $4,671,706. Additionally, Corporation Securities owed the bank $4,823,997, Public Service had loans at the bank of $4,043,208, and Commonwealth Edison had borrowed $1,115,517. Peoples Gas had sold the bank $180,000 of its bonds and had borrowed an additional $188,750. Martin Insull had also personally borrowed $600,843 from Traylor's friendly bank. Now federal regulators were reporting to each other that "failure of a number of [the Insull] concerns has forced sizable losses" at the First National Bank. But even after the bankruptcy filings, the regulators refused to stop Traylor's bank from publishing false financial statements. They were far more interested in keeping a lid on the crisis than in disclosing the bank's true condition.[60]

Refinancing the obligations of Middle West and the other Insull companies through the issuance of bonds was no longer an option because the market price of its shares had collapsed. Stock prices for Middle West had cratered from a high of $529 a share in 1929 to 25 cents a share in April 1932. The collapse of stock values began with IUI and Corporation Securities and spread to Middle West and its subsidiaries, then to Commonwealth Edison, Peoples Gas, and Public Service. The calamity soon spread to those banks of Chicago that were linked publicly with the demise of Insull's empire. It was well known by the middle of April that certain banks were holding at least $27 million in loans of Middle West, whose assets would be frozen in federal bankruptcy court. It was only a matter of time before depositors, thousands of whom were also stockholders and bondholders of Insull's companies, would withdraw their remaining savings from banks connected to Insull. Aware of the looming scenario, Dawes, Traylor, and the other leading bankers turned to the RFC to bail them out of their liquidity crisis.[61]

Insull issued a statement shifting the blame for his financial problems onto the Depression: "Economic conditions make it impossible to work out an immediate plan for the payment of about $22,000,000 in well secured bank loans, slightly over $7,000,000 in partially secured loans, and meeting of a maturity of $10,000,000 notes on June 1." The next day, in Wilmington, Delaware, five stockholders filed another petition seeking a receivership of Middle West, alleging that Insull and his directors had "negligently and improperly" procured loans for the subsidiaries totaling $25,176,000 without proper collateral and "negligently and improperly" invested $260 million of the companies' assets in stock of other Insull entities. Highlighting the problems of Insull's crumbling system, on that same day, Monroe County, Indiana, filed suit against Public Service Company of Indiana for $90,000 in damages, including $79,659 in back taxes that were unpaid between 1926 and 1931 because of "fraudulent methods" of assessment. To those reading the *Chicago Tribune*, the sky seemed to be falling on Insull.[62]

The negative disclosures about Middle West spurred a number of creditors to file involuntary bankruptcy petitions against IUI and Corporation Securities. On April 16, 1932, the Mississippi Valley Utilities Investment Company, a subsidiary of Middle West that had made speculative stock investments of $45 million mostly in IUI securities, was driven into bankruptcy. (Traylor's First National Bank was holding questionable loans of $1,050,000 to Mississippi Valley Utilities.) In short, Insull's three holding companies had invested approximately $450 million in the stock market at inflated prices and now their securities were worth only a fraction of what they had invested. Furthermore, the so-called investments were circular—holding companies investing in operating companies that, in turn, invested in each other and the holding companies. Insull's self-dealing efforts to solidify his control and power resulted in all of his companies sagging under huge debt.[63]

In another remarkable development, Judge Lindley appointed George A. Cooke, Insull's closest personal lawyer, and Calvin Fentress of Baker,

Fentress and Company, a brokerage company, as the IUI receivers. Lindley also appointed Patrick J. Lucey, another of Insull's lawyers, and Raymond J. MacNally, a member of A. O. Slaughter and Company, as the receivers for Corporation Securities.

The appointments of Cooke and Lucey demonstrated the influence that Insull still wielded within the Illinois judicial system. Judge Cooke, a former chief justice who had been a member of the Illinois Supreme Court from 1909 to 1919, had ruled in Insull's favor to reverse a lower court decision that had granted a $10 million rebate to the customers of Peoples Gas and subsequently became the attorney for not only Insull but Peoples Gas. Cooke, who was also close to the state auditor, Edward J. Barrett, received an appointment for his law firm, Cooke, Sullivan and Ricks, to represent the receiver of the closed Noel State Bank of Chicago.

Lucey, a Democrat, was elected the attorney general of Illinois in 1912 and held that office until 1917, when Governor Frank Lowden, a Republican indebted to Insull, appointed him to the Illinois Utilities Commission. In January 1929, Insull had given Cooke the opportunity to purchase 3,000 shares of IUI at $12 a share and Lucey the opportunity to buy 1,000 shares at that price. When the IUI stock was trading at a high of $149.25 in August 1929, Cooke, who had invested $36,000, was showing a paper profit of $411,750. Lucey's position was suddenly worth $149,250, so his paper profit amounted to $137,250 in eight months. They were now in a position to return the favor to their old benefactor.[64]

In his memoirs, Insull downplayed his role in the appointments of his lawyers, Cooke and Lucey, as co-receivers for IUI and Corporation Securities. Insull described a Sunday, April 10, 1932, afternoon meeting, at which he presided along with Junior, who now served as vice chairman of most of the Insull entities, to discuss the filing of the various receiverships during the upcoming week. It took place at the Chicago Club and attending were the major Loop bankers, including Melvin Traylor and Edward Brown, representing the First National Bank, which had loaned Insull's companies more than $26 million; Joseph Otis, representing the Dawes bank, which was holding more than $12 million of Insull paper; Abner Stilwell and other officials of Continental Illinois, which had the most to lose, having loaned Insull's companies nearly $60 million; and Harold Stuart, the president of Halsey, Stuart and Company. (According to the U.S. Senate's Committee on Banking and Currency, Stuart's company had procured "inordinate profits" in the financing of IUI and Corporation Securities of nearly $45 million. Three months later, Stuart would be instrumental in the raising of $5 million for the new Dawes bank, of which he was an organizing syndicate manager.) Also present at

Insull's strategy session were his lawyers Waldo F. Tobey of Isham, Lincoln and Beale, and Daniel Schuyler of Schuyler, Dunbar and Weinfeld.

Though the situation was tense, Insull and his son were meeting with men familiar to them. Like Cooke and Lucey, Otis, Stuart, Tobey, and Schuyler had been members of the insider's club who had purchased shares of IUI at $12 a share. (Stuart and Tobey would later be indicted, tried, and acquitted along with the Insulls.) As Insull "explained that practically the whole fortune of the Insull family was represented by their stock holdings in the two investment companies," he sounded as if he were discussing the appointment of trustees for his personal trust, instead of receivers of large publicly traded companies with thousands of stockholders and bondholders: "The only part that I took, with relation to the receiverships of the Insull Utility Investments, Inc., and the Corporation Securities Company of Chicago, was to ask, in view of the very large interests of myself and my family in the two investment companies, that Mr. George A. Cooke should be appointed co-receiver of the former, and Mr. Patrick J. Lucey should be appointed co-receiver for the latter." Rufus Dawes and even Calvin Coolidge had been discussed as possible receivers, but in the end Insull wanted his personal lawyers to be appointed, and he prevailed.[65]

One of Insull's most vociferous critics was Samuel A. Ettelson, a former Illinois state senator and former lawyer for Insull who had been a law partner of Daniel Schuyler's for many years. Ettelson would be criticized for collecting legal fees of $47,500 from the receivership of the South Side Savings Bank and Trust Company, when its depositors had received only 45 cents on each dollar of savings. And Ettelson had drawn fire for his role as the corporation counsel for the City of Chicago. Donald R. Richberg, a railroad union lawyer and Progressive Republican from Chicago whom Franklin Roosevelt appointed as the chairman of the National Recovery Administration, testified before the Senate Judiciary Committee: "Ettelson exercised the power of the corporation counsel's office to promote Insull's interests. His law partner, Daniel J. Schuyler, was a recognized channel of political influence over the administration."

Ettelson described himself to the House investigating subcommittee as "a sucker investor" because he had borrowed $150,000 from a bank and then gambled, along with his friends and family, on Insull's worthless Middle West stock. Ironically, Ettelson was one of the insiders whom Insull had allowed to buy IUI stock for half price at $12 a share in 1929. But now Insull's former confidant, who was a victim of his own greed, was on a crusade to destroy the man and the system that had been such an intricate part of his law practice for nearly two decades.

Ettelson testified that Insull had veto power over the judicial appointments of receivers and their lawyers: "Sam Insull, as I will demonstrate, had the power of veto over any appointment. . . . This slate was nominated by the bankrupt himself, because the banks always took the position that Sam Insull was these companies, he was dealt with as these companies. It was a one-man affair. He was the czar and the tyrant, to the point where he was nicknamed 'Samuel Insult.' That was his nickname. He just absolutely ran the show."[66]

Though bitter about his financial loss, Ettelson nevertheless made a compelling witness: "Now, this slate of receivers and counsel was presented to Judge Wilkerson. The record shows that Wilkerson refused to stamp his judicial approval on that slate. So Lindley came up here from Danville and he was persuaded to stamp with his judicial approval that slate and the names on that slate. That slate was named without any deviation. Not one word was changed in that slate. Not one name was changed. That was made by the order of the federal court. That is where it starts as far as the judicial proceedings are concerned."[67]

Insull's law firm, Isham, Lincoln and Beale, drafted and filed the bankruptcy petition against IUI on behalf of a friendly Iowa bondholder. It stated the obvious, that the company had spent more than $245 million for securities that were now worth a fraction of their original price. Additionally, there was the more than $32 million in loans that were payable on demand, plus the $10.5 million in default. Another of Insull's law firms, Schuyler, Dunbar and Weinfeld, drafted and filed the petition of bankruptcy against Corporation Securities, stating that it had borrowed tens of millions of dollars to purchase securities for more than $140 million at the height of the bull market.[68]

Samuel Insull's younger brother, Martin, now 62, was soon forced to resign as president of Middle West because he had "mismanaged the company in the most outrageous way." (He had been named senior vice president of the company in 1912 and had become its president in 1924.) Meanwhile, it was also reported that four large New York banks—the Chase National Bank, the Guaranty Trust Company, the Commercial National Bank and Trust Company, and the Central Hanover Bank and Trust Company—were auctioning off major blocks of stock held as collateral on demand loans to IUI and Corporation Securities that were in default. All told, the New York banks were holding 50,981 shares of Commonwealth Edison, 77,516 shares of Peoples Gas, and 24,554 shares of Public Service.[69]

Before the New York banks could auction off the Insull securities, Judge Lindley enjoined the sale. The injunction stopped the banks from selling the collateral, including nearly all of the assets of the two holding companies, which would have wiped out Insull's unsecured creditors and stockholders. Selling off everything of value to pay the loans in default at the New York banks would leave the holding companies as worthless shells. The only hope the stockholders and unsecured bondholders had was to delay such a sale until there might be a reversal of fortune on the stock exchanges. Such an event was unlikely since, for example, IUI's 6 percent debentures, of which $57,725,000 were outstanding, were selling at 12 1/2 cents for each $100 of par value.[70]

Complying with the injunction but claiming that the bankruptcy court lacked jurisdiction, the New York bankers postponed the auction of the blocks of stock held as collateral for the Insull loans. After lawyers representing the New York banks met with Judge Lindley, the auction was delayed again. Lindley left the injunction in force and admonished the lawyers, alluding to Shakespeare's *Merchant of Venice*: "I am not calling any of you gentlemen Shylocks, but when the rights of thousands of people are involved, common sense must be considered." The judge said it was "the duty of every one to prevent rocking the boat" because of the country's terrible economic condition. He then issued an order allowing the New York banks to receive dividends on the securities they were holding as collateral.[71]

It was becoming painfully clear to the investors in Insull's investment trusts that nothing would be left for them after the bankers had finished. Interest was focused on the New York banks because they were moving to sell their collateral; they were far more concerned about protecting their assets than about whether their actions might ignite a panic in Chicago. The large Chicago banks were also quietly holding the securities of the two trusts to secure their loans. Traylor's First National Bank had loaned $5 million to IUI, another $5 million to Corporation Securities, and yet another $5 million to Middle West, all three of which were now in receivership. Additionally, Chicago banks held major blocks of stock in the three Insull operating companies as collateral for loans. But the leading bankers of Chicago, anticipating runs on their banks, were reluctant to press for an auction. Many of the depositors were also holding worthless Insull paper, and it was feared that any precipitous action might spark a full-fledged panic.[72]

The public disclosures alarmed Traylor and the other Loop bankers, so they met in late May to plot a strategy. With so much at stake, they wanted to eliminate the problem quietly without further exciting their already concerned depositors. At the secret meeting, they decided that Insull had to resign. Insull abruptly ended his career just six weeks after Middle West went into receivership, followed by the bankruptcy filings of IUI and Corporation Securities, and when his three remaining operating companies were desperately attempting to refinance $70 million in debt. But the strategy backfired because Insull's sudden departure generated more adverse publicity.

Traylor and the other bankers chose Stanley Field, a close friend and personal adviser to Insull who had arranged much of Insull's financing from Continental Illinois Bank, to be the one to ask him for his resignation. When Field conferred with Insull in early June, the utility tycoon reluctantly agreed to relinquish his once unrivaled power. On June 6, Insull officially resigned as chairman from sixty-five corporations and as a director from eighty-five entities. After his resignations, he told reporters: "Well, gentlemen, here I am, after forty years a man without a job." But he would not be standing in a bread line. He planned to travel to Quebec and then sail for Europe and stay at a hotel in Paris.[73]

During the monotonous routine of his resigning ceremony, Insull also resigned as a receiver of Middle West. His position as a receiver had sparked controversy. Creditors and stockholders had demanded his resignation because of the obvious conflicts of interest. S. G. Lee, an attorney representing holders of Insull securities, had moved to intervene in the IUI receivership, charging that the receivers had not pursued illegal transfers of assets totaling $78 million. Lee had asserted that assets had been transferred to members of the Insull family at below-market prices. He had also demanded that the bankruptcy court order the receivers to file suit against Insull and his relatives, and against the officers and directors of the Insull entities, to recover corporate assets.[74]

Adding insult to the controversy were the rumors that Insull would simply leave his creditors behind and move overseas to his country estate in England. Having left England as a clerk, Insull now owned a large dairy and poultry farm where he entertained much like a member of the British royalty. Insull had converted an ancient structure into an impressive residence surrounded with lush landscaping. He built cottages for his farm workers and provided a large farmhouse for his manager. Traveling along country roads, guests approached the farm until a large gate greeted them. After the gate opened, they would drive down a private road for a half mile to end their journey at a home fit for a country gentleman.[75]

When word of Insull's resignations leaked at about 11:30 on the morning of June 6, there was a rapid rise in the shares of Commonwealth Edison, which closed the day up six points, at $61 a share. Public Service rose almost six points, closing at $40, and Peoples Gas closed up two points. All three companies had hit record lows in the previous ten days. Meanwhile, James Simpson, the chairman of Marshall Field and Company, at which he had worked for forty-one years, rushed back to Chicago from a hunting trip in India to be elected the new chairman of Insull's utility conglomerate. He had been a director for many years of Commonwealth Edison, and he was also deputy chairman of the Federal Reserve Bank of Chicago. (After he was named president of Marshall Field in 1923, the company built the Merchandise Mart, at that time the largest building in the world. Since 1920, Simpson had also worked closely with Insull to build the extravagant Chicago Opera House building.)[76]

In a hastily called meeting on that same June day, Owen Young, whose presence indicated his intimate involvement with Insull and the leading bankers and business leaders of Chicago, met privately at the Federal Reserve Bank of Chicago with Traylor; Philip Clarke, the president of the Dawes bank; George Reynolds, the head of Continental Illinois; and other leading bankers and industrialists. Wearing many hats, Young, who would be Dawes's partner in the organization of his new bank, combined his private interests as chairman of GE with his public role as deputy chairman of the Federal Reserve Bank of New York. When they emerged from the meeting, Young and the other participants refused to discuss with reporters how they were planning to respond to the crisis. Young did say that he had talked to Insull about his resignation earlier in the day.[77]

Two days later, a reporter for the *Chicago Tribune* asked the seventy-two-year-old Insull about his plans for the future, to which Insull responded: "I haven't any." Worth about $150 million on paper in 1929, Insull now had a negative net worth of at least $15 million. His brother Martin owed more than $7 million, and his son, Junior, owed hundreds of thousands of dollars to local banks. As one Chicago banker said, "They went down with the ship." That same day, information leaked from the independent audits of Commonwealth Edison, Peoples Gas, and Public Service that $85 to $90 million needed to be written off the books of the three companies to reflect properly the present value of their assets.[78]

Throughout June, negative articles about Insull's troubles ran parallel to stories about bank failures and the criminal trials of bankers. For months, the public had been reading about the plight of Insull, and by the third week of June they understood just how intertwined Chicago's major banks were in the Insull affair.[79]

Notes

1. T. B. Macaulay to O. D. Young, January 11, 17, 1933; Young to Macaulay, January 13, 1933, ODYP/SLU.

2. McDonald, *Insull*, 278; J. B. McDonough to Ferdinand Pecora, February 11, 1933, ISEP/NA; Insull, *Memoirs of Samuel Insull*, 213; "The Loss of Owen D. Young," 4; Case and Case, *Owen D. Young*, 612–14.

3. *Stock Exchange Practices, Insull*, 1731; "Witnesses Subpoenaed and Brief Abstracts of Their Testimony," n.d., ISEP/NA; "Insull Matter," memorandum, n.d., ODYP/SLU.

4. Statement of Owen D. Young, Washington, D.C., February 15, 1933, ODYP/SLU; Deposition of Gerard Swope, January 4, 1933, 379–84; and the deposition of Owen D. Young, December 16, 1932, 202–3, In re: Insull Utility Investments, Inc., Bankrupt, U.S. District Court of New York, SIP/LU; "The Loss of Owen D. Young," *Nation*, January 4, 1933, 4; Norman Thomas, "Owen D. Young and Samuel Insull," *Nation,* January 11, 1933, 35–37.

5. J. B. McDonough to Ferdinand Pecora, February 11, 1933; "Witnesses Subpoenaed and Brief Abstracts of Their Testimony," n.d., ISEP/NA; "Insull Matter," memorandum, n.d.; "Mr. Swope's Statement," n.d., ODYP/SLU; Deposition of Gerard Swope, January 4, 1933, 383–84, 388–464; and the deposition of Owen D. Young, December 16, 1932, 200–201, In re: Insull Utility Investments, Inc., Bankrupt, U.S. District Court of New York,, SIP/LU; *Stock Exchange Practices, 1933*, 1544–65; *New York Times*, January 5, 1933.

6. O. D. Young, "To the Board of Directors of the General Electric Company," December 2, 1932; with respect to the credibility of Young and Swope, see "Insull Matter," a memorandum resulting from an internal investigation at GE; "Mr. Swope's Statement," September 23, 1932; O. D. Young to Gerard Swope, September 16, 1931; "Memorandum Regarding Reorganization of Middle West Utilities," July 13, 1934, ODYP/SLU; Deposition of Gerard Swope, January 4, 1933, In re: Insull Utility Investments, Inc., Bankrupt, U.S. District Court of New York, 459, SIP/LU; A. A. Jamison to E. Ogden Ketting, February 18, 1932; Ketting to Jamison, March 19, 1932, EOKP/LU; Case and Case, *Owen D. Young*, 612–14.

7. *Stock Exchange Practices, 1933*, 1698–1703; T. B. Macaulay to O. D. Young, January 11, 17, 1933; Young to Macaulay, January 13, 1933, ODYP/SLU; J. B. McDonough to Ferdinand Pecora, February 11, 1933, ISEP/NA; Insull, *Memoirs of Samuel Insull*, 213; "The Loss of Owen D. Young," 4; Case and Case, *Owen D. Young*, 612–14.

8. "Insull Matter," memorandum, n.d., ODYP/SLU; *Chicago Tribune*, May 18, 1932; *Stock Exchange Practices, 1933*, 1698; "The Loss of Owen D. Young," 4; Thomas, "Owen D. Young and Samuel Insull," 35–37; Stuart, *Twenty Incredible Years*, 473; Williamson, "What Is the Relative Value?"

9. R. F. Clinch to C. G. Dawes, June 22, 1929; J. E. Otis to Dawes, July 24, 1929; C. G. Dawes to R. C. Dawes, November 10, 1930; R. C. Dawes to C. G. Dawes, October 30, 1931, CGDP/NUL; Various Comparative Data, Recovery Value of Collateral, December 31, 1939, as compared to December 31, 1940, RFC/NA; *Stock Exchange Practices, 1933*, 1698–1703; *Chicago Tribune*, April 16, June 22, 1932; *The Economist*, June 20, August 1, 1931; James, *The Growth of Chicago Banks*, 2:919; John Kenneth Galbraith, *The Great Crash 1929* (Boston: Houghton Mifflin, 1955), 71–72.

10. *Stock Exchange Practices, 1933*, 1698–1703; *Chicago Tribune*, January 17, 18, August 1, 2, 4, 5, 1929.

11. *Chicago Tribune*, July 24, August 2, 3, 19, 26, September 21, 22, 23, 24, 25, 26, 27, 28, 29, 1929, April 16, 1932; McDonald, *Insull*, 282.

12. Arthur R. Taylor, "Losses to the Public in the Insull Collapse, 1932–1946," *Business History Review* 36 (Summer 1962): 188–204. Arthur Taylor used three methods of valuation to determine what he described as "real value." He measured value in 1932, when Insull lost control of his conglomerate, first, by totaling the book value of the debt and equity carried on the balance sheets of the companies; second, by totaling the paid-in amounts received by Insull's companies when they issued their securities; and third, by totaling the market value of the securities in 1932. Taylor blended these three methods of valuation to assign an overall value he considered reasonable in light of the deflation being experienced during the Depression. The resulting values were higher than the market value in 1932, but they amounted to less than sums arrived at by relying exclusively on book value and paid-in value.

13. Ibid., 188, 191–93, 201–4. On December 18, 1931, Philip McEnroe, Insull's confidant who was a participant in the IUI insiders' stock syndicate along with Young and Swope, received a loan of $127,070 from the Continental Illinois Bank, secured by the worthless stock of IUI and Corporation Securities Company. *Stock Exchange Practices, 1933*, 1535–38, 1542, 1698, 1701, 1729–40; "Witnesses Subpoenaed and Brief Abstracts of Their Testimony," n.d., ISEP/NA; *Annual Report of the Interstate Commerce Commission* (Washington, D.C.: Government Printing Office, 1932), 258.

14. See Klein, *Rainbow's End*, 242–44.

15. Insull, *Memoirs*, 226; Hoover, *Memoirs*, 42; Schlesinger, *The Crisis of the Old Order*, 156, 158–59; Galbraith, *The Great Crash*, 109–12, 113–16; McDonald, *Insull*, 284–85; Hicks, *Republican Ascendancy*, 234; William E. Leuchtenburg, *The Perils of Prosperity, 1914–32* (Chicago: University of Chicago Press, 1958), 251.

16. *Stock Exchange Practices, 1933*, 1698; McDonald, *Insull*, 284–294.

17. Sherman, "Dawes," 117–21; McDonald, *Insull*, 278; Kennedy, *Banking Crisis of 1933*, 108; "Melvin A. Traylor: Homespun American," Traylor for President Club, 4–5, 16.

18. *Stock Exchange Practices, 1933*, 1698; Sherman, "Dawes," 117–21; Williamson, "What Is the Relative Value?"

19. E. Ogden Ketting to W. H. Dadd, February 8, 1932, EOKP/LU; Alfred P. Leyburn to Comptroller of the Currency, February 6, 15, 1932, USOCC/WNRC.

20. *Banking Law State of Illinois*, Section 10; *Stock Exchange Practices, 1933*, 1529–44, 1698.

21. "Recapitulation: Assets Pledged to Secure the Loan to the Central Republic Trust Company, Chicago, Illinois, and the Estimated Recoverable Value of the Same as of December 31, 1936," RFC/NA; *Stock Exchange Practices, 1933*, 1534–44; Taylor, "Losses to the Public in the Insull Collapse," 201–4; *Chicago Tribune*, July 2, 1932.

22. *Stock Exchange Practices, 1933*, 1529–34.

23. Minutes of Meeting of Board of Directors of Middle West Utilities Company, August 30, 1920, SIP/LU; *Banking Law State of Illinois*, Section 10; *Stock Exchange Practices, 1933*, 1529–34, 1698; *Economist*, August 1, 1931; *Callaghan's Illinois Statutes Annotated, 1925–1931 Supplement* (Chicago: Callaghan and Company, 1931), 99, 100; *Callaghan's Illinois Statutes Annotated* (Chicago: Callaghan, 1924), 1:690–92; Sherman, "Dawes," 117.

24. *Banking Law State of Illinois*, Section 10; *Callaghan's Illinois Statutes Annotated, 1925–1931 Supplement*, 99, 100; *Callaghan's Illinois Statutes Annotated*, 1:690–92; *Stock Exchange Practices, 1933*, 1529–34; Sherman, "Dawes," 117.

25. Ditchburne and Lounsbury to Samuel Insull; "Memorandum of conference with Mr. Eaton," SIP/LU; *Stock Exchange Practices, 1933*, 1529–34; Wasik, *The Merchant of Power*, 165–69.

26. In 1916, Judge Evans had been appointed by Woodrow Wilson to the U.S. Court of Appeals for the Seventh Circuit, which included the Chicago area, and served in that position until his death in 1948. "Insull Echoes," *Time,* January 1, 1934, 29; *Chicago Tribune*, June 9, 1932; Owen D. Young, "To the Board of Directors of the General Electric Company," December 2, 1932, ODYP/SLU; *Stock Exchange Practices, 1933*, 1529–34.

27. J. B. McDonough to Ferdinand Pecora, February 11, 1933, ISEP/NA.

28. McDonald, *Insull*, 278–82; "Samuel Insull: The Collapse," *New Republic*, October 5, 1932, 202.

29. *Stock Exchange Practices, 1933*, 1400; Busch, *Guilty or Not Guilty?* 139–42; Wasik, *The Merchant of Power*, 165–69, 180–81, 189–90.

30. E. V. Graham to Samuel Insull, August 12, 1929; Insull to Graham, August 27, 1929, SIP/LU; Busch, *Guilty or Not Guilty?* 139–42; McDonald, *Insull*, 281–82.

31. Ditchburne and Lounsbury to Samuel Insull; "Memorandum of conference with Mr. Eaton" Samuel Insull to Cyprus Eaton, June 3, 1930, SIP/LU; *Utility Corporations . . . Corporations Securities Co. of Chicago*, July 18, 1934, 721; Williamson, "What Is the Relative Value?"

32. Ditchburne and Lounsbury to Samuel Insull; "Memorandum of conference with Mr. Eaton," SIP/LU; *Stock Exchange Practices, 1933*, 1544–57, 1699; McDonald, *Insull*, 289.

33. J. E. Otis to Charles G. Dawes, May 1, 1931, CGDP/NUL; James, *The Growth of Chicago Banks*, 2:1030.

34. Insull, *Memoirs*, 208, 209; James, *The Growth of Chicago Banks*, 2:1030–31; Busch, *Guilty or Not Guilty?* 128–29.

35. Transcript of the Annual Meeting of Stockholders of the Commonwealth Edison Company, February 29, 1932, ODYP/SLU; *Chicago Tribune*, April 16, 1932.

36. Claim of the National City Bank of New York, November 15, 1938; Inventory, March 14, 1939, In the Matter of the Estate of Samuel Insull, Deceased, Docket 377, PCCC; Insull, *Memoirs*, 200, 201, 205; McDonald, *Insull*, 289–301; Wasik, *The Merchant of Power*, 196–97.

37. *Stock Exchange Practices, 1933*, 1510–13.

38. Deposition of Owen D. Young, December 16, 1932, 218–25, In re: Insull Utility Investments, Inc., Bankrupt, U.S. District Court of New York,, SIP/LU; Insull, *Memoirs*, 210; *Who's Who in Chicago and Vicinity: The Book of Chicagoans, 1931*, edited by Albert Nelson Marquis (Chicago: A. N. Marquis Company, 1931), 315.

39. Rufus Dawes to Charles G. Dawes, June 27, 1930, CGDP/NUL; Debtor's Petition, Creditors Whose Claims Are Unsecured, Schedule A-3, March 22, 1935, in the Matter of Charles Cutler Dawes, Bankrupt, Bankruptcy No. 59251, USDC/NDI; "Report of the President of A Century of Progress to the Board of Trustees," March 14, 1936, Library of Congress, Washington, D.C., 5–17; McDonald, *Insull*, 297–99.

40. McDonald, *Insull*, 289–301.

41. Statement of Assets and Liabilities of Charles G. Dawes, December 2, 1931, CGDP/NUL; Charles G. Dawes to himself, October 21, November 28, 1933, PRCP/ UI; Williamson, "What Is the Relative Value?"

42. Indicative of the complicated structure of Insull's system, a majority of the common voting stock of Midland United Company was owned by Commonwealth Edison, Peoples Gas, Middle West, Public Service, and other Insull entities. Taylor, "Losses to the Public in the Insull Collapse," 188 204; Thompson, *Confessions of the Power Trust*, 232–35.

43. *Chicago Tribune*, March 20, 24, 1932; Busch, *Guilty or Not Guilty?* 129; McDonald, *Insull*, 299.

44. Taylor, "Losses to the Public in the Insull Collapse," 188–204; Williamson, "What Is the Relative Value?"

45. The proposed loan package from the insurance companies would pay Commonwealth Edison's maturing one-year notes of $20 million; Public Service Company's maturing one-year notes of $15 million; Peoples Gas's maturing one-year notes of $15 million; Middle West's notes of $10 million due on June 1, 1932; and other Middle West obligations of $5 million. The insurance companies that would participate were: Sun Life Assurance Society of Canada, "because of its very extensive holdings of Insull equity stocks" (Insull met with its officials on April 7, 1932); Metropolitan Life Insurance Company; Prudential Life Insurance Company; New York Life Insurance Company; and Equitable Life Assurance Society. See Joseph E. Otis to Owen D. Young, March 29, 1932; and B. A. Mattingly to Otis, March 28, 1932, ODYP/SLU; Insull, *Memoirs*, 213. Edward N. Hurley, the chairman of the executive committee of Electric Household Utilities Corporation, was a director of Dawes's Central Republic Bank and Trust Company. In addition, Bernard E. Sunny, a director of GE and a member of the executive committee of Traylor's First National Bank, was also a director of Electric Household. *Moody's Manual of Investments, 1932*, 2664–65.

46. *Chicago Tribune*, March 31, 1932.

47. Ibid., April 7, 1932.

48. Ibid., April 6, 1932.

49. Ibid., April 7, 1932. Insull wrote in his memoirs, "Mr. Young was very insistent that, in some way or another, the Middle West Company must be saved, and that it would be a calamity if it failed." Despite his best efforts, Young could not save

Middle West. Nevertheless, Insull had nothing but praise for Young: "I cannot speak too highly of the services rendered by Mr. Owen D. Young during the whole of this troublesome period." Insull, *Memoirs*, 213–15.

50. *Chicago Tribune*, April 12, 1932; McDonald, *Insull*, 299–300, 310; Williamson, "What Is the Relative Value?"

51. *Chicago Tribune*, April 1, 5, 6, 9, 14, and 15, 1932.

52. *Report to the Committee on the Judiciary, House of Representatives, 73rd Congress, 2nd Session, on Receivership and Bankruptcy Investigation by the Subcommittee of the Committee of the Judiciary of the House of Representatives Investigating Receiverships and Bankruptcies at Chicago, Illinois* (Washington, D.C.: Government Printing Office, 1934), 35–42; *Stock Exchange Practices, 1933*, 1535–44; *Utility Corporations . . . Federal Trade Commission . . . Monthly Report . . . Middle West . . .* November 15, 1933, 18–19.

53. *Chicago Tribune*, April 15, 1932; *Report to the Committee on the Judiciary*, House of Representatives, 1934, 35–42.

54. *Stock Exchange Practices, 1933*, 1535–44; *Utility Corporations*, November 15, 1933, 18–19; *Chicago Tribune*, April 15, 1932; Williamson, "What Is the Relative Value?"

55. *Report to the Committee on the Judiciary*, 35–42; *Hearing before the Committee on the Judiciary, House of Representatives, 73rd Congress, 1st Session on Receivership and Bankruptcy Investigation, October 30 to November 4, 1933, March 19 to March 23, 1934, House of Representatives Subcommittee Investigating Receiverships and Bankruptcies, Chicago, Illinois* (Washington, D.C.: Government Printing Office, 1934), 440–57; *Chicago Tribune*, April 15, 16, 1932; *Moody's Manual of Investments: Industrial Securities, 1931*, 971; *1932*, 2664, 2665.

56. *Report to the Committee on the Judiciary*, 35–42; *Hearing before the Committee on the Judiciary, House of Representatives, 73rd Congress, 2nd Session on Receivership and Bankruptcy Investigation, April 21, 1934, May 2, 1934, House of Representatives Subcommittee Investigating Receiverships and Bankruptcies, Chicago, Illinois, Part 2* (Washington, D.C.: Government Printing Office, 1934), Testimony of Judge Walter C. Lindley, 889–914; "Judiciary: 'Almost Criminal,'" *Time*, May 28, 1934; McDonald, *Insull*, 219.

57. *Chicago American*, September 1, 4, 5, 6, 7, 10, 11, 12, 14, 1934; Stuart, *Twenty Incredible Years*, 530–32.

58. By April 1932, Central Republic Bank had made forty-one loans to Insull's companies totaling $11,157,069, or 80 percent of its capital. See receivership records of Central Republic Trust Company at the Cook County Courthouse. *Chicago Tribune*, April 16, 22, 1932; *Stock Exchange Practices, 1933*, 1698.

59. *Chicago Tribune*, April 15, and 16, 1932.

60. *Stock Exchange Practices, 1933*, 1699; Examiner's Report of Bowmanville National Bank of Chicago, September 21, 1932, USOCC/WNRC.

61. *Chicago Tribune*, April 15, and 16, 1932; see the RFC records of the Central Republic Trust Company at the National Archives.

62. *Chicago Tribune*, April 15, and 16, 1932.

63. Ibid., April 17, 1932.

64. Judge Lindley also named Eugene V. R. Thayer, a former chairman of the executive committee of the Dawes bank, as the receiver of Insull's Mississippi Valley Utilities Investment Company. *Chicago Tribune*, April 17, 1932; *Stock Exchange Practices, 1933*, 1425–26; 1699–1703; *Chicago American*, September 1, 1934; Insull, *Memoirs*, 166–67, 216, 218, 230–31; McDonald, *Insull*, 218, 220, 312, 319; Stuart, *Twenty Incredible Years*, 150; Dunne, *Illinois*, 3:148–49, 223–24.

65. Waldo Tobey's law partner, Gilbert E. Porter, at Isham, Lincoln and Beale, was also a personal lawyer of Insull's who represented his entities and was a stockholder of the Dawes bank. He was sued by the RFC and forced to pay $10,200 as his liability for being a stockholder after the bailout loans were made. Insull, *Memoirs*, 163, 167, 215–17, 224, 230–31; Wasik, *The Merchant of Power*, 187, 198–201; *Hearing before the Committee on the Judiciary, October 30 to November 4, 1933, March 19 to March 23, 1934*, 440–57; *Stock Exchange Practices, 1933*, 1692–93, 1699–1703; Supplemental Agreement . . . , January 3, 1933, PRCP/UI; Certificate of issuance of stock within authorized amount of Halsey, Stuart and Company, ISOS/ISA; "Syndicate Agreement between Frank Knox, H. L. Stuart and Rawleigh Warner, as Syndicate Managers and the Syndicate Subscribers," August 29, 1932, PRCP/UI; *New York Times*, September 13, 1931; *Chicago Tribune*, November 21, 1934.

66. *Hearing before the Committee on the Judiciary, October 30 to November 4, 1933, March 19 to March 23, 1934*, 440–57; *Chicago American*, September 1, 1934; Stuart, *Twenty Incredible Years*, 12, 21–22, 37, 101–3, 139, 244, 385, 441–42, 450, 527; Schlesinger, *The Crisis of the Old Order*, 3, 26, 36, 39, 42, 44, 51, 101, 113, 114, 120, 143–44, 147, 238–39, 255, 278, 422, 458–59; Frank Freidel, *Franklin D. Roosevelt: A Rendezvous with Destiny* (Boston: Little, Brown, 1990), 137, 228; McDonald, *Insull*, 178, 181, 219, 257, 310.

67. *Hearing before the Committee on the Judiciary, October 30 to November 4, 1933, March 19 to March 23, 1934*, 444–57.

68. Ibid., 440–57; *Chicago Tribune*, April 17, 1932.

69. *Chicago Tribune*, May 4, and 18, 1932; Wasik, *The Merchant of Power*, 200.

70. *Chicago Tribune*, May 6, 1932.

71. Ibid., May 12, 14, and 18, 1932.

72. Ibid., May 19, 25, 26, and June 1, 1932.

73. *Who's Who in Chicago and Vicinity*, 1931, 315; Sherman, "Dawes," 121; Insull, *Memoirs*, 222–23; *Chicago Tribune*, June 8, 1932; Wasik, *The Merchant of Power*, 200; McDonald, *Insull*, 302–4, 307, 308.

74. *Chicago Tribune*, June 7, 8, 1932.

75. Ibid., June 10, 1932.

76. Ibid., June 7, 10, 1932.

77. Ibid., June 7, 1932.

78. Ibid., June 7, 9, 1932; McDonald, *Insull*, 277.

79. *Chicago Tribune*, June 10, 18, 21, 22, 1932.

Chapter 3

Insiders at the Reconstruction Finance Corporation

"[The Dawes bailout] was upon the insistence of the two Democratic members of the Reconstruction board, sitting in the Federal Reserve bank meeting in Chicago, and upon the insistence of the leading Democratic banker of Chicago who was then mentioned as a candidate for the Presidency of the United States, and upon the insistence in New York City of the leading Democratic banker and a leading Democratic manufacturer, also mentioned for the Presidency; upon insistence of the other Democratic members of the Reconstruction Corporation."

—Herbert Hoover, November 4, 1932[1]

As Insull's house of cards collapsed around him, Charles Dawes was president of the Reconstruction Finance Corporation. Dawes, as he had done many times before, used his position of public trust to benefit himself and his family. In this instance of insider self dealing, he saved himself from the kind of fate that befell Samuel Insull. In using his connections at the RFC to salvage his own interests, he involved Herbert Hoover in a way that embarrassed the president as he began his campaign for reelection. The RFC made one of the largest loans in its history to the Dawes bank less than two weeks after he had resigned as head of the RFC in June 1932. Critics pounced on what appeared as a corrupt insider arrangement. Hoover's defense of the loan included the fact that it was made with the approval of three directors appointed on the recommendation of the leaders of the Democratic Party.

Hoover was correct, as if party affiliation somehow trumped self interest. Indeed, as part of his efforts at the RFC, Dawes made common cause with the leading Democratic appointee to the board, Jesse Jones, an operator on a par with Dawes. In early 1932, Dawes, the Republican, and Jones, the Democrat, were scrambling to save their troubled empires, so they worked together to benefit each other's financial interests. To advance their private agendas, they joined forces with Democratic appointees Harvey C. Couch and Wilson McCarthy—men who became beholden to Dawes and Jones—to dominate the RFC's board. Jones, Couch, and McCarthy then approved RFC loans to Chicago banks that were heavily indebted to the Dawes bank, while they were benefiting from their association with Dawes.

HOOVER'S RFC

When the Bank of England suspended gold payments for the pound sterling on September 21, 1931, a crisis of confidence swept through international financial markets. Watching gold reserves draining out of the nation's banks at an alarming rate, Herbert Hoover summoned the leading bankers of New York to a secret meeting on Sunday night, October 4, at Secretary of the Treasury Andrew Mellon's elegant residence on Massachusetts Avenue in Washington. The unofficial meeting was not held at the White House because Hoover said he wanted "to avoid public alarm and press speculation." The president urged these financial leaders to form a voluntary private credit organization with paid-in capital of $500 million to bail out troubled and closed banks, and he agreed—"if necessity requires"—to recommend to Congress the creation of an emergency federally funded lending agency.

At the prodding of Eugene Meyer the head of the Federal Reserve System, and George L. Harrison, the governor of the Federal Reserve Bank of New York, the member banks of the New York City Clearing House pledged $150 million to form the National Credit Corporation (NCC). Hoover was well aware that he needed to be seen as taking action to stimulate the economy or face certain defeat in the presidential election of 1932. Once the pledges were secured, he issued a press statement on October 6 to propose a "definite program of action." This program included not only the formation of the NCC but "if necessity requires . . . the creation of a Finance Corporation similar in character and purpose to the War Finance Corporation." The War Finance Corporation, which Meyer had headed as managing director, had been formed in 1918 to meet the credit demands of World War I. Later, it was used to combat the agricultural depression of the 1920s.[2]

Meyer and the nation's leading bankers would have preferred that Hoover immediately call a special session of Congress to create what would become known as the Reconstruction Finance Corporation. But the fact that he committed to create the federally funded agency if necessary was enough for them to move forward. One week later, Mortimer Buckner, chairman of the New York Trust Company, announced the incorporation of the NCC, along with the commitment of private banks to subscribe to $500 million of its debentures. Buckner was named president of the newly formed NCC, and George M. Reynolds was made chairman of the board. As the controlling stockholder of Continental Illinois Bank and Trust Company, Chicago's largest bank, and chairman of its executive committee, Reynolds was responsible for loaning nearly $60 million—representing 80 percent of its capital—to Insull's entities. If his bank failed, he would not only lose his powerful position and stock holdings, but he would also be liable, according to Illinois law, to its depositors and other creditors for the amount of his investment in the bank. In short, his family's fortune would be wiped out.[3]

Because member banks were jointly liable for its loans, the NCC's board was cautious with loan approvals. Reynolds' own bank was in desperate need of a massive bailout, which the NCC would never agree to provide. To make matters worse, he and the other directors of the NCC dragged their feet, waiting for Congress to rescue the banking industry. Hoover criticized the bankers' "procrastination," later recalling in his memoirs that the NCC was "ultraconservative, then fearful, and finally died." It was now clear to Hoover that the sand was rapidly running out of his administration's hourglass. His efforts to encourage volunteer action in the private sector were failing to revive the economy, so he changed course and endorsed the need for direct federal intervention.[4]

On December 8, 1931, during his third State of the Union address, eleven months before the presidential election, Hoover recommended that Congress create an emergency Reconstruction Finance Corporation, comparing it to the War Finance Corporation, which had continued to operate until 1929. Hoover foresaw keeping the RFC on a tight rein: "It may not be necessary to use such an instrumentality very extensively. The very existence of such a bulwark will strengthen confidence . . . [and] it should be placed in liquidation at the end of two years." During its existence, the RFC was "to make temporary advances upon proper securities . . . where such advances will protect the credit structure and stimulate employment." According to a supportive Meyer, the RFC would contribute to "the removal of fear" during its short duration.[5]

Desperately in need of a taxpayer bailout, the banking community took no chances and mounted a heavy lobbying campaign directed at skeptical senators. It was successful. Within a few weeks, on January 11, 1932, the full Senate approved the RFC bill, with only eight negative votes. Four days later, the House passed its version of the bill, on a vote of 335 to 55. On January

22, after receiving final congressional approval, the RFC bill was sent to the president.[6]

During the bill-signing ceremony, Hoover commended the congressmen for their "patriotism" and "devotion to the welfare of their country, irrespective of political affiliation." With so much riding on the success of the RFC, Hoover summoned Charles Dawes from London, where he was still serving as ambassador to Great Britain, and appointed him president of the new agency. Since the formation of the RFC marked the first time that the federal government committed to bailing out the banking industry with taxpayers' funds, the directors of the governing board would determine whether political considerations would unduly influence the agency. Hoover expedited passage of the RFC bill when he gave two powerful Democrats the power to nominate their candidate to the board: Speaker of the House John Nance Garner of Texas, the nation's highest elected Democrat and Roosevelt's future vice president; and Senator Joseph T. Robinson of Arkansas, the running mate of Alfred E. Smith in 1928 and the leader of Senate Democrats, who were in the minority by just one vote.

Garner nominated Jesse Jones of Houston, who the *Washington Post* described: "He is tall, gray haired and distinguished in appearance. He is retiring, has no hobbies save work, unless the Democratic Party and charity work might be hobbies, speaks publicly but infrequently, dresses conservatively and without regard for the mode." And Robinson's nomination was Harvey C. Couch from Arkansas. Couch was also a close friend of Owen Young, the man Hoover had described as "the leading Democratic banker and a leading Democratic manufacturer, also mentioned for the Presidency."[7]

Delegating the selection of two of the new agency's directors to the elected leaders of the opposition party in a presidential election year hardly made the agency nonpartisan. Although the Democratic leaders had negotiated that at least three Democrats would be legally required to serve on the RFC's seven-member board, their party had nothing to lose if the agency proved to be a failure. But the fate of Hoover's reelection could well rest on the agency's success in stimulating the economy.[8]

THE WEB OF SELF-INTEREST

But Hoover's concerns about his reelection and the state of the economy were not uppermost in the minds of the men who led the RFC. In early 1932, Dawes, the Republican, and Jones, the Democrat, feverishly trying to salvage their troubled business ventures, used the RFC to promote each other's interests. Joining in this effort were Democratic appointees Couch and Wilson McCarthy of Salt Lake City; together the four dominated the RFC's board. They proved to be kindred spirits.

Harvey Couch was a public utilities entrepreneur from Pine Bluff, Arkansas. One of Senator Joe Robinson's top campaign fund-raisers, Couch was a leader in the southern wing of the Democratic Party as well as the founder of the Arkansas Power and Light Company. By the time he was nominated in 1932, he was also a director of various railroads and banks in the South. Because Couch was also president of several power companies in Arkansas, Mississippi, and Louisiana, the progressive wing of the Republican Party expressed concern about his appointment. But he had a good relationship with Hoover after serving as the head of the president's Unemployment Relief Organization in Arkansas and on the Arkansas Drought Relief Committee. So Senator George Norris of Nebraska, the leading opponent of the "power trust," backed off, saying that he would not oppose Couch's nomination because the RFC was "President Hoover's baby."[9]

Actually, Couch's confirmation in the Senate was never in doubt because his companies, which included the Arkansas Power and Light Company, the Louisiana Power and Light Company, and the Louisiana and Arkansas Railroad, were anchor clients for Senator Robinson's Little Rock law firm, Robinson, House and Moses. While serving in the Senate, Robinson was also president of the Southwest Joint Stock Land Bank of Little Rock, and Couch sat on its board along with Robinson, whose law firm was general counsel of the bank. Following Roosevelt's election in November 1932, Couch, who had become a loyal ally of both Jones and Dawes, remained on the RFC's board for almost two more years.[10]

The third Democrat on the board, joining Couch and Jones, was Wilson McCarthy, who played a pivotal role though little has been written about it. Senator William H. King of Utah recommended McCarthy. A lawyer with ties to mining interests operating in the West, McCarthy had attended law school at Columbia University, graduating in 1913. Early in his career, he had been elected the district attorney for the Sake Lake City area and then appointed a district judge. He served for only two years as a judge, resigning to go into the practice of law in 1919. (But he would be referred to as Judge McCarthy for the rest of his career.) McCarthy stayed active in local politics and successfully ran for the state senate in 1926 as a conservative Democrat. He was appointed that year as a regent of the University of Utah, a post he held until Hoover appointed him to the RFC. He was also one of three original directors of the seven-member board who served after Roosevelt became president, resigning on September 30, 1933. Jones and Couch, who resigned in August

1934, were the other two directors who served during the new administration. Jones, Couch, and McCarthy all became part of Dawes's inner circle during the Hoover and Roosevelt administrations.[11]

Dawes and his Democratic friends exercised great authority at the RFC in part because they were its only full-time directors. The Republican appointees, Eugene Meyer, Odgen Mills, and Paul Bestor became part-time directors because they held other high-level, full-time posts. The four full-timers became fast friends, working closely together but also discovering that they had common interests and a similar self-interested approach to government service. Upon his arrival in Washington, McCarthy easily fit in with Dawes, Jones, and Couch, three wealthier and more influential men who would significantly contribute to his amassing a personal fortune of $1,225,900 when he died in 1956 (worth about $9,680,000 today).[12]

McCarthy's friendships with Dawes and Jones, in particular, would make the difference in the development of his personal fortune after he left Washington. And while McCarthy was at the RFC, he was instrumental in the bailouts of both the Dawes bank in Chicago and the Jones bank and other entities in Houston. The Jesse Jones connection provided McCarthy with long-term employment and influence as president of the Denver and Salt Lake Railway Company (D&SL), with a salary of $20,000 a year, and as trustee of the Denver and Rio Grande Western Railroad Company (D&RGW), with another salary of $12,516 a year. (The combined salaries were worth $508,000 in today's dollars). Both were based in Denver, and McCarthy engineered their merger in 1947. More importantly, nearly 40 percent of McCarthy's fortune, $457,282, was his ownership of 11,589 shares of common stock in the D&RGW, which he had accumulated during his employment as part of his compensation package. He amassed his significant stock holdings after the railroad company had run increasingly large deficits during the 1930s under his lackluster leadership. Even so, he was rewarded for his lobbying skills when he persuaded the RFC to restructure the railroad's loans to his great personal advantage, making this by far the best investment he ever made.

Throughout this period, McCarthy bragged about his connection with Jones. Writing to an acquaintance in 1935, McCarthy openly acknowledged that Jones had used his influence to have McCarthy appointed: "I do not know how permanent my present position is, as it was made available to me by Mr. Jesse Jones, Chairman of the Reconstruction Finance Corporation, who was anxious to have someone come here to protect the investment that the RFC had in the Denver and Rio Grande Western Railroad, which Company owns the stock of the Denver and Salt Lake Railway. This stock, however, is pledged with the RFC as security for about eight or nine million dollars which the D&RGW owes to the R.F.C."[13]

Image 3.1. Jesse Jones, as chairman of the RFC, approved loans to the Denver & Rio Grande Western Railroad and then directed the railroad company to hire Wilson McCarthy as its president. The photograph, a gift to McCarthy and his wife, was signed, "for my friends Wilson and Minerva McCarthy with great affection." As a director of the RFC, McCarthy approved millions of dollars of loans to the railroad company and then became its trustee and president. While a RFC director, McCarthy also approved loans to the Dawes bank and the Jones bank. (Courtesy, Utah State Historical Society)

As McCarthy walked through the revolving door at the RFC, he possessed intimate knowledge of the rapidly deteriorating financial condition of the troubled railroad company. As a director of the RFC, he had approved three loans totaling $8,350,000 to the D&RGW in 1932 and 1933. A review of its loan applications demonstrates that the railroad company should have been seeking bankruptcy protection instead of a government bailout. In 1924, after forcing creditors to forbear on their loans, the carrier had emerged from bankruptcy court and then enjoyed five years of prosperity. But by 1932 it was insolvent again. The railroad then submitted its first loan application to the newly formed RFC in February 1932, stating that its poor performance during the Depression year of 1930 was due primarily to the "subnormal year." The application completely ignored the company's dismal earnings in 1931, instead focusing on the robust earnings during the boom years of 1925 to 1929 in a misleading effort to justify the loan. Nevertheless, McCarthy and his colleagues at the RFC, along with members of the Interstate Commerce Commission, approved a $2.5 million loan package a few weeks later.

The D&RGW continued to borrow from the RFC after McCarthy's resignation. By December 22, 1934, when he became president of its subsidiary, the D&SL and the D&RGW had been issued twenty-eight RFC loans totaling $11,191,850. On November 1, 1935, the D&RGW defaulted on all of its RFC loans, and two and a half weeks later McCarthy was appointed the trustee of the D&RGW. For the next seven years, with McCarthy as its trustee, the D&RGW ran negative operating cash flows, increasing the indebtedness to the RFC to a total of $13,900,605 by January 1, 1943. In 1947, the D&RGW and the D&SL were consolidated and McCarthy was named the president of the successor entity, the Denver and Rio Grande Western Railroad Company, based in Denver. To facilitate the combination, the RFC issued $5,200,000 in "new first mortgage bonds," and $8,700,605 in "new income mortgage bonds" for a total of $13,900,605 in long-term debt from the reorganized D&RGW. Needless to say, the RFC suffered significant losses on these loans.[14]

Yet McCarthy had job security as long as Jones remained in control of the RFC. Jones also hired McCarthy as an attorney for the RFC while he was a railroad executive. Because of Jones's influence, McCarthy remained prominent in the railroad industry—which the RFC subsidized—for the rest of his career into the 1950s, even after Jones had been forced out of the RFC under a cloud of suspicion for, in large part, dictating who the management would be for the railroad companies and other entities receiving large loans from the RFC. Nevertheless, McCarthy remained loyal to Jones, telling his biographer: "Soon after the RFC was organized, we found that the old maxim that ability sits at the head of the table was doubly true at the RFC; for at the head of the table sat Jesse H. Jones. The major contributing influence to the greatness of the agency was the work and character of Mr. Jones."[15]

During the more than twenty years after his departure from the RFC, McCarthy also stayed close friends with Dawes and Couch, who owned the Louisiana and Arkansas Railroad. Couch, like Dawes, maintained his contacts at the RFC and other federal agencies throughout the 1930s and 1940s. In 1935, McCarthy visited with Couch in Arkansas to discuss railroad business and the Farm Credit Corporation, which had made significant loans to McCarthy's partner, Ashby O. Stewart, the president of the Pacific Coast Joint Stock Land Bank of San Francisco. Stewart was a good friend of Amadeo P. Giannini, the head of the Bank of America, also based in San Francisco, which, along with its entities, received nearly $95 million in loans from the RFC when McCarthy and Couch sat on its board. McCarthy then became the owner of a large securities position in the Pacific Coast Mortgage Company, formerly the Bankitaly Mortgage Company, which had borrowed $30 million from the RFC when he and Couch were directors of the RFC. Stewart had also been a major borrower from the RFC when McCarthy and Couch were its directors.

The remaining three initial RFC directors consisted of Republican members of the Hoover administration. Hoover named Eugene Meyer, governor of the Federal Reserve Board and an ex-officio member of the RFC board, to be the RFC's first chairman. When Hoover had nominated Meyer as head of the Federal Reserve in 1930, Congressman Louis T. McFadden, the Republican chairman of the House banking committee, had criticized Meyer as being too close to Wall Street and international bankers. But after Meyer's good friend, Bernard Baruch, the highly influential financier, told the *New York Times* that Hoover could not have appointed a better man than Meyer if he "had taken a thousand good men and rolled them into one," it became difficult to oppose the nomination. Baruch, the chairman of the War Industries Board, had employed the same kind of superlatives when Woodrow Wilson had nominated Meyer to be a director of the War Finance Corporation. Meyer's tenure as chairman of the RFC ended on July 31, 1932, after Hoover had asked Congress to amend the law to eliminate the governor of the Federal Reserve Board and the Farm Loan Commissioner as ex officio members of the RFC board. Hoover's reason was the "danger of a physical breakdown among the ex officio members in their endeavor to carry dual duties." But Secretary of the Treasury Ogden L. Mills, a close friend of Hoover's, remained on the RFC board as an ex officio member.[16]

Besides Meyer and Mills, the other ex officio initial member of the RFC was Farm Loan Commissioner H. Paul Bestor, a protégé of Meyer's and the conservative head of the Federal Farm Loan Board, to which Coolidge had appointed Meyer in 1927. Bestor had been a history professor at Yale before going to work for the Federal Land Bank of St. Louis during the Harding administration. He also had a close working relationship with Ogden Mills.

Secretary Mills, born to great wealth and social position, had been a New York City lawyer and then a congressman serving on the House Ways and Means Committee. In 1926, Al Smith defeated him in New York's gubernatorial race. Then President Coolidge appointed Mills, a conservative member of the Republican old guard who had become an expert on taxation and a critic of wasteful government spending, as undersecretary of the Treasury. Mills had supported Hoover early in his 1928 campaign and had joined the cabinet in February 1932 after Andrew Mellon had replaced Dawes as the ambassador to Great Britain. Mills had remained close to Hoover, representing him at the Chicago convention in 1932, and he was part of the president's inner circle during the 1932 campaign.[17]

The makeup of the RFC board changed in July 1932. To divert criticism leveled at the RFC because of the Dawes loans, Hoover gave the Democrats a majority on the agency's board when he appointed Atlee Pomerene (who served as a senator from Ohio between 1911 and 1923) as its chairman on July 26, 1932. Pomerene had gained national attention when Coolidge, Hoover's Republican predecessor, had appointed him as a special prosecutor in the Teapot Dome scandal. Later, he was Ohio's favorite son candidate at the 1928 Democratic National Convention in Houston, the same convention at which Jesse Jones was Texas's favorite son candidate. The *New York Times* called Pomerene's appointment as chairman a "surprise," and the *Washington Post* described it as a "bombshell."[18]

Hoover appointed Pomerene in an attempt to insulate the RFC from what he called a "demagogic attack" by Roosevelt's running mate, Speaker Garner, who was "clamoring for publication of all (the RFC's) bank loans." Pomerene followed the administration's line and lobbied to keep the operations of the RFC hidden from public scrutiny. But Pomerene had his own reasons to oppose disclosure: the Guardian Trust Company of Cleveland, whose board of directors included Pomerene, had received three RFC loans totaling $12,272,500 between April and June 1932, when its paid-in capital stock was only $7 million. And the Union Trust Company of Cleveland, which Pomerene's law firm represented and whose board included a partner in the law firm, Andrew Squire, had received a loan of nearly $14 million from the RFC. Both sets of loans would eventually be revealed to the public through Garner's efforts, and both banks, which were hopelessly insolvent, were closed in March 1933.[19]

After the lobbying efforts failed and Congress mandated publication of future loans, Pomerene and Hoover would blame the bank failures and subsequent bank holiday of 1933 on the publicity surrounding the RFC bank loans. However, the Dawes press conference on Monday, June 27, 1932, announcing that his bank had received large RFC loans, stopped the run on the Dawes bank, making a mockery of the administration's bank secrecy argument.[20]

Nevertheless, on July 14, 1932, the board of directors of the RFC, through its secretary, George Cooksey, urged Hoover to oppose "a provision inserted yesterday by the House of Representatives in the so-called 'Relief Bill' providing for the monthly publication of a report covering all of the activities of the Reconstruction Finance Corporation 'together with a statement showing the names of the borrowers to whom loans and advances were made, and the amount involved in each case.'" The directors stated that this provision would make the RFC's loans to banks and other financial institutions "public property," undoing "much that has been accomplished" and would "restrict its usefulness in the future." Furthermore, the publication of the RFC's loans to financial institutions "whose relations with the public are of a particularly sensitive character" would be "decidedly harmful" and would "thus destroy the very purpose for which [the RFC] was created." The board rejected the idea that "this kind of publicity is necessary in order to subject to constant scrutiny the actions" of the RFC. "The public interests" could be "fully safe-guarded" if the RFC opened its books to a select committee of the House or Senate. "In the unanimous opinion of the Board," it was determined that the disclosure provision was "against the public interest and may result in irreparable damage."[21]

On January 25, 1933, Jones lobbied Representative Howard "to suppress publication of the list" of RFC loans that were made from February 2 to July 20, 1932. Howard told the *New York Times* that he had to disagree with Jones's request, "It was shown clearly in the Dawes bank case that public confidence is increased, rather than destroyed, when it becomes known that the government has loaned money to any particular institution." But Jones, too, had his personal agenda: he was trying to stop the publication of the RFC's nearly $1.5 million loan to his Bankers Mortgage Company, which was made during the same week as the Dawes bailout. Yet Jones, always the politician, said in his memoirs that he had supported the publication of the RFC loans.[22]

Atlee Pomerene could not have been blind to the conflict-of-interest issues that the Dawes loans raised. However, Pomerene and Dawes were close friends who had gone to Cincinnati Law School together in the 1880s where they were members of an intimate debating society named the Quiz Club. Pomerene had brought up his concerns about his conflicting private and public interests to Hoover when they met at the president's fishing camp on the Rapidan River on July 24, 1932. Beside the RFC's loans to his clients, the troubled Cleveland banks, he disclosed that he and his law firm, Squire, Sanders and Dempsey, whose offices were in the Union Trust Building in Cleveland, represented the RFC's Cleveland office and were handling a substantial case load for the agency. Eager to defuse the Dawes issue in the campaign, Hoover chose to ignore Pomerene's conflicts of interest. So with the president's blessing, Pomerene remained a partner in the law firm and the

banks remained his clients during his reign as chairman. Pomerene's friendship with Dawes and his Democratic credentials were enough to make him
the preferred choice as head of the agency. Pomerene's approval of the final
$50 million disbursement to fund the new Dawes bank saved the Dawes fam-
ily fortune.[23]

While Pomerene held the chairmanship during the last seven months
of the Hoover administration, his private law firm continued to represent
the RFC and the troubled banks, generating substantial legal fees from all
of them. In 1933, the U.S. Senate's Committee on Banking and Currency
conducted an investigation of Pomerene's clients, the Union Trust Company
and the Guardian Trust Company, where he also sat as a director. The Committee issued a report in 1934 stating that the failure of the banks "was not
attributable, as has been maintained by the officers of the institution, to the
Michigan banking holiday, declared February 14, 1933, nor the national
banking holiday, declared March 4, 1933." The Senate committee's report
concluded:

> The evidence is overwhelming that the collapse of these institutions was a direct
> result of the unsound banking practices and mismanagement of the institutions
> over a period of years. . . . The dominant personalities of the Guardian Trust Co.
> and the Union Trust Co., in Cleveland, did not obviously regard themselves as
> public depositories burdened with the fiduciary duty of safeguarding the deposi-
> tors' funds, but rather deemed themselves private bankers dispensing the funds
> of their institutions to themselves and other powerful interests whose favor they
> sought to incur, to finance speculative and doubtful ventures. In order to secrete
> and conceal the losses sustained by these [breaches] of trust, incompetence, and
> mismanagement these banking officials resorted to a course of deception and
> prestidigitation, deluding and imposing upon depositors, stockholders, and gov-
> ernment bank examiners. To accomplish these frauds, these bankers sought and
> readily obtained the assistance and subvention of the banking institutions in the
> large commercial centers of the country. The utility of this surreptitious conduct
> was only transitory. The day of judgment could not be avoided. . . . The failure
> of the Guardian Trust Co. was not the result of unusual economic conditions, but
> rather the result of many years of mismanagement. Leniency in the granting of
> credit and laxity in collection gradually forced this bank into activities beyond
> the legitimate scope of banking. The bank became, in effect, a real-estate com-
> pany and the holder of worthless securities.[24]

Before accepting the RFC position, Pomerene had asked Hoover if he had
"any objections" to his seeking advice from his longtime friend, Charles
Dawes, about the issues pending before the RFC. Hoover saw no problem,
even though the Dawes loans had already caused a firestorm in his campaign

and the Dawes reorganization plan would be one of the first items Pomerene would have to address after he assumed the chairmanship.[25]

Meanwhile, Hoover left the day-to-day management of the RFC in the hands of the Republicans when he named Charles Miller, a lawyer and president of the Savings Bank of Utica, New York, as president of the RFC. Miller had been president of the New York Savings Bank Association and vice president of the New York Bar Association and was part of the Dawes and Young circle of friends. When Dawes was president of the RFC, it had been Young's unqualified recommendation that had persuaded Dawes to support Miller for the influential post of manager of the RFC's New York office. Miller was indebted to Dawes, and he would play a crucial role in the approval of the last $50 million installment of the Dawes loan in October 1932.[26]

JESSE JONES: THE BUSINESS OF POLITICS

Once Dawes left the RFC, Jesse Jones became its leading figure. He was no stranger to Herbert Hoover. They had become friends when Hoover was directing relief services in Europe during World War I. President Wilson had appointed Jones as the director general of military relief of the American Red Cross during the war because of his close ties to Colonel Edward M. House, the "master of manipulation," who was President Wilson's confidant. House had sat on the board of the Union Bank and Trust of Houston with Jones.[27]

While Jones was supervising the Red Cross's military relief, he became friends with Charles Dawes, the general purchasing agent during World War I. Their friendship would later result in their dominance of the RFC, and would confuse historians who, without comparing the recently released federal banking reports to the state bank liquidation records and the RFC documents, assumed incorrectly, simply because Jones was a Democrat, that his support of the Dawes loans was offered at arm's length.[28]

The career of Jesse Jones, who would become known as "Mr. Houston," as an entrepreneur and promoter began in 1898 when, at the age of twenty-four, he inherited the position of general manager of the estate of his deceased uncle, Martin Tilford Jones. This was quite a windfall since the estate held more than $1 million worth of lumber yards and timber properties in Texas and Louisiana. Moving to Houston from Dallas, Jones made the M. T. Jones Lumber Company his base of operations while developing his own highly leveraged fortune in the lumber, real estate, banking, and newspaper businesses.[29]

Just after the turn of the century, he used his friendship with the family of Edward House to borrow $500,000 on a preferential basis from their bank, T. W. House & Company, Houston's biggest bank. Thomas William House Jr., a co-executor along with Jones of the estate of Jones's deceased uncle, controlled the House bank. The failure of the bank during the Panic of 1907 did not terminate Jones's aggressive expansion plans; rather, it demonstrated to him the importance of being an insider in the Houston banking community.[30]

By 1905, Jones was already a founder, major stockholder, and director in the Union Bank and Trust of Houston, along with the House brothers. This position granted him full membership in Houston's elite banking fraternity, which included access to promoter loans from local bank and affiliated entities that were easy on credit terms and lenient on collateral. Using his banking privileges to the fullest extent, Jones managed to borrow $750,000 for the construction of the Rice Hotel and $500,000 to build the Chronicle Building, a total of $1,250,000 (about $26.6 million in today's dollars). The lender was the William M. Rice Institute for the Advancement of Literature, Science and Art (later Rice University), at a time when its total endowment was approximately $7 million.

The institution's chairman was James A. Baker, Jones's personal lawyer, who also served with him as a director of the Union Bank and Trust. Another founding director of the bank was William Marsh Rice Jr., whose uncle had endowed the institute and who was also a trustee of the Rice Institute when the Jones loans were approved. In 1910, Jones additionally arranged with his friends on the Rice board of trustees to obtain a ninety-nine-year lease on land sufficient to build his hotel, gratefully naming it the Rice Hotel. (Jones also negotiated an option granting his company an additional ninety-nine-year lease on the Rice land.) The Rice Hotel became the largest one in Houston at the time.[31]

Jones's ambition had also been served when, in 1908, he received a 50 per cent interest in the Houston Chronicle Publishing Company, which owned the *Houston Chronicle*, as partial payment for the construction of the newspaper's building. In 1926 he purchased the other half of the newspaper, and in 1931 he acquired the city's other major newspaper, the *Houston Post-Dispatch*, which later became the *Houston Post*. Jones used his position as part-owner of the *Houston Chronicle*, the city's foremost afternoon newspaper, to advance his political agenda. He directed the paper's editorial policy and endorsed Woodrow Wilson's candidacy. When Wilson was elected president in 1912, Jones's ever-helpful banking associate, Colonel Edward House, was able to provide him with access to the White House. In due course, Jones accepted the Red Cross appointment and worked both sides of the aisle, making almost as many Republican as Democratic friends. For two years, Jones was based in

Washington, D.C., where he became the liaison between the Wilson administration and the Red Cross. He enthusiastically staffed almost one hundred hospitals, helped build convalescent homes for those wounded in the war, and organized the distribution of tons of sweaters, socks, and other much-needed clothing. [32]

While in Washington, Jones also rubbed shoulders with former president William Howard Taft, John W. Davis, who was Wilson's solicitor general and the lawyer for the Red Cross, Bernard Baruch, Franklin Roosevelt, and Senator Warren G. Harding, who would be elected president in three years. These powerful friends enabled Jones to move in elite circles in Washington. And because of his close relationship with Colonel House and Wilson, he attended the Paris Peace Conference of 1919. [33]

Jones's entrance into the national arena had been augmented with the 1912 election of his brother-in-law, Daniel E. Garrett, to represent Texas in Congress. During the 1920s, Jones stayed close to Congressman Garrett and other members of the Texas congressional delegation, including John Nance Garner, who would become minority leader of the House Democrats by 1929. Jones also joined forces with senators Tom Connally, who would nominate Garner to be president in 1932, and Morris Sheppard, the "father of National Prohibition" who supported Al Smith in 1928 even though his presidential campaign favored the repeal of the Eighteenth Amendment.

After the midterm elections of 1930, which wiped away a 104-seat majority that the Republicans held in the House, the Democrats finally gained the majority by three votes when Speaker Nicholas Longworth and a few of his Republican colleagues died. John Nance Garner then became the new speaker on December 7, 1931. At the time, the *New York Times* described Garner: "He is as explosive as dynamite, as booming as a bass drum, as active as a cricket." When Garner's presidential bid failed, he threw his support to Roosevelt, which in turn resulted in Garner's unanimous selection as the vice presidential candidate in 1932. Garner's bourbon-drinking style and powers of persuasion were instrumental in the passage of Roosevelt's New Deal reforms. While Garner was vice president and Jones was head of the RFC, they remained in constant contact with each other, combining their individual power to enhance their collective influence within the Roosevelt administration. They effectively played the inside-outside game of politics together: when Garner was in the inner sanctum he protected the interests of Jones and vice versa.

Jones's credentials as a power broker were further bolstered with his membership on the Democratic National Committee and as a delegate to the 1924 and 1928 national conventions. In 1924, Jones enhanced his standing in

Democratic circles when he made a major effort on behalf of the seemingly hopeless presidential campaign of John W. Davis. A Wall Street lawyer who had represented West Virginia in the House from 1911 to 1913, and then had been Wilson's solicitor general and ambassador to Great Britain, Davis became the Democratic nominee on the 103rd ballot. His nomination broke a nine-day deadlock between Al Smith, the governor of New York, and William Gibbs McAdoo, Wilson's son-in-law who had been his secretary of the Treasury. Neither of them could secure the necessary two-thirds vote from the delegates.

After Davis received the nomination, he appointed Jones as his finance chairman. The two had become friends during Jones's Red Cross years. Davis faced the daunting prospect of running against Calvin Coolidge, a sitting president, during a period of prosperity. After the rancorous 1924 convention, several Democratic leaders sailed for Europe, but Jones, ever the loyal party member, rolled up his sleeves and started raising money and working with party leaders throughout the country, including Franklin Roosevelt, whose association with Jones also dated from his days at the Red Cross.[34]

As finance director of the Democratic National Committee, Jones sat on the three-member site selection subcommittee for the 1928 convention. Never one to miss an opportunity, Jones worked to persuade the committee to select Houston. He had made a commitment that Houston would build a convention hall that would hold twenty-five thousand people and that he would give or raise a $200,000 contribution to the party. To ensure that the offer made a properly dramatic impression on his Democratic colleagues, Jones attached a personal check for $200,000 to his proposal. When the committee selected Houston in a close vote over San Francisco, which had offered $250,000 but did not have Jones as its lobbyist, the *New York Times* proclaimed that the decision was "a personal tribute to Jesse H. Jones." Jones, who then "scurried about Texas raising money in order to reimburse himself," stood to profit from the decision more than anyone else because he owned dozens of buildings in downtown Houston, including the Rice Hotel, the Bristol Hotel, and more than half of the city's other hotels near the proposed site of the convention. Jones showed his gratitude in the name he chose for one of his properties: his recently constructed office building in Houston, where the staff of the Democratic convention would be located, became the Democratic Building.[35]

By the time the Democrats came to Houston in 1928, Jones was being touted as a vice presidential candidate on Al Smith's ticket. He had become the city's "leading citizen" and one of the wealthiest Texans—at least on paper. And during the convention, the Texas delegation nominated Jones, who

seemed to some to be "Democracy's Miracle Man," as its favorite son candidate for president. But the nomination was met with controversy. William
Clifford Hogg, a prominent businessman whose father was a former Texas
governor, attacked Jones in no uncertain terms. Hogg urged Texas governor
Dan Moody to reject the movement to nominate Jones because of his "stal-
wart avarice and piratical trading spirit."[36]

Jones's presidential aspirations fizzled after he received only the forty
votes of the Texas delegation and three votes from the Alabama delegation.
Nevertheless, the convention was a great success for both his hotel business
and his national prestige. Jones had built a penthouse apartment on top of his
newest building, the Lamar Hotel, where he entertained Democratic dignitar-
ies. It was where Mrs. Woodrow Wilson stayed with the Jones family during
the festivities. Jones had accomplished his goal. He was now a power to be
reckoned with in the Democratic Party. And Jones's fund-raising efforts on
behalf of the Democratic Party would pay off royally later, in 1932, when he
was appointed to the RFC's board.[37]

The Lamar Hotel, where Jones held court during the Democratic convention, was part of a building spree that he went on with bondholders' money
during the 1920s. By August 1925, he had been engaged in the marketing
of $4,850,000—about $59.4 million today—of mortgage-backed bonds
through the Chicago bond dealer and securities company S. W. Straus and
Company. Established in 1882, Straus and Company was located in its own
thirty-four-story building at Michigan Avenue and Jackson Boulevard in
Chicago. According to its offering circular, "for many years [it had] been
the acknowledged leader in the field of real estate financing." The company
also owned the Straus building at 565 Fifth Avenue in New York City and
the Straus buildings in San Francisco and Pittsburgh. Its forty-one offices
had more than one hundred thousand retail customers throughout the United
States and an affiliated Canadian company. Jones had issued real estate bonds
through Straus and Company before, but the issue he was putting together
was purportedly "the largest building construction loan ever underwritten in
the South."[38]

The Houston Properties Corporation bond issue epitomized the Jones
transactions. Jones owned the company and was its president. To be able to
sell bonds in Wisconsin—necessary because the state was a big bond market
for Straus and Company—Jones had to significantly increase the value of
the collateral he was pledging to secure the bond issue. Legally, he had only
two choices: either pledge additional properties or pay down the existing first
mortgage on the Rice Hotel to a level sufficient to comply with Wisconsin's
60 percent loan-to-value standard. (If properly adhered to, the Wisconsin law

would have provided a crucial safeguard for bondholders, given that the Rice Institute held a first mortgage of $742,000 on its leasehold site and the original hotel, which had a priority position over the second "general mortgage" that would be securing the mortgage-backed bonds.) Nevertheless, Straus and Company suggested a third alternative: deliberately inflate the appraisals of the pledged properties. Jones was faced with an ethical dilemma, but not for long. He set about inflating the appraisals to an extent that would mean that his bond offering circular would violate the antifraud provisions of Wisconsin. Jones's decision would eventually have horrific consequences for the nearly four thousand bondholders who were duped into buying his bonds.[39]

Jones used the transaction to enhance his relationship with Melvin Traylor and his First National Bank of Chicago. He told Traylor that although his contract indicated that he should use a New York bank, he preferred to use Traylor's Chicago bank. And on August 12, Jones wired Edward Eagle Brown, vice president of Traylor's First National Bank, to inform him that Straus and Company would be depositing $2.5 million into the Chicago bank the next day for the account of Houston Properties.[40]

Meanwhile, Jones was involved in big developments in New York City, and he wanted all of Houston to know it. He announced that Houston Properties had constructed, the previous year, a sixteen-story apartment building on Fifth Avenue "overlooking Central Park." And that his company was currently building a twenty-five-story office building "covering more than an acre of land on Madison Avenue" for approximately $10 million. A major tenant of the building would be Marshall Field and Company of Chicago. Finally, he proudly announced that he was "erecting a 15-stor[ied] apartment hotel on Park Avenue at 65th Street in the exclusive residential section of New York City."[41]

Numerous local investors had found Jones's announcement impressive enough to persuade them to invest in the bond issue of Houston Properties, which had nothing to do with the New York City developments. They were to regret doing so. By 1933, Jones's company had defaulted on all of its bond issues, financing every building mentioned in the press release, and had filed for protection and reorganization in the federal courts of Houston and New York.[42]

One thing can be said with certainty: The offering circulars containing the grossly inflated appraisals violated the antifraud provisions of the securities laws of Wisconsin, California, Indiana, Michigan, Missouri, Ohio, and Illinois. It can also be said that Jones definitely knew the appraisals were fraudulent and that the circulars contained misleading and false information. Four years later, on August 1, 1929, the financial statement for Houston

Properties would value the properties at $8,772,400 prior to depreciation, which was still $583,760 less than the value of the collateral used to sell the original bonds.[43]

After the Houston Properties bond issue, Jones's companies continued to raise capital selling 6 percent bonds to the public. Between 1925 and 1928, the Chicago investment banking houses led the nation when they issued nearly $800 million in mortgage bonds. A major part of the frenzy, Jones financed his hotels, office and apartment buildings, and theaters through Greenebaum Sons Investment Company, which Moses Ernest Greenebaum and James E. Greenebaum controlled. Here, once again, the money trail led back to the Dawes brothers since M. E. Greenebaum was also vice-chairman of the Dawes bank, and J. E. Greenebaum was its senior vice president. The Greenebaums abused their official positions at the Dawes bank, arranging loans to their personal company, which still owed $188,146 in delinquent loans to the liquidating shell of the Dawes bank in 1935. The insider loans had been pledged to the RFC to secure its loans to the Dawes bank. Before its demise, the Dawes bank had participated in the "wildly speculative" financing schemes with both Greenebaum Sons Investment Company and Straus and Company, and the bank was involved in more than four hundred real estate bond issues that defaulted on principal and interest payments to bondholders.

Greenebaum Sons Investment issued a 1928 offering memorandum for the purpose of raising $5.5 million of bonds for a New York City building project, which described the venture and Jones as follows: "The 10 East 40th Street Corporation is a wholly owned subsidiary of Houston Properties Corp., of which Jesse H. Jones, Esq., is president. The Houston Properties Corp. is the organization through which Mr. Jesse H. Jones of Houston, Texas handles his New York City operations. Mr. Jones is reported to have a net worth of about $10,000,000. Mr. Jones owns, in addition to real estate holdings, valuable oil properties in Texas."[44]

Jones was still riding high at the beginning of 1930, at least according to his January 1, 1930, financial statement, which included the Jesse H. Jones Company and its subsidiary companies. The statement, prepared for his financial institutions, showed his net worth to be $39,761,500 (or about $511 million in today's dollars). On paper, he was one of the richest men in America. Still, he recognized the concerns that banks would have relating to the high-risk business of developing hotels, apartments, office buildings, theaters, and other urban properties. A note on the bottom of the statement read: "All liabilities are owed by subsidiary companies, Jesse H. Jones Company, the parent corporation, owning 95%, or more, of the capital stock of the subsidiary companies, except Houston Properties Corporation, of New York, in which it owns 80%. The parent corporation is not endorser or guarantor on any obligation, and owes no debts." Jones was averse to personally endorsing any obligations of his real estate holding companies, even though their offering circulars implied that he was personally backing the projects. On the asset side of his statement, Jones valued his interest in Houston Properties Corporation at $5 million. His real estate in Texas "at independent appraisals" was stated as being worth $38,373,096, for a total of $43,373,096.

The financial statements of Jones's private companies were in a fluid state, with credits and debits flowing back and forth between the various entities. Jones's companies, in which he had few minority stockholders, also had interlocking directors. This enabled him to issue wire transfers from one entity to another without having to justify them. But his liquidity was thin, and many of the assets listed on the statement would soon file for bankruptcy protection. Experiencing difficulties with the cash flow of his properties, Jones abandoned any misgivings he had about the inflated building appraisals. In his survival mode, he stated that "independent and fair appraisals" supported all of the properties of the Houston Properties Corporation.[45]

By 1931, Jones was in such financial difficulty that he was speculating in the bonds of his own companies. On August 14, 1931, an official of his Houston Properties Corporation in New York City wrote Jones to advise him of the company's activities in the real estate bond market. He reported that Jones's agents were buying depressed bonds on several of Jones's properties, including 200 Madison Avenue, 10 East 40th Street, and Mayfair House. That week they were able to buy distressed 7 percent bonds that matured in 1940, on 200 Madison Avenue, for $71 on a bond with a face value of $100. They also purchased several 6 percent bonds that would mature in 1941, on 10 East 40th Street, for $51 and $52, although on those the price had recently gone up to $55 or $56 for each $100 bond. Jones's manager did not think they should buy at those prices, feeling that they might drop to as low as $40.[46]

The manager then shined light on their modus operandi, saying that he had told officials of Straus and Company that Jones's company planned to buy bonds with their surplus funds, then pay principal reductions with the full par amount of the bonds "in lieu of cash." He said: "They agreed to treat this proposal sympathetically, and will report later, but they are almost helpless to do other than accept." The bonds, having been purchased at depressed prices, would also be swapped at face value for future principal payments. This would create a default under the bond documents, but Jones's manager did not believe they would force a receivership. He further reported that the Houston Properties Corporation was currently $30,000 in arrears on its real estate taxes. He explained that they had no intention of attempting to arrange a loan with a bank to pay the taxes because it "would require all the stockholders endorsing the note." He reiterated that they were continuing "to maintain our policy of giving out no reports," but if asked they would say that the 200 Madison Avenue and 10 East 40th Street properties were generating sufficient income to meet their obligations. No mention would be made of the Mayfair House property; he had said earlier in the letter that they hoped to buy bonds on the Mayfair property "somewhere in the 60's," though they were currently trading at $73. Jones's manager complained: "There is considerable racketeering in bonds."[47]

Jones's real estate holding companies started defaulting on their bonds in 1931. Then in 1932, after he became a member of the RFC's board, Jones began filing bankruptcy petitions in federal court for at least a dozen of his companies, including the Houston Properties Corporation. Operating from his RFC office, Jones formed a myriad of entities run by his nephew, George A. Butler, who was a lawyer and head of Jones's reorganized properties, and Fred Heyne, his longtime employee who would become the co-executor of Jones's estate in 1956 and then the co-executor of the estate of Mary Gibbs Jones, Jones's wife, in 1962. Throughout the 1930s—while Jones was in Washington—these entities bought back the income bonds and voting trust certificates from scattered bondholders for pennies on the dollar. Thus, Jones was able to repurchase his foreclosed buildings and wipe out much of his debt.[48]

By 1934, after more than eight years, Jones had reduced the principal on the 1925 bond issue of $4,850,000 only $312,000, creating thousands of disgruntled bondholders. Many of the bondholders were upset with the reorganization plans. Because they did not have sufficient funds to hire counsel to represent them during the bankruptcy proceedings, they wrote letters individually to the court to complain. On May 9, 1933, after reading an article in the *San Francisco Daily News*, Emma Grigg, a widow and bondholder of the Houston Properties Corporation, wrote to the presiding federal judge in Houston to complain about Straus and Company, which had been the originating bond dealer for at least 211 real estate issues that were in default by 1934. Straus and Company and its principal subsidiaries were forced into bankruptcy court, where most of them were liquidated.

Grigg stated that Straus and Company "has been practically driven out of the state of New York for alleged dishonest and crooked practices and also that they are being investigated by the Attorney General of the State of Illinois." She went on to say that the company had "sold bonds by misleading and what were probably downright dishonest statements and appraisals." She told the

Image 3.2.   Jesse Jones, chairman of the RFC, and his nephew, George A. Butler, who was the lawyer and head of Jones's reorganized properties, working in the RFC's Washington office. (Courtesy, Library of Congress)

judge that the bond dealers had "a very unsavory reputation" in California and that virtually all of their bond issues were in default and were selling at about fifteen cents on the dollar. She asked the judge to examine carefully any reorganization plan that Straus and Company submitted because "hidden behind nicely worded statements generally lies a well laid plan to benefit either themselves, their friends or the former owners of the properties at the expense of the thousands of poor people to whom they sold the bonds."

Mrs. Grigg was not alone in her feelings of helplessness within a system in which she was represented by one of the "so called 'protective' committees controlled by S. W. Straus and Company." Another bondholder complained that "nearly every statement made about these properties at the time bonds were issued were exaggerated. Values were inflated; unconscionable commissions were paid to financiers and those connected with the properties."[49]

Ignoring the complaints of his bondholders, Jones quickly formed Rice Properties, Inc., of Houston in 1934 and purchased out of the bankruptcy court the Rice Hotel and the other properties that Houston Properties owned for a mere $25,000. Rice Properties then issued real estate bonds of $4,336,950 for a fifteen-year period, at an ostensible interest rate of 5 percent. But this was unlike the fixed interest rate of 6 percent on the original bonds, where the fixed rate helped to sell the bonds in the first place. In the new issue, Jones was able to convert the bonds for the first five years into "income bonds." This meant that the interest would be paid out of any net income available after paying operating expenses, including a management fee to Realty Management Company, which Jones also owned. So during the first five years of the bonds, until September 1, 1938, unpaid interest payments would not accumulate on the principal of the bonds.[50]

In 1937, more than four years after Jones had sought protection from the bondholders, Jones's Rice Properties, Inc., and the trustee of the bonds, Maurice A. Rosenthal, went back into federal court. They were seeking permission to use as much as $325,000 of the bondholders' money for the installation of an air conditioning system in the Rice Hotel, and the renovation of its dining room to make it look like a casino. According to the agreement with its bondholders, Jones's company was obligated to pay for the renovations. Instead, Jones and the trustee wanted court approval to amend the bondholders' agreement, which the bondholders approved during the 1934 reorganization, so that the improvements could be paid out of the "gross cash receipts." In this scenario, hotel revenues would be used to repay a loan from Jones's Realty Management Company, which had the management contract for the Rice Hotel. The bondholders would be required to subordinate their secured position and to further reduce their interest payments until that loan was also repaid. In addition, for a number of years the proposed renovations would curtail the interest payments to bondholders that was subject to net earnings and would eliminate its accumulation on the principal of the bonds.

Jones needed approval from the court since his plan was in direct violation of his agreement with the bondholders that resulted from the bankruptcy reorganization of his company. In that agreement between Jones's Rice Properties, Inc., and Maurice A. Rosenthal, trustee for the bondholders, Jones expressly promised "to maintain all buildings, structures and improvements now or at any time hereafter on said mortgaged premises . . . and from time to time to make or cause to be made all needful and proper replacements, repairs, renewals and improvements, so that the efficiency of said mortgaged property shall not be impaired." Clearly, the installation of an air conditioning system and renovations to the dining room of the Rice Hotel were the defined obligations of Jones's company.[51]

Following the court's suggestion, Jones's company sent notices of the proposed action to the bondholders, who still held $4,315,850 of the bonds. A number of them expressed their opposition to the renovation plans. "There is always money," one complained, "for attorneys, managers and financiers, most of whom are rich already, but very little money is available for the poor suckers who put up the actual money for construction. . . . Now that the case has been held and the pockets of the bondholders have been picked again the court is adjourned. Let all of we judges, financiers and attorneys go down to the Club and have a few high balls."[52]

The bondholders also raised questions about the high cost of the improvements (which would be equal to about $4,860,000 in today's dollars): "The amount to be spent, $325,000, is a very large sum to pay for the improvements mentioned. In fact it is sufficient to pay for the construction of a large hotel. The handling of these defaulted realty bond issues has been a national scandal."[53]

The Lamar Hotel, which was also going to be renovated and air conditioned with a similar plan, was another subject of controversy in the federal courthouse in Houston. The hotel had become the permanent home of most of the Jones family, including Jesse's aunt, Mrs. M. T. Jones, his sister, Ida (Mrs. Daniel E. Garrett), his brother, John Jones, and John's wife, all of whom had apartments in the hotel.

Jones and his wife lived in grand style at the Lamar. After they moved to Washington, they continued to fully maintain the top floor penthouse, which included "a servants" quarters, for their personal use. Whenever they returned to Houston, they were greeted with reverence as they walked through the Lamar's lobby. In 1927, when Jones built the hotel on property that had once been one of his lumber yards, he had acknowledged that Houston was not in need of such an elaborate hotel. Jones, who had a "gigantic ego," just wanted a luxurious place for him and his wife of seven years to live. As his friend Dawes remarked, Jones liked to keep an eye on his realm, looking down from the windows of his seventeenth-story penthouse.[54]

The letters of disgruntled bondholders were not read in open court, but they did become part of the official record of a hearing held in December 1937 before Federal District Judge T. Whitfield Davidson. A reading of the transcript of the hearing reveals why the bondholders were so upset. The exorbitant cost of the renovations immediately prompted further questions, in that the general contractor for the air conditioning work was Charles G. Hiney and Company. Charles Hiney's father was president of Bankers Mortgage Company, which was part of the Jones organization. During the hearing, it was also confirmed that entities of Jones owned the Houston Properties Corporation, Rice Properties, Inc., and Lamar Properties, Inc. Without giving a personal guarantee of any kind, Jones had been able to create two new companies and assume the assets of the old companies without reducing the principal amounts due on their bonds.

The Jesse H. Jones Company owned a controlling interest in the Hippo-drome Building and Amusement Company, which owned all of the preferred and common stock of Houston Properties Corporation. Hippodrome also owned a majority stake in the Southern Loan and Investment Company. And Jones controlled the Realty Management Company through Fred Heyne and George Butler. Butler was vice president of the Realty Management Company and Heyne, Jones's longtime right-hand man, was president.[55]

The trustee testified that Jones and his companies were not financially able to raise $325,000 or to make any capital contributions. And George Butler, Jones's nephew and head of Rice Properties, testified that Rice Properties had capital of only $25,000 and "it wasn't possible for the present equity owners [Jones and his entities] to make a capital investment. . . . The present equity owners were not in a position to finance the matter, the improvements." So the same Jones, who was listed in the offering circular of Houston Properties as having a net worth of $10 million when his company was selling bonds to the public in the 1920s, found it impossible in 1937 to contribute $325,000, either personally or through one of his companies, to improve the properties, despite his obligation to do so.[56]

Yet it was another Jones company, Realty Management Company, that made the loans for the renovations to both hotels. Jones did manage to find money to buy back the bonds at depressed prices. Working with bond dealers, Jones, through still another entity, purchased $1.8 million of the bonds for, at most, 68 cents on the dollar. He then presented the bonds to the trustee of the bondholders, who agreed to cancel $1.8 million of debt on the proper-ties and to release the Electric Building and the Kirby Theater from the real estate mortgage securing the original bond issue. After the cancellation of the bonds, just the Rice Hotel and Haverty Building secured the remaining $2.5 million of indebtedness.[57]

Jesse Jones filed for bankruptcy protection for eleven more major bond issues, including the Chamber of Commerce Building Company. Its president had been Jones's brother, John, when the bonds had been issued in 1922. The security for those bonds were the Chamber of Commerce Building and the fifteen-hundred-seat Palace Theater, located at the Northwest corner of Milam Street and Texas Avenue, in the block next to the prestigious Rice Hotel. The Chamber of Commerce building was a ten-story office and shopping complex with club quarters, later renamed the Milam Building. It had been built after Straus and Company sold $1 million of 6 percent bonds in 1922.

Jones's company began defaulting on principal and interest payments in November 1931. It also failed to pay any of its 1931 taxes, totaling $12,000, to the City of Houston, the Houston Independent School District, the state of Texas, and Harris County. By February 2, 1934, Jones's company owed

$897,936 to the bondholders, which included unpaid principal of $770,000, and unpaid interest of $127,936.[58]

As his influence and authority expanded within the Roosevelt administration, Jones, who many regarded as the second or third most powerful man in Washington because of the control he exercised over the economy, shielded his personal financial problems from public scrutiny with his complicated transactions and legal maneuvers. For example, when the Chamber of Commerce Building Company defaulted on its bonds, Jones changed its name to the Palace Building Company on April 25, 1932. Jones had also changed the name of its most valuable asset, the Chamber of Commerce Building, to the Milam Building. (Jones later said he named the building after Ben Milam, a hero of the Texas revolution, although it also happened to front on Milam Street and Texas Avenue.) During the years when Jones was in Washington, the building was managed through his company, Realty Management Company, which Butler and Heyne ran on a daily basis. But Jones continued to own and control the enterprise. All of the outstanding stock of the newly named Palace Building Company, whose president was Butler, was owned through Jones's Fidelity Securities Corporation, whose president was also Butler. The company promptly entered into a five-year management contract with Jones's management company, thus enabling it to steer tenants to other Jones buildings which his management company also managed, but that were in direct competition with the Milam building.[59]

The Houston Chronicle Building Company also had a second mortgage of $183,106 on the Milam Building. This company, with George Butler once again as its president, was controlled through the Houston Chronicle Publishing Company, which was controlled through the Jesse H. Jones Company. Its second mortgage provided an added incentive for Jones to regain control and ownership of the Milam Building to prevent his second mortgage from being wiped out at a public auction. After twelve years, the total debt on the building amounted to $1,081,042, more than the original $1 million bond issue. Consequently, the federal court in Houston determined that it was in "the best interests" of the bondholders for the mortgaged property to be sold on the courthouse steps.[60]

But Jones stepped in to structure a bankruptcy reorganization, thus preventing the sale of the building at a public auction. And this time he guaranteed that his bondholders would suffer even more losses in this bond issue than in most of his defunct bond deals. The situation seemed hopeless to the bondholders because the reported income from the building in 1933 had been only $22,670. Accordingly, they agreed to the Jones plan. It forced the bondholders to release their first mortgage on the buildings, and converted their secured bonds into 90 percent of the equity of a new company, thereby putting the bondholders in a vulnerable, unsecured position. Jones did not give them the option of converting the fixed-interest-rate bonds to net income bonds, which would be paid if income was available, and in some circumstances would even accrue unpaid interest. So when the new Jones entity, Milam Properties, Inc., failed, the former bondholders—who were now its nonvoting and unsecured stockholders—suffered horrendous losses.[61]

Jones retained only a 10 percent interest in the new company because, as he would later admit, it was "practically worthless" in and of itself. It had considerable value to him, however, in that he was able to eliminate the $897,936 mortgage on the building and relegate the bondholders into nonvoting stockholders, establishing a voting trust for their 90 percent interest, a trust which he controlled through its trustees. The reorganization plan explained the need for a voting trust as follows: "For the purpose of maintaining unity of control and a central point for the administration of the affairs of the new company, all of the shares of common stock of the new company will be issued to three trustees." Court filings revealed Jones's controlling influence over the voting trust, whose trustees were: Samuel J. T. Straus, who was supposedly the managing trustee protecting the interests of the bondholders; Fred Heyne, the operating head of Jones's entities for forty-nine years, and the local agent for Samuel Straus; and Jones's nephew, George Butler.[62]

Jones had no partners in his real estate operations to limit his authority or challenge his actions. His carefully constructed maze of companies also sheltered him from personal liability. Since each bond issue was in a separate Jones company, lacking a personal guarantee from Jones, his personal risk was minimal, especially since the financing was for more than 100 percent of the value of the properties. The only question became how much profit he would make.

As part of his effort to convince the bondholders to swap their secured debt position for an unsecured equity interest, Jones had argued in the reorganization plan that the location of the Chamber of Commerce Building had "retrogressed and the building is believed to be poorly located for the purposes for which it was designed. Of recent years, considerable difficulty has been experienced in obtaining tenants for the building; and, as a result of the fact that a great portion of the space has been vacant for a considerable period, the physical condition of the building has deteriorated."[63]

The default of the Chamber of Commerce bond issue could not be blamed entirely on the economic conditions associated with the neighborhood surrounding the hotel or even on the Depression, since it generated gross earnings of $88,554 in 1928, making it one of the most profitable buildings that Jones owned in Houston. But as Jones continued to capitalize on the lucrative bond issue frenzy, constructing as many buildings as his Chicago bond dealers could finance throughout the 1920s, he ended up competing against himself, and the Chamber of Commerce Building eventually started losing major tenants to his other newer buildings. Nevertheless, between 1929 and 1930 it still generated gross earnings of $67,112, prior to principal and interest payments to the bondholders. But by 1931, Jones had stopped paying state, county, and city taxes for the building, and by 1934 the delinquent taxes, with interest and penalties, amounted to $16,421. Because Jones had four other office buildings in Houston that were outperforming the Chamber of Commerce Building at that time, he allowed it to fall into disrepair, which compounded the problem of attracting tenants and violated the terms of his contract with the bondholders.[64]

Milam Properties, Inc., the bondholders' company that was managed through Jones's management company, operated at a loss, without issuing dividends, for a few years. Then Jones bought it from its trustees for fifteen cents a share. Given that each share represented $128 of debt, the bondholders received a fraction of one cent on the dollar. After years of having received no interest payments at all, the bondholders collected a total of about $1,161 out of the $897,936 that Jones's company owed them as of February 2, 1934. Ironically, faring somewhat better were the bondholders who disagreed with the Jones plan and refused to deposit their bonds, which amounted to $87,500, with the trustees. In 1934, they received 12.8 percent of their principal investment, a total of $11,190. It was the bondholders who trusted Jones, and were no doubt impressed enough with his status as the chairman of the RFC to go along with his plan, who received only one-tenth of one percent return on their investment, after waiting for a decade.[65]

If, as Jones would argue, the Milam Building and the Palace Theater had become "practically worthless" with the passage of time, why did he buy them back from his nephew George Butler and the other two trustees? Controlling the new company because of his close ties to the trustees, Jones was represented on both sides of the negotiating table, allowing him to purchase the two buildings after shedding their mortgages in bankruptcy court, quite a remarkable feat. In 1953, after the Milam Building had been depreciated for thirty years, its book value was still $1,968,616. But its fair market value was significantly more because Jones had refinanced the property years earlier and $2,465,000 still remained on that mortgage, which the Equitable Life Assurance Society held.[66]

Despite going through years of bankruptcy proceedings, in the early 1950s Jones's real estate empire was largely intact, although carrying a heavy debt burden. On August 31, 1953, the Jones real estate holdings in Texas showed a depreciated book value of $37,944,139, with debt of $32,257,435. Jones's

New York real estate companies had an even higher percentage of debt, with a book value of $12,222,941 against a debt of $11,148,860.[67]

As Royal F. Munger of the *Chicago Daily News* would observe in 1937: "The money raised by the sale of the bond issue[s] was then almost the only money that went into the building[s]. That was not illegal, but it was a dirty, rotten piece of business in which the public took the punishment, while the promoter[s] took the profits." But, as we have seen, the way Jones raised money for his buildings was, in fact, illegal because the grossly inflated appraisals in his offering circulars violated the antifraud provisions of the state securities laws in every state where the bonds were sold.[68]

Jones's grandiose plans to construct ornate hotels, office buildings, and theaters were designed to transform Houston into the premier commercial center of the South and Southwest. Instead, they had disastrous consequences for the thousands of investors who purchased his "gold bonds." His buildings changed the skyline of Houston, but they also resulted in bankruptcy reorganizations that cost investors more than $10 million of the $27.4 million worth of bonds that he sold to the public. The Jones investors would ultimately lose more than $149 million in today's dollars.[69]

As mentioned earlier, Jones also financed his real estate operations and other enterprises through financial institutions that he had formed or acquired. His rise to power had been greatly advanced when he gained control of the National Bank of Commerce in the early 1920s and was named its president and chairman of its board of directors. Throughout his thirteen years at the RFC, he remained chairman of the bank, which had become the largest bank in Houston.[70]

According to Jones, he had resigned as chairman of the board and president of one of his primary companies, the Bankers Mortgage Company of Houston, soon after he had arrived in Washington in April 1932. This was meaningless, however, except for the sake of appearance, because he remained the principal and controlling stockholder of the company, and the rest of its board of directors remained the same. Fred Heyne, Jones's longtime confidant and vice president of Jesse H. Jones and Company, which was located in the Bankers Mortgage Building in Houston, became president of the company and served on the board alongside John Jones, Jesse's older brother. Jesse completely trusted John, saying of him that "there was no nobler man, no finer friend, no more affectionate brother." Both Heyne and John Jones were also directors of Jones's National Bank of Commerce, as was N. Eugene Meador, a vice president and director of the mortgage company. Meador, the brother-in-law of Jones's wife, was the former general manager of the Jones lumber properties and the president of Jones's bank. Another director of the

Bankers Mortgage Company, A. D. Simpson, had worked since 1918 at the National Bank of Commerce, becoming its president after Meador's death in 1933. And yet another director of the mortgage company, Frank Andrews, was one of Jones's lawyers, who had known him "intimately for thirty years." These connections insured that although Jones was no longer on the board, he was still completely in control of his company.[71]

In June 1932, Jones was facing a liquidity crisis. So he directed his Bankers Mortgage Company to apply for a secret government loan from the RFC. With no publicity or due diligence, the RFC's board—without Jones's participation because of his conflict of interest—approved a $1.5 million loan for Jones's company, an amount worth about $23.6 million today. (The RFC disbursed $1,489,691 to Jones's mortgage company during the same week as the Dawes bailout.) The loan represented 74 percent of the purported $2 million of capital stock of the company, and 20 percent of the total assets of $7,284,067 it had held as of December 31, 1931.[72]

Jones had "appealed in vain" to restrict the release of information about the RFC's loans only to members of Congress. After he made news with his lobbying efforts, Jones wrote to Roosevelt, the newly elected president, insisting that he had "made no request" to keep the RFC loans confidential and that his visit to Capitol Hill had been "misinterpreted." Nevertheless, in an obvious attempt to cover himself, on February 2, 1933, less than a week after the Jones loan was made public, Jones dictated a memorandum to his secretary for his personal files, saying "that he had resigned his official connection with Bankers Mortgage Company, at Houston, and all other real estate operations soon after coming to Washington to accept directorship of the Reconstruction Finance Corporation." Jones did not suggest, however, that he had divested his controlling equity interest in the mortgage company or in his real estate companies.[73]

Despite the RFC bailout, Jesse Jones continued to be desperately short of cash throughout 1932 and 1933. And in July 1933, Jones, who was then chairman of the RFC, borrowed another $1,495,074 from the RFC through one of his entities named the Midland Mortgage Company, a subsidiary of the Bankers Mortgage Company that had been formed soon after Jones had joined the RFC. When word leaked about the Jones loans and the Fort Worth law firm of Boykin and Ray complained, Senator Duncan U. Fletcher, a Democrat from Florida who was the chairman of the Senate Committee on Banking and Currency, wrote to Jones for an explanation. With the heat turned up, Jones changed his story. On November 21, 1933, Jones made the following material misrepresentation to Fletcher and the banking committee: "I disposed of my interest and severed my connection with the [Bankers

Mortgage Company] in April 1932." But there had been no change of control of the Bankers Mortgage Company; Jesse Jones was still firmly in control of the company. Nevertheless, based on Jones's false statement and without any independent investigation, the Senate subcommittee on the RFC concluded, "Mr. Jones has not profited in any way from the making of the [RFC loans to the Bankers Mortgage Company and Midland Mortgage Company] and has no personal or individual interest therein."[74]

Fletcher's committee conducted its limited inquiry behind closed doors, failing to investigate the significant inconsistency between Jones's statements about his ownership of the Bankers Mortgage Company. In an effort to minimize publicity and to prevent another leak, "the rather lengthy statement of Mr. Jones had been passed from member to member until it had been read by all." Jones's confidential letter was revealing for its lack of candor. In it he had admitted that he "did not vote on or participate in the granting of either of these loans" because of his conflict of interest. (The obvious question was why had he abstained from voting on the loans if he had sold his interest in the companies that had received the RFC loans. Of course, the answer was that he had not "disposed" of his interest in the mortgage companies.) After misleading the committee, Jones lambasted the Fort Worth lawyers who dared to question his integrity: "the complaints which have reached you about these loans are not made from any honest motives but to aid unscrupulous lawyers who degrade an honorable profession and seek to use the courts of the land and the United States Senate to further their own unholy purposes."[75]

But even the RFC's injection of $3 million was not enough to solve Jones's liquidity problems. While he was in Chicago for the Democratic convention and at the same time as he was promoting the Dawes bailout, Jones procured a highly questionable $350,000 unsecured and undocumented loan from Melvin Traylor's First National Bank of Chicago. (The loan would be worth about $5.5 million in today's dollars.) Jones personally guaranteed the loan, which was in the name of the Houston Post Company. He had acquired the newspaper company in 1931 after its owner had suffered financial difficulties. Federal bank examiners severely criticized the loan for having "no credit information on file," since Jones had not submitted so much as a loan application or financial statement to Traylor. (Traylor, meanwhile, was promoting the bailout of the Dawes bank because he feared that its collapse would force his bank to close also.) Regulators further criticized the Jones loan because he received it without putting up any collateral and it was made to a fledgling newspaper business in another state, far outside the primary lending area of the Chicago bank.[76]

The idea of borrowing money for his cash-strapped companies from the vast resources of the RFC must have occurred to Jones soon after he arrived in Washington. Responding to his request, the law firm of Huggins, Kayser, and Liddel sent him a legal opinion on February 15, 1932, addressing the conflict-of-interest question. Jones was using the seven-member firm, which included his seemingly ubiquitous nephew, George Butler, to run interference for those of his Houston real estate entities that were defaulting on their bonds and filing for bankruptcy protection from their bondholders. As we have seen, Butler was a director of Jones's National Bank of Commerce and head of the reorganized Houston properties. Another member of the firm, W. O. Huggins, was the editor of Jones's *Houston Chronicle* and a director of Jones's National Bank of Commerce. In addition, he was a director of the Bankers Mortgage Company, as was another partner, Paul Kayser. Close to John Nance Garner, Huggins had convinced the vice president to lobby Roosevelt, unsuccessfully, to appoint Jones as secretary of the Treasury on the grounds that Jones was "strong with the Senators and Congressmen." Furthermore, as vice president of Milam Properties, Inc., another partner, Charles Reinhard, helped Jones buy the Milam Building and Palace Theatre from Milam Properties.

In all of this, Huggins, Kayser, and Liddel was hardly free of its own conflicts of interests. Nevertheless, the firm was quick to point out to Jones that there was no penalty in the RFC act for violations of its conflict-of-interest provision and that Jones's entities were free to borrow from the agency as long as Jones did not vote on the loan requests. For example, because Jones's "bank at Houston" had deposits in Dawes's Central Republic Bank, Jones recused himself when the RFC board formally approved the Dawes bailout.[77]

When Jones went to Washington, he remained the controlling stockholder of the National Bank of Commerce. Though he resigned as president of the bank, he stayed on as its chairman. Eugene Meador, the vice president of the Bankers Mortgage Company, served as the president of Jones's bank until his death about a year later. Then A. D. Simpson became the president of the Jones bank. The boards of Jones's mortgage company and his bank were interlocking, with Meador and Simpson being directors of both companies. Other interlocking directors on both boards were John Jones, Heyne, Huggins, and Sam Streetman. Thus Jones, the majority stockholder of both companies, continued to maintain tight control over their affairs.[78]

In early 1934, when Jones was the chairman of both the RFC and the National Bank of Commerce, the RFC purchased preferred stock of $2,500,000 in the Jones bank (a sum worth about $40.1 million today), which had capital stock of purportedly $1,000,000 and total assets of $26,365,268. When Jones closed the transaction, once again sitting on both sides of the table, the capital stock of his bank became $3,500,000, thanks to the U.S. government. This fortification of its capital allowed the Jones bank to increase its assets nearly $9 million by the end of that year as compared to the previous year, 1933, at a time when many other banks were experiencing a decrease in their assets. The bank enjoyed a total net profit of $612,452, as of December 31, 1934. This came to a robust 1.7 percent return on assets, a remarkable amount considering that Houston, like the rest of the country, was in the midst of the Depression. After the boost from the RFC, the Jones bank was performing better in the Depression year of 1934, with its net profit of $612,452, than in the boom year of 1929, when the bank's net profit, without the help of the federal government, was only $272,806.

In 1934, after receiving the federal injection of capital—designed to increase lending—the Jones bank more than doubled its profits, making far fewer loans than it had made in 1929. When a reporter asked Jones about his bank being "80 percent liquid," Jones said that "he had practically nothing to do with the management of that bank, but that he had urged it to make loans the same as any other institution." He added that the banks of Texas were "full of money." In October 1934, Jones's good friend, A. P. Giannini, was in Washington lobbying him to intervene on behalf of the Bank of America with the Federal Reserve Bank of San Francisco, which had refused to approve risky business loans originated at Giannini's bank. At the conclusion of his meeting with Jones, Giannini told a reporter that "Houston's National Bank of Commerce [the Jones bank] is one of the most prosperous banks in the country—and it is also one of the most liquid."[79]

The one-sided arrangement comes into clearer focus when the dividend record of the Jones bank is examined. Between 1922 and 1933, Jones and the other stockholders had been earning a 10 percent annual return on their $1,000,000 of capital stock. At the end of 1934, Jones increased the annual return to 12 percent, paying out dividends of $120,000. By contrast, on the government's investment of $2,500,000 of preferred stock, Jones declared and accrued $105,764, an annual return of 4.2 percent.

More important than the low rate of return was that the preferred dividends were not paid to the RFC, or even put into an escrow account; they were accrued. This meant that they appeared merely as a bookkeeping entry on the books of the Jones bank without affecting its cash flow. So the bank was allowed to use the RFC's investment and dividends for liquidity purposes or to make other investments, even though it was enjoying record profits.

In fact, the Jones bank did not redeem its preferred stock until December 12, 1944, a few months before Jones relinquished control over the RFC and more than eleven years after the RFC had made what was supposed to be a temporary advance to shore up his bank so it could make loans to businesses in Houston.[80]

For Jones, being chairman of the RFC had considerable financial rewards. He could afford to spend so much time in Washington because his position was so profitable for his banking, real estate, and other businesses. During the Depression, the Jones empire survived its cash-flow crises because his political power and authority enabled him to arrange sweetheart loans from banks seeking government assistance and allowed his own bank and other companies to receive bailouts from the RFC, which he dominated until 1945.

HOOVER AND THE BIG BANKS

Along with the shenanigans of Dawes and Jones, and their allies on the RFC board, Hoover misled the public about the agency that he had placed so much hope in to stimulate the economy and ensure his bid for reelection. To the critics who had complained that the chief beneficiaries of the RFC would be large banks in big cities—the very banks whose reckless speculation and imprudent lending practices had contributed so greatly to the stock market crash and the failure of so many businesses—the president insisted that, on the contrary, the RFC had been created to support small community banks. Eugene Meyer, while he was governor of the Federal Reserve Board and chairman of the RFC, also stated repeatedly that the bulk of the loans were going to small banks. Meyer testified to a Senate committee that 92 percent of the RFC loans were made to banks in cities with populations of less than ten thousand. Hoover and Meyer emphasized the *number* of banks receiving loans, rather than the *amount* of each of the loans.

Comptroller of the Currency John Pole, an old friend of Dawes's, also maintained that the banking crisis involved the smaller banks in the hinterlands and not the big money-center banks. And Pole joined in the charade, announcing three weeks after the RFC had been formed that it had loaned $24 million to banks "scattered all over the country." However, a closer look shows that $21 million of the $24 million went to only two banks. Actually, the RFC's first bank loan was a $15 million advance to the Bank of America National Trust and Savings Association of San Francisco (Bank of America). Instead of instilling confidence in the banking system, the misleading statistics and statements created grist for the RFC's critics to grind.[81]

Writing in 1933, Franklin Ebersole, an economist at Harvard University, concluded that Hoover had pursued a policy of deliberate misinformation about the lending activities of the RFC "to create a favorable state of mind upon the part of the general public by ignoring and obscuring the facts." During "the period of darkness"—from February to July 20, 1932—when the names of borrowers and the amounts of their loans were sealed from the public because of the Hoover administration's ongoing policy of secrecy, 23 percent of all the bank and mortgage loans that the RFC authorized— $184,900,000 out of $804,033,692—went to just two banking organizations, the Dawes bank and the Bank of America, formerly the Bank of Italy, which A. P. Giannini founded in 1904 (along with its affiliated Bank of Italy Mortgage Company). Giannini's bank was the largest outside New York and the fourth largest in the country, with more than $710.9 million in deposits as of June 30, 1932.[82]

Nonetheless, Hoover continued to promote the notion that the RFC was committed primarily to a policy of assisting small community banks. On March 8, 1932, he issued to the press a "confidential statement on the character of business undertaken" at the RFC "for background only," which was a clever way of limiting scrutiny and, thus, criticism of the agency. Hoover said the RFC had issued loans of nearly $61.8 million to 255 financial institutions, "most of them country banks," while failing to disclose that Giannini's bank and two other large banks had received more than $41 million of the $61.8 million of these loans.[83]

A week later, the White House released Hoover's telegram to the chairman of the Bank of Abbeville and Trust Company of Abbeville, Louisiana, acknowledging the RFC's assistance to the small rural bank. But the next day, on March 16, the RFC made a secret $25 million loan to Giannini's Bank of America, with no attendant press release. Hoover then issued a press conference statement on March 25, 1932, announcing that the RFC had authorized loans of nearly $127 million to 587 banks and trust companies located in forty-five states. According to Hoover, the "average per institution" loan was a mere $216,162. He stressed that "the great majority of these loans are to smaller communities." He further stated that less than $3.5 million had been authorized to banks located in cities with a population of more than one million, and that more than $116 million had been authorized to banks in communities with a population of less than six hundred thousand. At the time when Hoover issued his statement, however, more than 50 percent of these loans had been authorized to three large banks, including the Bank of America, which had received authorization for two loans that totaled $40 million, or 31.5 percent of all of the loans.[84]

On April 21, 1932, Dawes testified before Congress to answer questions raised about the loan policies of the RFC. He reaffirmed that the purpose of the agency, and the intent of Hoover and Congress in creating it, was "the relief of the people of the United States." The method of accomplishing this far-ranging goal was "through loans adequately secured" to banks, other financial institutions, and railroads. Dawes said the first item of business during the loan review process would be to determine if the applicant could provide the "adequate security" as Congress had mandated. Second, the RFC would consider the loan's "beneficial effect in the interest of the general public." Arguably, any loan to any financial institution would benefit some members of the public, so the emphasis had to be on its benefit to the general public.

Dawes stressed that only sixty-seven loans, a total of $5,994,300, had been authorized to closed banks that were in the process of reorganizing or liquidating. Receivers of failed banks could apply for loans, but so far the bulk of the authorized loans had gone to existing banks, approximately $243,248,769 to 1,520 banks between February 2 and April 19, 1932. He neglected to mention the $50 million in total loans for the Bank of America that his agency had approved, representing 20.5 percent of the RFC's authorized loans.[85]

When Representative Henry T. Rainey of Illinois, the future Democratic Speaker of the House, asked Dawes point-blank: "Have you made any loans to insolvent banks and railroads, hopelessly insolvent banks and railroads?" Dawes responded unequivocally. "We have not made loans to insolvent banks except to receivers as authorized by the law for the purpose of paying dividends to depositors. . . . We loan upon adequate security and to going banks. All our loans . . . are made upon adequate security, out of which it is expected that the loan will be paid in full and with interest. We make no unsecured loans."[86]

Dawes emphasized throughout his testimony that the RFC was "not giving money away" but instead "loaning it on adequate security." According to Dawes, the board considered loans on an individual basis, but they were made "primarily as to the adequacy of security" at the time the loan was made. When Rainey asked Dawes if he thought the RFC would lose money, Dawes responded that it would not "incur capital losses, taking into consideration its expenses as well as its income from interest received." Dawes's testimony would come back to haunt him in only two months, when he abruptly switched positions and became borrower instead of lender, since the strict collateral rule could not be applied to the Dawes bank because it was hopelessly insolvent.[87]

During his testimony before Congress, Dawes declared that because of the work of the RFC in its first few weeks, "the general withdrawal of bank deposits is stopped . . . bank deposits have ceased to fall and bank failures have been reduced to the minimum." He told the committee that "general confidence in our banking system has been restored. . . . The mass attitude is changed right now in the United States, from a condition of pessimism to one of comparative hopefulness." Dawes also said the nation was "approaching business recovery" and "prosperity." Dawes confidently proclaimed that "great credit" was due to the RFC for the "now changed mass attitude of the people."[88]

In an attempt to explain why the American people had lost confidence in the nation's business institutions, Dawes cited the "fundamental laws of human nature and human reaction." He said: "As natural laws have brought about that deflation, those same natural laws will bring about a return of prosperity to this country . . . it is how the great mass of the people, not think, but feel. And they are feeling better. . . . Anybody sitting on the board where I am sees things are getting better in this country." (When Dawes announced his resignation on June 7, seven weeks later, he said he was leaving because the nation was in such great shape.)[89]

While supporting the bailout of the banking industry, Dawes was a hard-nosed businessman when it came to relief of the general population or what might appear to be welfare payments to individuals. According to Dawes, it made no economic or moral sense for the government to accelerate a bonus to soldiers who had fought in the trenches of France, a bonus that Congress passed in 1925 but did not schedule to be paid until 1945.[90]

He denounced Representative Wright Patman's bill to issue $2.4 billion to expedite the bonus payments to these veterans. Speaking before Congress that April at the zenith of his credibility, Dawes—a general during World War I and a member of the American Legion—criticized the Patman bill as a formula for "complete economic ruin," a fiasco whose impact on the economy would be greater than the stock market crash of 1929. He recounted his experiences in formulating the Dawes Plan and "the devastating effects" of inflation on the German mark: "Well do I remember it, arriving in Berlin one morning and trying to buy a paper for 500,000 marks. The newsboy demanded 1,000,000." Delivering what might have been a knockout blow to the bonus bill, he raised his voice and shook his fist, declaring that the payments would inflate the dollar and "destroy the general confidence in the country which has now been re-established." When questioned, he fired back: "Why, damn it all, this issue of fiat money would undermine the credit of the country, invite the withdrawal of foreign deposits, and shake the soundness of the United States government." He admitted that he had not read the bills dealing with the bonus issue and he refused to study them: "O, hell, don't ask me to do that, I am busy. I got to work day and night on this Reconstruction corporation job." He ended his diatribe, proclaiming once again that, "Prosperity is bound to return as sure as the sun rises in the morning."[91]

Veterans' reactions to the former general's comments were, as might be expected, negative. When George Lawrence, the commander of the American Legion post in Winona, Minnesota, addressed a letter to Dawes at the "SO-CALLED RECONSTRUCTION CORPORATION," he posed the following question: "If the welfare of this country were so close to your heart as you would now have the people believe, will you explain why you hand out hundreds of millions of dollars for what was supposed to be 'RECONSTRUCTION PURPOSES' when, as a matter of fact, millions of dollars found themselves quickly in the hands of WALL STREET, which is directly the cause of the present HARD TIMES, but so-called 'DEPRESSION'?"

Dawes was unmoved. And when the angry veterans marched on Washington, he argued to Hoover that the "Bonus Expeditionary Force" was engaging in a rebellion that required military force to quell. Indeed, Eugene Meyer remembered "that Dawes wanted to meet the bonus marchers at the district line with troops with their bayonets fixed."[92]

On June 4 and 5, 1932, just before Dawes resigned as president of the RFC, Hoover held a conference with him and the other RFC directors at his 164-acre compound on the Rapidan River—excellent for trout fishing—a hundred miles from the White House in the Blue Ridge Mountains of Virginia. After the conference, the White House once again touted the administration's policy of lending to smaller banks in less populated communities, focusing again on the number of banks receiving loans, rather than the amount of those loans, along with the size of the communities where the banks were located. To back up the statement, the administration released statistics emphasizing that "of nearly 3,000 borrowing banks, more than 70 percent are located in towns of 5,000 in population or less; while 84 percent are located in towns of 25,000 in population or less; and that only 4.5 percent of money loaned to banks has gone to institutions in cities of over one million in population."

The distinction the White House drew between big cities—those with populations of more than one million—and small communities was also misleading. San Francisco had a population of less than one million, but was considered a big city in 1932. The skewed statistics, which mentioned no individual loan amounts or any names of recipient banks, allowed the administration to conceal the loans to Giannini's Bank of America.

Giannini's aggressive acquisition and expansion program during the 1920s had resulted in a banking organization that operated 410 affiliated banks and branches throughout California, suffering from extraordinarily high overhead

**Image 3.3.   President Herbert Hoover after a good day of trout fishing. Hoover person-
ally directed the bailout of the Dawes bank by telephone from his fishing camp on the
Rapidan River. (Courtesy, Library of Congress)**

expenses. With assets consisting of $115 million in slow, doubtful, and worth-
less loans, Giannini's banking system was on the verge of collapse. In addition, Giannini's Merchants National Trust and Savings Bank of Los Angeles,
which was part of the Bank of America chain of banks, had suffered a loss
of more than $5.5 million when four of its officers engaged in a bank fraud
conspiracy.

Had Hoover been forthcoming about the recipients of the loans and
explained that large loans to big-city banks were made in proportion to the
size of their assets and deposits, his critics would not have been silenced. But
more candor certainly would have enhanced his credibility and might have
engendered more support for the administration's recovery efforts. Instead,
his disingenuous statistical arguments made him an easy target. James Olson,
a historian of the RFC, confirmed the obvious when he wrote, "The critics
were right: the RFC did grant substantial loans to large banks." Proving this
point, on June 4, before traveling to Hoover's Rapidan River camp, the RFC
directors approved a fifth loan of $5 million for Giannini's bank, increas-
ing the total of the loans made to his entities to $62,500,000. Before the

RFC's shroud of secrecy was lifted, Giannini's financial institutions would receive two more loans, bringing the total loans for his money-center bank to $94,900,000.[93]

By the end of June 1932, the RFC had authorized 130 loans of more than $113 million to sixty-three banks in Chicago. Yet, the Dawes bank would receive $90 million, or 80 percent, of that amount. As Ebersole pointed out, "Much was said about the large number of loans made to small banks located in places of small population. But such statements and statistics were largely meaningless."[94]

When Hoover took "personal charge" of the bailout of the Dawes bank, which was the third largest bank in the nation's second largest city, his administration ignored the law, the RFC's policies, and its own rhetoric. Lines of authority became unimportant when the president started working the telephones from his Rapidan River camp on Saturday, June 25, 1932, throughout Sunday and until 3:00 Monday morning, June 27. In instructing the RFC directors "to save the Dawes bank," Hoover was making a last-ditch attempt to avert the financial and political disaster of a full-fledged banking panic in Chicago, which was hosting the Democratic convention at the time.[95]

Notes

1. William Starr Myers, ed., *The State Papers and Other Public Writings of Herbert Hoover* (New York: Doubleday, Doran, 1934), 2:445–46.

2. "Copy of Prepared Statement Read to Meeting of Nineteen New York Bankers Held at Secretary Mellon's Apartment, Sunday, October 4, 1931"; Herbert Hoover to George L. Harrison, October 5, 1931; Harrison to Hoover, October 7, 1931, GLHP/CU; Myers, *The State Papers of Herbert Hoover*, 2:4–7; Hoover, *Memoirs*, 81–86; Gerald D. Nash, "Herbert Hoover and the Origins of the Reconstruction Finance Corporation," *Mississippi Valley Historical Review* 46 (December 1959): 462–68; Mason, "The Determinants and Effects of Reconstruction Finance Corporation Assistance to Banks during the Great Depression," 6–11; James S. Olson, "The End of Voluntarism: Herbert Hoover and the National Credit Corporation," *Annals of Iowa* 41 (Fall 1972): 1104–13; Kennedy, *The Banking Crisis of 1933*, 31–33; James S. Olson, *Herbert Hoover and the Reconstruction Finance Corporation, 1931–1933* (Ames: Iowa State University, 1977), 26; Merlo J. Pusey, *Eugene Meyer* (New York: Alfred A. Knopf, 1974), 216–17.

3. *Stock Exchange Practices, Insull, February 15, 16, and 17, 1933*, 1698; Olson, *Hoover and the Reconstruction Finance Corporation*, 27–32; Kennedy, *The Banking Crisis of 1933*, 34–36; Ray Lyman Wilbur and Arthur Mastick Hyde, *The*

Hoover Policies (New York: Charles Scribner's Sons, 1937), 419–21; "Developments in President Hoover's Program to Stabilize Credit," *Congressional Digest* 10, no. 12 (December 1931): 300.

4. By the end of January 1932, the NCC had approved 644 loans totaling $144 million to 560 banks. Hoover, *Memoirs*, 97; David Burner, *Herbert Hoover: A Public Life* (New York: Alfred A. Knopf, 1979), 268–73; Olson, *Hoover and the Reconstruction Finance Corporation*, 28–32; Kennedy, *The Banking Crisis of 1933*, 34–36; Peter Fearon, *War, Prosperity and Depression: The U.S. Economy 1917–45* (Lawrence: University Press of Kansas, 1987), 109–25; *Wall Street Journal*, March 1, 1932.

5. Myers, *The State Papers of Herbert Hoover*, 2:41–57; *Washington Post*, January 16, 1932; Eugene Meyer, "From Laissez Faire with William Graham Sumner to the RFC," *Public Policy*, edited by Carl J. Friedrich and J. Kenneth Galbraith (Cambridge, Mass.: Harvard University, 1954), 24–25; Olson, *Hoover and the Reconstruction Finance Corporation*, 22–39; Kennedy, *The Banking Crisis of 1933*, 36–38; Martin L. Fausold, *The Presidency of Herbert C. Hoover* (Lawrence: University Press of Kansas, 1985), 152–54; Olson, "The End of Voluntarism," 1104–13; Pusey, *Eugene Meyer*, 157–70, 216–19.

6. *New York Times*, January 26, 1932; *Chicago Tribune*, January 26, 1932; Olson, *Hoover and the Reconstruction Finance Corporation*, 36, 38; Hoover, *Memoirs*, 102, 107; Kennedy, *The Banking Crisis of 1933*, 37.

7. *Washington Post*, January 26, 1932; Walter L. Buenger, "Jesse Jones," *Profiles in Power: Twentieth-Century Texans in Washington*, edited by Kenneth E. Hendrickson Jr., Michael L. Collins, and Patrick Cox (Austin: University of Texas Press, 2004), 76; Myers, *The State Papers of Herbert Hoover*, 2:445–46; Hoover, *Memoirs*, 107–8; Kennedy, *The Banking Crisis of 1933*, 36–38; Olson, *Hoover and the Reconstruction Finance Corporation*, 38–41; Bascom N. Timmons, *Jesse H. Jones: The Man and the Statesman* (New York: Henry Holt, 1956), 162–65.

8. Cecil Edward Weller Jr., *Joe T. Robinson: Always a Loyal Democrat* (Fayetteville: University of Arkansas Press, 1998), 99, 100, 107, 132–33; Olson, *Hoover and the Reconstruction Finance Corporation*, 38, 39; Hoover, *Memoirs*, 107–8; Timmons, *Jesse H. Jones*, 162–68; Donald W. Whisenhunt, ed., *The Depression in the Southwest* (Port Washington, N.Y.: Kennikat Press, 1980), 91–94; Edgar Eugene Robinson and Vaughn Davis Bornet, *Herbert Hoover: President of the United States* (Stanford, Calif.: Hoover Institution Press, 1975), 218.

9. Weller, *Joe T. Robinson*, 100, 107, 132–33; Winston P. Wilson, *Harvey Couch: The Master Builder* (Nashville: Broadman Press, 1947), 141–43, 156–57, 163–64; Stephen Wilson, *Harvey Couch: An Entrepreneur Brings Electricity to Arkansas* (Little Rock: August House, 1986), 29–106; Jones, *Fifty Billion Dollars*, 513; Hoover, *Memoirs*, 108; Olson, *Hoover and the Reconstruction Finance Corporation*, 40; *New York Times*, January 26, 1932; *Chicago Tribune*, January 26, 1932; James S. Olson, "Harvey C. Couch and the Reconstruction Finance Corporation," *Arkansas Historical Quarterly* 32 (Autumn 1973): 217–25; Robinson and Bornet, *Herbert Hoover*, 218.

10. Senator Huey Long, the fiery Democrat from Louisiana who relied on his friend Harvey Couch for political support and was a partner of his in a limestone quarry in Winn Parish, Louisiana, nonetheless made Couch's friend, Senator Robinson, an issue in May 1932 when he read a list of the Robinson law firm's clients, including Couch's companies, into the Congressional Record. The furor that was ignited by Long's attack on his party's leader resulted in Long resigning from all of his committee memberships. The controversy also forced Robinson to resign from his law firm. But he continued to be president of his Little Rock bank, and Couch continued to serve with him on its board. *The Martindale-Hubbell Law Directory* (New York: Martindale-Hubbell Law Directory, 1932), 1:35; *Moody's Manual of Investments, American and Foreign: Banks—Insurance Companies—Investment Trusts— Real Estate Finance and Credit Companies* (New York: Moody's Investors Service, yearly): *1931*, 1875; *1932*, 2014; *1933*, 2645; *1934*, 2575; *New York Times*, May 4, 1932; Weller, *Joe T. Robinson*, 130, 132–34; T. Harry Williams, *Huey Long* (New York: Vintage Books, 1981), 424–25, 796; William Ivy Hair, *The Kingfish and His Realm: The Life and Times of Huey P. Long* (Baton Rouge: Louisiana State University Press, 1991), 190–91, 194, 205, 236, 241, 262, 286.

11. Resume of Wilson McCarthy, WMP/UU; Jones, *Fifty Billion Dollars*, 513, 596; Hoover, *Memoirs*, 108; Olson, *Hoover and the Reconstruction Finance Corporation*, 41; Timmons, *Jesse H. Jones*, 165, 186.

12. Receipt for Inheritance Tax, State of Colorado, Department of Revenue, February 27, 1957, CCDC; "Petition for Probate of Will . . . and Affidavit of Decease," filed in County Court, City and County of Denver, Colorado, on February 24, 1956, WMP/UU; Williamson, "What Is the Relative Value?"

13. Intermediate Report of the Estate of Wilson McCarthy, approved by the court on April 22, 1957, CCDC; Wilson McCarthy to C. A. Magrath, July 8, 1935, WMP/ UU; Herbert Spero, *Reconstruction Finance Corporation Loans to the Railroads: 1932–1937* (Boston: Bankers Publishing Company, 1939), 112–21; Williamson, "What Is the Relative Value?"

14. The U.S. Railroad Credit Corporation also issued a $500,000 loan to the Denver and Rio Grande Western Railroad Company. Memorandum re: R.F.C. Loans to D&RGW, March 12, 1951; List of Loans from R.F.C. to D&RGW, n.d., WMP/UU; *Annual Report of the Interstate Commerce Commission*, 1932, 258; *Annual Report of the Interstate Commerce Commission* 1933, 129; Spero, *Reconstruction Finance Corporation Loans to the Railroads*, 114–21.

15. Jesse H. Jones to Wilson McCarthy, April 16, 1947 (telegram); McCarthy to Jones, April 23, 1947; Resume of Wilson McCarthy; Wilson McCarthy 1936 Income Tax Return, WMP/UU; Timmons, *Jesse H. Jones*, 216, 238.

16. C. G. Dawes to Eugene Meyer, January 3, 1923; Meyer to Dawes, January 5, 1923; Meyer to Dawes, March 22, 1926; Dawes to Meyer, March 27, 1926, EMP/LC; *Reconstruction Finance Corporation Act as Amended and Provisions of the Emergency Relief and Construction Act of 1932 Pertaining to Reconstruction Finance Corporation, July 21, 1932* (Washington, D.C.: Government Printing Office, 1932), 2; Pusey, *Eugene Meyer*, 149, 158, 204, 225–26; Olson, *Hoover and the*

Reconstruction Finance Corporation, 39; Kennedy, *The Banking Crisis of 1933*, 38; Jones, *Fifty Billion Dollars*, 514–20; Schlesinger, *The Crisis of the Old Order*, 42, 236–37; Helen M. Burns, *The American Banking Community and New Deal Banking Reforms, 1933–1935* (Westport, Conn.: Greenwood Press, 1974), 11; James S. Olson, "Herbert Hoover and 'War' on the Depression," *Palimpsest* 54 (July–August 1973): 30; Murray N. Rothbard, *America's Great Depression* (Kansas City: Sheed and Ward, 1975), 247; *Chicago Tribune*, May 18, 1932; B. M. Baruch to P. R. Pearson, June 24, 1935, CGDP/NUL; Agnes E. Meyer, "Diary of Mrs. Agnes E. Meyer," Oral History Research Office, Columbia University, February 11, 1932.

17. *New York Times*, October 12, 1937; Olson, *Hoover and the Reconstruction Finance Corporation*, 39–40; Jones, *Fifty Billion Dollars*, 513, 517, 519–20; Robinson and Bornet, *Herbert Hoover*, 19, 248, 268.

18. *New York Times*, July 27, 1932; *Washington Post*, July 27, 1932.

19. Phillip R. Shriver, "A Hoover Vignette," *Ohio History* 91 (1982): 74–78.

20. "Loans Authorized from February 2, 1932 to July 20, 1932 . . . , January 6, 1933," RFC/NA; "Is This a Trick"; "Is It Really Non-Partisan?"; "Passing the Buck"; "Handling a Hot One"; "Business Considerations First"; "The New R.F.C. Chairman"; "The Sacrificial Goat," n.d.s, clippings in Meyer's scrapbook, EMP/LC; *Baltimore Sun*, July 27, 1932; *New York Times*, January 27, 1933; Jones, *Fifty Billion Dollars*, 521, 522, 596; Olson, *Hoover and the Reconstruction Finance Corporation*, 73, 74; John T. Flynn, "Inside the R.F.C.: An Adventure in Secrecy," *Harper's Magazine,* January 1933, 165; Hoover, *Memoirs*, 168; Shriver, "A Hoover Vignette," 74–78; Harold U. Faulkner, *From Versailles to the New Deal* (New Haven, Conn.: Yale University Press, 1950), 163, 184–88, 207–8, 218.

21. G. R. Cooksey to the President, July 14, 1932, RFC/NA.

22. *New York Times*, January 26, 1933.

23. *Poor's Register of Directors of the United States and Canada, 1930* (New York: Poor's Publishing Company, 1930), 1568; *1931*, 1681; *1932*, 1639; Olson, *Hoover and the Reconstruction Finance Corporation*, 73, 74; Flynn, "Inside the R.F.C.," 165; Hoover, *Memoirs*, 168; Shriver, "A Hoover Vignette," 74–79; Jones, *Fifty Billion Dollars*, 69, 70, 521, 522.

24. *Stock Exchange Practices. Report of the Committee on Banking and Currency, 73d Congress, 2nd Session, Report No. 1455, June 6, 1934* (Washington, D.C.: Government Printing Office, 1934), 295, 301–2.

25. Shriver, "A Hoover Vignette," 81.

26. Charles Miller and Atlee Pomerene were not confirmed by the U.S. Senate, so their terms expired when Roosevelt was inaugurated in March 1933. "New Heads for Federal Aid," n.d., clipping in Meyer's scrapbook, EMP/LC; Shriver, "A Hoover Vignette," 78; Jones, *Fifty Billion Dollars*, 521, 522.

27. Walter L. Buenger, "Between Community and Corporation: The Southern Roots of Jesse H. Jones and the Reconstruction Finance Corporation," *Journal of Southern History* 56 (August 1990): 492–94; Walter L. Buenger and Joseph A. Pratt, *But Also Good Business: Texas Commerce Banks and the Financing of Houston and Texas, 1886–1986* (College Station: Texas A&M University Press,

1986), 42, 45, 46, 50; Robert C. Hilderbrand, "Edward M. House," *Profiles in Power: Twentieth-Century Texans in Washington*, edited by Kenneth E. Hendrickson Jr., Michael L. Collins, and Patrick Cox (Austin: University of Texas Press, 2004): 4–25.

28. Buenger, "Between Community and Corporation," 492–94.

29. *Houston Business Journal*, October 25, 2004; Joe R. Feagin, *Free Enterprise City: Houston in Political-Economic Perspective* (New Brunswick, N.J.: Rutgers University Press, 1988), 123, 131, 138; Buenger and Pratt, *But Also Good Business*, 75, 76; Timmons, *Jesse H. Jones*, 46; Buenger, "Jesse Jones," 67.

30. The House bank was one of the private banks that collapsed during the Panic of 1907 under the weight of bad loans. Buenger, "Between Community and Corporation," 485–87; Buenger and Pratt, *But Also Good Business*, 50.

31. James A. Baker was a partner in the Houston law firm of Baker Botts, and Baker. His grandson, James A. Baker III, was secretary of state under President George H. W. Bush. "Trust Deed and Chattel Mortgage, Houston Properties Corporation to Melvin L. Straus, Trustee, Securing $4,850,000," August 1, 1925, Melvin L. Straus, Trustee v. Houston Properties Corporation, Equity No. 560, USDC/SDT; "Texan's Realty Bond Issues Show Losses to Investor," newspaper clipping, *Chicago Sun*, March 4, 1945, EMP/LC; Buenger, "Between Community and Corporation," 487–88; Feagin, *Free Enterprise City*, 122, 123; Buenger and Pratt, *But Also Good Business*, 50; Buenger, "Jesse Jones," 69; Timmons, *Jesse H. Jones*, 79; Williamson, "What Is the Relative Value?"

32. Timmons, *Jesse H. Jones*, 77, 120–23, 160, 161; Feagin, *Free Enterprise City*, 122, 123; Jones, *Fifty Billion Dollars*, 72–74.

33. Norman D. Brown, *Hood, Bonnet, and Little Brown Jug: Texas Politics, 1921– 1928* (College Station: Texas A&M University Press, 1984), 380; Buenger, "Between Community and Corporation," 492–94.

34. "Reconstruction Finance Corporation," n.d., HHP/HHPL; Timmons, *Jesse H. Jones*, 134–50, 162; Bascom N. Timmons, *Garner of Texas: A Personal History* (New York: Harper and Brothers, 1948), 103–30; Richard Bailey, "Morris Sheppard," Patrick Cox, "John Nance Garner," and Janet Schmelzer, "Tom Connally," in *Profiles in Power: Twentieth-Century Texans in Washington*, edited by Kenneth E. Hendrickson Jr., Michael L. Collins, and Patrick Cox (Austin: University of Texas Press, 2004), 28–34, 42, 49–54; Boller, *Presidential Campaigns*, 218–22; Buenger, "Between Community and Corporation," 492–94.

35. Jones later expanded the Democratic Building and renamed it the C. and I. Life Insurance Building. See Timmons, *Jesse H. Jones*, 142–50, 154; *New York Times*, January 13, 1928; Buenger, "Between Community and Corporation," 495; Buenger, "Jesse Jones," 72–73; Brown, *Hood, Bonnet, and Little Brown Jug*, 378, 380; Feagin, *Free Enterprise City*, 121–23.

36. W. C. Hogg to Governor Dan Moody, June 19, 1928, JJC/UT; Buenger, "Between Community and Corporation," 495; Brown, *Hood, Bonnet, and Little Brown Jug*, 393, 394; Marguerite Johnston, *Houston: The Unknown City, 1836–1946*

(College Station: Texas A&M University Press, 1991), 274, 275; Timmons, *Jesse H. Jones*, 142–47.

37. Timmons, *Jesse H. Jones*, 147; Jones, *Fifty Billion Dollars*, 291–92; Hoover, *Memoirs*, 108; Brown, *Hood, Bonnet, and Little Brown Jug*, 396; Johnston, *Houston*, 274–77.

38. Trust Deed and Chattel Mortgage Securing $4,850,000 Six Per Cent First and General Mortgage Gold Bonds, August 1, 1925, Melvin L. Straus, Trustee v. Houston Properties Corporation, Equity 560, USDC/SDT; S. W. Straus Investing Corporation, 100,000 Unit Certificates, 6% Cumulative Preferred Stock, Series "A" $50 Par Value with Common Stock, filed on January 25, 1929; S. W. Straus and Company, Incorporated (A Delaware Corporation), filed on December 23, 1929; S. W. Straus & Co., Incorporated . . . 40,000 Shares Capital Stock . . . , filed on December 23, 1929, ISOS/ISA; "Released for Publication in Houston Sunday A.M. Newspapers, August 23rd," JJC/UT; "Record of Texan's Career Shows Bond Investors Lost," *Chicago Sun*, clipping in EMP/LC; James, *The Growth of Chicago Banks*, 2:966; Williamson, "What Is the Relative Value?"

39. J. C. Wright to Jesse Jones, August 8, 1925; "Financial Statement Houston Properties Corporation at the Beginning of Business August 1, 1925 (after giving effect to Straus Loan of $4,850,000.00)"; Leonard W. Martyr to S. W. Straus and Company, August 1, 1925, JJC/UT.

40. Jesse H. Jones to Melvin A. Traylor, August 6, 1925 (telegram); E. E. Brown to Jones, August 7, 1925 (telegram); Jones to Brown, August 8, August 12, 1925 (telegrams); "Maturities at Sundry Banks," August 13, 1929; "Maturities at Sundry Banks," July 24, 1930, and September 18, 1930, JJC/UT.

41. "Released for Publication in Houston Sunday A.M. Newspapers, August 23rd," JJC/UT.

42. "Released for Publication in Houston Sunday A.M. Newspapers, August 23rd," JJC/UT; See the testimony of George A. Butler in Maurice A. Rosenthal v. Rice Properties, Inc. and Maurice A. Rosenthal v. Lamar Properties, Inc., Equity Nos. 770 and 771, USDC/SDT; "Maze of Private Companies Screens Texan's Operations," March 3, 1945, EMP/LC.

43. Financial Statement Houston Properties Corporation, August 1, 1929, JJC/UT.

44. "Maze of Private Companies Screens Texan's Operations," *Chicago Sun*, March 3, 1945; "Texan's Realty Bond Issues Show Losses to Investor," *Chicago Sun*, March 4, 1945, clippings in EMP/LC; *Chicago American*, September 7, 1934.

45. "Consolidated Financial Statement of Jesse H. Jones Including Jesse H. Jones Company and Subsidiary Companies," January 1, 1930; "Bank Balances," August 12, 1929; "Daily Balances Due from Banks," August 12, 1929, JJC/UT; Williamson, "What Is the Relative Value?"

46. "Record of Texan's Career Shows Bond Investors Lost," *Chicago Sun*, March 2, 1945, clipping in EMP/LC; Houston Properties Corporation to Jesse H. Jones, August 14, 1931, JJC/UT.

47. Houston Properties Corporation to Jesse H. Jones, August 14, 1931, JJC/UT.

48. Melvin L. Straus, Trustee v. Goggan Building Company, Jesse H. Jones and Company and W. O. Huggins, Trustee, February 14, 1933, Equity No. 569; "Final Decree," February 2, 1934; "Special Master's Report of Sale," Samuel J. T. Straus, Trustee v. Palace Building Company, et. al., Equity No. 570, USDC/SDT; Affidavit for Inheritance Tax Appraisement, in the Matter of the Estate of Jesse Holman Jones, Deceased, filed March 15, 1957, JHJ/CCHC; Affidavit for Inheritance Tax Appraisement, in the Matter of the Estate of Mary Gibbs Jones, September 9, 1963, MGJ/CCHC.

49. Emma Grigg to Presiding Judge, U. S. Federal Court, Houston, Texas, May 9, 1933; Lillian Ewing, Secretary to Judge Kennerly, to Grigg, May 16, 1933, Melvin L. Straus, Trustee v. Houston Properties Corporation, Equity No. 560, USDC/SDT; *Chicago American*, September 7, 1934.

50. "Houston Real Estate Operations," January 31, 1945, JJC/UT; "Notice of Adoption and Filing of Plan of Reorganization and Summary Thereof," January 13, 1934; "Trustee's Preliminary Report," June 19, 1934, Melvin L. Straus, Trustee v. Houston Properties, Inc., Equity No. 560; "Houston Properties, Houston, Texas, Trust Deed and Chattel Mortgage, Rice Properties, Inc., to Maurice A. Rosenthal, Trustee," September 1, 1933; "Notice of Hearing" for October 15, 1937, Maurice A. Rosenthal, Trustee v. Rice Properties, Inc., Equity No. 770, USDC/SDT.

51. "Houston Properties, Houston, Texas, Trust Deed and Chattel Mortgage, Rice Properties, Inc., to Maurice A. Rosenthal, Trustee," September 1, 1933, 47–50, Maurice A. Rosenthal, Trustee v. Rice Properties, Inc., Equity No. 770, USDC/SDT.

52. "Notice of Hearing" for October 15, 1937; Georgie Anne Weeks to Honorable Judge, December 9, 1937; Mr. Malloy to President, Rice Properties, Inc., December 16, 1937, copy to Presiding Judge, Maurice A. Rosenthal, Trustee v. Rice Properties, Inc., Equity No. 770; Bella Dermody to Lamar Properties, Inc., December 9, 1937, Maurice A. Rosenthal, Trustee v. Lamar Properties, Inc., Equity No. 771, USDC/SDT.

53. Mr. Malloy to President, Rice Properties, Inc., December 16, 1937, copy to Presiding Judge; Georgie Anne Weeks to Honorable Judge, December 9, 1937, Maurice A. Rosenthal, Trustee v. Rice Properties, Inc., Equity No. 770, USDC/SDT; Williamson, "What Is the Relative Value?"

54. Timmons, *Jesse H. Jones*, 116–18; "Record of Texan's Career Shows Bond Investors Lost," *Chicago Sun*, March 2, 1945, clipping in EMP/LC; Bella Dermody to Lamar Properties, Inc., Attn: Maurice A. Rosenthal, December 9, 1937, Maurice A. Rosenthal, Trustee v. Lamar Properties, Inc., Equity No. 771; Bella Dermody to Rice Properties, Inc., Attn: George A. Butler, December 16, 1937, Maurice A. Rosenthal, Trustee v. Rice Properties, Inc., Equity No. 770, USDC/SDT.

55. Transcript of hearing before Honorable T. Whitfield Davidson in Maurice A. Rosenthal v. Rice Properties, Inc., Equity No. 770; and Maurice A. Rosenthal v. Lamar Properties, Inc., Equity No. 771, USDC/SDT.

56. Transcript of hearing before Honorable T. Whitfield Davidson in Maurice A. Rosenthal v. Rice Properties, Inc., Equity No. 770; and Maurice A. Rosenthal v. Lamar Properties, Inc., Equity No. 771, USDC/SDT; "Maze of Private Companies Screens Texan's Operations," *Chicago Sun*, March 3, 1945, EMP/LC.

57. "Houston Real Estate Operations," January 31, 1945, JJC/UT.

58. "Final Decree," February 2, 1934, Samuel J. T. Straus, Trustee v. Palace Building Company, Equity No. 570, USDC/SDT.

59. "Final Decree," February 2, 1934; Samuel J. T. Straus, Trustee, Operating Palace Building Company, Houston, Texas, May 1, 1932 to July 25, 1936; Notice of Adoption and Filing of Plan of Reorganization and Summary Thereof, June 30, 1934, Samuel J. T. Straus, Trustee v. Palace Building Company, Equity No. 570, USDC/ SDT; "Bank Balances," August 12, 1929, JJC/UT; Buenger, "Jesse Jones," 66; Rupert N. Richardson, Adrian N. Anderson, and Ernest Wallace, *Texas: The Lone Star State* (Upper Saddle River, N.J.: Prentice Hall, 1997), 371–72; Timmons, *Jesse H. Jones*, 82, 119.

60. Notice of Adoption and Filing of Plan of Reorganization and Summary Thereof, June 30, 1934, Samuel J. T. Straus, Trustee v. Palace Building Company, Equity No. 570, USDC/SDT.

61. "Chamber of Commerce Building, Houston, Texas, Trust Deed, Chamber of Commerce Building Company to Arthur W. Straus, Trustee, securing $1,000,000," November 1, 1922; "Final Decree," February 2, 1934; Samuel J. T. Straus, Trustee, Operating Palace Building Company, Houston, Texas, May 1, 1932 to July 25, 1936; Notice of Adoption and Filing of Plan of Reorganization and Summary Thereof, June 30, 1934, Samuel J. T. Straus, Trustee v. Palace Building Company, Equity No. 570, USDC/SDT.

62. "Houston Real Estate Operations," January 31, 1945, JJC/UT; "Final Decree," February 2, 1934; Samuel J. T. Straus, Trustee, Operating Palace Building Company, Houston, Texas, May 1, 1932 to July 25, 1936; Notice of Adoption and Filing of Plan of Reorganization and Summary Thereof, June 30, 1934; Samuel J. T. Straus, Trustee, Operating Palace Building Company, Houston, Texas, May 1, 1932 to July 25, 1936, Samuel J. T. Straus, Trustee v. Palace Building Company, Equity 570, USDC/SDT.

63. Notice of Adoption and Filing of Plan of Reorganization and Summary Thereof, June 30, 1934, Samuel J. T. Straus, Trustee v. Palace Building Company, Equity 570, USDC/SDT.

64. "Net Earnings 1928"; "Gross Profits before Deducting Administrative Expense, Interest, Depreciation, Amortization and Federal Income Taxes"; "Profit and Income Available for Interest and Amortization before Depreciation and Federal Income Tax," November 13, 1930, JJC/UT; Notice of Adoption and Filing of Plan of Reorganization and Summary Thereof, June 30, 1934, Samuel J. T. Straus, Trustee v. Palace Building Company, Equity 570, USDC/SDT.

65. "Final Decree," February 2, 1934, Samuel J. T. Straus, Trustee v. Palace Building Company, Equity No. 570, USDC/SDT.

66. Jesse Jones's nephew, George Butler, one of the three trustees of the former Jones bondholders who were now stockholders of Milam Properties, Inc., was also the law partner of Charles Reinhard, vice president of Milam Properties. "Houston Real Estate Operations," January 31, 1945, JJC/UT.

67. "Ownership-Description, Depreciated Book Value, and Indebtedness if any," August 31, 1953; "New York Corporation," June 30, 1953, JJC/UT.

68. Receiver's Petition No. 15, April 15, 1935, People of the State of Illinois, Ex. Rel. Edward J. Barrett, etc. v. Central Republic Trust Company, CCCC; Melchior Palyi, *The Chicago Credit Market* (New York: Arno Press, 1975), 69–72; W. A. Chadwell to Wilson, Supervisory Field Representative, Chicago, March 21, 29, 1955, RFC/NA.

69. Trust Deed and Chattel Mortgage Securing $4,850,000 Six Per Cent First and General Mortgage Gold Bonds, August 1, 1925, Melvin L. Straus, Trustee v. Houston Properties Corporation, Equity 560, USDC/SDT; "Released for Publication in Houston Sunday A.M. Newspapers, August 23rd," JJC/UT; "Record of Texan's Career Shows Bond Investors Lost," *Chicago Sun*, clipping in EMP/LC; Timmons, *Jesse H. Jones*, 82–83; Williamson, "What Is the Relative Value?"

70. Jones's National Bank of Commerce later became the Texas Commerce Bank, N.A., which was owned by the Texas Commerce Bancshares. The Texas Commerce Bancshares was acquired by Chemical Bank of New York in 1987. Chemical then merged with the Chase Manhattan Corporation, which later merged to become J. P. Morgan Chase Bank, currently the largest bank in Texas. *New York Times*, January 26, 1932; *Chicago Tribune*, January 26, 1932; James S. Olson, *Saving Capitalism: The Reconstruction Finance Corporation and the New Deal, 1933–1940* (Princeton, N.J.: Princeton University Press, 1988), 47; List of Candidates for Reconstruction Finance Corporation, January 1932, HHP/HHPL; Buenger, "Between Community and Corporation," 485–91, 499; Timmons, *Jesse H. Jones*, 114–15; *Houston Business Journal*, October 25, 2004; Texas Department of Banking, *Bank History National Banks*, 60, 69, 101, www.banking.state.tx.us/pubs/nbs.pdf.

71. After Roosevelt defeated Hoover, Frank Andrews, Jones's good friend who was a director of the Bankers Mortgage Company, wrote to Edward House to recommend Jones for a cabinet position in the new administration. In his letter to House, President Wilson's former adviser who was also close to Roosevelt and Jones, Andrews said that Jones was "true and loyal to his friends" and that he was "the outstanding citizen of Texas today. . . . Since the war he has done more toward the up building and development of Houston than any other single force in it." Frank Andrews to E. M. House, November 18, 1932; Jesse Jones to E. M. House, December 1, 1932, JJP/LC; *Moody's Manual of Investments: Banks, 1932*, 375, 454; *1933*, 504; *1934*, 377, 695; *1935*, 139, 554; *1936*, 380, 1534; Baruch, *Baruch*, 141–45; Memorandum to "JHJ personal files," February 2, 1933, JJP/LC; *New York Times*, January 27, November 21, 1933; *Washington Times-Herald*, January 27, 1933; Timmons, *Jesse H. Jones*, 114–15, 375; David G. McComb, *Houston: The Bayou City* (Austin: University of Texas Press, 1969), 168–70.

72. "Loans Authorized from February 2, 1932 to July 20, 1932, Inclusive and Changes in Such Loans from July 21, 1932 to January 6, 1933, Inclusive," RFC/NA; Minutes for Wednesday, November 8, 1933, U.S. Senate Committee on Banking and Currency, including Duncan U. Fletcher to Jesse H. Jones, n.d.; Minutes of the Meeting of November 21, 1933, Subcommittee on Stock Exchange Practices, including Jesse H. Jones to Duncan U. Fletcher, November 21, 1933; Minutes of Meeting of December 1, 1933, Subcommittee on Reconstruction Finance Corporation Matters, USS/NA; Williamson, "What Is the Relative Value?"

73. Jesse H. Jones to Franklin D. Roosevelt, January 26, 1933, FDRP/FDRL; Memorandum to "JHJ personal files," February 2, 1933, JJP/LC; *New York Times*, January 27, November 21, 1933; *Washington Times-Herald*, January 27, 1933.

74. "Loans of $100,000 or More to Mortgage Loan Companies Organized Since January 22, 1932. Authorized to November 18, 1933, Inclusive," RFC/NA; Jesse H. Jones to Duncan U. Fletcher, November 21, 1933; Minutes of Meeting of December 1, 1933, Sub-Committee on Reconstruction Finance Corporation Matters, USS/NA; Consolidated Financial Statement of Jesse H. Jones, including Jesse H. Jones Company (a Delaware Corporation Organized 1923) and Subsidiary Companies, January 1, 1930, JJC/UT; Fred J. Heyne to W. C. Costello, October 26, 1935, JJP/LC.

75. Minutes of Meeting of December 1, 1933, Subcommittee on Reconstruction Finance Corporation Matters; Jesse H. Jones to Duncan U. Fletcher, November 21, 1933, USS/NA.

76. Records of the Examining Division, Comptroller of the Currency's Office, USOCC/WNRC; Timmons, *Jesse H. Jones*, 160, 161; Johnston, *Houston: The Unknown City*, 288.

77. Huggins, Kayser and Liddell to Jesse Jones, February 15, 1932, JJP/LC; *Reconstruction Finance Corporation Act*, H. R. 7360, 72nd Congress, First Session, January 21, 1932, Sec. 3; "Know All Men by These Presents," August 10, 1936, Samuel J. T. Straus, Trustee v. Palace Building Company, et al., Equity No. 570, USDC/SDT; J. H. Jones to G. R. Cooksey, June 28, 1932 (telegram), RFC/NA; *Moody's Manual of Investments: Banks, 1932*, 375, 454; *1935*, 139, 554; Winston Wilson, *Harvey Couch: The Master Builder*, 160.

78. Jones was listed as the president of the National Bank of Commerce in 1934. *Moody's Manual of Investments: Banks, 1932*, 375, 454; *1933*, 504, 1950; *1934*, 377, 695; *1935*, 139, 554; *1936*, 380, 1534; Timmons, *Jesse H. Jones*, 114.

79. *New York Times*, April 3, 1934; Marquis James and Bessie Rowland James, *Biography of a Bank: The Story of Bank of America N.T. and S.A.* (New York: Harper and Brothers, 1954), 381–82.

80. On August 31, 1936, more than two-and-a-half years after the RFC's investment in Jones's bank, the RFC still owned $2,375,000 of preferred stock in Jones's National Bank of Commerce because Jones's bank had redeemed only $125,000 of its preferred stock. "Statement of Preferred Stock, Capital Note and Debenture Purchases in Amounts of $500,000.00 or more Authorized but Not Consummated at the Close of December 28, 1933"; "Preferred Stock Subscriptions and Debenture and Capital Note Purchases of $1,000,000 and Over Disbursed Up to and Including November 10,

1934"; "Banks in Which the Reconstruction Finance Corporation Had an Outstanding Investment as of August 31, 1936," RFC/NA; *Moody's Manual of Investments: Banks, 1932*, 454; *1934*, 377; *1935*, 139; John S. Spratt, "Banking Phobia in Texas," *Southwest Review*, 60 (Autumn 1975): 348–50.

81. "1,319 Loans to Banks by R.F.C., Says Meyer," n.d., clipping in Meyer's scrapbook, EMP/LC; J. Franklin Ebersole, "One Year of the Reconstruction Finance Corporation," *Quarterly Journal of Economics* 47 (May 1933): 477–79; James and James, *Biography of a Bank*, 353; Flynn, "Inside the R.F.C.," 161–65.

82. Myers, *The State Papers of Herbert Hoover*, 2:106–7; Ebersole, "One Year of the Reconstruction Finance Corporation," 469, 474–75; James and James, *Biography of a Bank*, 346–358; Lynne Pierson Doti and Larry Schweikart, *Banking in the American West: From the Gold Rush to Deregulation* (Norman: University of Oklahoma Press, 1991), 102–4, 134–40; Ester Matthews Applegate, "The Reconstruction Finance Corporation" (Master's thesis, University of Washington, 1932), 79; Gaines Thomson Cartinhour, *Branch, Group and Chain Banking* (New York: Macmillan, 1931), 135–36; Olson, *Hoover and the Reconstruction Finance Corporation*, 60; Jones, *Fifty Billion Dollars*, 19, 20; Flynn, "Inside the R.F.C.," 161–65.

83. Myers, *The State Papers of Herbert Hoover*, 2:139, Flynn, "Inside the R.F.C.," 163; Ebersole, "One Year of the Reconstruction Finance Corporation," 478–79.

84. White House Press Release, March 25, 1932, HHP/HHPL; Myers, *The State Papers of Herbert Hoover*, 2:142, 150; Flynn, "Inside the R.F.C.," 163.

85. Statement by Charles G. Dawes before the Committee on Ways and Means, House of Representatives, April 21, 1932, RFC/NA.

86. Ibid.

87. Ibid.; Jones, *Fifty Billion Dollars*, 72–81; "Total Indebtedness" of the Central Republic Trust Company, December 31, 1934 to December 31, 1943, RFC/NA.

88. Statement by Charles G. Dawes before the Committee on Ways and Means, House of Representatives, April 21, 1932, RFC/NA.

89. Ibid.; Flynn, "Inside the RFC," 164.

90. Eugene Meyer, "The Reminiscences of Eugene Meyer," Oral History Research Office, Columbia University, Transcript of interviews conducted by Dean Albertson in 1952 and 1953, 643–44; Agnes E. Meyer, "Diary of Mrs. Agnes E. Meyer," June 6, 1932; Roy Jenkins, *Franklin Delano Roosevelt* (New York: Henry Holt, 2003), 62–63.

91. "Dawes Assails Bonus Scheme," April 22, 1932, a clipping in CGDP/NUL. For a discussion of the Bonus Expeditionary Force, see Schlesinger, *The Crisis of the Old Order*, 256–65; Paul Studenski and Herman E. Krooss, *Financial History of the United States* (New York: McGraw-Hill, 1963), 356; and Hicks, *Republican Ascendancy*, 274–76.

92. G. W. Lawrence to C. G. Dawes, April 22, 1932; Member of Legislative Committee, Kentucky Post No. 1084, Veterans of Foreign Wars, to L. S. Ray, April 21, 1932; F. M. Hart to Arthur Capper, April 22, 1932, CGDP/NUL; Eugene Meyer, "The Reminiscences of Eugene Meyer," 643–44; Agnes E. Meyer, "Diary of Mrs. Agnes E. Meyer," June 6, 1932; Pusey, *Eugene Meyer*, 221–22.

93. White House Press Release, June 5, 1932, HHP/HHPL; Myers, *The State Papers of Herbert Hoover*, 2:203, 204; James and James, *Biography of a Bank*, 313–17, 350–56; Olson, *Hoover and the Reconstruction Finance Corporation*, 60.

94. Ebersole, "One Year of the Reconstruction Finance Corporation," 477–78; James, *The Growth of Chicago Banks*, 2:1029.

95. Agnes E. Meyer, "Diary of Mrs. Agnes E. Meyer," June 27, 1932; Hoover, *Memoirs*, 170, 171; *Reconstruction Finance Corporation v. Central Republic Trust Company, et al.*, November 7, 1936, 17 F. Supp. 263 (St. Paul, Minn.: West, 1937); Theodore G. Joslin, *Hoover Off the Record* (Garden City, N.Y.: Doubleday, Doran & Company, 1934), 249–52; Jones, *Fifty Billion Dollars*, 76.

Chapter 4

Insider Abuse at the Dawes Bank

"I realize how fortunate the student body is to hear you with admiration of the very fine feeling between you and the general and his love for the school, the town, and community. I just wish I might be there just to look on. May I extend greetings to you and the Dawes brothers and my love to the general."

—Harvey Couch to Owen Young, the keynote speaker at the commencement exercises of Marietta College, the alma mater of Charles Dawes, June 4, 1935[1]

After Charles Dawes announced that he was resigning from the Reconstruction Finance Corporation to return to Chicago to resume his position as the active head of the Dawes bank, rumors began circulating that he would replace Insull as a receiver of Middle West. Dawes "emphatically" denied the rumors, but the connection between the two men was widely reported and reinforced.

Dawes had been "honorary chairman of the board" and a voting member of his bank's board of directors between 1925 and 1932, during the period when he was serving as the vice president of the United States, the ambassador to Great Britain, and the president of the RFC. As we have seen, it was Charles, along with his brothers Rufus and Henry, and their cousin, William Dawes, a vice president and director of the bank, who controlled the Dawes bank. Charles Dawes, whose name and title were prominently displayed in the newspaper advertisements of the Central Republic Bank, owned only a small amount of the bank's stock in his own name, an amount he valued on his financial statement as being worth $16,899 as of December 2, 1931. Far more important, he was the largest stockholder of Dawes Brothers, Inc., the controlling shareholder of the Central Republic Bank.[2]

Dawes's announcement that he was resuming the chairmanship of the Central Republic Bank caused a flurry in its stock, temporarily increasing the value of its shares. But the increase was short-lived since the close affiliation between Insull and the bank was known to the public because of the bankruptcy filings of the Insull entities. The relationship with Insull, however, was only part of the problem. There was a pattern of insider abuse at the Dawes bank and all of the other Loop banks. The insider abuses were widespread as officers and directors received unsecured loans or loans secured with worthless collateral from their own banks and affiliated banks, loans which were never repaid. Then the RFC propped up the major Loop banks and their affiliates, issuing government loans backed by the same worthless assets.

Actually, the RFC's bailout of the Dawes bank, whose nonperforming loans to Dawes's family and other insiders exceeded its capital, began soon after Dawes arrived in Washington, months before the controversial bailout in June 1932. He had left his prestigious position in London because he understood the urgency of the situation for his family's bank. The Dawes bank was in such a deplorable condition that only he could save it. Like no one else, he knew how to operate quietly inside the offices of the RFC, the comptroller of the currency, and the Illinois auditor and banking commissioner. During the time Dawes was head of the RFC, it postponed the collapse of his bank, approving a number of loans to banks and other entities that were borrowers from the Dawes family's bank.

In May 1932, Dawes and his colleagues at the RFC approved a loan of $1,150,000 for Insull's Chicago, North Shore and Milwaukee Railroad Company, which had borrowed $550,000 from the Dawes bank. Joseph Otis, then the chairman of the Dawes bank, was also a director of Insull's railroad company, which went into a receivership in September 1932. The federal court appointed as co-receiver Britton I. Budd, Insull's handpicked railroad manager, who had borrowed $46,000 from the Dawes bank. Budd was also the president of Insull's Chicago Rapid Transit Company, which would go through a much more costly bankruptcy reorganization. The receivership of the Chicago, North Shore and Milwaukee Railroad Company would result in its investors suffering real value losses of $20,347,680, while the investors of the Chicago Rapid Transit Company would lose $47,623,474.[3]

When Charles rejoined his brothers and cousin on the board of directors of the Dawes bank, Rufus was in serious financial straits. Later on, more than three years after the RFC bailed out the Dawes family, Rufus Dawes and two of his sons would still owe $361,967 to the federal government, a sum worth about $5,660,000 today. As of October 31, 1935, $124,324 of the $361,967 Rufus owed was a direct obligation; the remainder were loans for his sons and business partners that Rufus had procured and guaranteed from the Central Republic Bank, and which, in turn, had been pledged to the RFC to secure its bailout loans.

When Charles Cutler Dawes, one of Rufus's sons, filed his bankruptcy petition on March 22, 1935, he owed the RFC $95,952, a sum that Rufus Dawes would continue to owe as the guarantor of his son's obligations. Rufus's son discharged his debts in bankruptcy court, but his father remained liable for the son's loan and its mounting interest. A stipulation between the RFC and the trustee in bankruptcy determined that the securities that were being held as collateral, first to secure the loan of Rufus's son and then pledged to the RFC to secure its loans to the Dawes bank, were "of no value." Rufus also owed $31,045 to the RFC as the guarantor for four loans that another son, William M. Dawes, had received between January and March 1932, a few months before the bank failed. William Dawes defaulted on these loans when they came due in April and June of that year. Instead of paying off the loans as guarantor after his sons had defaulted on them, Rufus defaulted on his obligations. Later, he negotiated a new repayment schedule with the RFC and then defaulted on that agreement. At the time of his death in 1940, he still owed the RFC $181,226.[4]

The trustee for the bankrupt estate of Charles C. Dawes was able to collect only $325. Nonetheless, Charles's uncle, Charles Dawes, had pledged his nephew's loans as collateral for the RFC bailout loans. As a result, the RFC would suffer a loss of $628,826.[5]

When the senior Charles Dawes was the U.S. ambassador to Great Britain, he had suffered a cash-flow problem because his $17,500 salary from the government was insufficient, even when combined with his investment income, to support his lifestyle and investments. Consequently, he had borrowed $16,372 from the Dawes bank on August 25, 1931, and another $5,000 from his bank on November 30, 1931. As mentioned earlier, he had also arranged a loan with J. P. Morgan and Company on October 20, 1931, which had an outstanding balance of $74,725 on December 2, 1931. Nonetheless, after the RFC bailed out the Dawes bank, Dawes certainly could have arranged financing to ensure that his brother and his nephew satisfied their debts to the RFC. He refused to do so and members of his very close family simply ignored their obligations.[6]

This pattern of abuse also included "trusted" officers of the Dawes bank. Joseph Otis, now the vice chairman of the Dawes bank, approved many a loan to Insull while participating in his sweetheart insider stock deals. Otis, the chairman and president of the Dawes bank in 1929, as well as a director of the Dawes brothers' Pure Oil Company, abused his position at the bank beyond his insider trading with Insull. He borrowed $85,900 in the name of the Joseph E. Otis Estate Land Trust to develop the Buckingham Building, an office building in downtown Chicago that was still unfinished in 1938. The directors of the Dawes bank had neglected to approve the filing of a lawsuit against their chairman's trust, though the bank had endured "actionable defaults" on the loan since 1929. Otis did not personally guarantee the loan, and the building was not pledged to secure it. Actually, the loan was "without endorsement or guaranty" of any kind and was not "secured by a direct pledge of collateral."

A close look at the liquidation records of the Dawes bank revealed the favors granted to the small group of Loop bankers in the form of unsecured loans from other banks and insurance companies. Indeed, the Otis trust had also borrowed $1,675,000 from the Northwestern Mutual Life Insurance Company, which had a first mortgage on the building, and $500,000 from the Chase National Bank of New York, on an unsecured basis. The trust owed another $68,485, which was also unsecured, to the Continental Illinois National Bank.

By 1938, the building was worth far less than the total of the loans of the Otis trust. Delinquent interest on the defaulted loans had reached approximately $150,000. The best the old Dawes bank, at which Otis had replaced Dawes as the chairman on October 5, 1932, could expect was "nominal" payments on its loan. When forming his new bank, Dawes had refused to purchase the $85,900 Otis loan, which remained unpaid on the books of the old Dawes bank after nine years of liquidation proceedings. Furthermore, the Otis loan was appraised at the full value of its principal and interest, and pledged as collateral to secure the RFC loans made to the Dawes bank. In reality, it was worthless and should have been charged off the books of the bank long before the government's loan was approved in June 1932.[7]

While Dawes was its president and the RFC was bailing out the Dawes bank through loans to its affiliated banks in Chicago, the RFC was also making loans that benefited Traylor's First National Bank. For example, the Alliance National Bank, after borrowing $670,673 from Traylor's bank, had received two loans from the RFC: one on May 18 and another on June 2, 1932. These loans were an attempt to ease the liquidity crisis at the bank, but the bank closed on June 15, 1932—with no publicity about its RFC loans.

The loan to the Alliance National Bank was not just an isolated questionable loan that the second largest bank in Chicago made to a single troubled bank. In fact, the largest loan that Traylor's bank made to a troubled bank was a $936,984 loan to the Dawes bank, which federal examiners criticized prior to the RFC bailout. In highlighting the problem loan to Washington, they noted that the bank's "officers feel [it] may be a slow workout." Examiners reported that Traylor's bank had also made bad loans to Charles Sumner Castle, director of the Dawes bank and former vice chairman of the National Bank of the Republic, in the amount of $8,135; and to Harry R. Moore, a vice president of the Dawes bank, in the amount of $5,900.

In another bailout attempt, the RFC made a loan of $300,000 to the Prudential State Savings Bank, which had borrowed $216,590 from Traylor's First National Bank. When the RFC approved the loan to the Prudential State Savings Bank, on March 1, 1932, Dawes had to recuse himself from voting on the application because of a conflict of interest. But his colleagues approved the loan, and less than four months later, the bank closed, on June 18, 1932—with no mention in the press that the bank had received the RFC loan.[8]

Traylor's bank also had on its books major problem loans of $617,866 to the Reliance Bank and Trust Company, which closed on Monday, June 20, 1932; and another worthless loan of $215,000 to the Peoples National Bank and Trust Company, which was controlled through the National Republic Bancorporation, an entity affiliated with the Dawes bank.[9]

Traylor, too, had used his position to enhance his personal fortune. He had personally borrowed $115,000 from the Drovers National Bank of Chicago, which was affiliated with the Dawes bank through interlocking directorates, at a time when examiners estimated his net worth to be $50,000. (Today Traylor's loan would be worth approximately $1,810,000 and his net worth about $785,000.) After receiving his loan, Traylor, as president of First National Bank, approved more than $35,000 worth of loans to officers of the Drovers National Bank, all of which the comptroller of the currency's office classified as "slow and doubtful paper." Sitting on the board of directors of the Drovers National Bank were two of the Dawes brothers' closest associates: Joseph Otis, chairman of the Dawes bank before the return of Charles Dawes, and Rawleigh Warner, vice president and treasurer of the Dawes brothers' Pure Oil Company and a director of the Dawes bank, who also served as an organizing syndicate manager, and then director, of the new Dawes bank. And Henry Dawes was a director of the Drovers Trust and Savings Bank, which was affiliated with the Drovers National Bank.[10]

NATIONAL BANK OF THE REPUBLIC MERGER

Sealing the fate of the Dawes bank was its affiliation with the National Republic Bancorporation, which owned a minority interest of 1,090 shares of the Dawes bank as a result of a merger and exchange of stock with its flagship bank, the National Bank of the Republic, on July 25, 1931. Waving a red flag to anxious depositors, after the merger with the National Bank of the Republic, Dawes's Central Trust Company of Illinois changed its long-time name to Central Republic Bank and Trust Company, which was a newly chartered state bank as of July 25, 1931. Meanwhile, the National Republic Bancorporation continued to own majority control of eight banks, including the United American Trust and Savings Bank, which failed on June 14, 1932, and the Madison Square State Bank, which closed the following day.[11]

After the combination of the Dawes bank with the National Bank of the Republic, five directors of the remaining National Republic Bancorporation, the holding company for the eight affiliated banks, joined the board of directors of the Dawes bank, and three of them became pivotal officers of the Dawes bank. Because of the interlocking directors between the Dawes bank and the National Republic Bancorporation, the collapse of the community banks affiliated with the latter signaled to the public that the Dawes bank was in serious trouble.[12]

Before the merger, the National Republic Bancorporation, through inter-locking directors and common stockholders, was affiliated with a total of twelve banks, with total assets of $253,650,000. After the Dawes bank merged with the National Bank of the Republic, the Dawes brothers remained in control of the successor institution. The affiliation between the National Republic Bancorporation and the failed banks was well known, according to Philip Clarke, the president of the Dawes bank and later a director of the Dawes brothers' Pure Oil Company. He observed that members of the chain banking group had advertised "their affiliation with National Republic Ban-corporation so extensively that many had come undoubtedly to regard them as branches of National Bank of the Republic." After the merger was completed, the Dawes bank sent a letter, on August 27, 1931, to the combined stockholders saying that management planned to issue annual dividends of $12 a share (12 percent per $100 of par value), bleeding the bank of capital desperately needed to charge off bad loans and face increasing demands of its depositors. Then, only a few months later, on March 31, 1932, the Dawes bank reduced the dividends to 2 percent per quarter, or 8 percent per year, which sent a message to its stockholders and depositors that the bank was facing problems.[13]

In their quest to control the third largest bank in Chicago, the Dawes brothers engaged for two years in "secret negotiations" with officials of the National Bank of the Republic. Those discussions intensified in the spring of 1931. The president of their bank, Philip Clarke, represented the Dawes brothers. Later when Clarke was caught up in a storm of controversy and litigation, he described five "favoring inducements" making the combination advantageous: (1) the banks were located directly across LaSalle Street from each other; (2) they had a similar amount of deposits, which, as of the date of the merger on July 25, 1931, was $112,310,706 at the National Bank of the Republic, and $121,278,033 at the Central Trust Company of Illinois; (3) in anticipation of future mergers, the Dawes bank had leased the old Continental Bank's magnificent building—complete with marble pillars in its lobby— paying rent of $780,000 a year, which was excessive for a bank the size of the Dawes bank; (4) the National Bank of the Republic needed more space; and (5) Vice Chairman Woodruff of the National Bank of the Republic, "the dominating administrative personality" of the bank, had suffered "a nervous breakdown" by the end of 1930. In a thirty-two-page "authentic record" of the Dawes bank that he prepared in 1936, Clarke did not, however, mention the troubled loans and securities investments of the Dawes bank, and he provided no reasons that would justify its merger with a bank so laden with nonperforming insider and illegal loans.[14]

Clarke wrote that the Dawes-controlled Central Republic Bank and Trust Company, "throughout the entire eleven months of its active existence, had to combat probably the most violent and unremitting decline in deposits that any major financial institution ever experienced." Actually, the whole time that Dawes was president of the RFC, his bank struggled with not only its own nonperforming loans but also the nonperforming loans of the National Bank of the Republic. Still, Clarke, groping to explain the old Dawes bank's collapse and "the motives for organizing" the new Dawes bank in October 1932, wrote, "the insidious gossip and rumor to which the Bank was being increasingly subjected, was directly attributable to a peculiar and heretofore unsuspected series of psychic influences created at the time of its organization." Clarke was upset about irresponsible brokers who ignored their "sense of public responsibility" and telephoned stockholders of the bank to suggest that they should sell their stock. The Cook County treasurer was said to be at fault, too, because he had withdrawn approximately $20 million in deposits from the bank in the fall of 1931. These factors exerted "tremendously adverse psychological influences" on the succeeding Dawes bank.

Clarke also pointed his finger at the *Chicago Tribune* for its reporting of the merger. He complained that the paper created an erroneous impression in the "public mind" because its Sunday, June 7, 1931, late edition had a front-page article, which created quite a commotion, about the problems at the Foreman group of banks and the reorganization plan to save Chicago's third largest banking group. Then the next day, the paper carried not only an article announcing the merger of the Dawes bank with the National Bank of the Republic, but an "equally conspicuous" article about Traylor's First National Bank acquiring the troubled Foreman State National Bank; and the First National Bank's affiliate, the First Union Trust and Savings Bank, acquiring the Foreman State Trust and Savings Bank. Both of the Foreman banks had collapsed under the weight of worthless insider loans.[15]

Indeed, the First National Bank took a giant step toward the abyss when it acquired the Foreman banks on June 8, 1931, in that the $26,745,199 it advanced to the Foreman State National Bank represented 107 percent of its paid-in capital. The transaction put Traylor's bank in a tenuous position, especially in light of its "treacherous" concentration of Insull loans. The loan also amounted to 53 percent of the First National Bank's combined capital and surplus, though the published capital and surplus accounts of the First National Bank were fraudulently overstated. By July 1932, the Foreman State National Bank, which was a liquidating shell of a company, still owed $17,578,186 to the First National Bank, a sum that represented 70 percent of the First National Bank's paid-in capital and 35 percent of its overstated capital and surplus.[16]

The acquisition of the Foreman banks also put at risk the Dawes bank and the other Loop banks that were members of the Chicago Clearing House, in that the clearing house guaranteed $10 million of the assets of the insolvent banking group. After the First National Bank's acquisition of the two major Foreman banks, on Monday, June 8, 1931, six of the Foreman community banks closed, along with three other unaffiliated community banks. The next day, twelve more banks failed, all members of the Bain banking chain, which John Bain controlled. Bain, a real estate promoter and major bank stock speculator, owned $1,192,061 worth of stock in eighteen Chicago banks, including the Foreman State National Bank, the First National Bank, the Continental Illinois, the National Bank of the Republic, and the Dawes bank. Bain's extensive bank stock holdings had been detailed in the *Chicago Evening Post* on June 6, 1931, the Saturday before the acquisition. The article traced the intertwined relationships among the city's bankers. More than thirty banks failed in the Chicago metropolitan area during the week of June 8 through 12, 1931. By the week's end, only five major Loop banks remained: George Reynolds' Continental Illinois, Traylor's First National, Dawes's Central Republic, the Harris Trust and Savings Bank, and the Northern Trust Company.[17]

Dawes was a promoter of his bank's merger with the National Bank of the Republic, but he wanted to ensure that he and his brothers ended up with control of the combined institution. Prior to Dawes's return to Chicago at the end of May 1931, Otis had informed him that Central Republic, despite its liquidity problems and instead of conserving its cash, had implemented a plan to quietly buy back its own stock on the open market as it fell in price. In this effort to halt its declining share price, which was adversely affecting the position of the Dawes brothers, the Dawes bank had already bought back $1,250,000 of its stock at an average price per share of $250. To announce the repurchase plan would, in Otis's opinion, lead "to alarm and vicious attacks that spell trouble of a dangerous character." Otis also indicated that the public market for utility bonds had been nonexistent for more than a year, and that the banks were providing the financing for Insull's expansion program. This explained, in part, the high concentration of Insull loans at the Chicago Loop banks, including the Dawes bank.[18]

Between May 29 and August 10, 1931, while Dawes and his brothers were negotiating and consummating the purchase of the National Bank of the Republic, the Dawes bank made seven loans, totaling $1,390,000, to the United American Trust and Savings Bank, which was controlled through the National Republic Bancorporation, the same holding company that controlled the National Bank of the Republic. The United American Bank was a small community bank that was in precarious condition. Its capital of $750,000 was severely impaired, and it had deposits of only $2,101,250 as of its December 31, 1931, call report.

By this time, the United American Bank's survival was critical to Charles Dawes and his brothers because of the questionable loans their bank had given it. Consequently, during the few months when Charles was president of the agency, the RFC made two loans totaling $525,000 to the United American Bank before it failed. The first loan of $300,000 was approved at a special RFC board meeting on February 11, 1932. Though Dawes attended the board meetings approving the loans to his affiliated bank, he did not "participate in the discussion" or vote to approve the loans, in compliance with the woefully inadequate conflict of interest provision of the RFC act. Nevertheless, Jones and his other colleagues on the RFC's board approved the loans, which were part of a group of loans that began the federal government's bailout of the Dawes bank during the desperate time between February and June 1932. At this point, it was becoming quite obvious to the Dawes brothers that the nearly $12 million of Insull loans from their bank would soon be worthless or frozen in bankruptcy court.[19]

After the United American Bank borrowed $525,000 from the RFC, it immediately paid down $506,072 of its loans to the Dawes bank, thereby reducing the Dawes bank's questionable loans nearly in direct proportion to the $525,000 total of the RFC loans. So when the United American Bank closed on June 14, 1932, the Dawes bank had been able to reduce its dubious credit risk to $883,928. But the unpaid balance of these loans still represented a major exposure for the Dawes bank, and after nearly three years of selling collateral, the defunct Dawes bank continued to owe $708,304 to the RFC.

While the RFC was making the two loans to the United American Bank, it entered into a security agreement allowing the Dawes bank to maintain a priority claim to collateral that had been pledged to it. After the United American Bank's loans from the Dawes bank were satisfied, the RFC would receive the remaining pledged assets to satisfy its loan. The agreement was between two creditors (the Dawes bank and the RFC) and the debtor bank (the United American Bank). When the agreement was negotiated, Dawes was the controlling stockholder of one creditor and president of the other creditor. Since these creditors had competing claims, this represented a classic conflict of interest. Once again, the RFC received the short end of the bargain and was forced to charge off its loans to the United American Bank, whose loans were thereby increased to a total of $594,000 of principal, not counting the lost interest payments. The RFC waited years—until June 30, 1947—to charge off the loans, long after Jones had left the government and even after the dissolution of the old Dawes bank.[20]

The RFC made the loans to the United American Bank even though the comptroller of the currency received a warning from Alfred P. Leyburn, the chief national bank examiner for the Chicago district, that the bank was in "deplorable condition." On November 9, 1931, Leyburn told Comptroller Pole that "it is only a question of time when some of the banks in the [National Republic Bancorporation] chain will be forced to suspend, which will be disastrous." Leyburn warned the comptroller that the Madison Square State Bank was also in "deplorable condition," despite the fact that the National Bank of the Republic had made an "undesirable" loan of $210,000 to a group of investors so they could purchase bad assets from the Madison Square State Bank when the National Republic Bancorporation acquired it. The worthless loan became an asset of the Dawes bank when it acquired the National Bank of the Republic, and it was used as collateral to secure the RFC loan to the Dawes bank. The Madison Square State Bank failed on June 15, 1932, and nearly three years later it still owed the Dawes bank $127,168. The $210,000 interbank loan was not enough to clean up the books of the Madison Square State Bank, which had paid-in capital of only $200,000. Three RFC loans to the bank totaling $215,000 in May and early June 1932, when Dawes was head of the agency, also failed to save it, because of its insider loans and other bad assets.[21]

On July 12, 1932, Oscar Nelson, the Illinois auditor and banking commissioner, and Oscar E. Carlstrom, the Illinois attorney general, filed a petition to dissolve the Madison Square State Bank. In it Nelson stated that an examination of the bank's books and records determined that the certified call reports of the bank "were and are erroneous and did not, and do not, correctly reflect the true value" of its assets. The examination also found that the bank's capital was so impaired that it was hopelessly insolvent, and that the bank had been "conducted in an unsafe manner" so a receivership was necessary to liquidate the bank to protect its depositors and other creditors.

When the receivership of the bank was eventually terminated, on March 6, 1941, the depositors had been paid only fifteen cents on the dollar for their deposits. Despite the level of depositors' losses, the receiver, Charles H. Albers, failed to collect money from any of the seventy-four stockholders other than the defunct National Republic Bankcorporation, which owned a majority of the bank's stock. But Albers reported that the receivership spent $31,816 on legal fees, a substantial amount for the small community bank, especially considering that the receiver had failed to take action against the bank's stockholders to collect on the stockholders' assessment obligations. Benefiting from the receivership in a significant way but not alienating the influential stockholders, Oscar Carlstrom represented the bank's receiver as a private lawyer after leaving the attorney general's office. Albers was also the receiver for the Dawes bank, and he refused to file suit against Charles Dawes and his brothers in that receivership.[22]

Alfred Leyburn, the federal examiner, knew that the Dawes bank, then called the Central Trust Company, was suffering from liquidity problems. But he had no idea of its true condition because officials of the state bank had issued fraudulent financial reports overstating the value of its assets. So, operating with incorrect information because he did not have access to state bank examination reports, Leyburn was encouraging the merger of the two troubled institutions in hopes of saving the National Bank of the Republic. Eager to consummate the merger, Leyburn did not force the National Bank of the Republic to charge off any of its bad loans or loan losses, even though his report listed problem loans of $15,570,373 and "illegal loans on own bank stock" and other advances on its stock of an additional $3,099,653.

The merger would be fatal for the Dawes bank because the National Bank of the Republic was laden with millions of dollars of worthless insider loans and worthless loans to the affiliated banks in the National Republic Bancorporation chain of banks. After most of the banks in the chain failed, the National Republic Bancorporation was insolvent, leaving behind its $356,720 loan at the Dawes bank, a loan that the RFC would later determine had an "estimated recovery value" of zero. Nevertheless, the Dawes bank pledged— and the RFC accepted—the valueless note of the National Republic Bancorporation as collateral for the RFC's loan.[23]

The financial call report of the National Bank of the Republic, published in the local newspapers, made the bank seem sound. The call report showed paid-in capital stock of $11 million, a surplus fund of $2.2 million, and undivided profits of $1,516,886. So the bank's capital accounts appeared strong at the end of the first quarter of 1931, a healthy 9 percent of the total assets of $160.4 million. But the comptroller of the currency's secret examination report of April 18, 1931, told a far different story. It revealed that the management of the bank had engaged in an illegal scheme to inflate the value of its stock, loaning nearly $2 million to directors and customers of the bank who purchased stock in the bank, and then secured the loans with the bank's own stock. The examiner said the "illegal advances [were] made in an effort to support a declining market for subject bank stock which proved to be a futile and expensive effort." It had also issued other illegal loans in the amount of $1,118,128 that were secured with its own stock but apparently were not part of the scheme to inflate the bank's share price. Thus, the bank had a total of $3,099,653 in illegal loans secured with its own stock.[24]

The bank that the Dawes bank would acquire in three months had other serious problems. To begin with, it had a troubled $899,467 loan to a group of speculators. The head of the group was W. A. Wieboldt, the chairman of the United American Bank. The loan was secured with 3,293 shares of that bank and 20,718 shares of the National Republic Bancorporation, its holding company. The bank examiner criticized the credit as a "heavy, undesirable loan that should be given attention and a definite program outlined for its liquidation." He also reported that none of the members of Wieboldt's group had provided personal financial statements to justify the considerable extension of credit. Including the $899,467 insider loan to Wieboldt's group, the bank had made a total of $2,229,429 worth of loans secured with the stock of the National Republic Bancorporation.[25]

The National Bank of the Republic also loaned $416,960 to the First American National Bank and Trust Company of Berwyn, Illinois, a loan that included a $28,221 overdraft. Additionally, the bank had other questionable loans to troubled banks, and when the merger with the National Bank of the Republic occurred, the Dawes bank became inextricably entwined with the debtor banks, and as each of them failed in June 1932, its own demise became more of a certainty.[26]

The officers and directors of the National Bank of the Republic had engaged in massive insider abuse. The loans they had made to themselves and their entities totaled $5,729,827, which represented 52 percent of the bank's paid-in capital of $11 million. And of the $5,729,827 in insider loans, $2,408,403 was unsecured.[27]

Worse still, the bank's officers and directors had taken their shenanigans outside of their board room. On the eve of the merger between the Dawes bank and the insolvent National Bank of the Republic, R. B. Wood, the president of Adams County State Bank in Adams, Wisconsin, complained to Comptroller of the Currency Pole: "There is not the slightest doubt but what there are irregularities on the inside and a great amount of this stock has been placed in the hands of those who were led to believe, by or through the officers of [the National Bank of the Republic], that there was great merit in the stock—a case of implied if not actual fraud on the part of those officers who were responsible for sending a member of their affiliate out to sell the stock."[28]

Wood was upset about the "very unethical conduct on the part of certain officers and/or directors of the National Bank of the Republic." His complaint came following his purchase of ten shares of the National Bank of the Republic at $75 a share. A salesman of the bank's securities affiliate, the National Republic Company, had sold the bank's stock to Wood. Shortly thereafter, the stock fell to $19 a share and then rose to $26 a share in early July 1931. Wood told Pole that "it is very evident that the [bank's] weakness was being carefully concealed by the officers and/or directors who were unloading the stock at a big price on an unsuspecting public . . . hoping thereby to save themselves and at the same time to maintain a high or fictitious market for the stock." Wood requested that the comptroller's office conduct a bank fraud investigation.[29]

But Wood's complaint fell on deaf ears in Washington. Comptroller Pole, an admirer of Dawes, knew that the Dawes bank was days away from completing the acquisition of the National Bank of the Republic, and for him to refer the complaint to the U.S. Attorney General's office for investigation would put the Dawes merger in jeopardy. The April 18, 1931, examiner's report of the National Bank of the Republic had already conveyed to Washington that the bank made nearly $3.1 million in loans secured with its own stock as collateral, "a large amount of which were illegal advances." Nevertheless, Pole's deputy comptroller, on July 15, 1931, dismissed Wood's complaint, saying that the comptroller's office lacked authority over the matter, and "if you have sustained any loss in this connection your remedy would be in the state courts against the party selling the stock."

The Dawes's merger was far too sensitive for the comptroller's office to take action on the formal complaint. The merger would eliminate a major problem bank from the jurisdiction of the comptroller's office, and it would enable the Dawes state bank to become the third largest bank in Chicago.[30]

INDICTMENTS OF THE ILLINOIS BANKING COMMISSIONER

There was a spectacular failure at the state level of regulations, too. The Dawes brothers operated their bank "in an unsafe manner" and published fraudulent financial statements with impunity because they had co-opted their regulator. Oscar Nelson, the statewide-elected auditor of public accounts and banking commissioner of Illinois, was deeply in debt to the Dawes bank. The Dawes bank had issued at least three loans to Nelson totaling $122,500, an amount worth $1,920,000 in today's money. If the bank failed, then Nelson's loans would immediately come due and become a matter of public record. So his financial and political survival depended on the bank continuing to operate even though it was insolvent by July 1931.[31]

But the compliant regulator's inaction allowed reckless bankers to operate within the state banking system, resulting in an epidemic of bank failures and his disgrace. On September 9, 1931, a Lake County grand jury indicted Nelson, at the urging of the local prosecutor, Ashbel V. Smith, for misfeasance of office and culpable omission of duty in connection with the failure of the Waukegan State Bank. When he launched the investigation, Smith, who had admitted that he "personally was a heavy loser in the crash of the Waukegan State Bank," declared that Nelson had "betrayed a public trust and become a traitor to his oath." After Nelson's indictment, his lawyers moved for a change of venue, arguing that the banking commissioner could not receive a fair trial in Waukegan due to the high emotions resulting from the bank failure. The motion was granted, and Nelson was tried before twelve McHenry County jurors in the old courthouse in Woodstock, Illinois, sixty-five miles northwest of Chicago.

Nelson's first criminal trial centered on the charge that his failure to initiate a receivership for the State Bank of Waukegan allowed the bank's officials to dissipate its assets between October 24, 1930, when he learned of the bank's insolvent condition, and June 17, 1931, when it finally closed. Circuit Judge Edward D. Shurtleff, sitting in Woodstock, gutted the case against the state regulator when he denied the admission into evidence of the state's examination reports of the Waukegan State Bank, even though the bank was closed and the fear of sparking a run on the bank could not be argued. Nelson's staff had prepared the examination reports and they would have worked against him, proving that the bank was insolvent in October 1930. Nelson's lawyers then moved to dismiss the charges on the grounds that the circuit court did not have jurisdiction to remove a statewide elected official for misfeasance in office, which would require impeachment proceedings in the legislature. Defense lawyers argued that "the financial welfare of the whole state of Illinois is being imperiled by the dragging on of this case. The insidious withdrawal of money from banks all over the state, inspired by this foolish prosecution, is too serious a problem for us to sit by idle and let this go on." Judge Shurtleff, who had earlier denied Nelson's motion to dismiss the indictment for lack of jurisdiction, granted the renewed motion to dismiss, and, in a very unusual move, ordered each of the jurors to sign a form acquitting Nelson of misfeasance.[32]

In a second indictment against Nelson, the Lake County grand jury also charged George Woodruff, the chairman of the National Bank of the Republic, which was the Chicago correspondent bank for the Waukegan State Bank, for conspiracy to defraud the depositors of the defunct Waukegan State Bank when it published false financial statements concealing its insolvent condition. The former president of the Waukegan State Bank, Norman O. Geyer, and William H. Miller, a vice president of the National Bank of the Republic and a director of the Waukegan State Bank, were also indicted for their role in the conspiracy to obtain deposits under false pretenses. Making the charges more sensational was the disclosure that Nelson owned sixty-six shares of stock in the National Bank of the Republic, which had been involved in several questionable transactions with the Waukegan State Bank.

When the National Bank of the Republic merged into Dawes's Central Republic Bank, on July 25, 1931, it held securities worth $841,000 that the Waukegan State Bank had pledged to secure a $450,000 loan from the national bank. (The national bank had two additional interlocking directors sitting on the board of the Waukegan State Bank. One of those directors, Edwin L. Wagner, also a vice president of the national bank, was "deep in debt," according to examiners of the office of the comptroller of the currency.) On May 13, 1932, the *Chicago Tribune* reported that Judge Shurtleff had declared: "A proper petition should be filed at once for a court order directing the Central Republic Bank and Trust Company of Chicago to return $841,000 in securities." The festering controversy spilled into the public domain when Judge Shurtleff removed the receiver for the Waukegan State Bank because of his failure to take action against the Dawes bank to recover the pledged securities.[33]

Attempting to gain some semblance of control over the utter chaos, the Dawes bank sought to reorganize and merge the Waukegan State Bank and the Waukegan National Bank, installing Charles Dawes's son-in-law, Melvin B. Ericson, as president of the succeeding institution. Ericson, who was married to Dawes's daughter, Carolyn, was vice president of the Houdaille-Hershey Corporation and a director of several Dawes entities, including Dawes Brothers, Inc., Metropolitan Gas and Electric Company, and the Union Gas and Electric Company.

Insull's personal lawyers at Schuyler, Dunbar and Weinfeld in Chicago were promoting the reorganization at the same time that they were representing the former president of the Waukegan State Bank, Norman Geyer, who was also under indictment for conspiracy to defraud its depositors. As part of the reorganization plan, the major stockholders of the new bank would be the Dawes bank and the interests of Samuel Insull, who had purchased the Waukegan Electric Light Company in 1902.

Judge Shurtleff, sitting in Waukegan, issued an order that protected Nelson. Stretching the impeachment argument to its illogical conclusion, the judge ruled that the bank examination reports of the Waukegan State Bank or other evidence showing Nelson's official misconduct were inadmissible in any of the bank fraud trials. Consequently, Smith, the state attorney, was forced to dismiss the charges against Nelson so he could prosecute William Miller, who was the first of the bankers to face a jury. During Miller's trial, the head bookkeeper at the state bank testified that the National Bank of the Republic had deposited a total of $1.25 million into the Waukegan State Bank over a period of eighteen months. The deposits were made just prior to publication of the state bank's quarterly financial reports in the local paper, and then the national bank had quietly withdrawn the funds a few days later. Though the state bank's published financial reports stated that its capital was $250,000, bank examiners testified that all but $52,000 of its capital had been wiped out because of worthless insider loans and other nonperforming assets. A conspiracy had been proved, according to the foreman of the jury, but the jurors believed that Miller was "a lesser figure and the ones to be punished were those higher up than Miller," so they acquitted him. When Dawes opened the City National Bank later that year in October 1932, he hired Miller as a vice president responsible for commercial loans.[34]

The frustrated prosecutor then dismissed the pending charges against the other bankers, saying that he did not "feel like putting the taxpayers of Lake County to further expense." But the indictments against Nelson, combined with the demands of the depositors for his impeachment, caused sufficient damage to convince the veteran politician to withdraw from the Republican primary. Running as a Democrat when his party's ticket was sweeping the state, Edward Barrett of Chicago, the statewide-elected treasurer, was elected state auditor, making him the new banking commissioner.[35]

PANIC STRIKES

During the so-called week of hysteria, lasting from June 20 through June 25, 1932, banks failed in record numbers as bankers faced prosecutors. Angry depositors, many of whom had lost most of their life savings in Insull's bankrupt entities, crowded the streets of Chicago to demand what was left of their

Image 4.1.   Depositors in Chicago demanding the return of their money in June 1932.
(Courtesy, Franklin D. Roosevelt Presidential Library)

money from banks weighed down with Insull loans. After two groups of stu-
dents were arrested for protesting in front of his home on Lake Shore Drive,
Insull quietly sailed for Europe. On June 22, he was reported to have arrived
in Paris, far away from process servers. News that Insull was hiding in Paris
fueled the panic that was threatening the survival of three of the major Loop
banks. They had financed Insull's reckless expansion and were left holding
the worthless paper of his shattered empire. Traylor's First National Bank,
Reynolds's Continental Illinois Bank, and Dawes's Central Republic Bank
were all suspect, and for good reason: they had bet heavily on a man who
was now on the run.[36]

Depositors became more alarmed than ever on Monday, June 20. John
Swanson, the Republican prosecutor for Cook County who was engaged in
a tough reelection campaign against Democratic State Senator Thomas J.
Courtney, leaked to a reporter that he planned to indict more bankers soon.
(Unknown to the press and the public was that Swanson and members of his
family were stockholders of the Dawes bank. The RFC later sued them to collect on their stockholder liabilities. Swanson refused to pay until he lost his
second appeal. He litigated against the RFC for three years to avoid paying
$400, worth about $5,980 in today's money.)

Setting up a special strike force to investigate criminal activities in Chicago's banks, Swanson had already gained some convictions. His bank fraud unit had completed audits on several more banks and was preparing to present evidence of criminal wrongdoing to grand jurors meeting in secret. Officials of one bank allegedly had misappropriated $1 million of depositors' money. Swanson, milking the investigation for publicity, refused to name the targets of the inquiry, creating more unrest among depositors in the area. (Despite the news coverage that he generated during his investigations, Swanson would lose in a landslide in November. Sharing the ticket with Hoover guaranteed his loss to state Senator Thomas Courtney.)[37]

Continuing to seek the limelight, Swanson praised local judges for rapidly disposing of the bank fraud cases, "which are of interest to almost every family in the community." During the first three weeks in June, Swanson won convictions against the following bankers for embezzlement and bank fraud: Elmer Langgruth, the president of the Peoples State Bank of Maywood; Walter Wolf, a clerk at the Continental Illinois Bank, who had embezzled more than $3 million; Carl A. Mueller, the president of the Laramie State Bank; Charles J. Wolf, the president of the Citizens State Bank of Melrose Park; Alexander Flower, the chairman of the Roosevelt-Bankers State Bank, and his brother, Samuel Flower; along with J. Chester Vastine, C. C. Dunkle, Lee A. King, Karl J. Heinzelman, and Earl D. Phillips of the Exchange State Bank; and Frank J. Gatz of the Stockmen's Trust and Savings Bank.[38]

With the glare of Swanson's sensational publicity and after experiencing depositor runs, the Bowmanville National Bank and the Reliance Bank and Trust Company were closed on Monday, June 20. In an unsuccessful attempt to lessen its liquidity crisis, the Reliance Bank had borrowed $617,866 from the First National Bank, a loan that had now become a worthless asset for Traylor's bank. Beyond that, F. O. Birney, the president of the Reliance Bank, had also procured a loan from Traylor in the amount of $12,500, and Thomas Lord, a director of the Reliance Bank, had another loan of $26,328 from Traylor's bank. The national bank examiners classified both as problem loans.[39]

Efforts of the RFC while Dawes was still president did not save either bank. In a bailout of the Bowmanville National Bank, the RFC made four secret loans before it failed, three of which the RFC approved while Dawes was president. (Dawes recused himself from voting on the loans because of his conflict of interest, but his colleagues approved them.) The losses of the Bowmanville National Bank would not be limited to its depositors and stockholders. When an examiner conducted a postmortem examination, he found that the bank owed $51,602 to the Central Republic Bank and Trust Company. To secure this interbank loan, Dawes's bank accepted the bonds of utility and

railroad companies that had subsequently suffered a depreciation of 40 percent. For the Dawes brothers and the other directors of the Central Republic
Bank to approve a loan of that magnitude when the officers and directors of
the Bowmanville National Bank had procured personal loans of $427,355
from their bank, representing 143 percent of its capital, was reckless and
irresponsible. Nevertheless, the Dawes bank's depreciated bonds would later
be used to secure the RFC loans.[40]

When the Bowmanville National Bank closed, its directors proposed to
Comptroller of the Currency Pole that the bank be reorganized and reopened.
In September, National Bank Examiner John F. Utt reviewed the records of
the bank to determine if the plan was feasible. After a thorough examination,
he recommended that the bank be liquidated:

> The examiner has come to the conclusion that the directors are simply trying to
> reorganize *to escape an assessment on the old capital stock* and to cover up their
> own worthless obligations and are *not* working for the good of the depositors. It
> is believed a 100% assessment should be levied without delay and that if there
> is any possibility of the Receiver being able to collect money from the directors
> because of their gross negligence, a lawsuit should be started against them. It is
> recommended the bank *not* be permitted to reorganize.[41]

The comptroller's office had known for years that the officers and directors
of the Bowmanville National Bank were abusing their fiduciary positions.
In April 1930, Deputy Comptroller John L. Proctor had criticized management for the "unsatisfactory conditions and policies" of the bank, especially
the "unwarranted" and excessive loans granted to John A. Schmidt, a bank
director, in violation of federal law. The comptroller's office had been aware,
specifically, of the illegal loans to officers and directors of the bank since at
least 1928. By early 1930, the insider loans exceeded 10 percent of all loans
and represented nearly the bank's entire capital. Still, the comptroller's office
failed to force the resignations of the officers or directors, preferring instead
to admonish them privately. Regulators also allowed the directors to issue
dividends, which depleted the bank's meager capital and deceived the public
about its true condition. Because of the extreme secrecy cloaking the comptroller's office, the public was unaware of the illegal activities at the bank.[42]

In addition to the insider abuses, most of the loans of the bank were secured
with dubious real estate mortgages. By September 1931, federal examiners
were reporting that officers and directors of the bank had made "liberal use of
the funds and many of these loans are now found to be of questionable value."
The bank was in such a "highly unsatisfactory" condition that examiners in
the field balked at certifying its solvency. They reported to Washington that

there was "absolutely no hope for corrective measures from [the] present board of directors." Frustrated examiners observed, "While this bank occupies a very desirable location and one that should be continued if possible, it remains that the directors as a whole are badly involved." They concluded that "a continued drain on the deposits is gradually bringing the situation to a point where a suspension will be necessary."

Yet the comptroller's office refused to take decisive action to limit depositors' losses. Deputy Comptroller Proctor merely wrote a letter complaining that the bank held "a menacing aggregate of slow and doubtful assets" totaling significantly more than twice the bank's capital. Proctor issued a dead-letter warning to the board of directors that the bank was in "a most unsatisfactory condition." Management flagrantly ignored regulators and did not even bother to require collateral or financial statements from one another as they continued to fund their own pet projects with depositors' money. Refusing to remove management or close the bank, submissive senior regulators in Washington allowed the plunder to continue unabated while depositors' losses mounted.[43]

On June 11, 1932, John P. O'Shaughnessy, vice president and director, and Elmer A. Suckow, cashier, of the Bowmanville National Bank, met in Washington with Deputy Comptroller Proctor to discuss the crisis at the bank. The two promoter-bankers, who had defaulted on their own loans at the bank, told Proctor that the institution could be saved if it received an additional loan from the RFC. And they said they needed further "leniency on the part of [the comptroller's office] and its representatives in Chicago." The directors revealed that the bank had already borrowed $290,000 from the National Credit Corporation (NCC), $185,000 from the RFC, and $48,826 from the Federal Reserve Bank of Chicago. Thus the federal government and the NCC had made loans totaling $523,826, which was 175 percent of the bank's capital. Additionally, the Dawes bank had loaned $51,602 to the insolvent bank, and the National City Bank of New York had loaned it another $50,000. When the interbank loans and NCC advance were added to the government assistance, the bailout had already come to more than twice the bank's capital. When using taxpayers' and depositors' money, O'Shaughnessy and Suckow, two free-wheeling promoters, recklessly made loans to themselves. Yet they told Proctor that they were unable and unwilling to put more of their own fortunes at risk to augment the bank's capital.[44]

Proctor's response to the visit from the two insiders, who had so abused their fiduciary positions, was to arrange an appointment for them at the RFC so they could attempt to borrow still more from the federal government. Instead of demanding the resignations of the officers and directors who were "hopelessly" abusing the bank, the comptroller's office refused to assess the stockholders for a capital injection because it would "only result in the suspension of the bank." To avoid this, Proctor had repeatedly instructed Alfred Leyburn, the chief examiner, to hold meetings with the directors to see if together they could find a way "to strengthen the bank."[45]

Though the condition of the Bowmanville National Bank remained confidential, agitated depositors found out enough through leaks, rumors, and newspaper articles to cause them concern. Consequently, they demanded the return of their money and forced the closing of the bank on June 20. Official secrecy, which kept confidential both the regulatory criticisms of the national banks and the names of the recipients of RFC loans, and which the Hoover administration was so strictly enforcing to prevent depositors from panicking, failed to prevent the panic that continued throughout the week of June 20 through 25.

Grabbing headlines that week was the bank fraud trial of John Bain, the former head of the Bain chain of thirteen state banks, his two sons, John H. and Robert A. Bain, and his son-in-law, W. Merle Fisher. The Bain banking chain—with $25 million in assets—had collapsed in June 1931, but Swanson, the prosecutor, had waited until his reelection campaign to pursue the case. On Wednesday, June 22, depositors read that the Bains had opened the Brainerd State Bank in 1928 with a $271,000 loan and then promptly borrowed 85 percent of the bank's capital. The Bain family looted its own banking chain, buying several tracts of real estate and then selling them to their banks at inflated prices.[46]

On June 21, two national banks and one state bank collapsed. The state bank, the Phillip State Bank and Trust Company of Chicago, had received a large loan from the Dawes bank. Then on May 17, 1932, it had received a $90,000 undisclosed loan from the RFC, when Dawes was its head. When the bank failed only a month later, it still owed the Dawes bank $55,256. The receivership records of the Phillip State Bank and Trust Company revealed that insider abuse caused its failure.[47]

The two national banks that closed on June 21, the Peoples National Bank and Trust Company and the Standard National Bank, were closely affiliated through an interlocking vice president who had engaged in a fraudulent scheme. The Peoples National Bank and Trust Company was controlled through the National Republic Bancorporation, which was affiliated with the Dawes bank. One of its directors, Hugo Otte, was a vice chairman of the Dawes bank and a director of the National Republic Bancorporation. The federal regulatory records of the two national banks tell a familiar tale of insider abuse. Even so, the RFC—with Dawes at its helm—continued to prop up the member banks of the National Republic Bancorporation chain, making seven loans to the Peoples National Bank. (These loans were made after the RFC had already loaned $100,000 to the United American Trust and Savings Bank, which was also controlled through the National Republic Bancorporation. The United American Trust and Savings Bank was on the verge of collapse because of its worthless insider loans and the weight of the $1,390,000 million loan from the Dawes bank.) The RFC loans to the Peoples National Bank might have provided liquidity that was desperately needed, but the interest and principal payment requirements of the government loans ensured the bank's insolvency.

Both the Peoples National Bank and the United American Bank were owned through the National Republic Bancorporation, the holding company that had owned the National Bank of the Republic before it merged into the Dawes bank and shared interlocking officers and directors with the Dawes bank, as well as being a stockholder of the Dawes bank. Another bank controlled through the National Republic Bancorporation was the Adams State Bank of Chicago. On March 10, 1932, the RFC's board (with the exception of Dawes, who abstained) had approved a $100,000 loan for the Adams State Bank, which represented 50 percent of the bank's capital of $200,000. The bank was tied through loans to the Dawes bank because of its prior affiliation with the National Bank of the Republic, now part of the Dawes bank. Despite the RFC loan, the Adams State Bank failed on June 30, 1932. When it closed, it owed its depositors $424,341, but by September 1934 it had paid only $30,149 to its depositors, or seven cents on the dollar.[48]

At a special board of directors' meeting on Saturday, March 12, 1932, the RFC's board of directors approved a $775,000 loan to the Peoples National Bank, which constituted 77.5 percent of its capital stock. Once again, in pro forma accordance with the conflict-of-interest section in the RFC act, Dawes did not "participate in the deliberation" of the loan or vote on the matter. But Jones, Couch, McCarthy, and Meyer voted for the loan.

Hugo Otte, the influential vice chairman of the Dawes bank, was a director of the Peoples National Bank, which was affiliated with the Dawes bank. Otte, who had personally guaranteed $25,000 of the bonds that were issued to finance the Chicago World's Fair, was well known to Dawes. In August 1931, after the first month of the Dawes bank merger with the National Bank of the Republic, Henry Dawes had remarked to his brother, Charles, that Otte was "working very hard" for the Dawes bank. After the collapse of both the Peoples National Bank and the Dawes bank, Philip Clarke recommended to Edward Hurley, the receiver of both the Middle West and the Midland Utilities Company, who had also been a director of the old Dawes bank, that he hire Otte to head Midland, the Indiana gas and electric company that Insull's son had managed.[49]

On March 25, 1932, less than two weeks after its first loan, the Peoples National Bank was back before the RFC's board with another loan request. This time the RFC approved, with Dawes abstaining, a loan of $90,000 to the bank, thereby raising to 86.5 the percentage of the RFC's loans to the bank's purported capital stock.[50]

During the first five months of the RFC's existence, when its board meetings and loan recipients were strictly confidential, the Chicago banks that were affiliated with the Dawes bank continued to line up for loans at the RFC while Dawes was head of the agency. One of them, the Cosmopolitan State Bank of Chicago, applied for and received approval on April 1, 1932, for a $425,000 loan from the RFC. But Alfred Leyburn, the chief national bank examiner for the comptroller of the currency's office in Chicago, had warned the comptroller of the currency a few months earlier of Cosmopolitan's precarious condition and insider loans. The Cosmopolitan State Bank had purported paid-in capital of $1 million, so the loan represented 42.5 percent of its capital stock. But its capital, including its surplus, was so seriously impaired that it was already insolvent at the time of the RFC loan. Dawes, whose bank benefited from the loan because the failure of its affiliated state bank would likely trigger a run on the Dawes bank, again recused himself from the discussion and did not vote on the loan. But, as usual, his colleagues approved the loan.

The National Republic Bancorporation, the stockholder of the Dawes Bank that also shared interlocking officers and directors with the Dawes bank, was the controlling stockholder of the Cosmopolitan State Bank. In a rare regulatory action with a political undercurrent, on February 17, 1933, Edward Barrett, the recently elected banking commissioner, closed the Cosmopolitan State Bank because it was being operated "in an unsafe manner." After an examination, Barrett determined that its officials fraudulently carried worthless assets on the books of the bank. Its capital was so impaired that the bank could not be reorganized, so its assets were placed in a receivership to be liquidated.

Barrett appointed William L. O'Connell, who had been "for years one of Chicago's best known politicians," as the receiver for the Cosmopolitan State Bank, which owed $1,731,413 to its depositors when it closed. The handling of the receivership was criticized when it was revealed that O'Connell had spent $99,913 of the cash assets of the bank on expenses during a period when the depositors had received none of their savings, all of which were frozen in the receivership. O'Connell had paid legal fees of $11,861 to the firm of

Nash and Ahern, whose members included Cook County Treasurer Thomas D. Nash, Alderman Roger J. Kiley, and Judge Cornelius J. Harrington.

Barrett also made the controversial appointment of his former employer, William T. Fleming and Company, as the official real estate appraiser for the state auditor's office. Barrett's former company received significant fees for appraising the real estate assets of the 146 defunct banks in Cook County. Depositors' committees representing the more than 600,000 depositors of the closed banks criticized the excessive legal, appraisal, and other fees as a waste of receivership assets.[51]

Insolvent promoter banks affiliated with the Dawes bank continued their pattern of abusing the RFC's loan program throughout April and May 1932. On April 1, 1932, the Austin State Bank of Chicago, another bank affiliated with the Dawes bank, applied for and received approval for a $190,000 loan from the RFC's board. Charles Castle, a director of both the Dawes bank and the National Republic Bancorporation, which controlled the Austin State Bank, was chairman of the Austin State Bank. Again, Dawes, with his conflict of interest, did not vote on the loan request at the RFC's board meeting. But Jones and his other colleagues approved the loan, which represented 38 percent of the purported $500,000 capital stock of the Bank.

A few days later, on April 5, 1932, the RFC approved a loan of $90,000 for still another bank affiliated with the Dawes bank, the First Englewood State Bank of Chicago. The loan, on which Dawes again abstained, represented 45 percent of its stated capital stock of $200,000. The First Englewood State Bank was also controlled through the National Republic Bancorporation, a stockholder of the Dawes bank, and four of its directors were directors of the Dawes bank. One of these, Lucius Teter, was chairman of the board of directors of the First Englewood State Bank. In fact, Teter sat on all three boards of directors: the Dawes bank, the First Englewood State Bank, and its holding company, the National Republic Bancorporation. Teter had been the vice chairman of the National Bank of the Republic, now part of the Dawes bank. Remaining loyal to Dawes, he stayed on the board of the old Dawes bank, the Central Republic Trust Company, even after it ceased conducting a banking business, which subjected him and the other directors of the defunct bank to intense litigation.

That same day, the Peoples National Bank, another affiliate of the Dawes bank, returned to the friendly RFC building for yet another loan, this time for $110,000, its third loan in less than a month. This one insolvent bank had now borrowed $975,000, representing 97.5 percent of its paid-in capital. Peoples National Bank was so impaired it was beyond restoration, especially since the RFC loans required 5.5 percent interest payments and were due in full six months after their issuance. Once more, Dawes abstained but Jones, Couch, McCarthy, and Meyer voted in favor of the loan, which had no hope of repayment.

On the surface, the Peoples National Bank had once seemed to be a well-capitalized community bank, with its $1 million of capital stock and $500,000 of surplus, which was published in the local newspaper. But, during the fall of 1931, the comptroller's office discovered that $185,000 had been embezzled from the Standard National Bank, a small Chicago bank that received its charter from Comptroller Pole in 1929. In early November, Leyburn secretly telegraphed Pole to inform him of that embezzlement and also to alert him that a recent examination of the Peoples National Bank showed a "precarious condition."[52]

Clarence R. Webster, vice president of both the Standard National Bank and the Peoples National Bank, was the ringleader behind the embezzlement at the Standard National Bank. The size of the theft put the Peoples National Bank in jeopardy because of its affiliation. Leyburn was much more interested in stopping newspaper leaks about the embezzlement than in prosecuting Webster and the other officers and employees who had conspired in the crime. Leyburn noted that the officers and directors of the Standard National Bank were now insolvent, since the bank stock they owned was worthless. As Leyburn told Pole, "the failure of any bank in the chain will undoubtedly cause the collapse of the entire chain and the effect on the banking situation in Chicago will be disastrous." The same argument would be made later to justify bailing out Dawes's Central Republic Bank and Trust Company.[53]

The Peoples National Bank owed $215,000 to the First National Bank, so its failure would have resulted in a significant loss for Traylor's bank. In light of the bank fraud conspiracy and the bank's "hopelessly incompetent" management, Leyburn's solution for saving the Standard National Bank and its affiliated Peoples National Bank was for the NCC and then the RFC to bail them out. Both banks received loans from the RFC. The board of the RFC, with the exception of Dawes, who, as usual, abstained from voting, approved a $60,000 loan to the Standard National Bank on March 23, 1932. But, predictably, that so-called solution failed to work for either of the two insolvent banks.

When the Peoples National Bank failed on June 21, 1932, it had received $1,635,000 in seven secret loans from the RFC between March 12 and May 28, 1932, which represented 163.5 percent of its capital stock. The Peoples National Bank failed because of massive insider abuse and fraud. The federal bailout strategy failed at twelve of the fifteen national banks that closed during the last two-and-a-half weeks of June 1932. (Only three of the failed national banks had not received RFC loans.) Indeed, all twelve of the failed banks had received secret loans from the RFC. Federal bank regulatory records also show that the RFC loans were not adequately secured, in violation of federal law. RFC loans, which remained confidential, were also ineffectual at twenty-three of the twenty-seven state banks in Chicago that closed in June. Only four of the closed state banks did not receive federal assistance.[54]

The federal bailout program was a dismal failure at the thirty-five banks in Chicago and Cook County that received secret RFC loans but then closed in June 1932. With Charles Dawes at the helm, the RFC made substantial loans to the troubled banks without requiring the removal of the same officers and directors whose insider abuse and fraud had put the banks in their deplorable conditions. Instead of working with national and state regulatory agencies to force the removal of the management of the troubled banks, the RFC loaned millions of dollars to hopelessly insolvent banks that rogue bankers controlled. The taxpayer funds were then used to bailout the bankers' pet projects as opposed to meeting the liquidity requirements of their banks. All of the banks receiving the secret government loans collapsed because of insider abuse and fraud and certainly not due to the nonexistent publicity surrounding those loans.

The spring of 1932 and the winter that preceded it were particularly stressful for many Chicagoans. The city was unable to pay the salaries of its sixteen thousand teachers and other municipal employees, and half of Chicago's working population was unemployed. Because of the city's failure to meet its payroll, many municipal employees were losing their homes after defaulting on mortgages and real estate taxes. One employee of the city of Chicago lost his home for failure to pay thirty-four dollars in real estate taxes after the city failed to pay his salary of $850, and others were homeless, sleeping in Chicago's parks.[55]

On Thursday, June 23, the *Chicago Tribune* reported that the Senate rejected "by an overwhelming vote" an amendment that would have allowed the RFC to make emergency loans to state and local governments to pay policemen, firemen, schoolteachers, and other unpaid municipal employees. The sponsor of the amendment, Senator James Hamilton Lewis, Democrat of Illinois, made an urgent appeal, declaring that it was better to send federal funds now than to send federal troops later to quell the "riot and revolt which would spread throughout the country."[56]

The measure resulted from a highly publicized lobbying effort in Washington. Mayor Anton Cermak, Melvin Traylor, and other local officials, bankers, and businessmen were seeking $81.5 million in loans from the RFC. Though the RFC continued to lack the authority to make direct loans to the city or the state of Illinois without an amendment to the RFC Act, it could have made loans to Chicago banks, which then could have bailed out the city and state. But Traylor and the Reynolds brothers were not interested in that approach, claiming that they already were holding excessive amounts of tax anticipation paper. Traylor publicly said: "Chicago cannot borrow its way out. The only method is to pay out." And privately he was saying that "under no circumstances would the Chicago banks put their names on any notes to the federal Reconstruction Finance Corporation where the only security was Chicago tax warrants." Absent from the Washington lobbying trip were officials of the Dawes bank, who were lobbying the RFC for their own bailout at the same time.[57]

More bad news appeared in the *Chicago Tribune* that Thursday. Reporting on the trial of John Bain, banner headlines declared that he had procured unsecured loans totaling $1,751,602 at eleven of his twelve banks, all of which had failed the previous year. Bain, a former plumber from Scotland, had been a power broker in Chicago for years and was still serving as a South Park commissioner. With anxious depositors packing the courtroom, the prosecution presented testimony to show how the Bain family had systematically defrauded its own banking chain. The headline next to the Bain article, which must have alarmed the depositors in other banks in Chicago, read: "5 State Banks and 1 National Closed in City." All too lethargic regulators failed to take action to close any of the banks.[58]

The one national bank that closed on Wednesday was the Jefferson Park National Bank, a promoter bank that failed because of reckless real estate ventures and insider abuse. The bank's president, Fred H. Esdohr, and its vice president and cashier, Rodney D. Andrews, would sit together on one side of the table, as the loan committee, while simultaneously sitting together on the other side of the table, as the bank's largest borrowers and real estate speculators. To support his speculative ventures, Esdohr borrowed extensively from the Dawes bank, in which he still owed $47,500 in December 1940. The staff of the RFC assigned to this loan an "estimated recovery value" of zero, which included collateral of 1,075 shares of the Jefferson Park National Bank. In 1940, Esdohr, in the name of the Jefferson Park National Company, still owed the Dawes bank $29,129, which had come due more than seven years earlier and the RFC staff valued at zero.[59]

Examiners from the comptroller's office criticized the bank's "heavy liability for money borrowed" and instructed the directors to "rapidly" reduce its indebtedness. Instead, Esdohr and Andrews had procured a loan for the insolvent bank from the NCC when his colleague, George Reynolds, head of the Continental Illinois Bank, was chairman of the NCC. And when Charles Dawes became president of the RFC, Esdohr and Andrews applied for and received a major loan from the RFC that would never be repaid. Next, Esdohr and his partner, Andrews, borrowed more money from their bank, keeping the circulation of currency flowing freely from the federal government into their pockets. Because regulatory secrecy shielded Esdohr and Andrews, they manipulated the system and survived for several years.[60]

Meanwhile, the regulators sat in the gallery and cheered. In April 1931, Examiner M. M. Ward and Alfred Leyburn, the chief examiner in charge, wrote in the bank's examination report, "Bank is conservatively and well managed. Officers strive to run a clean bank and appear to want to correct all matters criticized." The examiners were impressed with Esdohr, whose financial statement asserted a net worth of $150,000, and Andrews, whose net worth was supposedly $75,000. Regulators knew that Esdohr dominated the bank's daily affairs, but somehow they believed this was "beneficial." They also knew that Esdohr and Andrews had firm control of the bank. Esdohr and Andrews controlled the annual stockholders' meetings, monthly board meetings, and weekly loan committee meetings. They were the ones who approved the loans to their own real estate development company, the Esdohr and Andrews Company, and to the Jefferson Park National Company, a mortgage company that they controlled.

By April 6, 1931, the promoters had personally borrowed $52,912, or 18 percent of the bank's capital. Officers and directors, including Esdohr and Andrews and their entities, owed the bank at least $174,241, or more than 58 percent of the bank's capital of $300,000. The examiners were intimately aware of this brazen conflict of interest, yet they did not criticize the insider loans.[61]

The excessive insider loans occurred at a time when the bank was experiencing a liquidity crisis. As a result, the bank had borrowed $250,000 (representing 83 percent of its capital) from the Federal Reserve Bank of Chicago. The bank had also suffered a depreciation of $120,013 in its bond portfolio and had substandard loans and other assets of $173,872, over and above the loans to Esdohr, Andrews, and the other insiders. These bad investments alone nearly matched the bank's entire capital. Nevertheless, the examiners praised the directors, observing that they were "capable and believed to be familiar with the bank's affairs." And the conclusions of the April 1931 examination report gave the impression that the Jefferson Park National Bank was a model financial institution.[62]

Six months later, when the comptroller's office examined the bank again, the personal loans to Esdohr and Andrews had risen to $74,425, or 25 percent of the bank's capital. This time the regulators criticized most of the loans to the promoters as "unwarranted," recognizing that the bank was in "a very unsatisfactory and extended condition." During a meeting with the regulators, which did not occur until January 1932, the bank's board of directors agreed to immediately charge off $127,348 in losses. But since this sum did not involve the insider loans, the action was just a token. The directors also agreed not to declare a dividend, sending a signal to depositors that the bank was in trouble.[63]

While keeping the insider abuse at the bank a closely guarded secret, regulators failed to take decisive action to save the bank. Meanwhile, headlines in the *Chicago Tribune* continued to cause depositors concern. On Friday, June 24, 1932, the headline blared: "Trial Figures Show Losses of Bain Depositors: Receiver Lists Loans to Banker's Family." The article reported that loans totaling $2,156,207, either unsecured or backed with the worthless stock of the Bain banks, had been made to John Bain, his entities, or family members. The principal amount of the loans would ultimately result in a total loss. Bain's partners and the officers and directors of his banks who were not family members had borrowed an additional $2,922,972 from the affiliated banks. The twelve Bain banks had deposits totaling $13 million, but only $231,836 in cash. They had collected $884,000 in taxes under authorization from the county tax collector only six weeks before their collapse, but the tax receipts were now frozen in the liquidation process. Adding to the misery of the community was testimony describing twenty-four mortgage bond issues that the banks had sold to the public at "highly excessive" prices of nearly $6 million. All of the bond issues were now in default, resulting in millions of dollars of losses.[64]

The headline immediately following the Bain article read: "29 Year Old Head of Closed Bank Arrested by U.S." The article described how Francis Karel, the twenty-nine-year-old president of the First American National Bank and Trust Company of Berwyn (a Chicago suburb in Cook County), which had failed on the previous Saturday, had been arrested for embezzling funds from the bank. That same day, frantic depositors had forced the closing of three national banks and two state banks. Officials at Dawes's Central Republic Bank must have read the article with alarm. The Dawes bank made at least five loans, totaling $55,881, to Karel and his family. The loans were secured with shares of stock in the First American National Bank and Trust Company of Berwyn and two other local banks. (By December 31, 1940, the RFC would recognize that all of these loans and the collateral securing them had an "estimated recovery value" of zero. The only possible exception would be a promissory note in the amount of $1,750 that Karel had signed, requiring him to pay $250 semiannually.)[65]

The closed state banks were the Kaspar-American State Bank and the Central Manufacturing District Bank. Hugo Otte, with his ties to the Dawes bank and the National Republic Bancorporation, was a director of the Kaspar-American State Bank. The three national banks that failed on Friday, June 24, were the Midland National Bank, the National Bank of Woodlawn, and the Ravenswood National Bank. With interlocking boards of directors, the state banks and the Midland National Bank engaged in numerous interbank transactions benefiting the officers and directors of each of the banks. Worthless loans of their fiduciaries permeated the balance sheets of all of the banks that failed that day. Another common denominator among the defunct community banks was that they had concentrated their assets in speculative real estate loans.[66]

Different regulators supervised the Midland National Bank and the Central Manufacturing District Bank, but the same promoters controlled them. Records show that federal regulators had intimate knowledge of the chicanery being perpetrated, but no one in authority took action. Together, two promoters controlled two banks that failed on the same day: David E. Shanahan, chairman of the Central Manufacturing District Bank, and Frank L. Webb, its vice president and director, who held the same positions at the Midland National Bank. Webb was also the largest stockholder of the national bank, and his partner, Shanahan, owned the second largest position. More important, Webb was the largest borrower at the national bank. Examiners criticized his delinquent loans on numerous occasions and noted that "no progress was shown." To secure his loans at the national bank, Webb pledged his stock in the state bank, stock that was now worthless. Regulators in the field believed his personal loan guarantees were of "no value" and that his net worth was zero. They expressed grave concern about "numerous thinly margined loans predicated at least to a substantial portion on stocks in affiliated banks," including the Central Manufacturing District Bank. Yet the comptroller's office took no action to force Webb off the board of the Midland National Bank.[67]

Compounding the problem for federal regulators, the Midland National Bank had also borrowed $27,677 from Traylor's First National Bank. Traylor's bank would therefore suffer a loss if the Midland National Bank failed. Additionally, other officials of the Central Manufacturing District Bank, some of whom were bankrupt, had received numerous "objectionable" loans at the national bank. To procure the loans, officials of the state bank used its worthless stock and failed to provide financial statements. According to federal examiners, the loans ranged from "slow to worthless." But because of the policy of regulatory secrecy in Springfield, federal examiners had "no knowledge of the condition of the Central Manufacturing District Bank." Consequently, they did not know the value of the Midland National Bank's collateral or the creditworthiness of the officials of the state bank. Likewise, the policy of secrecy in Washington precluded state examiners from knowing the condition of the national bank and the value of its worthless stock that was pledged to secure loans at the state bank.[68]

Webb, the vice president of the Midland National Bank, and his partners on the board, violated the national banking code, making real estate loans exceeding the statutory limits and amounting to more than 50 percent of the deposits of the bank. The comptroller's office knew about the insider abuse at the Midland National Bank soon after its opening on January 18, 1927. The abuse had been documented in at least five examinations of the bank. Directors' loans were "subject to severe criticism" from career examiners, but their supervisors in Chicago and Washington still allowed the abuse to continue until the bank collapsed. In November 1931, Deputy Comptroller Proctor admonished the directors for their "dangerous" practice of making loans to insiders "predicated on bank stock" and other "inadequate security, especially when their financial standing does not warrant such extensions of credit." By May 1932, the comptroller's office in Washington was demanding that "all criticized loans of directors and their connections . . . should be paid or placed in satisfactory bankable condition." Proctor was also alarmed because of the depreciation in the bank's bond portfolio and the concentration in real estate loans exceeding the capital of the bank.[69]

Still the comptroller's office misled the public about the bank's deplorable condition. Regulators took a lenient posture of requiring only $25,278 of the loan and bond losses to be charged off the books of the bank. The rationale for the regulatory forbearance was that the bank would be too weak if the entire amount of worthless loans and bonds was charged off. The bank had purchased $20,748 of Insull Utilities Investment bonds, which were worthless but still carried on the books of the bank as being worth $550. Officials of the bank had speculated $274,364 in the corporate bond market. Now its corporate obligations had a market value of $112,359, representing a depreciation of $162,005. The biggest losers were public utilities, losing 74 percent; then railroads, losing 65 percent; and industrial bonds, losing 45 percent of market value. The bank's bond portfolio had gone down 59 percent between 1927 and 1932. Nevertheless, had the bank maintained adequate liquidity, and were it not carrying worthless insider loans on its books, it could have survived. The downturn in the economy had adversely affected the bond portfolio, but the capital, surplus, and undivided profits of the bank should have been sufficient to cover the paper losses. Even in a robust economy, management should not have maintained a loan-to-deposit ratio of 86 percent, a ratio that wiped out the bank's liquidity because most of the loans were secured with "exceedingly frozen" real estate.[70]

Evidence of a weakening economy and a lessening of confidence in the bank had been manifested through a precipitous drop in deposits over a twelve-month period. In April 1931, the bank had deposits of $1,535,011 (worth about $21,600,000 today), but by October those deposits had dropped to $794,707. In April 1932, they stood at $612,580. The drop between April and October 1931 was far greater than the drop between October 1931 and April 1932. An analysis of the loan portfolio shows that the bank had what appeared to be a conservative loan-to-deposit ratio of 54 percent in April 1931. Yet a closer look reveals that the loans were backed primarily with an amount of real estate that exceeded the lawful limit of real estate loans along with worthless bank stock. The speculative loans were also made to borrowers with weak financial statements. Thus it was impossible to liquidate the illegal loans at the same pace as the loss of deposits. As a result, the ratio of loans to deposits had risen to 78 percent by October 1931. The frozen assets remained relatively constant during the next six months, and by April 1932, the loan ratio was at 86 percent of deposits.[71]

The fixed assets of the bank remained constant and drained its liquidity. When the bank was organized in 1927, the directors owned the building. Then in 1930 they decided to liquidate their holdings in a classic insider deal. Ignoring the objections of examiners, the directors held a board meeting and decided to purchase the building from themselves without the benefit of an independent appraisal. As real estate speculators, they sold the building to the bank at an inflated price, thus tying up half of the bank's capital in its building, furniture, and fixtures. It was a good day for the directors, but it ensured the demise of the bank. When the panic spread, the bank's lavish facility and furnishings would not be enough to convince suspicious depositors that it was a safe place to keep their money.[72]

Depositors ended the tumultuous week with more bad news on Saturday, June 25. Three articles ran side by side in the *Chicago Tribune* describing bank failures, fraud, bribery, insider abuse, and depositor losses. The lead story announced the closing of the five banks discussed above, and beside it was the damaging headline: "Charge Banker Stole $10,000 to Pay as Graft." That article went on to describe in detail the arrest of Francis Karel, the president of First American National Bank and Trust Company of Berwyn, for embezzling $10,000 from the bank. The money went to bribe local politicians as part of an effort to sell a $100,000 building he owned to the city of Berwyn for use as a new city hall. And the city had purchased the building after local officials were paid a 10 percent "commission." He was also charged with falsifying the books of the bank to cover up the crime.[73]

In a third story in the *Chicago Tribune* that unnerving day, prosecutors revealed that all twelve Bain banks were insolvent and that the Bain family had defrauded their depositors. According to the article, the state had "shown the hopelessness of expectations by the thousands of depositors, whose claims aggregate $13,000,000, of ever getting any considerable amount in repayment." The Bain trial focused attention on the precarious condition of many of the banks of Chicago. With fraud and insider abuse so rampant, how could any bank be trusted?[74]

Meanwhile, it was on that very same Saturday, June 25, 1932, that President Hoover went to his fishing camp in the Maryland mountains to escape the heat of Washington and the stress of a week when angry depositors crowded into the lobbies of Chicago's banks. His respite would be short-lived.[75]

Notes

1. Harvey Couch to O. D. Young, June 4, 1935 (telegram), ODYP/SLU.

2. On merger agreements, Charles Dawes was listed as a voting member of Central Republic Bank's board of directors. *Chicago Tribune*, April 1, 1930, July 29, October 7, and December 31, 1931, April 5 and June 7, 8, 1932; "Dawes Resigns Presidency of Finance Body," n.d., clipping LYSP/ALPL; *Reconstruction Finance Corporation v. Central Republic Trust Company*, 267; Statement of Assets and Liabilities as of December 2, 1931, of Charles G. Dawes, CGDP/NUL; Olson, *Herbert Hoover and the Reconstruction Finance Corporation*, 58–61; Francis Murray Huston, *Financing an Empire: History of Banking in Illinois* (Chicago: S. J. Clarke Publishing, 1926), 2:31, 32; Dunne, *Illinois*, 3:21.

3. The tangled web among the Dawes bank, its debtor banks and other borrowers, and the RFC when Dawes was head of the agency is revealed by the RFC records, the comptroller of the currency's records, and the receivership records at the Cook County Courthouse. *Stock Exchange Practices, Insull*, 1535; Taylor, "Losses to the Public in the Insull Collapse," 201; *Moody's, Public Utility Securities, 1932*, 837, 838, 840; *1933*, 1174; *Annual Report of the Interstate Commerce Commission*, 258; Wasik, *The Merchant of Power*, 114, 135.

4. Stipulation and Affidavit of H. A. Mulligan, July 12, 1935, In the Matter of Charles Cutler Dawes, Bankrupt, In Bankruptcy No. 59251, USDC/NDI; Order of Declaration of Heirship, January 30, 1940; and Claim of the Reconstruction Finance Corporation, July 3, 1940, In the Matter of the Estate of Rufus C. Dawes, Deceased, PCCC; Receiver's Petition No. 27, October 30, 1935, People of the State of Illinois, Ex. Rel. Edward J. Barrett, etc. v. Central Republic Trust Company, CCCC; *Who's Who in Chicago*, 243; Williamson, "What Is the Relative Value?"

5. Demand Notes of Charles Cutler Dawes to the order of Central Trust Company of Illinois in the amounts of $75,000, on September 11, 1929; and $1,500, on December 31, 1930; Claim of RFC and Affidavit of H. A. Mulligan, July 12, 1935; Stipulation between RFC and Maurice Klein, trustee; Trustee's First and Final Report and Account, January 2, 1936; Final Distribution Sheet, March 9, 1936; Trustee's Supplemental Final Report, April 7, 1936, In the Matter of Charles Cutler Dawes, Bankrupt, In Bankruptcy No. 59251, USDC/NDI.

6. R. J. Taylor to Ira Moore, July 18, 1933, RFC/NA; Statement of Assets and Liabilities as of December 2, 1931, CGDP/NUL.

7. Receiver's Petition No. 92, People of the State of Illinois, Ex. Rel. Edward J. Barrett v. Central Republic Trust Company, January 29, 1938, CCCC; *Reconstruction Finance Corporation v. Central Republic Trust Company* (1937), 267, 278; *Moody's, Industrial Securities, 1930*, 3101; *1931*, 2985; *1932*, 2392; *1934*, 1570.

8. Records of the Examining Division, Comptroller of the Currency's Office, USOCC/NA; Minutes of a Meeting of the Board of Directors of the Reconstruction Finance Corporation, March 1, 1932, RFC/NA.

9. Melvin Traylor's bank also carried bad debts of $27,677 from the Midland National Bank, which closed on June 24, 1932, and $26,000 to its affiliate, Midland Utilities Company; plus a $14,752 loan to South Ashland National Bank, which closed on June 25, 1932. *Chicago Tribune*, July 3, 1930; Records of the Examining Division, Comptroller of the Currency's Office, USOCC/WNRC.

10. Rawleigh Warner was so close to the Dawes brothers that he was named chairman of the board of directors of the Pure Oil Company in 1947 after Beman Dawes retired as the chairman. Arlington C. Harvey, *History of the Pure Oil Company, 1914 to 1941* (Chicago, 1941), 30, 31; Petition of First National Bank of Chicago for Proof of Will and Letters Testamentary, February 28, 1934; and Executor's First and Final Account, March 3, 1939, In the Matter of the Estate of Melvin A. Traylor, Deceased, PCCC; Records of the Examining Division, Comptroller of the Currency's Office, USOCC/WNRC; "1877—Henry May Dawes—1952," *Pure Oil News*, 35, no. 6 (November 1952): 4, 5; *Moody's, Banks—Insurance Companies—Investment Trusts—Real Estate Finance and Credit Companies, 1931*, 235–36; *1932*, 102; *1933*, 378–79; *1934*, 370–71; *1935*, 29–30; *1936*, 292; Williamson, "What Is the Relative Value?"

11. Edward P. Vollertsen to Comptroller of the Currency, October 5, 1931, USOCC/NA; "The Record of Central Republic Bank and Trust Company," Philip R. Clarke, April 16, 1936, PRCP/UI; *Moody's Manual of Investments: Banks, 1932*, 1180, 2749; Joseph William Charlton, "The History of Banking in Illinois since 1863" (Ph.D. diss., University of Chicago, 1938), 41–42.

12. John A. Lynch, a founder of the National Bank of the Republic in 1891 and its president for thirty-two years, had owned $1,355,140 of its stock. He had also been its chairman of the executive committee, and he was selected to hold the same powerful position at the Dawes bank, a position he continued to hold even after the Dawes bank ceased conducting a banking business. After the merger, Lynch had become a major stockholder of the Dawes bank, owning 3,553 shares with a par value of $100

a share. As such, in the RFC's stockholder assessment lawsuit, he was ordered to pay $355,300 to the receiver of the old Dawes bank. John W. O'Leary, who succeeded Lynch as the president of the National Bank of the Republic, continued as a director of its holding company and became a vice chairman of the Dawes bank. Hugo Otte, the former vice chairman of the National Bank of the Republic and a director of the affiliated Peoples National Bank and Trust Company, was named a vice chairman of the Dawes bank. Otte owned 302 shares of the Dawes bank and would be ordered to pay $30,200 to its receiver. Two other directors of the National Republic Bancorporation were named to the board of the Dawes bank: Lucius Teter and Charles Castle. Teter was the former vice chairman of the National Bank of the Republic and current chairman of the First Englewood State Bank, which was still controlled by the holding company (he owned 401 shares of the Dawes bank and would be ordered to pay $40,100). Castle was the former vice chairman of the executive committee of the National Bank of the Republic, and was the chairman, and former president for twenty-four years, of the affiliated Austin State Bank, a community bank formed in the Village of Austin in 1891. Charles Castle's son, Ward C. Castle, who had been the executive vice president of the National Bank of the Republic, also was made a vice president of the Dawes bank and remained an officer and director of the National Republic Bancorporation. Charles Castle owned 460 shares of the Dawes bank and his estate would be ordered to pay $46,000; Ward Castle, who owned only two shares, was ordered to pay $200 to its receiver. Decree, May 1, 1937, RFC v. Central Republic Trust Company, USDC/NDI; Examiner's Report of the Condition of the National Bank of the Republic, April 18, 1931, USOCC/NA; *Moody's Manual of Investments: Banks, 1931,* 1503–7; *1932,* 1181; *1933,* 2000; *Chicago Tribune,* July 2, 1932; *Chicago Evening Post,* June 6, 1931; Dunne, *Illinois,* 3:253–54.

13. "The Record of Central Republic Bank and Trust Company," Philip R. Clarke, April 16, 1936; Answer of City National Bank . . . McIlvaine v. City National Bank . . . June 21, 1937, PRCP/UI; *Reconstruction Finance Corporation v. Central Republic Trust Company* (1937), 274–76; see the advertisement of the National Republic Bancorporation and its affiliated banks in the *Chicago Tribune,* July 3, 1930; R. G. Thomas, "Concentration in Banking Control through Interlocking Directorates as Typified by Chicago Banks," *Journal of Business of the University of Chicago* 6, no. 1 (January 1933): 5; *Moody's Manual of Investments: Industrial Securities, 1935,* 2036; *1936,* 2537; *1937,* 2462.

14. "The Record of Central Republic Bank and Trust Company"; Memorandum of John T. Clyne, n.d.; Answer of City National Bank . . . McIlvaine v. City National Bank . . . June 21, 1937, PRCP/UI; *Chicago Tribune,* October 20, 1931.

15. Dawes had been interested in acquiring the Foreman chain of banks, which had more than $200 million in deposits at its peak in 1929. But the Dawes bank had already committed to more than it could digest with the acquisition of the National Bank of the Republic. "The Record of Central Republic Bank and Trust Company"; Memorandum of John T. Clyne, n.d., PRCP/UI; Records of the Examining Division, Comptroller of the Currency's Office, USOCC/WNRC; James, *The Growth of Chicago Banks,* 2:946–47, 996–1002, 1004–5, 1014; *Chicago Tribune,* June 7, 8, 1931.

16. Records of the Examining Division, Comptroller of the Currency's Office, USOCC/WNRC.

17. Ibid.; James, *The Growth of Chicago Banks*, 2:996–1006; *Chicago Evening Post*, June 6, 1931; Thomas, "Concentration in Banking Control through Interlocking Directorates as Typified by Chicago Banks," 5; *Chicago American*, September 6, 1934.

18. J. E. Otis to Charles G. Dawes, May 1, 1931, CGDP/NUL.

19. Minutes of a Meeting of the Board of Directors of the Reconstruction Finance Corporation, February 11, February 16, 1932, RFC/NA; Receiver's Petition No. 15, April 29, 1935; Receiver's Petition No. 141, May 15, 1934; Recapitulation for filed claims, United American Trust and Savings Bank, Closed June 14, 1932; Receiver's Petition, May 15, 1946, People of the State of Illinois Ex. Rel. Oscar Nelson as Auditor of Public Accounts of the State of Illinois v. United American Trust and Savings Bank; Receiver's Petition No. 27, October 30, 1935, People of the State of Illinois, Ex. Rel. Edward J. Barrett, etc. v. Central Republic Trust Company, CCCC.

20. Receiver's Petition No. 2, July 25, 1932; Receiver's Petition, May 15, 1946, People of the State of Illinois Ex Rel Oscar Nelson as Auditor of Public Accounts of the State of Illinois v. United American Trust and Savings Bank, CCCC.

21. Alfred P. Leyburn to Comptroller of the Currency, November 9, 1931; Examiner's Report of the Condition of National Bank of the Republic, April 18, 1931, USOCC/NA; Receiver's Petition No. 27, October 30, 1935, People of the State of Illinois Ex. Rel. Edward J. Barrett, etc. v. Central Republic Trust Company, CCCC; *New York Times*, January 27, 1933.

22. Bill for Dissolution, July 12, 1932; Release of Claim of RFC against Madison Square State Bank, Chicago, Illinois, January 25, 1939; Petition of Charles H. Albers, Receiver of Madison Square State Bank for Order Approving His Final Report . . . Public Account, n.d.; Arthur C. Lueder to Charles H. Albers, March 6, 1941; Statement of Liquidation, February 28, 1941, People of the State of Illinois, Ex. Rel. Oscar Nelson, as Auditor of Public Accounts of the State of Illinois v. Madison Square State Bank, SCCC; *Banking Law State of Illinois*; *Moody's Manual of Investments: Banks, 1931*, 1506; Stuart, *Twenty Incredible Years*, 119, 179, 213, 218, 226, 247, 370, 485–87, 505, 545.

23. "Bill of Complaint," November 21, 1934, People of the State of Illinois, Ex. Rel. Edward J. Barrett, Auditor of Public Accounts v. Central Republic Trust Company, CCCC; Recapitulation . . . Central Republic Company . . . and the estimated recovery values assigned to the same as of December 31, 1940, RFC/NA.

24. Examiner's Report of National Bank of the Republic, April 18, 1931, USOCC/WNRC.

25. Examiner's Report of National Bank of the Republic, April 18, 1931, USOCC/WNRC; *Moody's Manual of Investments: Banks, 1931*, 1507.

26. The National Bank of the Republic had also made a bad loan of $75,000 to the Albany Park National Bank and Trust Company; a $41,500 loan to Carl W. Zepp, one of its directors, which was criticized by federal bank examiners as an "old debt"

and "slow work-out"; a $40,000 loan to the First National Bank of Riverside; and a $27,103 loan to the National Bank of Commerce, among others. Examiner's Report of National Bank of the Republic, April 18, 1931; Alfred P. Leyburn to Comptroller of the Currency, June 16, 1931, USOCC/WNRC; Receiver's Petition No. 15, April 29, 1935, People of the State of Illinois, Ex. Rel. Edward J. Barrett, Auditor of Public Accounts v. Central Republic Trust Company, CCCC.

27. Examiner's Report of National Bank of the Republic, April 18, 1931, USOCC/WNRC.

28. R. B. Wood to J. W. Pole, July 8, 1931, USOCC/NA.

29. Ibid.

30. Examiner's Report of National Bank of the Republic, April 18, 1931; R. B. Wood to J. W. Pole, July 8, 1931; E. H. Gough to Wood, July 15, 1931, USOCC/WNRC.

31. Order, People of the State of Illinois . . . v. Central Republic Trust Company, RFC/NA; "Bill of Complaint," November 21, 1934; "Order Appointing Receiver," November 21, 1934, People of the State of Illinois . . . Edward J. Barrett, Auditor of Public Accounts of the State of Illinois v. Central Republic Trust Company; Receiver's Petition No. 113, January 31, 1939, People of the State of Illinois . . . v. Central Republic Trust Company, CCCC; *McIlvaine v. City National Bank*, PRCP/UI; *Moody's Manual of Investments: Banks, 1935*, 750; Dunne, *Illinois*, 4:312–13; Williamson, "What Is the Relative Value?"

32. *Chicago Tribune*, September 1, 9, December 31, 1931, January 1, 4, 5, 1932.

33. "Examiner's Report of the Condition of the National Bank of the Republic," April 18, 1931, USOCC/WNRC; *New York Times*, September 19, December 22, 1931; *Chicago Tribune*, September 1, 2, 9, 19, 30, October 2, 3, 27, 30, November 7, 17, December 15, 1931, May 13, 17, 21, 29, June 30, July 1, 7, 8, 9, 12, 13, 15, 28, 1932.

34. "Examiner's Report of the Condition of the National Bank of the Republic," April 18, 1931, USOCC/WNRC; *Who's Who in Chicago*, 298; *New York Times*, September 19, December 22, 1931; *Chicago Tribune*, September 1, 2, 9, 19, 30, October 2, 3, 27, 30, November 7, 17, December 15, 1931, May 13, 17, 21, 29, June 30, July 1, 7, 8, 9, 12, 13, 15, 28, 1932; Platt, *The Electric City*, 173–75; "City National Bank and Trust Company of Chicago Statement," December 31, 1932, ODYP/SLU.

35. Dunne, *Illinois*, 4:312–13; *Chicago Tribune*, February 23, September 16, 1932; Stuart, *Twenty Incredible Years*, 46.

36. *Chicago Tribune*, May 15, June 18, 22, 1932; McDonald, *Insull*, 307, 312; Insull, *Memoirs of Samuel Insull*, 232–33.

37. *Chicago Tribune*, June 20, 1932, November 21, 1934; Decree of Judge James H. Wilkerson, May 1, 1937, RFC v. Central Republic Trust Company, et al., Equity No. 14189, USDC/NDI; Stuart, *Twenty Incredible Years*, 135, 356, 362, 373, 376, 466, 488, 500, 501, 544; Complaint, RFC v. Central Republic Trust Company, et al., In Equity No. 34-C-24606, CCCC; McDonald, *Insull*, 308–12; Busch, *Guilty or Not Guilty?* 131; Williamson, "What Is the Relative Value?"

38. *Chicago Tribune*, June 20, 1932.

39. Ibid., June 21, 1932; Examiner's Report of Bowmanville National Bank of Chicago, September 22, 1931, USOCC/WNRC. The receivership records of Reliance Bank in the Cook County Courthouse contain a wealth of information about the insider abuse at the bank. The records of Bowmanville National Bank were preserved by the comptroller of the currency's office in Washington and are now public after being sealed for more than six decades.

40. The RFC's board approved the first loan of $290,000 to the Bowmanville National Bank of Chicago on April 7, 1932. Examiner's Report of Bowmanville National Bank of Chicago, September 22, 1931, USOCC/WNRC; Minutes of a Meeting of the Board of Directors of the RFC, April 7, 1932, RFC/NA.

41. Emphasis in original. Examiner's Report of Bowmanville National Bank of Chicago, September 22, 1932, USOCC/WNRC.

42. J. L. Proctor to Board of Directors, Bowmanville National Bank of Chicago, April 10, August 30, 1930; Deputy Comptroller to Cashier, June 12, 1930, USOCC/WNRC.

43. J. L. Proctor to Board of Directors, Bowmanville National Bank of Chicago, October 27, 1931, Examiner's Report of Bowmanville National Bank of Chicago, September 22, 1931, USOCC/WNRC.

44. J. L. Proctor to Board of Directors, Bowmanville National Bank of Chicago, October 27, 1931; Examiner's Report of Bowmanville National Bank of Chicago, September 22, 1931; Proctor to File of Bowmanville National Bank of Chicago, n.d., USOCC/WNRC.

45. J. L. Proctor to A. P. Leyburn, April 6, 1932; Leyburn to Comptroller of the Currency, April 11, July 15, 1932, USOCC/WNRC.

46. *Chicago Tribune*, June 22, 1932; Thomas, "Concentration in Banking Control through Interlocking Directorates as Typified by Chicago Banks," 5, 6, 11; Esbitt, "Bank Portfolios and Bank Failures during the Great Depression: Chicago," 456.

47. Receiver's Petition No. 27, October 30, 1935, People of the State of Illinois, Ex. Rel. Edward J. Barrett, etc. v. Central Republic Trust Company, CCCC. The Phillip State Bank and Trust Company became the successor bank to Phillip State Bank in 1922 and assumed the deposits of the Illinois State Bank of Evanston in 1931. James, *The Growth of Chicago Banks*, 2:1347.

48. Peoples National Bank and Trust Company of Chicago was the successor bank to Peoples Stock Yards State Bank in 1929. Records of the Examining Division, Comptroller of the Currency's Office, USOCC/WNRC; Auditor of Public Accounts Trust Department . . . United American Trust and Savings Bank . . . December 31, 1931; Official Publication . . . United American Trust and Savings Bank . . . December 31, 1931, IAPA/ISA; James, *The Growth of Chicago Banks*, 2:1002–4, 1330, 1332, 1345, 1378; *Chicago American*, September 11, 1934.

49. Minutes of Meetings of the Board of Directors of the RFC, March 10, 12, 25, 1932, RFC/NA; Henry M. Dawes to Charles G. Dawes, August 26, 1931, CGDP/NUL; Philip R. Clarke to Edward N. Hurley, October 10, 1932, PRCP/UI; McDonald, *Insull*, 231–32, 275.

50. Minutes of a Meeting of the Board of Directors of the RFC, March 10, 12, 25, 1932, RFC/NA.

51. Minutes of a Meeting of the Board of Directors of the RFC, April 1, 1932, RFC/NA; Alfred P. Leyburn to Comptroller of the Currency, June 16, November 9, 1931, Records of the Examining Division, Comptroller of the Currency's Office, USOCC/WNRC; Bill of Complaint, February 27, 1933, People of the State of Illinois . . . v. Cosmopolitan State Bank, CCCC; *Chicago American*, September 1, 4, 11, 12, 14, 1934.

52. A. P. Leyburn to Comptroller of the Currency, November 2, 4, 1931, USOCC/WNRC.

53. A. P. Leyburn to Comptroller of the Currency, November 4, 1931, USOCC/WNRC.

54. The following twelve national banks in Chicago and Cook County, which received secret loans from the RFC, closed during the last two-and-a-half weeks of June 1932: Standard National Bank, Peoples National Bank and Trust Company, Alliance National Bank, Bowmanville National Bank, Hyde Park Kenwood National Bank, Jefferson Park National Bank, Jackson Park National Bank, National Bank of Woodlawn, Midland National Bank, First National Bank and Trust of Chicago Heights, First American National Bank and Trust of Berwyn, and First National Bank of Wilmette. Only three of the fifteen failed national banks did not receive loans from the RFC: Ravenswood National Bank, South Ashland National Bank, and First National Bank of Riverside. The following twenty-three state banks also received secret loans from the RFC and then failed in June: Adams State Bank, Citizens State Bank, United American Trust and Savings Bank, Empire Trust and Savings Bank, Devon Trust and Savings Bank, Prudential State Savings Bank, Commonwealth Trust and Savings Bank, Kenwood State Bank of Chicago, First Englewood State Bank, South Shore State Bank, Woodlawn Trust and Savings Bank, Cottage Grove State Bank, Reliance Bank and Trust Company, Universal State Bank, West Irving State Bank, Central Manufacturing District Bank, North Avenue State Bank, Chicago Bank of Commerce, Congress Trust and Savings Bank, Phillip State Bank and Trust Company, Logan Square State and Saving Bank, Madison Square State Bank, Pinkert State Bank of Cicero, Northbrook State Bank, and Division State Bank. The Kaspar American State Bank of Chicago, Chatfield Trust and Saving Bank, Old Dearborn State Bank, and South Shore State Bank were the only four state banks that failed in June that did not receive assistance from the RFC. "Loans Authorized from February 2, 1932 to July 20, 1932 . . . , Illinois," RFC/NA; Examiner's Report of Peoples National Bank and Trust Company of Chicago, October 19, 1931, USOCC/WNRC; Minutes of a Meeting of the Board of Directors of the RFC, March 23, 1932; "List of Reconstruction Finance Corporation Loans," CGDP/NUL; Charles W. Calomiris and Joseph R. Mason, "Contagion and Bank Failures during the Great Depression: The June 1932 Chicago Banking Panic," *American Economic Review* 87, no. 5 (December 1997): 863–83.

55. Olson, *Hoover and the Reconstruction Finance Corporation*, 59, 60; Calomiris and Mason, "Contagion and Bank Failures during the Great Depression,"

867–68; Jesse H. Jones, *Fifty Billion Dollars*, 176–78; Burner, *Herbert Hoover*, 275; Gottfried, *Boss Cermak of Chicago*, 257–58; *Chicago Tribune*, June 23, 26, 1932; Schlesinger, *The Crisis of the Old Order*, 250.

56. *Chicago Tribune*, June 23, 1932.

57. Victor Watson to Lawrence Richey, June 21, 1932 (telegram); Richey to Watson, June 23, 1932; "Copy" of Memorandum, June 21, 1932; James Joseph Burke to Herbert Hoover, June 20, 1932 (telegram); C. H. Hanson to Herbert Hoover, June 20, 1932; White House Memorandum from M. H. H., June 21, 1932, HHP/HHPL; *Chicago Tribune*, June 9, 20, 21, 22, 23, 24, 1932; for a good discussion about the rise and political clout of Anton Cermak, see "Anton J. Cermak: The Man and his Machine," in *The Mayors: The Chicago Political Tradition*, ed., Paul M. Green and Melvin G. Holli (Carbondale: Southern Illinois University Press, 1987), 99–110.

58. *Chicago Tribune*, June 23, 1932; James, *The Growth of Chicago Banks*, 2:1031.

59. Examiner's Report of Jefferson Park National Bank of Chicago, April 9, 1931, USOCC/WNRC; Various Comparative Data, Recovery Value of Collateral, December 31, 1939 as compared to December 31, 1940, RFC/NA.

60. R. D. Andrews to Comptroller of the Currency, December 22, 1931, Jefferson Park National Bank Records; Examiner's Report of Jefferson Park National Bank of Chicago, April 9, 1931, USOCC/WNRC; "List of Reconstruction Finance Corporation Loans," CGDP/NUL.

61. Examiner's Report of Jefferson Park National Bank of Chicago, April 9, 1931, USOCC/WNRC.

62. Ibid.

63. Board of Directors to Comptroller of the Currency, April 21, 1932; J. L. Proctor to Board of Directors, January 11, 1932; A. P. Leyburn to Comptroller of the Comptroller, January 7, 1932, USOCC/WNRC.

64. *Chicago Tribune*, June 24, 1932.

65. Ibid.; "*RECAPITULATION*: Assets Pledged to secure loans of Central Republic Trust Company, Chicago, Illinois and the estimated recovery values assigned to the same as of December 31, 1940," RFC/NA.

66. *Moody's Manual of Investments: Banks, 1931*, 417; *Chicago Tribune*, June 25, 1932; "Expense of Examiner While in Closed Bank," September 14, 1932; A. P. Leyburn to Comptroller of the Currency, July 19, 1932; Deputy Comptroller J. L. Proctor to Board of Directors, May 14, 1932; Board of Directors to Comptroller of the Currency, June 20, 1932, all in Midland National Bank Records, USOCC/NA.

67. Examiner's Report of Midland National Bank, April 27, 1932, USOCC/WNRC.

68. *Chicago Tribune*, June 25, 1932; Examiner's Reports of Midland National Bank, October 13, 1931, April 27, 1932, USOCC/WNRC.

69. Examiner's Report of Midland National Bank, April 27, 1932; J. L. Proctor to Board of Directors, November 21, 1931, May 14, 1932, USOCC/WNRC.

70. Examiner's Report of Midland National Bank, April 27, 1932; Deputy Comptroller J. L. Proctor to Board of Directors, May 14, 1932, USOCC/WNRC.

71. Examiner's Reports of Midland National Bank, April 22, 1931, October 13, 1931, April 27, 1932, USOCC/WNRC.

72. Examiner's Reports of Midland National Bank, February 1, July 23, 1930, April 22, October 13, 1931, April 27, 1932, USOCC/WNRC.

73. *Chicago Tribune*, June 25, 1932.

74. Ibid.

75. Memorandum of Eugene Meyer, June 27, 1932, EMP/LC; Hoover, *Memoirs*, 169–71; "Dawes' Reply for Court-draft," CGDP/NUL; Joslin, *Hoover off the Record*, 230–31, 248–53.

Chapter 5

Dawes Plays His Hand

"You ought to think about the country as well as yourself."

—Eugene Meyer to Charles Dawes on June 26, 1932[1]

When Charles Dawes abruptly resigned from the Reconstruction Finance Corporation in the middle of June 1932, on the eve of the Republican convention in Chicago, he made it sound as though the Depression was coming to an end: "Now that the balancing of the national budget by Congress is assured, the turning point toward eventual prosperity in this country seems to have been reached." As he left Washington, however, his own bank was on the verge of collapse. And he later described what he found upon his arrival in Chicago: "Depositors seeking to withdraw their money from Chicago banks filled the streets around them to such an extent that reserves of police, mounted and on foot, were required to control the crowds. The banking situation in Chicago was unprecedented in its history."[2]

Like the other major banks of Chicago, the Dawes bank had lost significant deposits during the previous year. After the merger with the National Bank of the Republic on July 25, 1931, the bank's deposits had stood at $240,746,647. In less than a year, by the end of May 1932, they had dropped nearly $100,000,000, to $147,688,097, losing an average of about $9.3 million a month. But during the first three weeks of June 1932, the Dawes bank lost more than twice that, with slightly over $20 million leaving its vault. By the end of the third week of June, depositors were panicking and deposits fell to $127,686,092. In the six days from Monday, June 20, through Saturday, June 25, $13,552,230 was withdrawn. On that Saturday, depositors crowded into the lobby, taking out a total of $4,618,523 on that one day.[3]

As he watched at close range the evaporation of his family's fortune, Dawes pulled as many strings as he could muster to pressure Hoover and his administration to save his bank. Facing a liquidity crisis, on Friday, June 24, he applied to his former agency for a $16 million loan, an amount worth about $251 million today. The assumption was that the loan, which would represent 114 percent of the bank's capital even before writing off any of the Insull loans or sour real estate loans, was of sufficient size to allow his bank to withstand the panic. According to the RFC's lending policy that was established when Dawes was its president, the loan would have to be repaid in full, including interest on an annual basis of 5.5 percent, six months from the date of its issuance. Thus the Dawes bank would be committed to turning over $16,440,000 to the RFC in December 1932.

But since at this point the bank's liabilities exceeded its assets, it could not have repaid or even serviced a $16 million loan. To avoid liquidating the bank when the balloon payment was due, the RFC would have had to extend the loan, thus making the annual interest payments alone $880,000. These interest payments, without any repayment of principal, would have added an intolerable overhead burden to the bank, which was already suffering from severe negative cash flow. In other words, the $16 million loan made no financial sense on any level.[4]

In deference to their former president, the directors of the RFC did not require Dawes to follow any of the normal loan application procedures and guidelines established to ensure that loans were properly made and adequately secured. The loan was in such obvious conflict with normal RFC standards that Dawes did not even bother to fill out a loan application. Nevertheless, the loan was approved just one day after Dawes asked his colleagues to replenish his bank's treasury.

Just two days later, on Sunday, June 26, instead of drawing on the $16 million loan commitment he had just received, Dawes threatened instead to liquidate his bank unless the RFC bailed out *all* of his depositors. He told his colleagues at the RFC that this would require a sum of $95 million, an amount worth nearly $1.5 billion today; nothing less was acceptable. Of that amount, the major Loop banks would have to loan $5 million to his bank. His audacity and the magnitude of his demands were remarkable.

As a comparison, A. P. Giannini's Bank of America and its affiliated Bank of Italy Mortgage Company had received loans of $94.9 million from the RFC, an amount similar to that given the Dawes bank. But Giannini's bank had deposits of $710.9 million and a purported net worth exceeding $100 million as of June 30, 1932, while the Dawes bank had $112.3 million in deposits and a supposed net worth of $24 million on that date. Nonetheless, Giannini's bank was forced to seek the RFC bailout because it held $120.5 million in nonperforming loans and other problem or worthless assets. When Dawes was president of the RFC, he and Jones had led the effort to make what was also a questionable bailout of Giannini's bank.[5]

Dawes's bailout demand was nearly six times the bank's $16 million loan request that the RFC's directors had approved only one day earlier. Fully aware of the strength of the cards he held, Dawes refused to negotiate the terms of the loan package: either the bank would receive the entire $95 million or he would close its doors. At that point, presumably, the pretense would end and no amount of cajolery would be capable of stopping the resulting panic that would surely engulf the banks of Chicago and perhaps then spread throughout the nation's banking system.

Reflecting on that "dramatic-in-the-extreme" Sunday, Jesse Jones, the Democratic director of the RFC who shepherded the bailout, described Dawes as "the coolest man in the room." Why the loan package had increased so much overnight and to such a specific amount would not become apparent for another two-and-a-half weeks, when Dawes would finally reveal to the RFC a reorganization plan involving the liquidation of the old Dawes bank and the formation of a new Dawes bank.[6]

Charles Dawes was in control of the situation that weekend because he had the votes on the RFC board. Harvey Couch of Arkansas, one of the three Democratic RFC directors, was a solid vote that Dawes could count on. As Winston P. Wilson, one of Couch's sympathetic biographers, wrote, "The close relationship between Couch and Dawes on the RFC developed into one of the finest friendships in the country." Relying on Couch's unpublished memoirs, Wilson quoted Couch's recollections about the granting of the Dawes loans: "Friday I contacted the General, Mel Traylor, and others out there to see if the situation was under control, as I wanted to attend the [Democratic] convention. I recall that General Dawes said: 'You are needed more in Washington than you are out here. You had better stay there.'" Dutifully, Couch followed Dawes's instruction and remained in Washington that fateful weekend. Couch said he stayed in contact with Dawes throughout the weekend, relaying messages between Dawes, Hoover, the RFC's staff and other directors. (Couch and Paul Bestor were the only two RFC directors in town that Sunday.)[7]

A skilled diplomat who was also an opportunistic entrepreneur with a flair for the dramatic, Dawes executed the ceremonial part of his plan at noon on June 26, 1932. He assembled at his bank more than thirty of the most prominent bankers and businessmen of Chicago. Sitting at the head of the same table at which forty-one loans totaling $11,157,069 had been approved for Insull's entities, Dawes was in firm control. Beginning the tense meeting with the high drama typical of his reparation meetings in Paris or armament conferences in Geneva, the former ambassador flatly announced that his bank would not open its doors on Monday morning. He explained that the "smart" depositors had been withdrawing more than $2 million a day, and it was time to take action. Otherwise, the deposits of the "friendly, trusting" (and uninformed) customers would be frozen while the bank was liquidated.[8]

Jesse Jones, who admitted that history would record that he was "the fall guy" in the sordid affair, later said that, on Sunday, June 26, Melvin Traylor had summoned him to this meeting from the hotel room where he was staying during the Democratic convention then being held in Chicago. Traylor's first order of business that day became bailing out the Dawes bank in order to save his own Insull-plagued bank. It was just the previous day that Traylor, in an effort to calm angry depositors, had perched himself on the base of one of the marble pillars in his ornate lobby to assure his anxious customers that their savings were safe at the seventy-year-old institution. In addition to the problematic Insull loans and other nonperforming insider loans, Traylor's bank also had on its books a troubled loan of $936,984 to the Dawes bank, which bank examiners had recently criticized.[9]

During a week of power politics, Jones and Traylor proved once again that when big money is involved, there is no distinction between political parties. Jones, still considered a possible Democratic vice presidential candidate, was supposedly an independent director of the RFC representing the Hoover administration. Traylor was also a dark horse Democratic presidential or vice presidential candidate. Yet one day they were maneuvering on the floor of the Democratic convention to nominate a ticket that could beat Hoover, and the next day they were working with Hoover to save the bank of Dawes, a Republican titan.[10]

Mayor Anton Cermak of Chicago, a participant in Insull's syndicate of insiders who was later killed by a bullet aimed at the newly elected president, Franklin Roosevelt, was promoting Traylor as a conservative alternative to Roosevelt, while Speaker of the House John Nance Garner was suggesting that Traylor would be the best running mate with Roosevelt. A collapse of the Chicago banks, which would include Traylor's First National Bank, on Monday, June 27, the first day of the Democratic convention, would certainly eliminate Traylor's chance to be on the ticket. But, more important, a banking panic in America's heartland would also destroy Hoover's chances of being reelected.

After quelling the panic at his bank on the Saturday before the start of the convention, Traylor realized that reassuring speeches would no longer mollify his frantic depositors. Next time, he would have to lock the doors. Desperate times seemed to require desperate measures, and Traylor was prepared to take whatever action was necessary to save his bank, his career, and his fortune.[11]

Eugene Meyer, the chairman of the RFC who was serving simultaneously as the head of the Federal Reserve Board, was offended but not surprised with the way Dawes handled the situation. When the RFC was being organized, Meyer had opposed the appointment of Dawes as its president, in part because he did not think Dawes was a prudent banker. "I hadn't seen anything in Mr. Dawes' record [he said in the early 1950s] to make me think he was a very good banker."[12]

Meyer, who was "a most able man with long experience" according to Hoover, chaired the meeting of the RFC board that approved the original $16 million loan request from the Dawes bank on Saturday, June 25, 1932. Meyer then left Washington on a noon train headed for Mount Kisco in Westchester County, thirty-eight miles north of New York City, where Seven Springs Farm, his weekend retreat, was located. After Meyer had arrived at his farm, Governor James B. McDougal of the Federal Reserve Bank of Chicago called to assure him that "the situation in Chicago had quieted considerably."[13]

Around 12:30 p.m. on Sunday, June 26, Meyer received a telephone message to call Howard P. Preston, manager of the Chicago RFC loan agency, "as soon as possible." Preston told Meyer that "General Dawes, whose bank had indicated it would apply for $40,000,000, of which $16,000,000 was authorized Saturday morning, was going to close his bank unless he could get assurance of loans from the Reconstruction Finance Corporation in sufficient amounts to pay off all his deposits in full." On the next day, Meyer prepared a memorandum memorializing his conversations and the events. In it he said that he was "very much disturbed and immediately talked to Dawes about the situation." He recalled that Dawes maintained that "the disturbance that existed and the seepage that was going on in his commercial accounts would make it necessary for his bank to borrow large amounts and show the borrowings on its statement; that, in such circumstances, the bank inevitably would close, and that, therefore, in justice to all the depositors, he could not afford to do anything except close the bank." Meyer observed, "I got the impression that he was looking out for General Dawes as well as for the depositors, and that his notifying me on a Sunday morning that he was going to close the bank the next morning, was unfair and improper and not in the interest of his bank or of the community."[14]

After talking to Dawes by telephone, Meyer had lunch at Seven Springs with George Harrison and W. Randolph Burgess, respectively the governor and deputy governor of the Federal Reserve Bank of New York, to discuss "the Chicago situation and its possible repercussions in other districts and the banking situation in general." Meyer and Harrison then talked by telephone with Secretary of the Treasury Ogden Mills, Owen Young, Melvin Traylor, and several others before Meyer, Harrison, and Burgess returned to New York for a Sunday afternoon meeting at the Federal Reserve Bank. Meyer had invited Mills to attend the meeting, and Harrison had invited Thomas W. Lamont of Morgan and Company to join them, in an effort to entice other New York banks to participate "in anything that might be done." Lamont in turn brought S. Parker Gilbert, his partner who had been responsible for implementing the Dawes Plan, along with Owen Young. Gilbert had developed a close friendship with Dawes when he had worked with him and Young during the German reparations crisis.[15]

Owen Young, whose company, GE, had significant funds on deposit at the Dawes bank, was in Van Hornesville, New York, but he was on the telephone orchestrating events behind the scenes on behalf of Dawes, with whom he was also in constant communication. Young supported Dawes's determination to force a decision that night. As he told Harrison, "we would know as much tonight as we would within 24 hours." Young worked in concert with Jones, Traylor, and Reynolds to bring Harrison around, along with Meyer.

Harrison had been stressing the problems that the RFC staff was "having in finding 'adequate security'" to justify a $90 million loan and the need for a twenty-four-hour delay, and Meyer was also questioning Dawes's motives. Nonetheless, the RFC proposed to Dawes that Sunday that his bank accept a $50 million loan, which would have been much more than enough to meet depositors' demands. In refusing the RFC's overly generous proposal and threatening to close his bank, Dawes himself had created the real crisis that weekend.[16]

Melvin Traylor was also lobbying the decision makers by telephone. The involvement of Traylor, the vice chairman of the RFC's Advisory Committee for the Chicago district and the vice president of the Federal Advisory Council of the Federal Reserve Board, was critical. The RFC's examiners in Chicago had "reported that their examination of the assets of the Central Republic Bank appeared to show that on the basis of present values the capital of the bank [would be] wiped out with some additional loss." But Traylor and George Reynolds, the head of the troubled Continental Illinois Bank, which was in the same bad shape as Traylor's bank, took issue with the RFC's professional staff. They argued that the Dawes bank was solvent and would be able to repay the loan over a number of years. Supporting them were, not surprisingly, the vice president of Traylor's First National Bank, Edward Brown, the president of Reynolds's Continental Illinois Bank, James R.

Leavell, and the vice president of Reynolds's bank, Abner Stilwell, who would stay particularly close to Samuel Insull Jr. throughout the next three decades. When the New York banks refused to participate in the bailout, after Dawes held firm on his arbitrary deadline to close his bank, it was Traylor and Reynolds who had to agree to make additional loans from their banks to the Dawes bank to pay all of the Dawes depositors.[17]

Meanwhile, from Chicago, Traylor and Jones both called Hoover at his Rapidan River camp to recommend the Dawes bailout. Traylor told Hoover that the Dawes bank was "the focal danger point" of the entire crisis. He asked the president for "substantial" assistance from the RFC, adding: "If we do not get such support by Monday every Chicago bank, ours among them, of course, will have to close its doors."

Throughout the day and night of that Sunday—June 26—and into the early morning hours of Monday, according to Randolph Burgess, the deputy governor of the Federal Reserve Bank of New York, "the main question was whether full and adequate security could be found to justify a loan sufficient to put the bank in a position to meet all deposit liabilities." The RFC was relying on Jones, McCarthy (the other RFC director in Chicago attending the Democratic convention), Traylor, and Reynolds to determine if the collateral was sufficient to repay the loan according to a reasonable amortization schedule. But Dawes's actions in the very near future would prove that he had no intention of repaying the loan as an obligation of a going concern. Instead, he clearly intended to liquidate his bank, telling Harrison by telephone around 8:00 on Sunday night that "total deposits less secured deposits are about $107 million and that therefore the total commitment would have to be for $108 million, which would take care of expenses of liquidation as well as depositors." Dawes then added that "certain excess collateral" at the Federal Reserve Bank of Chicago, which would have to be released, plus other cash assets of the bank, would enable a $90 million loan to be a sufficient amount "to do the trick."

During these conversations, Harrison was taking copious handwritten notes, from which he dictated a confidential memorandum to his secretary on July 6, 1932. When Harrison asked Dawes what action he was going to take if he received the full RFC loan commitment, Dawes responded in plain language that "it would be his purpose early in the morning to make an announcement that owing to the inability of the bank to carry on as a going concern the bank will liquidate its deposits and thus invite the depositors to come in and take their money." Dawes's stated intent clearly violated federal law. Therefore, much of the rest of that evening was dedicated to structuring the transaction to at least make it appear that the loan complied with the law.

However, despite this restructuring, Dawes did exactly what he had said he was going to do, in violation of the letter and spirit of the RFC act: he liquidated his bank.[18]

After talking with Traylor and Jones, Hoover immediately went into action. He ordered the federal examiner in charge to "rush a report" to Jones and McCarthy. Neither Jones nor McCarthy had supervisory authority over the RFC's loans being made to banks. Jones, who was prohibited from voting on the loan or participating in the decision-making process because his Houston bank had deposits in the Dawes bank, supervised the RFC's railroad loans, along with Couch. And McCarthy, along with Paul Bestor, supervised the agency's agricultural credits.[19]

Any reputable loan committee of any financial institution would have summarily denied the Dawes demand. But the RFC did not operate like a loan committee in the private sector. And this was an election year. As has been noted, Hoover would face certain defeat if the Chicago panic spread throughout the nation. Jesse Jones conceded in *Fifty Billion Dollars: My Thirteen Years with the RFC (1932–1945)* that it was impossible to "examine a large bank in a few hours," since that would be insufficient time for examiners to determine the value of the assets of the bank, as the law required. Nonetheless, he asserted that after just "skimming the bank's condition with several Chicago financiers and the RFC staff," he was able to determine that the huge loan was supported by its assets (despite its millions of dollars of nonperforming paper, including the Insull loans). So the loan was applied for and approved in less than a day.[20]

After making his hasty "horseback appraisal" of the Central Republic Bank, Jones told Hoover that he would recommend the extraordinary loan, despite Jones's after-the-fact abstention from voting on it because of his conflict of interest. On Tuesday, June 28, a day after the RFC board approved the Dawes bailout, Jones wired George R. Cooksey, who was secretary to the RFC board: "Our bank at Houston has had a small account with the Central Republic and therefore I do not wish to be recorded as voting on any loan to it."

The same federal law that prohibited Jones from voting on the Dawes loans also specifically prohibited him from participating in the deliberation: "No director . . . of the [RFC] shall in any manner, directly or indirectly, participate in the deliberation upon or the determination of any question affecting his personal interests, or the interests of any corporation . . . in which he is directly or indirectly interested." But when Jones was blowing his own horn in his memoirs, he confirmed: "I told the President that I was willing to take the responsibility of making the loan." Indeed, the official minutes of the RFC's board meeting on June 27, 1932, which approved the

Dawes bailout, read: "Secretary Mills reported to the meeting that Directors Jones and McCarthy, who . . . are on the ground, had said to him over the long distance telephone last night that they unequivocally recommended the loan."[21]

At the time, Jones took the firm position that a loan package of $95 million, 95 percent of which would come from the RFC, would be necessary to save the Dawes bank and prevent a banking panic in Chicago. So, after talking to Dawes by telephone, Hoover directed Jones to save it. Hoover then participated in conference calls between Chicago, Washington, and New York throughout the day. The president understood the repercussions of the RFC making loans of that magnitude to the bank of its own recently resigned president, who was also a former Republican vice president. He was relying on Jones and McCarthy, two Democratic directors, to provide the political cover to justify it. Criticism of the bailout would be embarrassing, but Hoover could reasonably expect that the details of the loan package would be kept secret until after the election because of his official policy that all of the RFC's bank loans were strictly confidential. No matter what, it was certainly preferable to the alternative of a national banking holiday.[22]

In New York City, the emergency meeting at the Federal Reserve Bank lasted throughout the afternoon and night into the early morning hours. Meyer's original memorandum describing the meeting read: "Traylor and Reynolds urged the approval of loans by the Reconstruction Finance Corporation in amounts *sufficient to pay all depositors so that the bank could go into liquidation*" (emphasis added). After being edited by hand, Meyer's memorandum read: "Traylor and Reynolds urged the approval of loans by the Reconstruction Finance Corporation in amounts *equal to the deposits of the bank*" (emphasis added). Meyer's original memorandum accurately reflected what happened that night. But had he left it in its original form, it would have been an admission that Dawes and the RFC directors had intentionally violated the law. Meyer's handwritten revisions acknowledged and addressed the legal sensitivity of the situation.[23]

Dawes's statement to Meyer on Sunday confirmed that under "the circumstances, the bank inevitably would close" when its large borrowings were made public. Dawes also expressed his intention to liquidate the bank to the RFC's senior staff assembled in Washington. They included Morton G. Bogue, general counsel of the RFC and a Republican from New York, who had worked with Meyer when he was special counsel to the War Finance Corporation; George Cooksey, the secretary of the board, who was formerly a director of the War Finance Corporation; and Lynn P. Talley, special counsel to the board.[24]

Lynn Talley had talked to Dawes from his room at the Carlton Hotel in Washington earlier in the day. A banker in Dallas and Houston and governor of the Federal Reserve Bank of Dallas, Talley was loyal to Jones, his close friend since 1910. Then later that day, Howard Preston, manager of the Chicago RFC office who had worked for Talley when he had been the chairman of the Bank of America in San Francisco, and RFC examiners—Milford and Buss—had begun reviewing the voluminous books and records of the Dawes bank. Early in the evening Dawes called Talley, the special counsel, in Washington to emphasize that "something would have to be done today." Trying to persuade Dawes to be reasonable, Talley reminded him about the resolution of the Tennessee banking crisis involving the East Tennessee National Bank. After the RFC had loaned $6 million to the Knoxville bank in February, the crisis had been abated. But Dawes was undeterred, insisting that the crisis in Chicago was different.[25]

While Dawes continued to demand a loan commitment, he also continued to make his intentions clear. A top staff member put it succinctly: "It was our understanding, gained from the conversation with General Dawes that the General, even if he succeeded in getting loans in sufficient amount to pay off all his depositors, would proceed to liquidate the bank." Talley, Cooksey, and Bogue of the RFC telephoned Meyer and "called his attention to this fact." Meyer immediately put Secretary Mills, an ex officio member of the board, on the telephone. The staff members repeated Dawes's intentions to him. As general counsel, Bogue advised Meyer and Mills that it would be illegal for the RFC to provide loans to the Dawes bank "in contemplation of liquidation." Meyer and Mills agreed that "the Corporation could not think of making loans on any such basis or understanding, and that if loans were made by the Corporation it would have to be definitely understood that the bank would continue in business as a going institution." Bogue kept advising all of the participants during several conversations throughout the long night that "the Corporation could not legally make any loan to a bank in Illinois if liquidation was contemplated."[26]

Meyer and Mills relayed Bogue's legal advice to Jones, who was totally involved, despite a federal law strictly prohibiting his involvement. Later, Jones called Bogue directly to discuss "the legal situation." Jones read to Bogue the following language drafted in Chicago to certify the Dawes loans: "From the information which we have received from the officers and directors of the bank and the confidence which we have in their representations, and from the report of the Clearing House examiner in November 1931, we believe the loan fully and adequately secured." Bogue was not impressed with the out-of-date examiner's report, telling Jones that "the proposed certificate had many qualifications and did not say a great deal." As he pointed out, the bank had not been examined for more than seven months, a volatile period during which it had lost tens of millions of dollars in deposits. Because of the rapid deterioration of its loan and securities portfolios, including the worthless loans and bonds of the insolvent Insull entities, it was not the same bank in June 1932 as it had been when the report was made.[27]

Jones immediately reported this turn of events to Dawes and McCarthy. They decided to telephone Washington to convince the senior staff that the bank did not contemplate liquidation. A short time later, McCarthy told Bogue that Dawes had said "emphatically that if loans were made in an amount equal to his deposits after offsets, the bank would continue in operation as a going concern; in other words, that the loans were not to be obtained in contemplation of liquidation." McCarthy also read Bogue the new language that had been drafted for members of the advisory committee to sign: "We believe from the information which we have received that the loan applied for by this bank of $95,000,000 will be fully and adequately secured." At that point, the loan application had not even been filed. McCarthy and Jones expressed no concerns about the condition of the collateral; they were concerned only about consummating the deal.[28]

Dawes must have been sitting right next to McCarthy during these conversations because when McCarthy finished his conversation with Bogue, he handed the telephone to Dawes. Sounding like the current president of the agency instead of a loan applicant, Dawes told Bogue: "We are making this loan in contemplation of paying off what deposits are demanded. I have told the New York people we are making the loan as a going institution for the purpose of taking care of current demands. That is our whole purpose. We will make no statement about it." A staff member wrote the next day that Dawes's comment about not making a "statement" related to the "impression which [the Washington staff] had gained in earlier conversations with Chicago that, if the necessary loans were made, the General would still proceed to liquidate the bank and announce that he had sufficient money to pay off all depositors."[29]

According to Meyer's handwritten notes, at 12:45 a.m., Jones took the lead and telephoned him to urge "the importance of making the loan and said that it was absolutely necessary in order to save the situation." In that early morning call, Jones informed Meyer that the Chicago bankers hoped the New York banks "would take a $10,000,000 participation." Jones also indicated that "the money would only be taken down as needed." In a follow-up to the Jones call at 1:00 a.m., McCarthy stressed to Meyer and Mills "the dangers of the situation, and the fixed determination of the General not to open unless he could get the assurance of $95,000,000." McCarthy repeated that Dawes had "emphatically" said that "the loans, if granted, would be for the purpose of keeping the bank open and not in contemplation of liquidation." Dawes then called Mills and Meyer to emphasize once again that he planned to keep the bank open if he received the $95 million. And once again, they reiterated that "the Corporation could not and would not make any loan if it was his intention to liquidate the bank."[30]

Dawes was lobbying hard to explain why he needed so much money. Philip Clarke, president of both the Central Republic Bank and the new Dawes bank, later confirmed that "the primary purpose and accomplishment of the RFC loan" was to meet the demands of all of the depositors. Certainly based on Dawes's statements throughout that fateful Sunday afternoon and evening, it's quite evident that he never intended to keep his old bank open.[31]

As the meetings stretched into the night, the participants friendly to Dawes made the following generous proposal: "Dawes should take a loan of, say, $40,000,000 to $50,000,000 for Monday, June 27, and then, as the Secretary of the Treasury [Mills] suggested, upon further consideration it might be possible for the Corporation to go as high as $70,000,000 if arrangements could be made on Monday for $10,000,000 from banks in New York and $10,000,000 from the banks in Chicago." But by then there was so much uncertainty about Dawes's intention to liquidate his bank and the condition of its assets that the New York banks refused to commit any funds at all, and the Chicago banks reduced their participation and exposure by 50 percent.[32]

Finally, Meyer told the staff in Washington that the $95 million rescue plan seemed to be necessary because "directors Jones and McCarthy, who were on the ground, unequivocally recommended that the loans be made." Jones's close friend, Talley, called Preston, the agency manager in Chicago, and discussed the situation with him. Preston still believed that "the New York banks would participate to the extent of $10,000,000, but no arrangements had been made to that effect." The New York banks had discussed providing loans totaling $10 million if Dawes received $40 to $50 million from the RFC and the Chicago banks and if they had "a day in which to consider the matter." Since Dawes refused to give the New York bankers that day, they prudently went home without making a commitment.

Faced with the ultimatum and fearing a panic, officials of the other four Chicago Loop banks agreed to lend the Dawes bank a total of $5 million, as Dawes continued to demand that the RFC increase its commitment to the full $90 million. Traylor's First National Bank loaned the Dawes bank $2,055,765, which when combined with its previous loan of $936,984 gave it a total exposure of nearly $3 million to the Dawes bank. (Traylor's loans to the Dawes bank would contribute greatly to the impairment of his bank's capital, necessitating its own bailout the following year.) Reynolds's Continental Illinois Bank loaned $2,189,645 to the Dawes bank.

(This imprudent credit would contribute to the necessity for the RFC bailout it too would need the following year.) The Northern Trust Company of Chicago loaned $403,520, and the Harris Trust and Savings Bank made a loan of $351,070.[33]

Dawes, as the controlling stockholder, called a special stockholders meeting of his bank for 1:00 a.m. on Monday. During the meeting he was elected a director, and then a special board of directors meeting was convened. The first order of business was to elect Dawes chairman of the board, after which he formally presented to his brothers and the other directors his plan to borrow $95 million from the RFC and participating Chicago banks. The board authorized the loan application, which was still incomplete, and agreed to pledge all of the bank's assets as security.[34]

Dawes submitted the loan application "between 2:30 and 4:00 o'clock on the morning of June 27, 1932" to Ralph Buss, the RFC examiner in Chicago who was reviewing the assets of the Central Republic Bank. At a 9:00 a.m. emergency board meeting in Washington, the RFC directors, without so much as reviewing the loan application, approved the $90 million loan. Buss later testified that "none of the usual routine" was followed. In fact, "there was no application submitted to the examiners in Washington before the $40,000,000 was advanced." The Reviewing Committee failed to make a report to the RFC's board before the application was approved and the money disbursed. Buss prepared a report "after the loan had been approved and after the advances had been made."[35]

According to the RFC's underwriting procedures, the Advisory Committee of the RFC's Chicago Loan Agency had to approve the loan and certify that it was "fully and adequately secured." The chairman of the Advisory Committee was George Reynolds, Dawes's good friend, who was also chairman of the executive committee of the Continental Illinois Bank. Their cozy relationship had been enhanced when Dawes bought stock in the Peoples Trust and Savings Bank of Chicago, which Reynolds and his son Earle, the bank's president, controlled.

After the loan application was completed, it was submitted to the RFC's Advisory Committee for the Chicago district during the early morning hours of June 27. But the process was delayed because Reynolds could not be located. Finally, after searching the bank, Jones found Reynolds "flat on his back, loudly, peacefully snoring" in one of the bank's closets. Reynolds was awakened, and the application was presented to him for approval. He and Traylor, who was vice chairman of the Advisory Committee, summarily approved the Dawes loans and certified in a statement that they would be "fully and adequately secured, the security to be of a face or book value of approximately $118,000,000 and including all the assets of the bank."[36]

Reynolds, formerly chairman of the National Credit Corporation and a past president of the American Bankers Association, had previously weathered banking panics in Chicago. He had been the spokesman for the city's banking community in 1914 when Lorimer's chain had crashed. Reynolds also had been active in Republican politics throughout his business career, and President Taft had offered him the cabinet post of Secretary of the Treasury, which he had turned down.[37]

When Mills and Meyer left New York on the 2:00 a.m. train for Washington, where they would attend the emergency board meeting of the RFC at 9:00 a.m. on Monday, June 27, the Dawes bank had not yet submitted a loan application. Without the benefit of a facsimile machine, there was no way that the directors could review the loan application and the list of collateral before or during the board meeting. So the Dawes demands precluded the board's exercise of due diligence and the discharge of its statutory fiduciary responsibilities. Beyond the question of the legal sufficiency of the collateral was the legal requirement that "no loan or advancement shall be made by the [RFC] for the purpose of initiating, setting on foot, or financing any enterprise not initiated, set on foot, or undertaken prior to the adoption of this Act [January 22, 1932]." Again, federal law clearly prohibited Dawes from using the loan proceeds for the purpose of financing a new bank, which is exactly what he would be proposing to do.[38]

To induce the directors to approve the loan, Dawes specifically guaranteed that the loan was for ongoing operations and not for liquidation purposes. The minutes of the Monday board meeting recorded only a few select events of Sunday evening: "General Dawes assured the members of the Board by telephone last night that the loan applied for is for current requirements, including the payment of deposits, in order to keep the bank open and not in contemplation of liquidation." The RFC directors attempted to insulate themselves from such a plain violation of the law. They made Dawes's promise a covenant of the loan agreement when they sent him the following telegram: "Relying upon your assurance already given that loan applied for is for current requirements and to keep bank open and not in contemplation of liquidation."[39]

Dawes obviously understood that without his promise to keep the bank open no loan could be authorized. So he did what it took, confirming his commitment and the loan covenant: "Your telegram received. Am glad to know that relying upon my assurance already given that loan applied for is for current requirements and to pay depositors in order to keep bank open and not in contemplation of liquidation." But within two weeks, he would propose a plan to liquidate the Central Republic Bank and to form a new bank. Philip Clarke would later explain that the reorganization plan was designed to eliminate the "possibility of stockholder liability suits [which] would be indefinitely deferred if not permanently removed." Opening a new national bank and taking the prime commercial loans and deposits of the Central Republic Bank with him, Dawes would leave depreciated assets and immense liabilities, including the $95 million worth of loans, in the Central Republic Bank, which became a bankrupt shell of a company.

The false statement that Dawes made to induce the RFC directors to issue the loan violated Section 16(a) of the RFC Act, which provided for criminal sanctions. Hoover's attorney general, William D. Mitchell, failed to pursue the individual complaints filed at the Department of Justice against Dawes for fraudulently obtaining the loan. No charges were brought against Dawes despite the fact that Section 16(a) had received prominence in "Circular No. 1 of the Reconstruction Finance Corporation," which was issued in February 1932, when Dawes was president of the agency. It read: "False statements and overvaluation of such security are subject to the penal provisions of the Act." The first circular of the newly constituted agency also quoted Section 16(a): "Whoever makes any statement knowing it to be false, or whoever willfully overvalues any security, for the purpose of obtaining for himself or for any applicant any loan . . . shall be punished by a fine of not more than $5,000 or by imprisonment for not more than two years, or both."[40]

When the RFC directors approved the bailout package, they violated federal law and their fiduciary obligations because they failed to complete the due diligence examination of the bank's assets. Federal law mandated that no loan could be approved without being fully secured, and the prudent man rule required that no loan could be approved without the directors knowing the quality of the bank's loan portfolio. In that portfolio the Insull loans violated a fundamental principle of the Illinois banking code prohibiting reckless loan concentrations. The Dawes bank's loans to the Insull group of entities represented gross mismanagement because they were issued to a single control group, exceeding by more than 300 percent the loans-to-one-borrower prohibition in the Illinois banking code.[41]

Even ignoring the bankrupt Insull companies and counting each of the forty-one Insull loans as fully performing assets, the $90 million RFC loan still constituted 346 percent of the net worth of the Dawes bank. Without writing the Insull loans or the numerous other nonperforming loans off its books, the Central Republic Bank and Trust Company had a net worth, on paper, of only $26 million, including capital of $14 million, and a fictitious surplus and undivided profits category of $12 million. Thus the RFC directors made a loan to their former president that was more than three times the inflated book value of the bank. Repayment of the principal amount of $90 million according to the terms of the loan was impossible, and the debt service burden crushed the bank.[42]

Any banker as clever as Dawes would know that the terms of the RFC loan guaranteed a speedy default. The loan was to mature in full "on or before" December 24, 1932, at which time the bank would be required to repay the entire $90 million and six months of interest, which carried an annual interest rate of 5.5 percent. The interest payment alone for the first six-month period of the RFC loan would have amounted to $2,475,000. Additionally, the interest payment required on the other $5 million loan from the participating Chicago banks would have been $137,500 for the first six months. Even if the RFC loan had been renewed every six months, the annual interest payment would have been $4,950,000, and the annual interest payment for the other part of the loan package would have been $275,000. Without any principal reduction, the weight of the debt service requirements would have forced the bank to close its doors.[43]

In short, the bank was bankrupt the moment it accepted the funds from the RFC and the Chicago banks. When the loans were approved, the Dawes bank had at least $100 million in deposits, most of which were earning 3 percent interest. Assuming that the bank was paying only 2 percent on its deposits, it would have to pay $2 million annually to its 120,000 depositors. So the bank was obligated to pay at least $7,225,000 to its secured and unsecured creditors before paying any of its overhead, which included the annual rent of about $1 million and salaries for a large staff.

Offsetting the bank's interest expenses and overhead was approximately $107 million of supposedly performing loans, which excluded the nonperforming Insull loans. But even if all of these remaining assets were fully performing, they would have yielded only 4 5/8 percent annually, for a total of $4,948,750. The mismatch of interest income to interest expense, combined with the bank's annual rent and other overhead expenses, created huge operating losses—a negative cash flow of hundreds of thousands of dollars a month. Without even considering the default of the RFC loan itself, the bank's negative cash flow alone would have assured its insolvency.[44]

Philip Clarke, the bank's former president, would later admit that the bank was hopelessly insolvent even before the RFC loans were funded. In 1937, an attorney representing stockholders of the old Dawes bank that were hostile to Clarke and Dawes alleged that the two had engaged in a conspiracy to defraud the other stockholders of the bank. Responding to the allegation, Clarke pointed out that the bank had suffered such a "tremendous decrease in earning assets that the bank for some time had been unable to avoid substantial operating losses." In fact, the expenses of the bank were "exceeding income by at least $2,000,000 annually . . . it had become an uneconomic unit and it was thoroughly obvious that proceeding as it was, a receivership was inevitable."[45]

At 8 a.m. on that Monday, June 27, just before the RFC board meeting in Washington, the Federal Reserve Bank of Chicago, acting on behalf of the RFC, advanced $10 million to the Central Republic Bank and Trust Company. Far from keeping the bailout a secret, Dawes issued the following statement to the press:

> The demands on the Central Republic Bank and Trust Company during the past week made necessary recourse to borrowing to meet them. These loans have been completed and place the bank in an impregnable cash position. The loans negotiated are for current requirements and to pay depositors and are not for the purpose of liquidation.[46]

Two days later the RFC advanced another $30 million to the Dawes bank. On that same day, June 29, Dawes requested an additional $30 million, which the Federal Reserve Bank disbursed. But the last disbursement of $30 million, which would have a relative value of about $471 million today, caused an overdraft at the Federal Reserve Bank of Chicago in the account of the United States Treasury. Consequently, the Central Republic Bank had to return the $30 million, leaving a loan balance of $40 million due to the RFC, as well as the $5 million that the Loop banks had already advanced. At that point, the RFC had still not received a completed application or a list of the collateral securing the loan.[47]

The last advance of $50 million—which had not been needed during the June panic—was not made until October 6, 1932, in exchange for a promissory note from the old Dawes bank, after Dawes had organized the new bank that became the recipient of the funds. By then the panic had long since subsided, so the loan could no longer be justified from a policy standpoint as a "curbing of disaster," as even Meyer later attempted to do.[48]

Writing in 1938, F. Cyril James, a respected professor of finance at the University of Pennsylvania, confirmed that the crisis had passed several months before the issuance of the final $50 million loan: "By the end of July, therefore, Chicago was filled with a sense of relief. For the moment, there were no serious threats of storms, and it was possible to survey the actual situation. . . . As a matter of fact, only ten banks failed in Cook County between July 1 and December 31, 1932."[49]

In the absence of a banking panic in Chicago in October, the $50 million advance represented a glaring example of favoritism, especially when compared to Hoover's attitude toward the appeals for relief from Governor Gifford Pinchot of Pennsylvania, whom Hoover later described as one of the "pseudo liberals." With Hoover's signature, the Emergency Relief and Construction Act became law on July 21, 1932, appropriating $300 million for direct loans to states provided that no state received more than 15 percent of the total amount. A few days before the emergency legislation became effective, Governor Pinchot applied for a $45 million loan from the RFC. Suggesting that Pennsylvania had not done enough for its unemployed citizens, the board members of the RFC unanimously rejected the state's application for federal relief—including Atlee Pomerene, the RFC's new chairman, who implied that Pinchot was engaged in pork barrel politics, and Jones, who would lecture Pinchot about patience.

Pinchot, a Republican who made his name as a conservationist when he was Theodore Roosevelt's chief of the Forest Service, then sent Hoover an urgent telegram:

> After two months of constant effort to get help for Pennsylvania's one million two hundred fifty thousand totally unemployed and their wives and children, the Reconstruction Finance Corporation still persists in its cruel, needless and unexplained refusal to advance what Pennsylvania has every right to ask and to get. The Reconstruction Finance Corporation shows either complete inability or complete unwillingness to realize the situation in Pennsylvania and the pitiful need for help. Tens of thousands of families are living on two dollars a week or less and the need for relief grows greater day by day.

Responding much differently than when he was working the telephones for Dawes and instructing the RFC's directors "to save the Dawes bank," Hoover lectured Pinchot about the law and the RFC's lending procedures:

> I feel that if you will study the law creating the Reconstruction Finance Corporation you will realize that it was set up as an independent agency by the Congress with specific directions in the law for its conduct by its Board of Directors, giving to them sole authority in determination of loans. I have no authority or right therefore to direct the Board to make specific loans or advances you request. The Board is a non-partisan body of eminent, patriotic and sympathetic men. They are engaged in unceasing investigation of every application. They are giving earnest and full consideration to information supplied to them and endeavoring to extend every aid to distress and proved need within their authority. I am sure you will find they will act fully in this spirit.

Pinchot was not impressed, so he sent another telegram to Hoover:

> Your answer to my appeal is a deep disappointment. The senseless arbitrary embargo which the Reconstruction Finance Corporation is enforcing against

the starving in Pennsylvania remains. I cannot concede that you are power-less to help. Whatever may be your legal authority over the Reconstruction Finance Corporation, its members are your appointees and would unques-tionably respect your wishes. You suggest that I study the law. I did so most carefully before making application and found in it no requirement whatever beyond the application and certification of need by the Governor, which I made two months ago. Your board has read into the law fine spun red tape which Congress never wrote into it and is using it to starve our unemployed. Red tape does not interest the hundreds of thousands of destitute families in Pennsylvania now on the verge of winter without resources and without hope. What they want is help. All the help private charity, the commonwealth, and the nation can give will still fall far below their bitter need. Our people are rightly indignant. . . . Through its harsh and needless delay the board is pun-ishing the poor. . . . A California project proposed since Pennsylvania made its appeal has received a loan of forty million dollars. For California red tape can be cut. Why not Pennsylvania? You yourself have given the guarantee that no one shall starve in this country. I ask you to make that guarantee good in Pennsylvania. I seek your friendly assistance in righting a great wrong to mil-lions of innocent people in direst need. What is theirs by every human right the Reconstruction Finance Corporation is withholding.

Pinchot then publicly complained to Pomerene that Hoover was far more concerned about the few who were rich than the many poor people of his state. Hoover may have considered Pinchot a liberal maverick, but he was still a prominent member of the Republican Party. The rejection of Mayor Cermak's appeal for emergency funds for the schoolteachers who were "sleeping on benches in Chicago," the Dawes bailout, the Bonus Army fiasco, and now the controversy over the denial of relief funds for Pennsyl-vania, all were sending the wrong signals in the middle of Hoover's reelec-tion campaign.[50]

Beyond the political ramifications, the last Dawes loan was another clear violation of law. Long after the defeat of Hoover, on March 28, 1935, Everett C. McKeage, a San Francisco lawyer, filed a formal complaint with Roosevelt's attorney general, Homer S. Cummings (the articulate former chairman of the Democratic National Committee from Stamford, Connecti-cut, where he served three terms as mayor), demanding the prosecution of Dawes under the criminal provisions of the RFC act. McKeage quoted the relevant section, which he correctly stated was "found in its penal sections, wherein any violations of the [RFC act] is denounced as a crime and appropri-ate penalties therefore are provided":

No loan or advance shall be approved under this section, or under the Recon-struction Finance Act, directly or indirectly, to any financial institution any officer or director of which is a member of the board of directors of the Reconstruction Finance Corporation, or has been such a member within twelve months preceding approval of the loan or advance.[51]

In response to the furor surrounding the Dawes loans, Congress included the provision as part of the Emergency Relief and Construction Act, which became law in July 1932 after the original authorization of the Dawes loans but well before the $50 million advance. McKeage asked: "Do not these provisions of the [RFC act] brand the acts in procuring and making the so-called Dawes loan a crime? Such a conclusion, seems to me to be inescapable." But prosecuting Dawes would also mean, at a minimum, the embarrassment of Jones, and no charges were brought.[52]

A FLAWED PROCESS

Herbert Hoover defended the Dawes loans on the campaign trail and in his memoirs, arguing that Melvin Traylor, along with Jesse Jones and the other Democratic RFC directors, had given their "unqualified" support for the bailout. But again Jones could not and did not actually vote to approve the Dawes loans because his bank in Houston had deposits at the Dawes bank, constituting a conflict of interest. The strong-willed Democrat, appointed to the RFC board as a gesture to Speaker John Nance Garner, had a secret reason for assisting Dawes and Traylor. As mentioned earlier, at the time of the Dawes loans, Jones had procured a $350,000 unsecured and undocumented loan from Traylor's First National Bank of Chicago. That unsecured loan would be worth today about $5.5 million—an extraordinary loan to a small company or an individual, even had his net worth on paper been substantial. But Jones was facing a personal liquidity crisis, and Traylor's bank did not bother to ask him to provide a financial statement.

Adding to the historical smokescreen, Hoover published his memoirs in 1952, during the height of Senator Joseph McCarthy's influence. In them, he still defended the bailout, blaming the panic and subsequent runs on the Dawes bank on a "systematic propaganda of alarm carried on by telephone." Hoover even went so far as to suggest that "some information uncovered later indicated that it was a communist operation." In fairness to Hoover, it should be noted that Philip Clarke, the president of both the old and new Dawes banks, also viewed the old Dawes bank's problems as caused by a "campaign of communistic activity." Under siege and finding himself in the middle of a storm of controversy and litigation in 1936, a defensive Clarke blamed much of the bank's difficulties on: "A campaign of communistic activity that was principally concentrated against Central Republic on the undoubted theory that the latter's statement showed a much heavier depletion than that sustained by any of the other downtown institutions and thus less strength to withstand continued attack. Hardly a day passed in January or February of 1932 that depositors did not come to the bank to advise that they had been anonymously telephoned to remove their deposits immediately from Central Republic as the bank would close within a week. A separate department was organized within the bank to collaborate with federal authorities in apprehending those responsible for these depredations and conclusive proof was soon obtained that the operation was that of a group of communists. It was ultimately rooted out and stopped but not before adding substantially to the bank's withdrawals." In blaming the communists, Clarke neglected to mention the worthless loans on the old bank's books or the loans to the other failed banks. Nor did he mention the concentration of Insull loans or the bad real estate loans and insider loans to the Dawes family and the bank's directors. In 1936, when Clarke was blaming the old bank's problems on a communist conspiracy, it still owed more than $47,265,061 to the RFC, an amount worth more than $732 million in today's money. Nevertheless, Clarke maintained that the real problem had been that "Central Republic became a helpless victim of the unreasoning hysteria of the times."[53]

During his campaign and in his memoirs, Hoover made a number of glaringly false statements. One such statement was that the Dawes bank was in good condition and "had ample securities which in normal times could have paid out their depositors leaving a large margin." Hoover also asserted falsely that "the assets had been valued by the examiners of the Reconstruction Corporation" before the loan was made. In fact, as we have seen, Hoover and his RFC had no way of knowing the condition of the Dawes bank when the bailout occurred because the examiners, contrary to law, regulation, and policy, had not completed their work or even made a report. More remarkable still was Hoover's statement that "the loans offered by the cooperating banks and the Reconstruction Corporation were never fully called for and have since been largely repaid, and every danger in connection with that episode is now over." But Dawes had drawn the last $50 million of his $90 million loan when his new bank opened during the first week of October, only a month prior to Hoover's speech. In his memoirs, Hoover also made the incorrect statement that "General Dawes had not owned any interest in [the Central Republic Bank and Trust Company of Chicago] since he became Vice President of the United States in 1924, but he felt a responsibility for it and believed that his prestige might pull it out of trouble." However, as we know, Dawes and his brothers had continued to own a controlling interest in their family bank while

Dawes was in Washington and London. Hoover also erroneously claimed that the collateral for the RFC loan was of such high quality that "the government could lose no money." But on December 31, 1937, five years after the Dawes bank had defaulted on the loan, the RFC projected that it would recover only 30 percent from the commercial loans of the Dawes bank that had been pledged as collateral. At that point in the liquidation process, the RFC was facing huge losses because the Dawes bank still owed $46,879,256, while the appraised recoverable value of all of the collateral securing the loan was only $17,881,987. Equally alarming for the RFC, the indebtedness had been reduced by a mere $385,805 during the entire previous year. And, by the end of 1938, the bank's total indebtedness had actually increased by $102,379 because of unpaid interest being added to principal. Between December 31, 1936 and December 31, 1943—a seven-year period—the indebtedness was reduced by only $2,941,143. At the end of 1943, the bank still owed $44,323,918 on a loan that had been due in full eleven years earlier. The relative value of the amount that was outstanding on the loan in today's dollars was $550 million.[54]

Spinning his web, Jones made a national speech on August 29, 1932, titled "Work of the Reconstruction Finance Corporation." It was carried on radio affiliates of the National Broadcasting Company. Jones sent a printed copy to Dawes, addressed to "General Dawes with affectionate regards." In the speech, which was made after the Dawes loans had been severely criticized, Jones argued the point that the RFC was "non-partisan" and stressed that its established procedures and standards for the processing of loans enabled it "to act with more dispatch in meeting emergency situations."[55]

He elaborated on those procedures and standards, explaining in detail that loan applications were first filed at the RFC's local branch office, then the branch manager reviewed them independently along with the local advisory committee, which was composed of bankers and businessmen. Only after the local manager and advisory committee conducted a "thorough examination" of the collateral that was to secure each loan was the application forwarded to Washington, along "with a full description of the collateral." Furthermore, even after passing the collateral test, the loan had to be verified as intended for a proper purpose that was in the public interest. In Washington, it was then "reexamined [independently] by a special examiner and a review committee," after which they would make separate recommendations to the board of directors.

Jones also emphasized that the RFC's legal department had to review and certify that the loans were "fully and adequately secured," that doing so was "a provision of the law and not one of policy adopted by the board." All these elaborate procedures were intended to allow the directors to be "able to act with a fair degree of intelligence, both as to the collateral offered and the public interest involved." Jones made the loan application process and the directors sound prudent and reasonable. However, as we have seen, the Dawes loans had in no way been handled according to the procedures he so meticulously outlined in his speech.[56]

After Hoover left office and the Dawes loans became ensnared in a federal lawsuit, Ralph Buss, a senior RFC examiner from Washington, testified that his examination of the Central Republic Bank had begun on Friday, June 24, 1932, when he was dispatched to Chicago to determine whether its condition and assets warranted a $16 million loan, representing 114 percent of the bank's capital. A few hours into the examination, it was stopped. Buss told the court, "The actual examination of the collateral was not attempted due to the lack of time." Nevertheless, the first loan application was approved the next day at a special Saturday RFC board meeting, a clear violation of the RFC's procedures and federal law. Indeed, the examination of the bank's assets was not finished until some time after July 7, 1932.[57]

Buss immediately called Charles Dawes when the examination was halted. Dawes assured Buss that the stockholders' liability, as a mandate of the Illinois banking code, would provide additional security for the loan since many of the bank's stockholders were in a position to pay their assessments if the bank failed. In backing up Dawes, Philip Clarke, president of the Central Republic Bank, told Buss that the stockholders' liability was worth between $7 and $8 million dollars, about "fifty cents on the dollar." This resorting to the stockholders' statutory assessments to secure a loan was extraordinary. Out of the two hundred banks that Buss had examined, he had reviewed the stockholders' liability only twice, both times in an effort to boost worthless and nonperforming assets.

But Buss was less than impartial; he was a willing participant. After returning to Washington, the young examiner wrote Dawes, the senior statesman, "to express my great admiration for your courage and wisdom in trying circumstances, as well as my gratification in having had the privilege of working with you."[58]

Buss also testified that he and his boss, W. R. Milford, who was chief of the RFC's examining division, "did not use the same general method employed by bank examiners who are making a bank examination." The records they examined were woefully inadequate because they "did not review each individual piece of collateral that appeared in the assets of the bank." They merely accepted the value of the assets as they appeared on the financial statements that the bank's officers had prepared. Simply put, the RFC failed to perform an independent evaluation of the bank's assets. The Illinois banking commissioner would later find, and the Circuit Court of Cook County would confirm, that the assets of the bank as stated in its financial statement were "erroneous and did not, and do not, correctly reflect the true value thereof; and that the value of certain items of resources did not, and do not, equal the amounts, respectively, for which said resources were carried on the books of said [bank]."[59]

Yet Milford was another that Dawes entranced. In an effusive letter, he wrote: "My recent visit to Chicago was both pleasing and interesting. The high regard I have always entertained for you was strengthened beyond any human power to disturb by the fine attitude you maintained throughout the recent negotiations." He concluded: "The many kindnesses extended to me and my associates during our stay in Chicago are greatly appreciated. If at any time I can be of service to you, please do not hesitate to command." So Milford could hardly be viewed as an impartial examiner of the Dawes bank, either.[60]

If Buss and Milford had properly examined the Dawes bank before the RFC loans were approved, they would have discovered that its bad investments were not limited to loans to Insull's entities or to the Dawes family and other insiders. For example, the involvement of Dawes in the reconstruction of Germany and Europe had led to his bank making investments that proved to be imprudent in the external loans of Germany and other European paper. Dawes and Owen Young had become confidants when they served on the German reparations committee, known as the Dawes Committee, in 1924. As a consequence of the Dawes Plan, J. P. Morgan and Company, which would become Dawes's personal banker, became the lead investment banking firm for the German External Loan of 1924, in which the Dawes bank participated. Then in 1930, Young authored his own plan for easing the German reparations crisis, resulting in the German Government International Loan (the Young Loan), part of which also ended up in the Dawes bank's portfolio. In addition, the Dawes bank made a highly risky investment of $761,327 in the German government's two-year dollar treasury gold notes, which would go into default in 1934, after Adolf Hitler's rise to power.

The Dawes bank's German notes were part of the collateral securing the bailout loan package of the four participating Chicago banks, including Traylor's First National Bank, which had a large foreign department that had suffered significant losses. Traylor's bank also made a questionable investment of $840,142 in the German notes, and it had charged off its books $375,501 "caused by the violent drop in sterling exchange." By the end of July 1932, Traylor's bank had also charged off $308,407 in other foreign investments, including securities of the Swedish Match Company and obligations of the Hungarian government. Nonetheless, when Traylor's bank participated in the Dawes bailout, the Dawes bank pledged securities of the Swedish Match Company and Hungarian government, which national bank examiners had already identified as "frozen assets," as collateral to secure the loans.[61]

The participating banks would suffer significant losses on their loans to the Dawes bank. They reached an agreement with the RFC in 1936 to accept $29,562 in cash and foreign securities having a total face value of $970,594, but "no market value," and to relinquish the remaining unpaid indebtedness of the Dawes bank, totaling $1,237,195. By the end of 1936, the banks judged that the prospects of recovering on the foreign securities were greater than continuing with the liquidation of the old Dawes bank, in spite of the fact that $761,327 of the securities were obligations of the German government, and $159,760 of them were obligations of the Hungarian Central Mutual Credit Institute of Budapest.

Jones's RFC agreed to the settlement and release, which removed the foreign securities from its books. Before the Dawes loans were made, Congress had prohibited the RFC from making loans that were secured by foreign securities, so the RFC structured an agreement with the four participating Chicago banks to pledge the foreign securities as collateral for their $5 million loan. But the RFC was still considered the primary beneficiary of the collateral, as the receiver's report in 1935 indicated: "Endorsed four new Participation Certificates [of German government bonds] in blank for the benefit of the Reconstruction Finance Corporation."[62]

As collateral for the RFC loans, the Dawes bank also pledged notes secured with German obligations. In June 1945, the RFC purchased from the receiver, at one dollar each, government and corporate bonds from Germany that had been pledged as collateral. In his petition for permission from the court, the receiver said:

> The [foreign] bonds, being all of German origin, have no market value whatsoever, trading therein having been suspended at the outbreak of hostilities. In view of the situation existing in Germany at this time with respect to its financial position and the effect thereof on the corporate issues included and the possibility of irreparable damage to plants and installations of the issuing corporations, a nominal value of $1.00 per issue has been agreed upon and assigned to these securities for acquisition purpose.[63]

Prohibiting any pledge of foreign securities as collateral for an RFC loan was another one of the sound principles underlying the intent of Congress to require well-secured loans, as were the criminal sanctions designed to

prevent misrepresentations in the loan application process. But neither provision made much of an impression on Dawes or his colleagues. So despite
his specific promise to the contrary, less than two weeks after the Hoover
administration had bailed out his bank, he proposed liquidating the insolvent
Central Republic Bank and Trust Company and organizing a new bank with
a clean balance sheet.[64]

Notes

1. Pusey, *Eugene Meyer*, 223.
2. "Text of General Dawes' Letter of Resignation as President of the Reconstruction Finance Corporation," June 6, 1932, HHP/HHPL; "Dawes' reply for Court-draft,"
CGDP/NUL; *Chicago Tribune*, June 19, 22, 1932.
3. John J. McDevitt Jr. to Lawrence Richey, June 29, 1932 (telegram), HHP/
HHPL; *Reconstruction Finance Corporation v. Central Republic Trust Company*
(1937), 267; Answer of City National Bank, McIlvaine v. City National Bank, PRCP/
UI.
4. *Reconstruction Finance Corporation v. Central Republic Trust Company*
(1937), 267–68; Testimony of Gerald S. Hadlock, Narrative Statement of the Evidence, RFC v. Central Republic Trust Company, Equity No. 14189, USDC/NDI;
Williamson, "What Is the Relative Value?"
5. A. P. Giannini's bank, the Dawes bank, and the RFC also had in common an
employee, Walter Ladd Vincent. Vincent began as the cashier of Giannini's Bank of
Italy in San Francisco; he then joined the RFC in Washington and was involved in the
issuance of the Dawes loan; later he became a vice president of the Dawes bank and
finally president of the Central Illinois Securities Company, a Dawes company. *New
York Times*, April 16, 1939; James and James, *Biography of a Bank*, 311, 313–17,
353, 358; "Memorandum to the Board of Directors," by M. G. Bogue, June 15, 1932,
EMP/LC; Williamson, "What Is the Relative Value?"
6. Jones, *Fifty Billion Dollar,* 74–75.
7. Wilson, *Harvey Couch: The Master Builder*, 156, 158; Wilson, *Harvey Couch*,
90–93. Minutes . . . of the Board . . . of the RFC, June 27, 1932, RFC/NA; "Dawes
Sued for RFC Loans," *Chicago Tribune*, November 20, 1934; "Dawes Stockholders
Face 14 Million Loss," clippings in PRCP/UI.
8. Sherman, "Charles G. Dawes," 125–26; Jones, *Fifty Billion Dollars*, 74–75;
New York Times, April 14, 1929; S. J. Woolf, "Mr. Dawes Views the Panorama of
Life," *New York Times Magazine*, January 22, 1928; Bliven, "Charles G. Dawes,
Super-Salesman," 263–67.
9. Records of the Examining Division, Comptroller of the Currency's Office,
USOCC/NA; Jones, *Fifty Billion Dollars*, 72–81. Without offering any proof, Cyril
James, in his two-volume work, *The Growth of Chicago Banks*, published in 1938,
did not totally discount the hypothesis of "a political motive" behind the panic. He

pointed out that most of the "alarmist propaganda from sources that have never been traced" was directed against just one bank, the supposedly sound First National Bank of Chicago headed by Melvin Traylor, the possible presidential candidate at the upcoming Democratic convention. But James concluded that "pandemonium broke loose" only after the Carroll chain of banks and then eight community banks failed on Thursday, June 23, and Friday, June 24, 1932. James, *The Growth of Chicago Banks*, 2:1032, 1033.

10. For a discussion of the Democratic convention, see Elliot A. Rosen, *Hoover, Roosevelt, and the Brains Trust: From Depression to New Deal* (New York: Columbia University Press, 1977), 243–75; "Melvin A. Traylor," Traylor for President Club, 4–5, 16; Jones, *Fifty Billion Dollars*, 72–81; Sherman, "Dawes," 121, 124–25; Wicker, *Banking Panics of the Great Depression*, 114.

11. Timmons, *Garner*, 158, 160, 163–67; "Melvin A. Traylor," Traylor for President Club, 15–17.

12. Meyer, "The Reminiscences of Eugene Meyer," 602–3; Agnes E. Meyer, "Diary of Mrs. Agnes E. Meyer," January 18, 24, 1932; "Memorandum" by Eugene Meyer, June 27, 1932, EMP/LC.

13. "Memorandum" by Eugene Meyer, June 27, 1932, EMP/LC; Testimony of Ralph H. Buss, Narrative Statement of the Evidence, *Reconstruction Finance Corporation v. Central Republic Trust Company* (1937), 268–72; Hoover, *Memoirs*, 108, 168; James, *The Growth of Chicago Banks*, 2:1033–36.

14. "Memorandum" by Eugene Meyer, June 27, 1932, EMP/LC.

15. Ibid.; Pusey, *Eugene Meyer*, 223–24; Hicks, *Republican Ascendancy*, 142; W. Randolph Burgess to Governor Harrison, "Memorandum on Events of Sunday, June 26, 1932," June 28, 1932; Governor Harrison to Confidential Files, "Central Republic Bank and Trust Company of Chicago (Meeting Sunday night, June 26)," June 26, 1932, two memorandums dictated by Harrison from his handwritten notes on July 6, 1932, GLHP/CU.

16. Governor Harrison to Confidential Files, "Central Republic Bank and Trust Company of Chicago (Meeting Sunday night, June 26)," June 26, 1932; W. Randolph Burgess to Governor Harrison, "Memorandum on Events of Sunday, June 26, 1932," June 28, 1932, GLHP/CU.

17. W. Randolph Burgess to Governor Harrison, "Memorandum on Events of Sunday, June 26, 1932," June 28, 1932, GLHP/CU; Decree of Judge James H. Wilkerson, May 1, 1937, RFC v. Central Republic Trust Company, Equity No. 14189, USDC/NDI; McDonald, *Recovering the Past*, 84.

18. W. Randolph Burgess to Governor Harrison, "Memorandum on Events of Sunday, June 26, 1932," June 28, 1932; Governor Harrison to Confidential Files, "Central Republic Bank and Trust Company of Chicago (Meeting Sunday night, June 26)," June 26, 1932, GLHP/CU.

19. In his memoirs, Hoover failed to mention that the RFC had already approved the more than sufficient $16 million loan to the Dawes bank. Hoover, *Memoirs*, 168–71, 225; Olson, *Herbert Hoover and the Reconstruction Finance Corporation*, 47; W. Ernest Thompson, "Melvin A. Traylor, 1878–1934," *Southwestern Historical*

Quarterly 67 (October 1963): 232; Joslin, *Hoover Off the Record*, 249–51; Wilson, *Harvey Couch: The Master Builder*, 160.

20. Flynn, "Inside the R.F.C.: An Adventure in Secrecy," 164–65; Jones, *Fifty Billion Dollars*, 75–79; Timmons, *Portrait of an American*, 319–24; Hoover, *Memoirs*, 169–71; Sherman, "Dawes," 126–28; *Reconstruction Finance Corporation v. Central Republic Trust Company* (1937), 268–72.

21. Jesse H. Jones to George R. Cooksey, June 28, 1932 (telegram); Minutes of a Meeting of the Board of Directors of the Reconstruction Finance Corporation, June 27, 1932, RFC/NA; Jones, *Fifty Billion Dollars*, 75–79; *Reconstruction Finance Corporation Act*, Section 3, January 21, 1932, RFC/NA; Timmons, *Portrait of an American*, 319.

22. Hoover, *Memoirs*, 169–71; Pusey, *Eugene Meyer*, 224; Jones, *Fifty Billion Dollars*, 76–77; Sherman, "Dawes," 126; Joslin, *Hoover Off the Record*, 249–51.

23. "Memorandum" by Eugene Meyer, June 27, 1932, EMP/LC.

24. Staff members were busy making telephone calls from their Washington offices on that Sunday. As a consequence, the participants left a detailed record describing the events of the day. One staff memorandum, which reflected copious note-taking, said that Meyer had told them, "General Dawes had stated emphatically that he would not open his bank [Monday] morning unless he could get loans in an amount sufficient to pay off all his depositors." "Memorandum," by Harrison, June 27, 1932, EMP/LC; W. Irving Shuman to James A. Farley, December 30, 1932; "Memo for Messrs. Farley and Howe," n.d., FDRP/FDRL.

25. Jesse Jones would later nominate Lynn Talley to be head of the Commodity Credit Corporation, a lending arm of the RFC. Talley was the chairman of the Bank of America from the fall of 1931 until February 15, 1932, when Elisha Walker of New York lost control to A. P. Giannini. After Giannini took control of the Bank of America again, he terminated Talley. But by then Jones, Talley's mentor, was settling into his position at the RFC, so he brought Talley to Washington. Talley and Dawes shared a mutual friend in Walker, who would later in the year become a director of the new Dawes bank. Comptroller Pole was also close to both Dawes and Talley. Jones, *Fifty Billion Dollars*, 517–18; James and James, *Biography of a Bank*, 319, 326, 332, 336, 339, 340, 341, 344, 353; Wilson, *Harvey Couch: The Master Builder*, 156–164; Olson, "Herbert Hoover and 'War' on the Depression," 30; W. Irving Shuman to James A. Farley, December 30, 1932; "Memo for Messrs. Farley and Howe," n.d., FDRP/FDRL; Olson, *Saving Capitalism*, 144–45; Kennedy, *The Banking Crisis of 1933*, 38–39; "Memorandum to Mr. Harrison" by M. G. Bogue, June 27, 1932; "Memorandum" by Eugene Meyer, June 27, 1932; "Memorandum" by Harrison, June 27, 1932, EMP/LC.

26. "Memorandum to Mr. Harrison" by M. G. Bogue, June 27, 1932; "Memorandum" by Eugene Meyer, June 27, 1932, EMP/LC; Hoover, *Memoirs*, 108–9.

27. "Memorandum to Mr. Harrison" by M. G. Bogue, June 27, 1932; "Memorandum" by Harrison, June 27, 1932, EMP/LC.

28. "Memorandum to Mr. Harrison" by M. G. Bogue, June 27, 1932; "Memorandum" by Harrison, June 27, 1932, EMP/LC.

29. "Memorandum to Mr. Harrison" by M. G. Bogue, June 27, 1932; "Memorandum" by Harrison, June 27, 1932, EMP/LC.

30. Handwritten notes of Eugene Meyer, June 27, 1932; "Memorandum" by Eugene Meyer, June 27, 1932, EMP/LC.

31. "Memorandum" by Eugene Meyer, June 27, 1932; "Memorandum to Mr. Harrison" by M. G. Bogue, June 27, 1932; "Memorandum" by Harrison, June 27, 1932, EMP/LC.

32. "Memorandum to Mr. Harrison" by M. G. Bogue, June 27, 1932; "Memorandum" by Harrison, June 27, 1932, EMP/LC.

33. Receiver's Petition No. 54, People of the State of Illinois, Ex Rel. Edward J. Barrett v. Central Republic Trust Company, December 30, 1936, CCCC; "Memorandum to Mr. Harrison" by M. G. Bogue, June 27, 1932, EMP/LC; Sherman, "Dawes," 125–30; *Reconstruction Finance Corporation v. Central Republic Trust Company* (1937), 267–73; Jones, *Fifty Billion Dollars*, 77–78.

34. *Reconstruction Finance Corporation v. Central Republic Trust Company* (1937), 268.

35. Testimony of Gerald S. Hadlock, Narrative Statement of the Evidence, RFC v. Central Republic Trust Company, USDC/NDI; Jones, *Fifty Billion Dollars*, 603.

36. *Reconstruction Finance Corporation v. Central Republic Trust Company* (1937), 268–72; *Chicago Tribune*, May 21, 1930; Jones, *Fifty Billion Dollars*, 78–79; Sherman, "Dawes," 123–24, 128.

37. *Chicago Tribune*, June 12, 1910; *Chicago Sun*, January 3, 1943; Jones, *Fifty Billion Dollars*, 47–49, 78–79; James, *The Growth of Chicago Banks*, 2:1087–90.

38. "Memorandum" by Eugene Meyer, June 27, 1932, EMP/LC; Testimony of Gerald S. Hadlock, Narrative Statement of the Evidence, RFC v. Central Republic Trust Company, USDC/NDI; *Reconstruction Finance Corporation Act*, Section 5, January 21, 1932, RFC/NA; Ebersole, "One Year of the Reconstruction Finance Corporation," 472–73. Congress amended the RFC act, effective August 1, 1932, to eliminate the provision that prohibited the RFC from financing the formation of de novo banks. *Reconstruction Finance Corporation Act as Amended . . . July 21, 1932*, 4.

39. *Reconstruction Finance Corporation v. Central Republic Trust Company* (1937), 271–72.

40. Ibid., 272; *Circular No. 1 of the Reconstruction Finance Corporation, Information for Banks and Other Financial Institutions Desiring to Apply for Loans under the Reconstruction Finance Corporations Act*, February 1932 (Washington, D.C.: Government Printing Office, 1932), 2, 4, 5; *Reconstruction Finance Corporation Act*, Section 16, January 21, 1932, RFC/NA; Ebersole, "One Year of the Reconstruction Finance Corporation," 467.

41. *Reconstruction Finance Corporation v. Central Republic Trust Company* (1937), 263; Sherman, "Dawes," 128–30; Jones, *Fifty Billion Dollars*, 76; *Stock Exchange Practices, Insull*, 1529–34, 1698; *Callaghan's Illinois Statutes Annotated, 1925–1931*, 99, 100; *Callaghan's Illinois Statutes Annotated*, 1924, 1:690–92.

42. *Reconstruction Finance Corporation v. Central Republic Trust Company* (1937), 263; Sherman, "Dawes," 128–30; Jones, *Fifty Billion Dollars*, 76.

43. *Reconstruction Finance Corporation v. Central Republic Trust Company* (1937), 263.

44. "Central Republic Bank," PRCP/UI; *Chicago Tribune*, June 11, 1932; *Reconstruction Finance Corporation v. Central Republic Trust Company* (1937), 263, 267–73.

45. "Central Republic Bank," PRCP/UI.

46. Statement of Charles G. Dawes, n.d., PRCP/UI.

47. Proof of Claim of RFC against Central Republic Trust Company, Chicago, Illinois, March 16, 1935; Original Note of Central Republic Bank and Trust Company, October 6, 1932, People of the State of Illinois, Ex. Rel. Edward J. Barrett, Auditor of Public Accounts v. Central Republic Trust Company, CCCC; *Reconstruction Finance Corporation v. Central Republic Trust Company* (1937), 272–73; Plaintiff Exhibit 32, RFC v. Central Republic Trust Company, USDC/NDI; Ebersole, "One Year of the Reconstruction Finance Corporation," 474; Williamson, "What Is the Relative Value?"

48. Pusey, *Eugene Meyer*, 224.

49. James, *The Growth of Chicago Banks*, 2:1041.

50. Gifford Pinchot to the President, September 20, 21, 22, 1932 (telegrams); Herbert Hoover to Pinchot, September 20, 1932 (telegram); "Copy" of Memorandum, June 21, 1932, HHP/HHPL; Hoover, *Memoirs*, 152; Olson, *Hoover and the Reconstruction Finance Corporation*, 72, 73, 82–85; Burner, *Herbert Hoover,* 276–77; Leuchtenburg, *The Perils of Prosperity*, 131; Douglas Brinkley, *The Quiet World: Saving Alaska's Wilderness Kingdom, 1879–1960* (New York: Harper Collins, 2011), 57, 72–85, 91, 102, 107, 108, 110, 111, 117, 119, 120, 155, 158, 205, 206, 220, 314.

51. Everette C. McKeage to Homer S. Cummings, March 28, 1935, RFC/NA.

52. Olson, *Hoover and the Reconstruction Finance Corporation*, 72; Schlesinger, *The Crisis of the Old Order*, 31, 44, 103, 299, 303, 479; Kennedy, *Freedom from Fear*, 258, 328, 331, 345.

53. Hoover, *Memoirs,* 168–71; "The Record of Central Republic Bank and Trust Company," Philip R. Clarke, April 16, 1936, PRCP/UI; Examiner's Report of National Bank of the Republic, April 18, 1931, USOCC/NA; Schlesinger, *Crisis of the Old Order*, 238; Dorothy Horton McGee, *Herbert Hoover: Engineer, Humanitarian, Statesman* (New York: Dodd, Mead & Company, 1959), 266–67; Eugene Lyons, *The Herbert Hoover Story* (Washington, D.C.: Human Events, 1959), 316–17; Wilson, *Harvey Couch: The Master Builder*, 141–43, 160; Wilbur and Hyde, *The Hoover Policies*, 434; Minutes of Board, June 27, 1932, RFC/NA; Records of the Examining Division, Comptroller of the Currency's Office, USOCC/WNRC; Williamson, "What Is the Relative Value?"

54. "Reconstruction Finance Corporation v. Central Republic Trust Company, et al.," Bill of Complaint; Request for Admissions, January 24, 1941; Stipulation

No. 3 between RFC and Certain Defendants, "The 'Union Agreement,' Memorandum of Agreement," June 8, 1931, Exhibit A; "Notice of Stockholders," June 24, 1931, Exhibit B, RFC v. Central Republic Trust Company, No. 14189, USDC/NDI; *Chicago Tribune*, July 2, 1932; Sherman, *Dawes*, 96; *Reconstruction Finance Corporation v. Central Republic Trust Company* (1937); *Moody's, Banks—Insurance Companies—Investment Trusts—Real Estate Finance and Credit Companies*, 1931, 558; Total Indebtedness as of 12/31/34 to 12/31/43; "Recapitulation, Assets pledged to secure the loan to the Central Republic Trust Company, Chicago, Illinois, and the estimated recoverable value assigned to the same as of December 31, 1937, RFC/NA; Myers, *The State Papers . . . of Herbert Hoover*, 2:431–49; Williamson, "What Is the Relative Value?"; Herbert Hoover and Calvin Coolidge, *Campaign Speeches of 1932* (New York: Doubleday, Doran, 1933), 212–19, 216.

55. Jesse H. Jones, "Work of the Reconstruction Finance Corporation," August 29, 1932, National Broadcasting Company, CGDP/NUL.

56. Ibid.

57. Ralph Buss later became an official of the Federal Reserve Bank of Detroit. Testimony of Ralph H. Buss, Narrative Statement of the Evidence, RFC v. Central Republic Trust Company, USDC/NDI; *Reconstruction Finance Corporation v. Central Republic Trust Company* (1937), 267.

58. Testimony of Ralph H. Buss, Narrative Statement of the Evidence, RFC v. Central Republic Trust Company, USDC/NDI; *Reconstruction Finance Corporation v. Central Republic Trust Company* (1937), 267; Ralph H. Buss to C. G. Dawes, July 14, 1932, CGDP/NUL.

59. W. R. Milford later became a managing director of the Federal Reserve Bank of Baltimore. Testimony of Ralph H. Buss, Narrative Statement of the Evidence, RFC v. Central Republic Trust Company, USDC/NDI; *Banking Law State of Illinois*, Section 10.

60. W. R. Milford to C. G. Dawes, July 13, 1932, CGDP/NUL.

61. Receiver's Petition No. 27, October 30, 1935; Receiver's Petition No. 54, People of the State of Illinois, Ex. Rel. Edward J. Barrett v. Central Republic Trust Company, December 30, 1936, CCCC; Statement of Assets and Liabilities as at December 2, 1931, of Charles G. Dawes, CGDP/NUL; German External Loan 1924 (Dawes Loan), German Government International Loan 1930 (Young Loan), J. P. Morgan and Company, June 28, 1935; Lee, Higginson and Company to Central Republic Trust Company, May 3, 1935, and May 6, 1935 (telegram); Walter E. Braunl to W. R. Vincent, July 12, 1935; Assistant Manager to R. J. Taylor, November 27, 1936; "Germany to Pay U.S. 1 3/4 Billion on Old Debts," *Chicago Tribune*, February 27, 1953; *Reconstruction Finance Corporation v. Central Republic Trust Company* (1937), 274; Sherman, "Dawes," 131; O. D. Young to C. G. Dawes, August 2, 1935, CGDP/NUL; Timmons, *Portrait of an American*, 215–26; Tarbell, *Owen D. Young*, 297; Kennedy, *Freedom from Fear*, 8–9.

62. Receiver's Petition No. 54, December 30, 1936; Order on Receiver's Petition No. 54, December 31, 1936, People of the State of Illinois, Ex. Rel. Edward J. Barrett

v. Central Republic Trust Company, December 30, 1936, CCCC; P. M. Black to F. M. Murchison, April 26, 1934, RFC/NA.

63. Order on Receiver's Petition No. 164, May 12, 1944; Receiver's No. 180, June 20, 1945, People of the State of Illinois, Ex. Rel. Edward J. Barrett v. Central Republic Trust Company, CCCC; Upham and Lamke, *Closed and Distressed Banks*, 159.

64. "Memorandum to the Board of Directors" of Lynn P. Talley, July 15, 1932, EMP/LC.

Chapter 6

Playing the Young Card

"City National Bank and Trust Company open for business this morning. I can conceive of no greater satisfaction in life than the ability to render such service as you have done in this accomplishment. I cannot express my feeling of personal appreciation."

—Henry Dawes to Owen Young, October 6, 1932[1]

Seeking approval of his controversial new proposal, Dawes played the Young card. In early July 1932, shortly after the bailout, Dawes invited his old friend Owen Young to a weekend strategy session at the Dawes home in Evanston, Illinois. Dawes needed Young's credibility and clout to keep the three Democratic directors of the Reconstruction Finance Corporation in line. Young also enjoyed the confidence of Hoover, who had wanted him to replace the resigning Meyer as chairman of the RFC. Though Young declined the offer, his stature was at its zenith during the summer of 1932 when Dawes asked him to lobby the RFC on his behalf.

As deputy chairman and a member of the executive committee of the Federal Reserve Bank of New York, Young held a powerful post. And as chairman of the banking and industrial committee of the Federal Reserve Bank, he was responsible for encouraging private lending activity in the business community. As we have seen, before the Democratic convention, Young had even been widely regarded as a leading presidential candidate because of his business credentials and expertise in foreign affairs. No less a personage than Will Rogers had declared Young the "Democratic white hope." A favorable biography was also released just before the Democratic convention. The book, Ida Tarbell's *Owen D. Young: A New Type of Industrial Leader*, canonized Young as a "political paragon." What the pundits did not know at the time was that Young was financially ruined because of his stock market speculations.[2]

Since they were unaware of his financial difficulties, Young was still the favorite of many of the most powerful members of the Democratic Party's conservative faction. They were determined to stop Roosevelt, the liberal governor of New York. Democratic Party rules required a two-thirds vote to secure the nomination, and the anti-Roosevelt forces were trying to marshal enough delegates to block his nomination. Young was the frontrunner as a dark horse candidate if the convention was deadlocked. Yet during the middle of May, Young made a Sherman-like statement withdrawing his name from consideration: "So may I say definitely and finally that I cannot, for reasons which are so controlling as not to be open to argument, accept a nomination for the Presidency if made."[3]

Young's withdrawal immediately made Melvin Traylor the dark horse candidate among conservative Democrats. Mayor Cermak of Chicago quickly announced that his mentor had significant strength among the Illinois delegation. Traylor also gained support in the delegation of his native state of Kentucky and among the delegates from Texas, where he had lived until 1911, becoming a lawyer and then a banker there. Traylor was married to a Texan, Dorothy Arnold Yerby, of Hillsboro. The Texas delegates were also supporting Speaker of the House Garner. Consequently, during the middle of June, Roosevelt's political confidant, James A. Farley, met with Traylor in Chicago to discuss the possibility of him running as the vice presidential candidate. But Traylor was by necessity focusing on keeping his bank open, not advancing his political career.[4]

Democratic insiders believed that Young's gracious withdrawal from the presidential sweepstakes would result in a high-ranking position for him in the Roosevelt administration. That perception was important to Dawes, who could not have selected a more effective lobbyist to advance his new plan. On July 13, 1932, sixteen days after Dawes had received the first $10 million advance from the RFC, Young stood before its directors to present the new Dawes plan, which on its face violated the Reconstruction Finance Corporation Act. According to the minutes of that meeting, Young stated that "he desired, first, to advise the Board that he had no personal interest whatever in the matter except his personal friendship for General Dawes, who had asked him to come to Chicago and spend the weekend with him."

Young misled the directors when he failed to disclose that the company of which he was chairman, General Electric, would become a major stockholder in the new Dawes bank. Young also neglected to inform the directors that his company had substantial deposits at Dawes's Central Republic Bank, which would be lost if the bank failed. Young's GE would use its deposits in the old

Dawes bank to buy two thousand shares of the new bank at $125 a share, for a total investment of $250,000, an amount worth about $3,930,000 today. Thus, the U.S. government would end up loaning the new bank the money to pay GE for its deposits in the old bank, after which GE would buy stock in the new bank, thereby simultaneously getting Young off the hook while enabling Dawes to raise the capital necessary to open it.[5]

Harvey Couch pointed out that Young had traveled to Washington several times to lobby the directors to approve the new Dawes plan. Dawes made sure that the Democratic directors were aware that leading Democrats planned to invest in the new bank. Before the board approved the Dawes plan to form a new bank, which would take possession of the proceeds of the RFC loan, including the last $50 million installment, Couch was told about the $250,000 of the bank's stock that Young's GE would be purchasing. Young's misleading disclaimer did not seem to concern Couch, who must have known that Young was splitting hairs—that he had no personal interest in the new Dawes bank aside from GE's interest. Instead, Couch was impressed that Young's company would be a major stockholder in the new Dawes bank. As he said, "There was no way then that [the RFC] could legally purchase stock, so we went out with [Dawes's] friends and other interested ones and raised $5 million in stock."[6]

Approval of the Dawes plan was sealed when Bernard Baruch, mentor to the Republican chairman of the RFC, Eugene Meyer, and a longtime Democratic power broker, agreed to buy $100,000 worth of the new bank's stock, an amount equal to about $1,570,000 today—a big number then and now. Baruch's involvement also helped to secure the votes of Couch and Wilson McCarthy, two of the three Democratic members of the RFC. Couch and Baruch both counted Senator Joe Robinson, the leader of Senate Democrats, as one of their best friends. Baruch also held sway over McCarthy because of his influence among the Democratic members of Congress, including Speaker John Garner—Roosevelt's running mate.

Dawes covered his bets in the presidential sweepstakes when he gained the support of Baruch, Young, and Traylor, all of whom were advisors to Roosevelt and his campaign. While Dawes was busy raising capital for his new bank, on August 30, 1932, Roosevelt sent letters to "only a few people whose judgment I value," which included Baruch and Traylor. Writing from the Executive Mansion in Albany, Roosevelt asked them to become part of "a small group to hold themselves in readiness for consultation" on many "matters relating to issues and policies of various kinds." Roosevelt emphasized that this part of his "task has nothing to do with those who are engaged in the strictly political management of the campaign, but has in a sense a more personal relationship."

Image 6.1. Bernard Baruch, a Democratic power broker who was a major stockholder of the new Dawes bank, at Franklin Roosevelt's White House (Courtesy, Library of Congress)

Roosevelt was also consulting his old friend, Owen Young, during and after the campaign. After his election, Roosevelt told Traylor: "I shall have need of all the counsel and support which such public-spirited citizens as you can give, and I know that I may count on you." And during his second week in the White House, Roosevelt sent a handwritten note to Baruch, whom he addressed as "my dear Bernie," saying: "I do hope you will come down & see me soon."[7]

Baruch was one of the most significant contributors to the Democratic Party. Between the 1928 and 1932 elections, Baruch contributed at least $50,000 to the national party. He had also contributed at least $33,500 to Smith's presidential campaign in 1928. And at the Democratic convention, Baruch had been the one to walk across the floor of the convention carrying a letter from his close friend, Owen Young, declining the nomination should it be offered to Young.[8]

Wilson McCarthy, the lawyer from Salt Lake City whom Dawes had cultivated during his stint at the RFC, believed the national crisis of confidence was persisting since he failed to see any meaningful recovery in the banking system. McCarthy warned Dawes that the entire system might collapse in the near future. His pessimism did not affect his support for Dawes's latest proposal, despite Dawes's prior promise to the directors that the $90 million loan "was not made in contemplation of liquidation." As soon as Young presented the new Dawes proposal to the RFC directors, McCarthy confirmed to Dawes in writing that he supported the proposal for a new bank. He then quickly requested a few personal favors. Most important, McCarthy asked Dawes, as former ambassador to Great Britain, if he would write letters of introduction for his only son, Dennis, who was living in London. For a young man trying to become established in a foreign country, a letter of recommendation from a former ambassador was invaluable. McCarthy also asked Dawes if he would send one of his pipes to Dr. John J. Galligan, an admirer of Dawes who was one of McCarthy's friends in Salt Lake City. Finally, McCarthy complained that both Jones and Couch had autographed pictures of Dawes hanging in their apartments. Sounding more like a hero worshiper than an impartial official facing a tough decision about the propriety of dispensing $50 million of scarce government funds when the emergency had subsided, McCarthy requested his own autographed picture from Dawes. He closed his letter telling Dawes that he was always available to be of service to him.[9]

Playing the insider's game, Jesse Jones's support for the Dawes loans had been enhanced when Traylor made him the $350,000 loan from a bank whose survival depended on the Dawes bailout. Dawes had also proven his friendship to Jones when he agreed to lease space in Jones's office building in Houston over the objections of his brother. In addition, Jones was good friends with Young, who had endorsed Jones's appointment to the RFC's board. Jones also had a cordial relationship with Baruch, despite the harsh words he had exchanged with Baruch during the campaign of 1924 when Jones was the finance director of the Democratic National Committee. During that difficult campaign, Jones had criticized Baruch for giving only $25,000, though even that made him one of the largest Democratic contributors. (Jones and other Democrats had hoped that Baruch would give as much as $200,000 to the campaign.) According to the Jones camp, the friendship between Jones and Baruch was "never more than partially restored." However, the correspondence between the two men throughout the 1930s indicates that they remained close friends, and Baruch was kind to Jones in his memoirs. Baruch wrote that he had recommended Jones for the RFC post, adding that Jones was "as smart as any man I have ever met." Baruch also revealed that he had

**Image 6.2.   Charles Dawes gave his autographed photograph to his "friend" Wil-
son McCarthy, who acted like a hero worshiper of Dawes when he approved the
unprecedented bailout package for the Dawes bank. (Courtesy, Utah State Historical
Society)**

"declined" a seat on the RFC board because he believed he could be more
effective as a "free agent."[10]

  (Baruch would be content to remain a stockholder in the new Dawes bank,
the City National Bank of Chicago, until a few months after Roosevelt's RFC
filed suit against Dawes Brothers, Inc., and other stockholders to collect their
stock assessments in the defunct Central Republic Bank. At that point, in
June 1935, Baruch seemed to be worried about his exposure as a stockholder
of Dawes's new bank, so he expressed his desire to sell his stock in the City
National Bank, saying that he did not want to hold any stock that was subject
to an assessment. After returning from a trip to Europe and without receiving

a response to his earlier letter, Baruch wrote again, saying that he had purchased eight hundred shares of the bank as a favor to Dawes and that it was no longer necessary for him to be a stockholder. This time Dawes immediately replied to the request, assuring Baruch that he would personally buy the stock from him.)[11]

Less than a week after Young's presentation on Dawes's behalf, and before the examining division and legal staff had investigated the new Dawes proposal, Wilson McCarthy, the pivotal RFC director, wrote Dawes saying he wanted approval of the new plan "speeded up." He also mentioned that he was "hoping President Hoover might be able to persuade Owen D. Young" to join the RFC. Word in the halls of the RFC's offices was that Hoover had offered Young the chairmanship and Traylor the presidency. But Traylor and Young both declined Hoover's overtures to join the agency.[12]

Even with McCarthy's ringing endorsement, Young had to misrepresent the reasons for the insolvency of the old Dawes bank when he presented the new Dawes plan to the RFC board. Young indicated to the compliant directors that, after the bailout, the condition of the Central Republic Bank had suddenly become hopeless because of the bank's excessive interest expense on the RFC loan. He said the bank's assets yielded 4 percent annual interest, while the interest rate on the RFC loan was 5.5 percent annually. Young also mentioned that the high overhead of the bank, including the annual rental obligations of at least $780,000, was adding to the deficit. What Young did not mention was that the Insull loans and other troubled assets were generating no income.[13]

Young also suggested that the loss of $27 million in deposits after the RFC bailout loan was approved was adding to the bank's difficulties. But he failed to acknowledge that the loss of deposits also significantly reduced the bank's overhead, in that the bank had to pay interest to far fewer depositors. The mismatch of assets and liabilities was created when the bailout loans were added to the liability side of the bank's balance sheet, in addition to the deposits. By July 13, the bank had liabilities of $100 million of deposits and the recently disbursed part of the rescue package of $45 million. The $45 million of bailout loans carried an annual interest rate of 5.5 percent, and in the middle of a depression, no bank could make sufficient loans to offset that interest expense. On the asset side, the loans of the Insull companies in bankruptcy and the nonperforming loans to the Dawes family and other insiders were either worthless or worth merely a fraction of their book value.[14]

So sixteen days after the Dawes bank had been bailed out, Young was arguing that the bank had suddenly become insolvent and that only two options remained. One was that a receiver could be appointed to liquidate the Central Republic Bank, resulting in the receiver calling for the full amount of the loan commitment. But this was a spurious argument since there would be no way that a receiver of the old Dawes bank could fully secure the remaining $50 million commitment. The best alternative, according to Young, was that a new bank could be formed to assume the deposits of the Central Republic Bank. The new bank would also need the unfunded $50 million loan commitment to assume the deposits of the Central Republic Bank. Dawes, as chairman of the City National Bank, would then be able to use the loan proceeds to purchase from the RFC between $20 and $30 million of the old bank's "prime collateral" at face value, reducing the loan amount by a corresponding amount.

Dawes would soon scale back the asset purchase. He sent Philip Clarke, his bank president, to Washington to lobby the RFC's directors to reduce this requirement, which showed that the assets worth keeping were far less than initially indicated. Managers of the syndicate formed to raise the capitalization of the new bank told potential investors that no more than $15 million worth of loans of the old bank would be purchased. They wanted the new bank to "keep itself at all times in a condition of extreme liquidity," a policy in opposition to the Congressional mandate of the RFC "to provide emergency financing facilities for financial institutions, to aid in financing agriculture, commerce, and industry." As we have seen, when Hoover signed the RFC act, he said specifically that the agency had been "created for the support of the smaller banks and financial institutions, and through rendering their resources liquid to give renewed support to business, industry, and agriculture."

According to Clarke, "the new bank must not be crippled or prejudiced in the public mind by being burdened with an undue amount of the old bank's assets, in fact in my opinion it must have no specific obligation as respects the old bank's paper." The loan portfolio of the old bank was in such bad shape that Dawes's right-hand man insisted that the new bank had to maintain a "position of high liquidity" and abstain from acquiring too much questionable paper from the old bank, which would suffocate it from the outset with problem loans.[15]

Dawes proposed that the new bank purchase "selected" collateral from the RFC, including loans of customers whose deposits the new bank assumed, using the proceeds of the RFC loan. This maneuver enabled Dawes to select collateral from the old bank that the RFC purchased and then sold to the new bank. The clever procedure insulated Dawes from allegations of self-dealing that could be lodged against him and his new bank in the receivership proceedings of the old bank. However, the RFC's legal department believed there was "no reason why the RFC should make a commitment to purchase any of the 'selected' collateral without a definite appraisal thereof and commitment of the new bank to purchase it from the RFC."[16]

The new Dawes plan did not receive rubber-stamp approval, as had the initial bailout. With three new directors on the agency's board, the RFC's staff attempted to conduct a due diligence of the new Dawes plan. But Dawes could count on the support of Howard Preston, the manager of the RFC's Chicago office who would later become the president of the Hamilton National Bank of Knoxville, Tennessee. According to Clarke's contemporaneous memorandum, Preston visited Dawes at his stately office in the Central Republic Bank on July 18, 1932. At that meeting, which included Henry Dawes, Preston "suggested that in his opinion it would be feasible to organize a new bank . . . for the purpose of carrying on the commercial banking business" of the old bank, and that "$3,000,000 of capital would be sufficient." He told the Dawes brothers that he believed "such a plan would be favorably received" by the RFC. Later in July, the RFC's chief bank examiner, John K. McKee, and a staff lawyer, Allen E. Throop, traveled to Chicago and met with the Dawes brothers for three days, discussing "various plans for the organization of the new bank."

Dawes stayed in contact with Young by telephone, and then the Dawes brothers and their lawyer, Harry B. Hurd, who was also a director of the Central Republic Bank and would become a director of the new Dawes bank, took the train to New York City to meet with Young on Saturday, July 30. After weekend strategy sessions with Young, Henry Dawes took the train to Washington where he met with Atlee Pomerene (the new chairman of the RFC's board), Charles A. Miller (the RFC's new president), Jones, Couch, and McCarthy. On August 3, Henry Dawes made a presentation to the RFC's board of directors. Jones took the lead, asking a number of questions about "deposits, assets, earnings, and the plan itself," even though he was prohibited from participating or voting on the matter because of the deposits of his Houston bank in the Dawes bank.

At that meeting, the RFC's board appointed a committee to review the new Dawes plan, composed of Pomerene (as its chairman), Bogue, Talley, and McKee. Over the next two days, Henry Dawes and Harry Hurd met with Pomerene's committee and the full board, resulting in a stalemate. The staff was insisting that the capital of the new bank should be at least $5 million and that the new bank should purchase not less than $25 million of the old bank's assets. Morton Bogue, the RFC's general counsel, questioned whether the double liability of the stockholders of the old Dawes bank would survive the transfer of its deposits without the approval of its stockholders. Hurd, the lawyer for the Dawes brothers, was "strongly of the opinion that there was not the slightest chance" that the stockholders of the old bank would be released from their liability.[17]

Henry Dawes then called Young to apprise him of the situation, requesting that he come to Washington to meet privately with the board. Young promptly took the train to Washington, and "met with the board in executive session, no others being present," on Saturday, August 6. During this secret meeting, another issue was raised: did Chicago really need a fifth Loop bank? That question sent Henry Dawes back to Chicago on Sunday to confer with his brother and Melvin Traylor. On Monday, Traylor and Henry Dawes were on a train headed to Washington, along with Hurd, Clarke, Edward Brown, the executive vice president of Traylor's bank, and Abner Stilwell, the vice president of the Continental Illinois Bank whose private company, Stilwell & Co., was a stockholder of the Dawes bank.

The next day, Henry Dawes, Traylor, and the others met in Washington with the RFC's board and then adjourned to a more critical meeting in Jones's office where Young joined them. Traylor and Stilwell agreed that their banks "would do all they could to keep the business of Central Republic for the new bank, and would reassure present and future depositors as to the soundness of the new institution and would even consider loaning money to individual subscribers on stock of the new bank." Recognizing the poor quality of the assets of the old Dawes bank, Traylor and Stilwell refused to purchase "a large amount of the paper remaining in the hands of the Reconstruction Finance Corporation." Henry Dawes, Traylor, and the other bankers, looking out for their own banks, which were entwined with each other, "insisted that if the new bank were to be a success it should not be started with the burden of servicing and liquidating the loans" of the RFC.[18]

Henry Dawes, the former comptroller of the currency, stated that it would be "unsafe" for the new bank to purchase more than $15 million of the collateral pledged to the RFC. In fact, the Dawes brothers only agreed to "absolutely" purchase from the RFC $10 million of the prime paper that it was holding as collateral for the bailout loans. They demanded and received an agreement providing that "the other $5,000,000 would be acquired, subject to the right of City National [Bank] during an agreed period, to substitute the $5,000,000 of assets, or any part thereof, for an equivalent amount of the collateral assets retained" by the RFC. The loans the bank purchased from the RFC were those found to be of the highest quality after they were "submitted to the Chief National Bank Examiner of the Comptroller's Bureau and the Clearing House Examiner of the City of Chicago, for their scrutiny and advice." An officer of the new Dawes bank reported that "no piece of paper has been accepted which the examiners do not believe to be good," and that officials of the bank had "access to all of the notes pledged by the Central Republic Bank." Instead of maintaining the best assets as collateral to repay its $90 million loan, the RFC and Comptroller Pole's office actually worked with the Dawes brothers to assure that their new bank was highly profitable, thereby guaranteeing greater losses to the RFC.[19]

The comptroller of the currency's office, always friendly to the two former comptrollers, would also issue a legal opinion declaring that the contract between the old and new Dawes banks and the RFC would in no way "render the [new bank] liable for, directly or indirectly, any obligations of the [old bank] of any kind or character whatsoever other than the said deposit liabilities." The new bank "would not, by entering into the transaction, become liable for the repayment of any part of the loans" to the RFC. That legal opinion would later provide substantive grounds for the U.S. Circuit Court of Appeals for Chicago to affirm the dismissal of a lawsuit seeking $70 million in damages from the Dawes brothers and their new bank.[20]

Gardner Cowles, a conservative Republican and newspaper publisher from Des Moines, Iowa, raised another alarming aspect of the new plan. Cowles was Hoover's close friend, who the president had nominated to fill Dawes's seat on the RFC's board on June 23, 1932, and confirmed by the Senate five days later, joining the board on July 5. Responding to a question from Cowles, Young said that Dawes had "an arrangement with the landlord" of the palatial bank building located at 208 South LaSalle Street. This "arrangement" allowed the new bank to continue leasing the same office space that the old Dawes bank had previously been leasing, with one difference: the lease, which had been $780,000 a year for the old Dawes bank, was now just $150,000 a year for two years. An obvious question was why the old Dawes bank had been unable to obtain the same deal as the new bank. When disgruntled stockholders of the old Dawes bank asked the same question in 1937, Clarke indicated that the bank was in such bad shape at that time that its management could not offer "any assurance to the landlord that the old bank could have continued in business." But Clarke did not reveal that the old bank had paid the landlord a substantial lump sum payment "in cancellation of all their future liability under these leases." So the assets of the old bank were used to subsidize the new bank, at a significant loss to the RFC.[21]

Young also neglected to disclose to the RFC's board that Clarke was one of the landlords. The Dawes bank was located in a building that was owned through a real estate trust named 208 South LaSalle Street Building Corporation, which in turn was owned through the Utilities Power and Light Realty Trust, a holding company. Harley L. Clarke, a director of the Dawes bank, was president of the holding company, and he and Philip Clarke were two of the three trustees who controlled the 208 South LaSalle Street Building Corporation. When Philip Clarke was negotiating on behalf of the Dawes bank, he was also negotiating with himself and his co-trustees.[22]

JONES SPRINGS INTO ACTION

When it became apparent that the Washington legal staff was opposing the new Dawes plan, Jones sprang into action, sending a telegram and making a telephone call to Melvin Traylor, his personal banker. Jones also sent a telegram to Young. Both Traylor and Young sat on the board of GE, which would benefit from the new bailout plan. Jones wired Traylor: "Our board and Mr. Young anxious to have you meet him and the board here Tuesday August Ninth for further consideration of reorganization matter." On the same day, Jones wired Young: "Have just talked with Traylor and he will be here Tuesday with one or two associates."[23]

When Meyer initially selected Morton Bogue as the RFC's general counsel, Jones and Hoover had opposed him. Meyer prevailed, and now Morton objected to the new plan on several grounds: The new Dawes bank, the City National Bank of Chicago, would be acquiring the goodwill of the Central Republic Bank, "a substantial amount of business through the deposit liabilities assumed, and, presumably, also a substantial amount of trust department business; yet under the terms of the plan, the new bank would pay nothing for such good will and for such business." Indeed, the Dawes bank had advertised that it had 207 tellers to service its 200,000 customers, representing "one out of every five homes in Chicago," and "seven of the eight outstanding leaders" in the meat packing industry, and "fifteen of the twenty-one leading railroads bank with Central Republic."

A significant legal question remained as to whether the liability of the old bank's stockholders could be preserved if the RFC approved the new plan. A Chicago law firm, Mayer, Meyer, Austrian, and Platt, advised Bogue that the tendency of the Illinois courts was to construe the stockholders' liability statute in ways to benefit depositors of an insolvent bank, even though its directors might have engaged in insider abuse and illegal conduct. Consequently, the transfer of the RFC loan proceeds from the old Dawes bank to the new Dawes bank, which could be determined as an unlawful use of the RFC loan proceeds, would not necessarily nullify the well-established stockholders' liability. But Bogue could expect a stockholder to raise the defense that the RFC "at the time it made the advance, knew that the money was to be used by the old bank for an *ultra vires* [that is, beyond the scope of its corporate authority] purpose or to consummate an *ultra vires* purpose which could not be effectuated if the money had not been advanced." Dawes himself, through Dawes Brothers, Inc., would raise that defense when the RFC filed suit to recover assessments from the stockholders of the old Dawes bank. Beginning in 1934, the Dawes brothers vigorously litigated the issue of stockholder liability even though Charles Dawes had promised to include the stockholder assessments as part of the collateral, which Illinois law mandated.

Under the new plan, the RFC would "lose the general obligation of a going institution," resulting in the expenditure of considerable money to liquidate assets held as collateral. In addition to high expenses, the Dawes plan would "burden" the RFC with the complex problems associated with the liquidation of deflated real estate and other assets. Bogue resented that Dawes's "proposed plan amount[ed] to a dictation by a borrower of the manner in which the Corporation should proceed in connection with a loan which it has already made." Dawes refused to accept any liabilities of the Central Republic Bank, except the deposits that were to be funded with the RFC loans. Thus, Dawes's new City National Bank would be the beneficiary of the RFC loans but would not be liable for its repayment or a guarantor of the loan. All other liabilities of the old Central Republic Bank, including $30 million of secured deposits and the bank's building lease, would remain obligations of that insolvent shell of a company.

It was also revealed that the old bank owed $16 million in loans to New York banks, loans secured with a first lien on a substantial portion of the same prime collateral that the RFC had used to meet the legal requirement to secure, "fully and adequately," the bailout loans. Because the RFC held a second position on at least $16 million of collateral, the appointment of a receiver for the old bank would trigger a foreclosure action by the New York banks that would "wipe out the equity of the RFC therein." If the $16 million of collateral was extinguished, the RFC would be holding more than $27 million of troubled collateral, including the nearly $12 million of Insull's worthless or nonperforming loans. Additionally, as a result of the July 22 board meeting, the RFC had returned $20 million of assets to the old bank. The loss of more than $47 million of collateral, reducing the RFC's collateral from $118 million to $71 million, would mean that the Dawes loans of $90 million would not be "fully and adequately secured." From any point of view, to approve the new Dawes plan would just as clearly violate federal law as approving the original loan to the old bank did.

Bogue sent a memorandum to the RFC directors warning them about the "legal difficulties" surrounding the Dawes plan. Because Dawes made clear that he did not "wish to go to the stockholders [of the Central Republic Bank] for approval of the plan or for authority to make the various transfers contemplated in the plan," Bogue was alarmed that a sizable percentage of the stockholders would be released from liability. Even if the Dawes control group of stockholders were to approve the plan, the minority stockholders could be released from liability.

After "careful study," the legal department concluded that approval by only the board of directors of the Central Republic Bank would give the minority stockholders a strong defense against a stockholder assessment action. Illinois law did not "authorize any transfer of assets by an Illinois bank except upon the assumption of all liabilities by the transferee bank." But according to the Dawes plan, more than $50 million in cash and "prime collateral" would be transferred to the new Dawes bank, "leaving the old bank liable to the New York banks, the Federal Reserve Bank, [and the RFC]," as well as to the Chicago banks. Bogue was concerned that the stockholders of the old bank "might successfully claim the transfer was not authorized by law, that the law was designed to protect them against claims by appropriate assumption agreement, which had not been obtained in this case."[24]

Bogue cautioned his superiors that the RFC would not benefit "simply as a creditor by any plan which would leave as its only source of realization the residue of the pledged collateral contemplated by the plan, and no clear-cut liability enforceable against the stockholders." The general counsel was disturbed that the RFC would be taking an unprecedented step purchasing assets that Dawes selected and then selling those assets to the new Dawes bank. It seemed obvious at the time that Dawes planned to handpick the "prime collateral," then let the RFC and the other stockholders fight it out in court. (Three years later, Dawes joined with the old bank's stockholders, using frivolous defenses to resist the attempts of Roosevelt's RFC to collect the stockholders' assessments.)[25]

On August 4, the staff reported to the RFC's board that approval of the plan would require certain conditions:

1. The new bank should have a minimum capitalization of $5 million;
2. The new bank should lend 50 percent of its deposits to the borrowers of the old bank, reducing the RFC loans by a like amount;
3. The new bank should service the real estate and trust departments of the old bank, dividing the profits 40 percent to the new bank and 60 percent to the old bank, until the RFC loans were paid in full;
4. The New York banks and the Federal Reserve Bank of Chicago, which held millions of dollars of the Central Republic Bank's assets, should sell the collateral without hurting the RFC's position;
5. The new bank should collect the collateral pledged to the RFC for no fee, only out-of-pocket expenses;
6. The Central Republic Company, the securities affiliate of the old bank, should indemnify the RFC for the stockholders' liability and not pay the stockholders a dividend during the life of the loans;

7. At least a majority, and preferably two-thirds, of the present stockholders should approve the plan; and
8. Bogue, the general counsel, should supervise the implementation of the plan.

The RFC's board of directors rejected the staff report. Part of the problem was that the Washington staff could not rely on independent advice from its Chicago law firm, Fisher, Boyden, Bell, Boyd, and Marshall, which also represented Dawes's Central Republic Bank and Trust Company. Walter T. Fisher, a partner in the firm, was the Chicago Counsel for the RFC, and Darrell S. Boyd, also a partner in the firm, was a director of the old Dawes bank.[26]

The new Dawes plan gave the RFC directors definitive grounds to rescind, had they so wished, the $50 million unfunded portion of the $90 million loan commitment and to demand immediate payment of the already funded portion of $40 million and interest, in that the loans were contingent on Dawes's promise that the loans were for "current requirements" and "not in contemplation of liquidation." But Dawes did not plan to continue operating the old Dawes bank. After being a regulator and then a banker for thirty-five years, Dawes knew that his bank could not possibly repay, by December 1932, the RFC loans of $90 million, plus six months of interest at an annual rate of 5.5 percent. He and his brother Henry well understood how to combine the bank chartering and liquidation process.[27]

As a result of the Dawes controversy, Congress amended the RFC law, as of July 21, 1932, to prohibit the RFC from making a loan—"directly or indirectly"—to a bank having an officer or director who was a former director of the RFC "within the twelve months preceding approval of the loan." The amendment prohibited the final disbursement of $50 million that was used to fund the new Dawes bank in October 1932. Organizing a new national bank to assume just the deposit liabilities and prime assets, leaving the rest of the liabilities and problem assets to be liquidated, was not permitted under the Reconstruction Finance Corporation Act.[28]

Nothing had changed between June 27, when the RFC formally approved the $90 million loan commitment, and July 13, when Young presented the new Dawes plan, except the loss of $27 million in deposits, which, while reducing the bank's earnings, also reduced its expenses. Young made his presentation one day after the RFC examiners completed their investigation of the collateral that secured the ill-advised loans. On July 12, more than two weeks after the loan commitments, the examiners finally presented the report of collateral to the RFC's board of directors. This report demonstrated conclusively that the RFC had violated federal law in approving the bailout.[29]

Despite having a negative net worth, the bank had not needed a $95 million bailout to weather the short-lived panic. It had cash on hand of $18,620,916 on June 25, 1932, which was not pledged to secure the RFC's loans. That cash position would have given the RFC adequate time to examine thoroughly the assets of the bank that were to be used as collateral for the loans. Certainly, the original $16 million loan application which had been approved on Saturday, June 26, combined with its $18.6 million in cash, would have been sufficient to keep the bank open. Even if the RFC had stopped after funding only the original loan, the bank would have had $34,620,916 in liquidity, more than enough to survive.[30]

When Dawes waved his magic wand and produced the $95 million bailout, the Central Republic Bank's net worth had been ravaged. The bank held tens of millions of dollars of worthless or nonperforming Insull loans, bad real estate loans, troubled loans to the Dawes family and other insiders, and depreciated securities. As a consequence of nonperforming loans and "heavy interest charges," the Central Republic Bank suffered devastating losses during July, August, and September 1932—$168,912 in July, $94,526 in August, and $125,344 in September. It had no choice except to liquidate its holdings, and on October 6, 1932, the state bank ceased to operate.[31]

As uncertainty hung in the air, Dawes found himself having difficulty raising the $5 million needed to open the new bank, an amount worth about $78.5 million today. Dawes later said: "To raise that enormous sum at that time in 1932, and in so short a time, seemed practically impossible. . . . The sword of Damocles hung by a thread over the situation for weeks, but somehow the miracle was accomplished, and the $5,000,000 for the stock of a new bank was raised."[32]

Harvey Couch, whom Hoover had considered but did not appoint as Dawes's replacement as the RFC's president, said that it was he and other directors who "went out with [their] friends and other interested ones and raised $5 million in stock" for the new Dawes bank. Dawes also enlisted his old friend and partner Owen Young to sell bank stock subscriptions. Young, whom Dawes named to his new bank's "Advisory Committee for the selection of a Board of Directors and staff of officers of the New Bank," had already agreed, as we have seen, to have GE buy $250,000 of the bank's stock. He used his considerable influence both to save the fortune of the Dawes brothers and to prevent a significant loss to his own company.[33]

Without this active fund-raising support from the RFC directors, Dawes could not have raised $5 million for a new bank in less than three months during 1932. The fund-raising activities of the directors were improper, violating their fiduciary obligations to the RFC. When they should have been rescinding approval for the original Dawes loans, as they had done with other RFC loans when the circumstances of the loan applications had changed, Couch, McCarthy, and Jones were instead soliciting potential stockholders for the new Dawes bank. Throughout September, the three directors were working in concert with Young and Dawes to sell enough subscriptions to minority stockholders to put Dawes "over the top" in the capitalization of his bank.

Despite these extraordinary fund-raising efforts, Dawes was unable to raise the entire $5 million, so he quietly arranged for the Central Republic Company, an affiliate of the old bank, to purchase $1.7 million of the new bank's capital stock, giving it a 34 percent equity position. The stock of the Central Republic Company was held in a trust that Dawes controlled for the benefit of the stockholders of the old Dawes bank. But the RFC did not require that the 13,600 shares in the new bank, which the Central Republic Company distributed to the Dawes brothers and the other stockholders of the old bank in December 1933, be used as collateral to secure the bailout loans.[34]

On September 16, at the height of Dawes's fund-raising activities and in the middle of the presidential campaign, Hoover wrote to Dawes to say that he had heard from their mutual friend Henry M. Robinson that "some of your worries are coming to an end." Robinson, who was preoccupied with Hoover's reelection, was a director of Young's GE and president of the Security-First National Bank of Los Angeles. He had been a member of the Dawes reparations committee, along with Owen Young. He had remarked to Hoover that Dawes was "looking much better and getting to be [his] old self again." The president added in his letter to Dawes: "I just wanted you to know that I have felt deeply for you in your troubles, in addition to carrying a certain amount of my own."[35]

Though the Dawes reorganization plan violated federal law, the directors took no action to approve or disapprove the plan to form the new Dawes bank. But they authorized the new Dawes bank's purchase of $15 million "of the more desirable paper" from the assets of the old Dawes bank, treating the transaction as a principal payment on the $90 million of RFC loans. Meanwhile, the frantic fund-raising activities continued.[36]

The deference shown to Dawes was a far cry from the way the RFC had treated community bankers, who lacked political clout at the national level, when Dawes was president of the agency. A few weeks before Dawes resigned, G. W. Merz, a banker from Akron, Ohio, complained to Congressman Francis Seiberling that the RFC was acting on a "cold blooded business basis" when it evaluated collateral used to secure loans. Seiberling forwarded the letter to President Hoover, and Dawes was asked to respond. Taking a hard line, Dawes said Merz was wrong because federal law mandated that every loan had to be "fully and adequately secured." But only a few weeks later, the RFC applied a much different standard in granting Dawes his loans.[37]

Two days before the collapse of the Central Republic Bank, Dawes, the former comptroller of the currency, filed a national bank application with his friends at the comptroller of the currency's office in Washington. The bank charter application was approved the next day, and, on October 6, 1932, the City National Bank and Trust Company of Chicago opened its doors. As planned, the new bank received the proceeds of the RFC loan to cover the deposits of the old bank, including the final loan installment of $50 million. The City National Bank assumed all of the old bank's prime commercial, savings, and checking deposits, amounting to $72,330,629 of the defunct state bank's deposits, but none of its bad loans. So Dawes's new bank enjoyed the benefits of low-interest or no-interest depositors' funds without accepting responsibility for the RFC loans, though it had accepted the proceeds from the bailout.[38]

The formation of the City National Bank provided Charles Dawes and his brothers with a new beginning. When the bank opened it immediately became one of Chicago's five largest banks, possessing a valuable banking franchise and low-cost deposits funded by the Hoover administration. To summarize, the federal government allowed the Dawes brothers, as the controlling stockholders of the new bank, to acquire a banking business that had been operating for thirty years without paying anything to the RFC or to the stockholders of the old bank, which could have been used to fund their obligations to the RFC. Additionally, when the RFC directors allowed Dawes to purchase the $15 million of prime assets, they removed from their books the most valuable assets of the old Dawes bank, thereby denying the RFC the benefit of future appreciation of those assets during a liquidation process that would last for more than twenty years. Those income-producing assets would make the new Dawes bank a profitable institution the day it opened its doors, an unheard of achievement for a newly formed bank. Indeed, Philip Clarke remarked that the RFC loans enabled the old Dawes bank to transfer or pay off all of its other liabilities, which "assured the Central Republic of a leisurely, as contrasted with a forced, liquidation."

Dawes and his brothers enjoyed unrivaled control of the City National Bank. They owned or controlled more than twenty-four thousand shares of the bank's forty thousand outstanding shares through Dawes Brothers, Inc., the Central Illinois Securities Corporation, and the Central Republic

Company. Dawes could also count on the proxies of his friends, including GE's 5 percent, which Owen Young controlled, and Bernard Baruch's 2 percent of the shares. Controlling the profitable new bank was far easier for the Dawes brothers than controlling the old bank, which had four thousand stockholders, because the new bank had only seventy-one stockholders, and forty-eight of those stockholders owned 99.5 percent of the bank's voting shares. No market existed for the shares of the new bank, which the Dawes brothers and their good friends held closely.[39]

Dawes formed the new bank with the same officers and directors who had wildly speculated with Samuel Insull. Though the pension plan of the old bank was terminated, most of the officers retained their former titles at the new bank. The minority stockholders of the old bank were given the opportunity to purchase stock in the new bank, but they were gun-shy, having already suffered a double loss of their investment in the old bank, since they were responsible for a 100 percent capital assessment under Illinois law. The Dawes brothers were also liable for that assessment, but they would enjoy the lucrative benefits of being the majority stockholders of a major money-center bank.[40]

The Federal Reserve Bank of Chicago credited a $62,121,060 check from the Central Republic Bank to the order of the City National Bank. It included the $50 million final installment of the RFC loans and the remaining cash from the initial loan disbursements, as well as proceeds of the loans from the Loop banks. The old bank also transferred cash credits of $10,209,569 to the new bank, representing 100 percent of the low-cost deposits of $72,330,629 that the new bank assumed. The transactions were worth, in today's dollars, about $1.14 billion. In the understated words of Jesse Jones, Dawes had "played his hand well."[41]

On October 6, 1932, prior to the opening of the new Dawes bank at 208 South LaSalle Street—the same location as the old bank, with the same tellers and even the same checks and passbooks—Dawes hired the advertising firm of Batten, Barton, Durstine and Osborn Corporation to organize a public relations campaign. In an effort to retain the old bank's valuable customers, the campaign included newspaper and radio advertisements for both the Central Republic Bank and the City National Bank, and direct mailings to depositors, stockholders, customers, and correspondent banks. The public relations firm prepared statements for Dawes, Clarke, and Otis, who assumed both the chairmanship and presidency of the old Dawes bank, which Dawes and Clarke had previously held. (Dawes's cousin, William Dawes, also remained a vice president and director of the old bank.) The old Dawes bank announced its retirement from commercial banking but its continuation of the trust and real estate departments, which the new bank would manage, and its investment affiliate, the Central Republic Company, a major stockholder of the new bank.

To postpone litigation as a way to avoid criminal prosecution, especially since his friend the Republican Cook County prosecutor, John Swanson, was in political trouble, Dawes delayed the liquidation of the old bank despite its hopeless insolvency. Dawes then issued a misleading press release announcing that the old bank had the "opportunity for realization of its assets to be made carefully during a prospective period of business recovery." An internal circular distributed to the employees of the old Dawes bank stated that it had to "proceed in orderly liquidation by divesting itself of its deposits and having them assumed" by the new Dawes bank.

The Batten, Barton firm also worked with Reynolds, the head of Continental Illinois Bank, and Traylor to coordinate their upbeat statements to the media. So the Dawes bank issued a press release declaring that "Chicago bankers feel that the new bank, with its position of extreme liquidity, launches forth under unusually favorable conditions and at a time when indications point to improvement in general business conditions." Reynolds and Traylor then made positive statements to advance the publicity campaign. Dawes and Clarke had not been satisfied with the publicity that followed the merger of the old Dawes bank with the National Bank of the Republic just fifteen months earlier, and they were not taking any chances of bad press this time. This was their last opportunity to regain the confidence of their depositors, all of whom had been bailed out by the RFC loans.[42]

Philip Clarke, who was facing a $90,000 liability as a stockholder of the old Dawes bank, was rewarded for his loyalty to the Dawes family. Soon after the new bank opened, the Dawes brothers and their board increased Clarke's salary to $36,000 a year and awarded him a bonus of $10,000, respectively worth about $565,000 and $157,000 in today's money. This prompted the deputy comptroller under Roosevelt's new comptroller of the currency, J. F. T. "Jefty" O'Connor, to admonish the board, on June 27, 1933: "It is very apparent that the bank's earnings do not warrant the payment of such a high salary to its president."[43]

Instead of losing money during the first year of operations, like most new banks, the City National Bank was highly profitable from the day its doors opened. During its second year of operation, the nascent bank was $400,000 more profitable than even Dawes had projected. At the end of 1934, Dawes reported to Young, whose company was one of the largest stockholders of the new bank, that the bank was operating "splendidly" and had realized during the second year a gross profit "in the neighborhood of $1,000,000."

After "charging off organization expenses, all known losses, and establishing proper contingent reserves," which the old bank had failed to do, the new bank booked about $300,000 in undivided profits for the year. During the middle of the Great Depression, Dawes had generated a 6 percent annual return for the $5 million equity investment. Yet Dawes told Young that "in any normal year, with even subnormal interest rates, the net earnings of the bank should be over $1,500,000 to $2,000,000," representing an annual return of 30 to 40 percent for the Dawes family and the other investors. Dawes, who was reaping the rewards of the RFC loans, low-cost deposits, and prime assets, observed that business opportunities were the best he had ever experienced.[44]

Dawes assured Young that he was not bragging: "I am recounting this, not in a boastful spirit, but because the experience gained from a crisis in my own affairs in a great Depression taught me the quality of your friendship. I know in my heart that you are pleased with such news." Dawes, an entrepreneur for four decades who had survived the Panic of 1893 and the Panic of 1907, observed that he had never seen such a highly profitable enterprise that was not exposed to "the risks incident to even normal business times and conditions." Young had helped Dawes turn a business disaster into the opportunity of a lifetime. Along with the phenomenal success of the bank, Dawes disclosed that A Century of Progress, the Chicago World's Fair of 1933, of which Young had been such an instrumental organizer, had repaid its loans from Dawes and his entities of more than $1.5 million.[45]

From October 6 to the end of 1932, deposits in the new Dawes bank increased from $72,330,629 to $80 million. Deposits rose another $4 million in 1933 and then leaped to $97 million by the end of 1934, an incredible amount for a two-year-old institution. The bank also enjoyed a banner year in 1935, when deposits reached $121 million, and it continued to grow throughout 1936, with deposits rising to $128 million. This pattern of growth continued unabated, and by 1941, deposits had risen to $185 million.[46]

With low-cost deposits and no liability for the RFC loans, the City National Bank made millions of dollars from its grand opening on October 6, 1932, to May 24, 1946, when the old bank was finally dissolved, leaving the RFC with millions of dollars of losses. During those years, which included the boom period of World War II in Chicago, the RFC received an infinitesimal amount of interest. Needless to say, the RFC should have forced the new bank to comply with the terms and conditions of the original loan agreement, including the payment of principal and interest. Instead, the new Dawes bank was allowed to generate windfall profits that were distributed to Dawes and his family in the form of salaries and benefits and dividends.[47]

Notes

1. H. M. Dawes to O. D. Young, October 6, 1932 (telegram), ODYP/SLU.

2. Herbert Hoover to Henry B. Steagall, July 8, 1932, HHP/HHPL; Stephen A. Schuker, "The Candidacy That Never Was: Owen D. Young and the Presidential Election of 1932," *Statesmen Who Were Never President*, edited by Kenneth W. Thompson, Miller Center Series on Statesmen Defeated for President (Lanham, Md.: University Press of America, 1996), 2:127, 130, 133–36; Tarbell, *Owen D. Young*, viii, 147, 300, 302; Pusey, *Eugene Meyer*, 225; Case and Case, *Owen D. Young*, 582.

3. *Chicago Tribune*, May 17, 18, 1932; Schuker, "The Candidacy That Never Was," 127, 130, 133–36; Baruch, *Baruch*, 237, 238; Case and Case, *Owen D. Young*, 564–72.

4. M. H. McIntyre to Louie (no last name), November 1, 1931, FDRP/FDRL; *Chicago Tribune*, May 17, 18, June 14, 1932; Thompson, "Melvin A. Traylor," 226–30; "Melvin A. Traylor: Homespun American," Traylor for President Club, 14, 15.

5. *Reconstruction Finance Corporation v. Central Republic Trust Company*, 273–75; Sherman, "Charles G. Dawes," 131–32; O. D. Young to C. G. Dawes, August 2, 1935, CGDP/NUL; Williamson, "What Is the Relative Value?"

6. Congress later amended the RFC law to authorize the agency to purchase preferred stock in troubled banks. Proof of Claim of RFC against Central Republic Trust Company, Chicago, Illinois, March 16, 1935; Original Note of Central Republic Bank and Trust Company, October 6, 1932, People of the State of Illinois, Ex. Rel. Edward J. Barrett, Auditor of Public Accounts v. Central Republic Trust Company, CCCC; Wilson, *Harvey Couch: The Master Builder*, 141, 142, 162, 163; Williamson, "What Is the Relative Value?"

7. Franklin D. Roosevelt to Bernard M. Baruch, August 30, 1932; Baruch to Governor Roosevelt, December 20, 1932; Roosevelt to Baruch, March 13, 1933, BBP/PU; Franklin D. Roosevelt to Melvin A. Traylor, October 30, 1932; Traylor to Roosevelt, November 9, 1932 (telegram); Roosevelt to Traylor, December 1, 1932; Owen D. Young to the President, March 4, 1933 (telegram); Roosevelt to Young, March 9, 1933, FDRP/FDRL.

8. Bernard Baruch to Eugene Meyer, January 22, 1932 (telegram); Baruch to Meyer, August 20, 1942, EMP/LC; Owen Young to B. M. Baruch, "Memorandum," June 24, 1932, BBP/PU; B. M. Baruch to P. R. Pearson, June 24, 1935, CGDP/NUL; Hoover, *Memoirs*, 219–20; Agnes E. Meyer, "Diary of Mrs. Agnes E. Meyer," February 11, 1932; Rothbard, *America's Great Depression*, 247; Baruch, *The Public Years*, 183–84, 208; Margaret L. Coit, *Mr. Baruch* (Boston: Houghton Mifflin, 1957), 425; *Chicago Tribune*, May 18, 1932; Case and Case, *Owen D. Young*, 430, 475–76.

9. Wilson McCarthy to C. G. Dawes, July 19, 1932, CGDP/NUL; Olson, *Herbert Hoover and the Reconstruction Finance Corporation*, 41, 58, 59; Timmons, *Portrait of an American*, 319–20.

10. Bernard Baruch to Eugene Meyer, January 22, 1932 (telegram), EMP/LC; Bernard M. Baruch to Jesse H. Jones, October 6, 1933; Jones to Baruch, October 31, 1933, BBP/PU; Baruch, *The Public Years*, 183, 184, 234, 301–3; Timmons, *Jesse H. Jones*, 137; Case and Case, *Owen D. Young*, 550, 580.

11. B. M. Baruch to P. R. Pearson, June 24, August 8, 1935, CGDP/NUL.

12. Jones, *Fifty Billion Dollars*, 521; Wilson McCarthy to C. G. Dawes, July 19, 1932, CGDP/NUL; Case and Case, *Owen D. Young*, 582; Hoover, *Memoirs*, 168.

13. *Reconstruction Finance Corporation v. Central Republic Trust Company* (1937), 273–76; "Central Republic Bank," PRCP/UI.

14. "Central Republic Bank"; "To the Organization of the Central Republic Bank and Trust Company," n.d., PRCP/UI; Proof of Claim of RFC against Central Republic Trust Company, Chicago, Illinois, March 16, 1935; Original Note of Central Republic Bank and Trust Company, October 6, 1932, People of the State of Illinois, Ex. Rel. Edward J. Barrett, Auditor of Public Accounts v. Central Republic Trust Company, CCCC; *Reconstruction Finance Corporation v. Central Republic Trust Company* (1937), 270, 272–76.

15. *Reconstruction Finance Corporation v. Central Republic Trust Company* (1937), 274; "Central Republic Bank"; "Memorandum to A.W.H.," September 22, 1932; Rawleigh Warner to H. Wendell Endicott, September 21, 1932; "The National Bank and Trust Company of Chicago," August 29, 1932, PRCP/UI; Reconstruction Finance Corporation Act, January 21, 1932; Myers, *The State Papers . . . of Herbert Hoover*, 2:106–7.

16. "Memorandum to the Board of Directors" of Morton G. Bogue, n.d., EMP/LC; Mayer, Meyer, Austrian and Platt to Morton G. Bogue, September 26, 1932, RFC/NA.

17. Philip R. Clarke to Charles G. Dawes, n.d., PRCP/UI; *Reconstruction Finance Corporation Act*, Section 3, January 21, 1932, RFC/NA; *Reconstruction Finance Corporation v. Central Republic Trust Company* (1937), 274–75; Jones, *Fifty Billion Dollars*, 606; Wilson, *Harvey Couch: The Master Builder*, 160.

18. Philip R. Clarke to Charles G. Dawes, n.d., PRCP/UI; Decree of Judge James H. Wilkerson, May 1, 1937, RFC v. Central Republic Trust Company, Equity No. 14189, USDC/NDI.

19. Report to Philip R. Clarke, October 11, 1932; Andrew J. Dallstream to Philip Clarke, November 8, 1945; Opinion in the U.S. Circuit Court of Appeals for the Seventh Circuit, No. 8757, October Term and Session, 1945; *United States of America, On the Relation of Raymond J. Nitkey, and Raymond J. Nitkey in His Own Behalf, Plaintiff-Appellant, v. Charles G. Dawes, et al., Defendants-Appellees*, PRCP/UI.

20. Andrew J. Dallstream to Philip Clarke, November 8, 1945; Opinion in the U.S. Circuit Court of Appeals for the Seventh Circuit, No. 8757; *On the Relation of Raymond J. Nitkey, and Raymond J. Nitkey in His Own Behalf, Plaintiff-Appellant, v. Charles G. Dawes, et al., Defendants-Appellees*, PRCP/UI; *New York Times*, March 12, 1946.

21. *Reconstruction Finance Corporation v. Central Republic Trust Company* (1937), 275; "Central Republic Bank"; Robert H. McCormick to Philip R. Clarke,

September 20, 1932; Robert H. McCormick to Rawleigh Warner, September 20, 1932, PRCP/UI; Jones, *Fifty Billion Dollars*, 596; Olson, *Hoover and the Reconstruction Finance Corporation*, 74.

22. *Moody's . . . Public Utilities Securities*, *1931*, 946–47; *1932*, 2047–48; *1933*, 1367–69.

23. J. H. Jones to M. A. Traylor, August 6, 1932; Jones to O. D. Young, August 6, 1932, JJP/LC; *Moody's . . . Industrial Securities*, *1932*, 2346; *1933*, 864.

24. "Memorandum to the Board of Directors" of Morton G. Bogue, n.d.; "First Quarterly Report of R.F.C.," April 1, 1932, EMP/LC; *Chicago Tribune*, November 24, 1931, May 3, 11, June 14, 1932.

25. "Memorandum to the Board of Directors" of Morton G. Bogue, n.d., EMP/LC; "First Quarterly Report of R.F.C.," April 1, 1932.

26. *Reconstruction Finance Corporation v. Central Republic Trust Company* (1937), 275–76; *Martindale-Hubbell Law Directory* (New York: Martindale-Hubbell Law Directory, 1933), 1:279; Thomas L. Marshall to Philip R. Clarke, December 29, 1932; Statement of Central Republic Trust Company, December 31, 1932, PRCP/UI; *Chicago Tribune*, June 30, 1932.

27. "Memorandum" by Eugene Meyer, June 27, 1932, EMP/LC; Pusey, *Eugene Meyer*, 223–24; *Reconstruction Finance Corporation v. Central Republic Trust Company* (1937), 274, 291, 297.

28. *Reconstruction Finance Corporation v. Central Republic Trust Company* (1937), 274, 291, 297.

29. Ibid., 267–72, 274, 276, 297.

30. Ibid., 267, 269, 276.

31. Ibid., 277, 278.

32. "Dawes' reply for Court—draft," CGDP/NUL; *Chicago Tribune*, September 17, 1932; Williamson, "What Is the Relative Value?"

33. "The National Bank and Trust Company of Chicago," August 29, 1932, PRCP/UI; Wilson, *Harvey Couch: The Master Builder*, 162, 163; Sherman, "Dawes," 132–33; Pusey, *Eugene Meyer*, 225.

34. O. D. Young to C. G. Dawes, September 14, 19, 1932 (telegrams); C. G. Dawes to O. D. Young, September 15, 1932 (telegram), CGDP/NUL; "Notice of Distribution of Capital Stock of Central Republic Company to Stockholders of Central Republic Trust Company," December 9, 1933; "Balance Sheet, Central Republic Company, Chicago," November 30, 1933, PRCP/UI; *Chicago Tribune*, November 19, 1932.

35. Herbert Hoover to Charles G. Dawes, September 16, 1932, CGDC/EHC; Address of Jesse H. Jones, chairman of the RFC, Honoring Owen D. Young . . . May 20, 1936, RFC/NA; Case and Case, *Owen D. Young*, 274, 277, 283, 289, 309, 311, 313, 499, 602; Hoover, *Memoirs*, 17.

36. *Reconstruction Finance Corporation v. Central Republic Trust Company* (1937), 276; R. J. Taylor to Ira Moore, July 18, 1933, RFC/NA.

37. G. W. Merz to Francis Seiberling, May 12, 1932; Seiberling to Lawrence Richey, May 13, 1932; Herbert Hoover to C. G. Dawes, May 14, 1932; C. G. Dawes to Hoover, May 18, May 25, 1932, CGDP/NUL.

38. *Reconstruction Finance Corporation v. Central Republic Trust Company* (1937), 263, 273–78, 280; Timmons, *Portrait of an American*, 321; Williamson, "What Is the Relative Value?"

39. Complaint, *McIlvaine v. City National Bank*, SCCC; Answer of City National Bank, *McIlvaine v. City National Bank*; Rawleigh Warner to Philip R. Clarke, January 3, 1933; Philip R. Clarke to W. Irving Bullard, October 10, 1932, PRCP/UI; R. J. Taylor to Ira Moore, July 18, 1933, RFC/NA.

40. Complaint, *McIlvaine v. City National Bank*, SCCC; Answer of City National Bank, *McIlvaine v. City National Bank*, PRCP/UI.

41. *Reconstruction Finance Corporation v. Central Republic Trust Company* (1937), 280; *McIlvaine v. City National Bank*, SCCC; Jones, *Fifty Billion Dollars*, 80; Williamson, "What Is the Relative Value?"

42. "Outline of Procedure for Release of Publicity and Advertising Covering Readjustment of the Central Republic Bank and Trust Company and Launching of the City National Bank and Trust Company," n.d.; "To the Organization of the Central Republic Bank and Trust Company," n.d.; Philip R. Clarke to Our Correspondents, October 6, 1932; Board of Directors, Central Republic Bank and Trust Company to the Stockholders of Central Republic Bank and Trust Company, October 5, 1932; "Central Republic to continue trust and loan departments," statement by Joseph E. Otis, n.d.; "Chicago Gets New Loop Bank Today"; "Central Republic Retires from Commercial Banking," News Materials for Release Thursday morning, October 6, PRCP/UI; "City National, Gen. Dawes New Bank, Launched: Takes Over Central Republic Savings," *Chicago Tribune*, October 7, 1932.

43. Gibbs Lyons to Board of Directors, City National Bank and Trust Company, June 27, 1933, PRCP/UI. When J. F. T. O'Connor was comptroller of the currency, he was regarded as a "California politician and vibrant personality." Ross M. Robertson, *The Comptroller and Bank Supervision: A Historical Appraisal* (Washington, D.C.: Office of the Comptroller of the Currency, 1968), 127, 128, 134, 173; Williamson, "What Is the Relative Value?"

44. *Reconstruction Finance Corporation v. Central Republic Trust Company* (1937), 280, 281; C. G. Dawes to D. G. Wing, October 13, 1934; C. G. Dawes to O. D. Young, December 31, 1934, CGDP/NUL.

45. C. G. Dawes to O. D. Young, December 31, 1934, CGDP/NUL.

46. *McIlvaine v. City National Bank*, SCCC; C. G. Dawes to O. D. Young, June 20, 1941, CGDP/NUL.

47. *Chicago Tribune*, October 7, 1932; *Chicago Tribune*, May 25, 1946; Sherman, "Dawes," 132–39.

Chapter 7

The Winners and Losers

"I have erred but my greatest error was in underestimating the effects of the financial panic on American securities and particularly on the companies I was trying to build. I worked with all of my energy to save those companies. I made mistakes, but they were honest mistakes. They were errors in judgment and not dishonest manipulations."

—Samuel Insull, May 12, 1932[1]

Charles Dawes and his brothers and their families were big winners following the panic that gripped major banks in the Loop at the end of June 1932. Dawes's remarkably audacious brinkmanship rescued his family's fortune, but he had to resort to fraudulent tactics. Nevertheless, his brazen influence peddling ensured that he would continue to be a major player in Chicago and on the national scene until his death in 1951.

Insull was the biggest loser in wealth and reputation in the collapse that brought down his empire. Despite his reckless and corrupt activities, albeit with the complicity of the nation's top political leaders, Insull could argue, which his son Junior did through Forrest McDonald, that he had succeeded in his career because he made electricity increasingly available at lower and lower prices.

Ultimately, in 1953, Congress closed down the RFC. It continued to be engulfed in controversy and the same charges of political corruption that marked the Dawes bailout surrounded other activities, most notably a loan to the Baltimore and Ohio Railroad Company. In that case, as in the Dawes loans, there was ample evidence of political influence and self-dealing. The RFC lasted as long as it did because it was shrouded in secrecy throughout its existence, which hid the impact of its revolving door on its lending practices.

RFC officials participated in the granting of loans and then moved from the agency to the businesses that had benefited from those loans.

INSULL FLEES

As the federal government was bailing out Dawes and his family, removing the Insull loans from their bank's balance sheet, prosecutors launched a criminal investigation of Samuel Insull and his family and associates, in September 1932. Several months earlier, Insull's Middle West Utilities Company and his Midland Utilities Company, along with his two investment trusts, Insull Utility Investments and Corporation Securities, had all sought protection from their creditors in bankruptcy court. Public investors in Insull securities would suffer real value losses of about $638 million as a result of the collapse of the Insull empire. Adding to the public furor, the receivers of Insull's companies disclosed that brokerage fees had run into the millions of dollars and that members of Insull's "secret syndicate lists" had profited handsomely from inside information.[2]

As Swanson, the Cook County state's attorney, had revealed that September, Insull had established two secret syndicates composed of bankers, businessmen, and politicians. These privileged few had been given the right to purchase shares of IUI at well below market prices. Soon Dwight H. Green, the ambitious Republican federal prosecutor for Chicago, who Hoover appointed but he would remain the U.S. attorney under Roosevelt for long enough to prosecute Insull, held his own press conference to announce an investigation of Insull and his companies. Not to be preempted by his federal counterpart, Swanson then convinced a Cook County grand jury to indict Insull and his brother Martin in October 1932, just before his reelection bid failed. Following Swanson's lead, the grand jury charged the Insull brothers "with stealing and embezzling $66,000 from Middle West Utilities Company."

A few months later, in February 1933, Green's federal grand jury indicted Insull and sixteen other defendants—including his son Junior; Harold Stuart of Halsey, Stuart & Company, Insull's securities firm; Stanley Field, a director of the Edison Company and the Continental Illinois Bank; and Waldo Tobey, Insull's personal attorney at Isham, Lincoln and Beale, who was also a member of the IUI syndicate of insiders—for defrauding thousands of purchasers of the stock of Corporation Securities Company and marketing through the U.S. mails "the worthless stock of this corporation at highly inflated and fictitious prices." Green, who would serve as governor of Illinois from 1941 to 1949, returned to the grand jury in May 1933 to obtain another indictment against Insull, his son, and Harold Stuart, this time for bankruptcy fraud.[3]

A year earlier, Insull's wife, Gladys, had joined him in Paris, where they spent the next several months living in a hotel. But after Swanson's Cook County grand jury indicted Insull in October 1932, he fled France to avoid being extradited and prosecuted. As he said in his memoirs: "I had been advised that I had been made the center of a political campaign, and not having any idea of 'putting my head in the lion's mouth,' I decided to leave Paris." With his wife remaining in France, Insull traveled to Milan, Italy, by train with his son, Junior. He then leased a small plane and flew to Tirana, the capital of Albania, and then on to Salonika, Greece. After the turbulent trip across the Adriatic Sea, which happened to be Insull's first ride in an airplane, he was delighted to board a train to Athens, where he stayed at the luxurious Grande Bretagne Hotel. But he was now a seventy-two year old fugitive.[4]

When Insull arrived in Athens on October 9, 1932, Greece had not yet ratified an extradition treaty with the United States, but the next month Greece and the United States exchanged treaty ratifications. Almost as important, Insull had enjoyed a longtime friendship with Sir Basil Zaharoff, who may have been the most influential man in Greece. As a result, Insull managed to stall extradition, hiring Greek lawyers to vigorously resist deportation. Nearly two years elapsed before prosecutors were able to bring America's most famous fugitive to trial. After losing several attempts to extradite Insull, Roosevelt's administration increased its pressure on the Greek government, which finally capitulated. On March 13, 1934, before his temporary visa expired, Insull chartered a dilapidated vessel, the S.S. *Maiotis*. To disguise himself, Insull darkened his white hair and mustache before he sailed from Greece. Then the drama on the high seas began as Congress quickly passed legislation allowing officials of the U.S. government to arrest Insull in countries that had extradition treaties with the United States.[5]

When it was learned that Insull had landed in Istanbul for supplies, the American ambassador demanded that the government of Turkey arrest him even though Turkey had not ratified the extradition treaty, which it had signed in 1923. Nevertheless, Turkey complied with the State Department's demands. Turkish officials boarded the Greek vessel and arrested Insull, causing a furor in Greece. After three nights in a sleazy jail and a few legal formalities, the Turkish court released Insull to the custody of a State Department official. He was then shipped ignominiously back to the United States. After a long but relaxing journey, a refreshed Insull arrived in Chicago in May 1934 to proclaim his innocence to a waiting throng of reporters.[6]

Insull's federal trial began in October 1934 before Judge James H. Wilkerson, who had been on the federal bench for twelve years and was best known for his sentencing of Al Capone to eleven years in prison. Insull and the other defendants were charged with fraudulently manipulating the market for the securities of his Corporation Securities Company when they traded large blocks of its stock at fictitious prices through affiliated companies. The essence of the government's case was that Insull and his alleged co-conspirators had used the U.S. mail to steal more than a hundred million dollars from thousands of ordinary people through stock manipulation.

Wilkerson and Insull had been friends for decades, so the conduct of Insull's trial was far more polite than Wilkerson's stern admonitions cast at Capone during his trial. When it was finally time for Insull to face the music, there was no better place for him to be than in Judge Wilkerson's courtroom. They had developed a close relationship during the early 1900s when Wilkerson was serving in the Illinois legislature and then when he served as the Cook County attorney from 1903 to 1904. He went on to be a special federal prosecutor from 1906 to 1911, during which time he prosecuted the Standard Oil Company, resulting in a $29 million judgment against it. In 1911, President Taft appointed Wilkerson as Chicago's U.S. Attorney and Woodrow Wilson reappointed him to the post, in which he served until 1914. He then entered the private practice of law, joining the firm of Brundage, Wilkerson, and Cassels. After Governor Lowden, a Republican, was elected in 1916, he appointed Wilkerson to the Public Utility Commission of Illinois, where he was subsequently named chairman. So Wilkerson was head of the agency that regulated Insull's utility companies. During this time Wilkerson headed a local charity that Insull supported significantly. While serving on the commission, Wilkerson served alongside Patrick Lucey, one of Insull's lawyers who would later become the receiver of Insull's Corporation Securities. Wilkerson's law partner, Edward J. Brundage, then a two-term attorney general of Illinois, appointed Wilkerson as a special assistant attorney general specifically to prosecute Len Small, the Republican governor who had been elected in 1920 and who was subsequently acquitted of misappropriation of state funds. Attorney General Brundage had also supported Wilkerson in 1922 when President Warren Harding appointed him to the federal bench. After Wilkerson became a federal judge, according to a House investigator, "fees of $1,000,000, it was said, were the first year given to Mr. Brundage as the payment of a political debt." Hoover later nominated Wilkerson to the Circuit Court of Appeals, but the Democrats in the Senate thwarted his confirmation.[7]

The government called more than 135 witnesses, including receivers, employees of Insull's defunct companies, accountants, and purchasers of Insull securities from throughout the country. After the prosecution finished its side of the case, following a month of tedious but incriminating testimony, it seemed that Insull's defense team faced an uphill struggle. To counterbalance the sheer volume of evidence against Insull and the other defendants, the defense made a brilliant strategic move: as their first witness, they called Insull, whose appearance was that of an elderly and courtly gentleman. Nearly seventy-five years old, Insull had dictated his memoirs in preparation for this moment. When he took the stand and began his story, the jurors were entranced. By the time he described how he had risen from being Thomas Edison's private secretary to heading the largest utility system in the nation, the prosecution's case was a shambles. Insull finished his rags-to-riches-to-rags story, confiding to the jury that he was totally broke. He left them with the impression that, like them, he, too, had been a victim of the Depression.[8]

A scant two hours after the jurors began deliberations, the announcement came: Insull, his son, and the other defendants were innocent of all of the mail fraud charges. Young was delighted when he heard the news that Insull and Junior were acquitted of the federal charges. He immediately wrote to both men to extend his "heartiest congratulations and best wishes." Young observed that Insull had "excited the admiration of all" during "the long struggle" in which he "so valiantly defended" himself. He confided that he had "very great reservations" when Insull stayed out of the country for so long when criminal charges were pending against him. But Young added that the acquittal showed that Insull had taken the right course of action during a period of time when "the general demand for sacrifices" was so strong. Young told Insull that it was "fair to say that with the peculiar situation existing in Chicago, you might, under the tension of that high feeling, have been made a victim." Young also expressed his "greatest joy and satisfaction" to Junior, emphasizing his courage and loyalty: "You loyally stood by in times of prosperity, and what is even more important you stood by in times of adversity."[9]

Still, Young, whose reputation had been tarnished because of his relationship with Insull, did not think it was a good idea to contribute to Insull's defense fund. Charles A. Munroe, formerly the vice president of Peoples Gas Light and Coke Company who had given $9,278.50 to Insull "since his trouble," wrote Young in April 1935, to solicit his help so Insull could "clean up his bills in connection with his trials." Young responded that he and Swope could not provide assistance: "For a reason I shall explain to you when I see you."[10]

But Insull's ordeal was not over, since he still faced a state embezzlement charge and a federal bankruptcy fraud indictment. In March 1935, he and his brother Martin were tried in state court for allegedly embezzling $66,000 from the Middle West Utilities Company. When the Insulls were acquitted for lack of evidence after a short trial, the state prosecutor dismissed the other state charges.[11]

Franklin Roosevelt's new U.S. attorney, Michael L. Igoe, also attempted to send the Insulls to prison in June 1935. Yet Igoe, who had resigned from the U.S. House of Representatives to become the federal prosecutor for Chicago, had his own conflict of interest since he had been one of Insull's insiders who subscribed to the IUI syndicate in 1930. When Insull, Son and Company filed its petition for bankruptcy in 1933, Igoe owed $7,629.91 to it for the IUI stock subscription. While the trustee of Insull's defunct company was pressing Igoe for payment, Igoe was prosecuting Insull and his son. In 1939, the trustee of Insull, Son and Company filed a report listing the collections received from the insiders of the IUI stock subscription, showing that Igoe—then a U.S. district judge in Chicago whom Roosevelt appointed—had still paid only $3,282.88.[12]

When Igoe's office filed criminal charges against Insull, his son, and Harold Stuart, the indictment alleged that they had illegally transferred assets out of the Corporation Securities Company, just before its bankruptcy filing, to the benefit of certain creditors, including Owen Young's General Electric Company. Young, indebted to Insull for several sweetheart stock deals, returned those favors, arranging for GE to loan Insull's company $2 million in December 1931, receiving $1.25 million worth of securities to secure the loan. When the government finished its case, the defense moved to dismiss the charges for insufficient evidence. Judge John C. Knox, who had been assigned from the southern district of New York, agreed that the government had failed to meet the burden of proof and dismissed the case. But until Insull's death in Paris on July 16, 1938, he would remain entangled in civil litigation resulting from the collapse of his empire.[13]

By then Insull's estate owned no real estate and no securities and contained only $1,031 in cash. It also held a residual interest in a trust established with the Dawes bank on June 14, 1932, to satisfy claims of creditors. Insull had transferred all of his valuable real estate and personal property into the trust. Even so, his estate's residual interest in the trust was worthless since the value of Insull's assets was only $933,000, while the unpaid claims of his creditors totaled about $19 million.

The posthumous public auction of Insull's securities only realized $2,170,841, so when this amount was combined with the dividends from the pledged collateral on November 1, 1938, Insull still owed, in just one instance, $2,617,212 of principal and $865,633 of interest on his 1932 personal loan of $5 million to the National City Bank of New York.[14]

Prosecutors failed to convict Insull of a crime, in large part, because he went down with his ship. Insull seems to be a more sympathetic figure than Dawes and his banker colleagues in the Loop, whose fortunes were saved because of repeated government bailouts. But what is indisputable is that

Insull manipulated the financial system and violated the banking laws to build and maintain control over his utility domain. In the process, he also breached his fiduciary duties to his stockholders and creditors, decimating the life savings of those who believed his misleading and false statements that concealed the insolvent condition of many of his companies.

What is also indisputable is that officials of the Dawes bank, Traylor's First National Bank, and the Reynolds brothers' Continental Illinois Bank published false financial statements, which fraudulently concealed the deplorable conditions of their banks. Still, the publicity surrounding the collapse of the Insull empire exposed the speculative and illegal lending practices of Chicago's bankers, which continued unabated even after the stock market crash of 1929, and significantly contributed to the failure of the Dawes bank and Chicago's panic in June 1932.

Unlike Insull, however, the Dawes brothers did not have to worry about being prosecuted at the state level because their chief regulator, Oscar Nelson, was a major borrower of the Dawes bank, and the Cook County prosecutor, John Swanson, was one of its stockholders.[15]

DEBTS UNPAID AND LAWSUITS

It was only a few weeks before Hoover's defeat that Dawes opened his new institution, the City National Bank, drawing on the last $50 million installment of the loans from the Reconstruction Finance Corporation to the Central Republic Bank, the old Dawes bank. Inevitably, when the Dawes loans became due in full on December 24, 1932, the old Dawes bank defaulted on the principal and interest. The continuing default of interest proved that the collateral pledged to secure the loan was woefully inadequate. As long as Hoover remained in the White House—until March 1933—no efforts were made to collect on the Dawes loans. Even after Roosevelt's inauguration, with Jesse Jones named as chairman of the RFC, the agency's ongoing reluctance to file a collection action against Dawes and the other stockholders of the Central Republic Bank remained the unofficial stance of the new administration.

Charles Dawes and Franklin Roosevelt had a cordial relationship. At a private dinner in 1931 when Dawes was the ambassador to Great Britain and Roosevelt was the governor of New York, Dawes had explained to Roosevelt that the Chicago World's Fair "was in dire straits." Roosevelt had privately agreed to support the Dawes project, despite publicly supporting fiscal belt-tightening, proclaiming that there were "fifty ways in which the [state] budget can be cut." A few months later, on January 26, 1932, after Hoover had tapped

Image 7.1.   Chairman of the RFC Jesse Jones pounding his fist to make a point to Chairman Henry B. Steagall and the House Banking and Currency Committee. (Courtesy, Library of Congress)

Dawes to be president of the RFC, Roosevelt submitted a supplementary budget to the New York legislature that included a $75,000 appropriation for the state of New York's participation in the Chicago World's Fair. Dawes later told Roosevelt that "this action in itself and in the example it set for the other States was an indispensable element in a final success." And in 1935 Dawes made the following positive comment about the Roosevelt administration: "Anybody who thinks the New Deal hasn't helped the banks, doesn't know a damn thing about banks."[16]

The RFC's inaction was made possible because the machinations of Dawes and his colleagues were kept hidden from the public, a policy of official secrecy that continued throughout the Roosevelt administration. But many of the stockholders of the Central Republic Bank—the ones who had not only lost their entire investment in the old Dawes bank but had been required to pay an additional stockholders' assessment equal to their original investment—understood all too well what Dawes and his partners had done. Edgar B. Penney, the restrained vice president and treasurer of C. A. Mosso Laboratories of Chicago, expressed to Dawes the opinions of the stockholders who had trusted him. Penney, who had owned twenty shares of the old Dawes bank on October 6, 1932, and later would be ordered to pay $2,000 to its receiver, thought the Dawes plan to liquidate the old bank for the benefit of the new bank was "very unfair and bordering on a dishonest high finance manipulation."[17]

Penney wrote a diplomatic letter to Dawes on September 20, 1932. In it he noted that he and his wife, Minnie F. Penney, a national committee-woman from Nebraska when Dawes was nominated for the vice presidency, had invested in the Central Republic Bank because they trusted and admired Dawes. But the Penneys believed the formation of the new bank was "an attempt to profit by the present established business, leaving all excess rental leases, 'cats and dogs' of all descriptions, to be taken care of by the old bank." Penney could not understand how the City National Bank could succeed with the same officers as the old bank, "especially if all stockholders in Central Republic see their investment wiped out by the proposed liquidation." Penney said that, at a minimum, Dawes should hold a stockholders' meeting, where all of the cards would be "laid on the table" and the stockholders would be allowed to vote on Dawes's reorganization plans. Dawes ignored Penney's advice and continued to refuse to hold a stockholders' meeting to approve the controversial reorganization plan prior to its implementation. Dawes did, however, approve the holding of a special stockholders' meeting, on November 19, 1932, to ratify the reorganization, six weeks after the new Dawes bank had been formed.[18]

A stockholder of the old Dawes bank, Fred Franz, rejected the offer to subscribe to the new Dawes bank: "How can you insult my intelligence by asking me to subscribe to your new fly by nite venture, the City National Bank & Trust Company? As a former stockholder of the National Bank of the Republic under the mismanagement of George Woodruff and after con-solidation with the Central Trust Company, I have learned a great deal about our Chicago bankers and their unethical business tactics. . . . My friends and myself have no intentions of trusting you and your associates with our sav-ings. Last month I even disposed of my box in your safety vault."[19]

Yet Harold Greist, a friend of Philip Clarke, the president of the new Dawes bank, wrote Clarke to say that he had read Clarke's statement in the newspaper and was pleased that "the new City National Bank owes nothing to the Reconstruction Finance Corporation. . . . There seem to be a great many people who do not realize that the loan of the Reconstruction Finance Corpo-ration is against Central Republic and not City National." Greist concluded his letter to Clarke saying that his statement in the newspaper "should help somewhat to alleviate the ill feeling of the stockholders." Privately, Clarke was even more revealing: "The paramount objective, of course, was the frustration of receivership with the forced liquidation and stock liability suits that would accompany it."[20]

The stockholders of the old Dawes bank knew they were liable for the par value of the worthless shares they were holding. One such stockholder was Edward Menkin, who told Clarke that he was opposed to transferring the old bank's deposits to the new Dawes bank "unless you satisfy me that there will be no stockholders liability." As he put it, "I am entitled to know the diagnosis of the baby's ailment which was born on July 27, 1931 [when the old Dawes bank merged with the National Bank of the Republic], and died on October 6th 1932 [when the old Dawes bank ceased conducting a banking business], what was the sickness?"[21]

More than two years elapsed before Edward J. Barrett, the newly elected state auditor and banking commissioner, appointed a receiver for the old Dawes bank. Barrett, a Democrat, was a fresh face who had been elected as the Illinois state treasurer in 1930 at the age of thirty. After Oscar Nelson, the Republican state auditor, was indicted, Barrett decided to run for the powerful post which also regulated all of the state-chartered banks of Illinois.

The ambitious Barrett finally took action to liquidate the old Dawes bank on November 21, 1934—long after it had ceased conducting a banking business. Philip Clarke later complained about "the element of politics" that "influenced appointments" in the receiverships of failed banks in Chicago, resulting in unnecessarily "heavy expenses." As if proving this point, Barrett appointed William O'Connell, a powerful Democratic politician who had supported Lawrence Sherman, Dawes's Republican confidant, when he was running for the Senate. And O'Connell's credentials were solid in the Roosevelt administration because he had voted for Roosevelt when he was a delegate to the Democratic convention in 1932. O'Connell had also been a director of the South Side Savings Bank and Trust Company of Chicago, which closed on June 6, 1931. He was paid $25,000 a year (about $401,000 today) as the receiver for the Dawes bank for a part-time position, but he defaulted on an $18,000 loan from the South Side Savings Bank and still owed $11,000 on the loan in September 1934, about which he explained: "Times have been hard, and money hard to come by. I have paid what I could."

Barrett also named the law firm of Igoe and Flaherty as counsel for the Dawes receivership. The firm's senior partner, Michael Igoe—later Roosevelt's federal prosecutor in Chicago—was formerly a state representative and had been a delegate to the 1932 Democratic convention, where he had nominated Melvin Traylor for president as the "favorite son" candidate for the Illinois delegation, which was led by Traylor's protégé, Mayor Cermak. Igoe continued to play the lucrative receivership game, and the receiver of the defunct Lincoln Trust and Savings Bank of Chicago retained his firm in 1934.[22]

Illinois Attorney General Otto Kerner also joined with Barrett to file a complaint against the Central Republic Trust Company. The complaint stated that an examination of the defunct bank's books and records "disclosed purported resources" or assets of $78,094,390 on November 20, 1934. The examination determined that the assets of the old Dawes bank "were and are erroneous and did not and do not correctly reflect the true value thereof and that the value of certain items of resources did not and do not equal the amounts, respectively, for which said resources were carried on the books of said corporation." The examination also found that the condition of the defunct bank was so poor that the impaired capital could not be restored. Furthermore, the bank "was operating with an insufficient portion of its assets in cash or readily convertible securities; and the business of said bank was being conducted in an unsafe manner." Barrett had determined that the old bank was in such bad shape that it could not be reorganized and thus had to be liquidated.[23]

The old Dawes bank still owed $61,692,993 on the RFC loans (about $988 million today), a sum which had been in default since December 24, 1932. And the purported assets of $78,094,390, which were theoretically available to pay back the loans, had been grossly overstated by the officers and directors of the bank. The situation was hopeless, so the banking commissioner seized the bank and wiped out the stockholders' equity of $15,400,000, representing $14,000,000 of capital and surplus of $1,400,000. Not only did the stockholders lose their investments of 140,000 shares, with a par value of $100 each, they would now face a lawsuit to collect on the stockholders' liability, which would be equal to their investment in the defunct bank.[24]

The receivership to dissolve the old Dawes bank, which would continue until May 24, 1946, ended the charade. Simultaneous with the receivership in 1934, and even though Jones remained as head of the RFC, the agency filed suit against Charles Dawes, his brothers Henry and Rufus and other Dawes family members, the Dawes Brothers, Inc., and other Dawes entities, along with about four thousand other stockholders of the Central Republic Bank. In addition to being forced to pay the full amount of their investment, which had been lost, the stockholders of the old Dawes bank also had to pay for the litigation to establish the RFC's claim against their personal assets. The collection agents of the federal government would hound the individual stockholders and their heirs for the next two decades. If the assessment was not paid before a stockholder's death, the RFC would file a claim against the estate to force the sale of real estate or any other property that could be located to satisfy the RFC judgment. To finance these efforts, the RFC would use the resources of the federal government to collect judgments, which included the debtors' income tax returns.[25]

The day the RFC filed suit against Dawes—November 19, 1934—he arrived in Hot Springs, Arkansas, on the same train with Owen Young. They were attending a high-powered gathering that Harvey Couch, who had resigned from the RFC that August before the suit against Dawes had been filed, had organized. The event was held at Couch's rustic lodge, Couchwood, located on an island on Lake Catherine, which was named for Couch's only daughter. Couch and Senator Joe Robinson greeted Dawes and Young at the railroad station and then they traveled to Couchwood, where "everything [was] off the record."[26]

Finally, nearly two years after the old Dawes bank had defaulted, the RFC began its attempt to recover its unprecedented losses from the stockholders of the bank. Its lawsuit sought to collect assessments on the bank's outstanding stock, which Charles Dawes had pledged as collateral for the bailout. Under the Illinois banking code:

> Every stockholder in any bank . . . shall be individually responsible and liable to its creditors, over and above the amount of stock by him or her held to an amount equal to his or her respective shares so held, for all its liabilities accruing while he or she remains such stockholder.

Charles Dawes was the largest stockholder of Dawes Brothers, Inc., which had a net worth of more than $2.5 million by 1935. And he and his brothers and their entities controlled the Central Republic Bank. But despite his promises, Dawes vigorously resisted the stockholder assessments, which were a primary condition of the RFC loan and a strict obligation under the Illinois banking code and constitution.[27]

To do so, lawyers for Charles Dawes and his family made the frivolous argument that Dawes Brothers, Inc., a privately held Dawes concern, acted outside the scope of authority provided in its articles of incorporation and outside the general corporation laws of Maine, where it was incorporated, when it bought stock in the Central Republic Bank. Thus the company was not liable to the RFC or any other creditor of the bank. A federal judge rejected Dawes's position, holding that Charles Dawes, his brothers, their entities, and other Dawes family members were liable for the full assessments on their stock.[28]

The actual ownership position and documented legal maneuvers of Charles Dawes and his brothers were in direct conflict with the version given in Jones's memoir. In his memoirs, Jones wrote: "Though the Dawes family interests willingly paid their assessments in full in the liquidation of their bank, we had to go to court to collect from some of the Central Republic's other 4,000 stockholders." It is remarkable that Jones would publish such a statement, having watched, at close hand, Dawes and his family members aggressively fight to delay payment of the inevitable stockholder assessments for years. But Dawes's old friend, former senator Lawrence Sherman, conceded that "it was a disaster [for the old Dawes bank] to be in such a condition as to require such extraordinary steps."[29]

Dawes lost the RFC suit on May 1, 1937, when U.S. District Judge James Wilkerson declared that the Dawes brothers and other Central Republic Bank shareholders were liable for $10,500,000, which would be about $157 million in today's money. Judge Wilkerson, the judge in the Insull mail fraud case, had firsthand knowledge of Dawes's business practices. As Chicago's U.S. Attorney, he prosecuted William Lorimer after his banking chain collapsed, so he was intimately aware of Dawes's role in the Lorimer scandal. Now Judge Wilkerson ordered the Dawes Brothers, Inc. to pay $978,600 (an amount worth about $14.6 million today). He also ordered Henry Dawes to pay $23,800, Rufus Dawes to pay $25,200, and their cousin, William Dawes, to pay $11,000. Their bank president, Philip Clarke, was ordered to pay $90,000. After the lawsuit was filed, Charles Dawes paid the amount of $5,200, the nominal sum that he owed on his individual shares of stock. However, throughout the litigation he personally directed the family's defense against the RFC's lawsuit.[30]

When Dawes formed the new national bank, he enhanced his family's patrimony and enabled his old bank to repay the loan at its leisure with inflated dollars. On July 23, 1935, after the new bank had been operating less than three years, Guy Huston and Company, a Chicago-based investment banking firm, recommended to its customers that the City National Bank's stock be considered as a "permanent holding" in their portfolios, "an investment that would certainly appreciate greatly in value." As evidence to support their recommendation, the investment bankers said: "Seldom, if ever before, has a new bank been set up with deposits almost twenty times its capital stock paid in to it in cash, a volume of business that would ordinarily take a generation to acquire by a newly organized bank." Citing the June 29, 1935, statement of condition, they observed the bank's "extreme liquidity" that "showed cash and government bonds in the amount of approximately $79,000,000 as against deposits of $102,872,000." By that time, no dividends had yet been paid, but the investment firm opined that "potential earnings per share are unusually high." A few months earlier, Dawes had blown his own horn to Owen Young, "I am enjoying freedom from debt, and have ample reserves."[31]

After Judge Wilkerson ordered the stockholders "to pay forthwith" in cash the $100 of par value for each share of stock that they owned in the old Dawes bank, Wynnett W. McIlvaine, a stockholder and former employee of the bank, filed a class action suit against Charles Dawes, his old and new banks, and the receiver of the old bank, Charles H. Albers, who had been appointed as the successor receiver after O'Connell died on July 24, 1936. McIlvaine sought to recover in excess of $8 million for the fraudulent conversion of the banking and trust business and goodwill of the Central Republic Bank and Trust Company.

(The Central Republic Trust Company, formerly the Central Republic Bank and Trust Company, had issued 140,000 shares of stock that were outstanding at the time of the RFC bailout. Judge Wilkerson ordered stockholders to pay $100 a share for each of the shares that they held, a total of $14,000,000. As a result, stockholders paid $11,234,848 to the receivers of the old Dawes bank, who made payments to the RFC on its loans.)[32]

The McIlvaine suit was based on the allegation that Dawes had fraudulently misrepresented to the RFC and to the board of directors of the Central Republic Bank that the $95 million bailout was "for the purpose of paying the depositors and to keep the bank open, and not in contemplation of liquidation." McIlvaine contended that despite his promises to the contrary, Dawes "within a few days thereafter . . . began to promote the organization of a new national bank for the purpose of acquiring the banking and trust business [of the Central Republic Bank]." The suit alleged that Dawes and the officers and directors of the old bank, who became the officers and directors of the new bank, were "charged with the responsibility of preserving the assets of [the Central Republic Bank] for the stockholders and creditors." But "in violation of said fiduciary relationship," they had transferred the banking business and "valuable good will" of the old bank to the City National Bank "without the payment of any consideration therefor and without the receipt of anything of value by the old bank."[33]

More than a year after the McIlvaine suit had been filed, Judge James F. Fardy dismissed the action on procedural grounds. Fardy emphasized that he was not ruling on the merits of the complaint or the "legality of the transactions attacked in the suit." Instead, he ruled that the lawsuit could not be brought on behalf of the stockholders but should have been filed in the name of the Central Republic Bank, which was in liquidation proceedings in another state court division. The only person empowered to bring such a suit was the receiver of the old Dawes bank, and two of them had already refused to sue Dawes for fraud. The civil case against Dawes, which also suffered from statute-of-limitation problems, suffered a similar fate at the appellate level.[34]

Starting in 1932 and continuing into the early 1950s, the taxpayers of the United States subsidized the Dawes family and their entities with tens of millions of Depression-era dollars—so much so that on December 31, 1934, a month after it had finally been forced into a receivership, the old Dawes bank owed the RFC $61,817,705, an amount worth $990 million today.[35]

A staff report of the RFC prepared, as of December 31, 1943, titled "Recovery Value of Collateral," reveals the final chapter of the Dawes saga. The report verified that the Dawes bank owed $44,323,918 as of that date, but it estimated that the recovery value of its remaining loans, investment securities, real estate paper, and other assets pledged to secure the loan was worth only $10,504,857, which included a $1 million increase that occurred during World War II in the market values of the securities. Yet even this estimate of the recovery potential of the aged collateral was dubious because the bank, and then its receivers, had been liquidating assets since October 1932, and the principal of the loan had been reduced at a slow pace.[36]

Using the optimistic recovery prediction and $10,500,000 in judgments collected from the stockholders of the old Dawes bank as a result of litigation, the amount available to repay the outstanding indebtedness was—at best—a total of $21,004,857, leaving a final loss to the RFC of $23,319,061 (an amount worth more than $289 million today), as of December 31, 1943.[37]

Though his influence with Franklin Roosevelt was waning, Jones was still chairman of the RFC in 1944, a presidential election year. In spite of the election being held during the war, Thomas E. Dewey, the hard-charging Republican governor of New York, was mounting a serious challenge to Roosevelt. Fearing the consequences of the election and Jones's loss of control of the RFC, the Jones group inside the agency attempted to clean up its books with respect to the Dawes loans. Disguising the extent of the loss to taxpayers, much as Jones had done throughout the 1930s with his bondholders, the RFC allowed the receiver of the old Dawes bank to reduce its indebtedness by swapping part of the debt in exchange for the questionable collateral, giving the nonperforming assets inflated values. In a number of transactions, the RFC arranged to purchase the stale assets by simply reducing the outstanding loan amount. Accepting title to the assets in lieu of cash payments, the RFC reflected on its books that the old Dawes bank owed only $9,726,467 on May 31, 1945, for the Dawes loans that had matured in December 1932.

Throughout that difficult period, when the United States was in the midst of the Great Depression and, later, World War II, the new Dawes bank—the City National Bank of Chicago—employed Dawes and members of his family and generated more than $9.25 million in after-tax profits for them and the limited number of stockholders. It also financed many of the entities of the Dawes brothers, including the Pure Oil Company. The City National Bank was the bedrock underpinning of the Dawes family during these troubled times, which witnessed a federal indictment of Henry Dawes and the Pure Oil Company.

In August 1936, a federal grand jury sitting in Madison, Wisconsin, indicted twenty-three major oil companies and fifty-eight executives—including the Dawes brothers' company and Henry Dawes—for conspiracy to fix gasoline prices in violation of the Sherman Antitrust Act. Prosecutors argued that the oil companies reaped $70 million in "illicit profits" through their scheme to raise and maintain artificial gasoline prices in the Middle West during 1935 and 1936. After spending two million dollars in legal fees during a trial that lasted 111 days, the Pure Oil Company, the Shell Petroleum Corporation, and fourteen other oil companies, along with Henry Dawes and twenty-nine other executives, were found guilty of conspiracy. And when a Madison grand jury issued a second indictment against the Pure Oil Company and Henry Dawes and the other companies and oil executives, the Dawes company and the other companies reached an agreement with prosecutors to pay fines and costs of a total of $385,000. As part of the settlement, antitrust charges against Dawes and the other top executives were dropped. Meanwhile, Henry Dawes and the other defendants filed a motion before the federal judge, Patrick T. Stone, to set aside the jury verdict in the first Madison trial. Judge Stone dismissed the charges against Dawes but upheld the conviction of the Dawes brothers' Pure Oil Company and a vice president of the company, R. H. McElroy Jr. After the government appealed Stone's ruling, the U.S. Supreme Court, in May 1940, upheld Dawes's dismissal and the conviction of the Pure Oil Company and McElroy in a comprehensive decision. Justice William O. Douglas wrote the decision in the Pure Oil case, which strengthened the price-fixing laws.[38]

While the government continued to liquidate assets of the old Dawes bank in 1947, the new Dawes bank proudly issued a pamphlet titled "Fifteen Years October 6th 1932—1947." On its cover stood a great lion, his magnificent head silhouetted against the rising sun. The pamphlet tells a remarkable success story, despite what the comptroller of the currency's office deemed "the excessive overhead expenses of the bank," which included high salaries for Dawes and its other officers.

The stockholders' equity was $5 million when the bank began in 1932. Fifteen years later it stood at $12,853,803, and that was after it had distributed dividends of $1,400,000 to the Dawes brothers and its other stockholders. So the bank generated an after-tax profit of $9,253,803 during that fifteen-year period.

As one of the most profitable banks in the country during this period, the Dawes bank did not generate the bulk of its profits by making loans. When it began, less than 21 percent of its assets were in loans, and fifteen years later its loans still comprised less than 26 percent of its assets. By then, U.S. government securities and cash represented 71 percent of its assets. And thanks to the government's subsidy—given that during all of those years, the new Dawes bank charged off a total of only $107,838 in loans—the Dawes brothers were able to enjoy their considerable profits with few risks and few of the customary operating expenses.[39]

THE DEMISE OF THE RFC

A pervasive policy of secrecy hid the illegal and reckless banking practices at Charles Dawes's Central Republic Bank, Melvin Traylor's First National Bank, and the Reynolds brothers' Continental Illinois Bank. The fraud and insider abuse at the Dawes bank and the other Loop banks were concealed from the public, as well as from the Department of Justice. Officially sanctioned secrecy prevented prosecutors from understanding the cozy relationships between directors of the RFC and many of the recipients of the agency's loans. Indeed, many of its loans went directly to entities that the RFC's directors controlled, including Jones's bank and mortgage companies.[40]

Although the Dawes bailout damaged the reelection campaign of Herbert Hoover, Charles Dawes's credibility and reputation remained solid enough to be of great assistance when individuals complained to the Department of Justice and when his own stockholders sued him for fraud. He managed to elude the charges because of official secrecy, clever legal maneuvers, and the aura of respectability that he was still able to project. The stockholders in the Central Republic Bank on the other hand, not only lost their entire investment in his bank but also paid a substantial penalty in the form of stock assessments, which were equal to their initial investment. The policy of regulatory and RFC secrecy tarnished the judicial system and denied to the stockholders and prosecutors knowledge they should have had regarding the complicity and corruption that was rife at the RFC.[41]

Had prosecutors known what the bank regulators and RFC examiners knew, Dawes could have been charged with defrauding the U.S. government. Moreover, if the Dawes stockholders—and the public—had known about the Dawes brothers' cozy relationships and the deplorable condition of the Dawes bank, approval of the last installment of the Dawes bailout, which was $50 million, could have been rescinded before the 1932 presidential election. This would have resulted in a savings of approximately $785 million in today's money to the cash-strapped federal government. But the well-protected secrecy shrouding the RFC and the banks that it bailed out allowed the abuses to flourish and to go undetected until now.

In addition, the leading bankers of Chicago, who had engaged in insider abuse while recklessly funding Insull's expansion program, were never prosecuted for issuing fraudulent financial statements or held liable for their gross negligence. Far from holding the bankers accountable for their participation in Insull's pyramid scheme, government officials instead bailed out the three Loop banks they knew to be most culpable.[42]

The Reynolds brothers' Continental Illinois Bank was the largest U.S. financial institution outside of New York. As we have seen, Insull cemented his relationship with the bank through the grant of preferred insider status to a total of thirteen of its officers and directors, including the Reynolds brothers. These same officials then obligingly concentrated 80 percent of the bank's capital in nearly $60 million of Insull's problem loans. In all, Insull borrowed more than $97 million from the three Loop banks controlled by the Reynolds brothers, Dawes, and Traylor. During 1932 these three banks published fraudulent call reports, representing that the Insull loans and other nonperforming assets were worth 100 cents on the dollar. Inevitably, several months after the panic had subsided Continental Illinois Bank was forced to write off $110 million of worthless assets, including the Insull loans.

George Reynolds and his brother, Arthur, who was the bank's chief executive officer, had not only grossly mismanaged the bank but had also procured large personal loans from it. And the machinations of the Reynolds family extended beyond its primary bank. The family also controlled the Peoples Trust and Savings Bank of Chicago, in which Dawes was a stockholder. This bank borrowed $16,421,642 from the Continental Illinois Bank in June 1932 to pay off its depositors, including themselves, in full. The Peoples Trust and Savings Bank then went into a voluntary liquidation on June 10, 1932, which left the Continental Illinois Bank with a loss on its loan of $5,576,041 of principal, and $677,340 of interest.

Nevertheless, the RFC, under the leadership of its new chairman, Jesse Jones, would bail out the Continental Illinois Bank's stockholders, including the Reynolds brothers, purchasing nearly $50 million of its preferred stock on December 22, 1933, a bailout worth about $828 million today. Soon after this bailout, A. P. Giannini hired Arthur Reynolds as vice chairman and chief executive officer of the Bank of America in San Francisco. Reynolds's appointment received the blessing of Comptroller of the Currency J. F. T. O'Connor, a political operative from California who continued to handle sensitive political assignments for Roosevelt even after being named chief regulator for the country's national banks. For five years prior to his selection to the powerful post, Comptroller O'Connor had been the law partner of Senator McAdoo, who had lobbied Roosevelt for his appointment, and he had also been a loyal friend of Bernard Baruch and Giannini.[43]

When Jones took over the RFC, he changed roles with his good friend and banker, Melvin Traylor, becoming lender instead of borrower. And in December 1933, Jones's RFC bailed out Traylor's bank, purchasing nearly $25 million of its preferred stock, an amount worth about $414 million today. This preferred stock purchase was authorized under a provision of the Emergency Banking Act of 1933, which Traylor had lobbied Congress to pass and became law during Roosevelt's first week in office. The sale of so-called equity was far more profitable for Traylor's bank than merely borrowing $25 million from the RFC on a short-term basis would have been, in that no payments of principal were required.

Jones also approved terms that left control of First National in the hands of Traylor and the same board of directors responsible for making the bad loans that had put the bank into its unsound condition in the first place. And Traylor and the other directors had approved for themselves and the other stockholders dividends of $26,662,500 between June 1929 and June 1932, a period of only three years. This extraordinary amount equaled more than the entire subsequent RFC bailout.[44]

Although it took more than two decades, the RFC was finally dismantled in 1957 after multiple charges of "political and personal favoritism" and several congressional investigations. Accusations of favoritism at the RFC had continued beyond the Hoover administration, and throughout the Roosevelt and Truman administrations. After World War II, there were a number of congressional investigations into the agency's operations and loans. In particular, two subcommittees of the Senate Committee on Banking and Currency investigated the RFC and held hearings between 1947 and 1951, concluding that favoritism had been shown on a bipartisan basis and that Democrats had received their fair share of largess. They also concluded that throughout the agency's existence, a revolving-door syndrome had plagued it, with officials routinely participating in the issuance of large loans to companies that they would subsequently join as officers and directors.[45]

One of the controversies that would lead eventually to the demise of the RFC involved loans of more than $85 million issued to the Baltimore and Ohio Railroad Company, a company whose top management later comprised a number of former employees of the RFC. After five former RFC officials joined its top management, the railroad company was able to gain approval in bankruptcy proceedings to extend its loan maturities for twenty years. Calling for an investigation in 1945, Burton Wheeler, the liberal Democrat from Montana who was chairman of the Senate Committee on Interstate Commerce, said: "It seems to me rather shocking that government officials charged with lending huge sums of money such as those lent to the B&O should shortly thereafter become officers and directors of the company to which the money was lent." Senator Wheeler stressed that "at least $82,000,000 of these loans are unpaid today. This is the largest sum outstanding in the form of loans by the government to any single railroad company."[46]

Breaking ranks with his colleagues, Cassius M. Clay, one of the former RFC officials who had been the general counsel of the B&O during its bankruptcy proceedings, testified before the Senate that the bankruptcy plan had been "a fraud upon the jurisdiction of the federal courts, and I think that is an offense that smells to heaven."[47]

Ironically, it was Hoover who called for the liquidation of the RFC when he headed the Hoover Commission on Organization of the Executive Branch of the Government, which issued a report to Congress in 1949. At the time, the RFC still had more than five thousand employees and thirty-one branch offices. The Hoover commission report concluded that "direct lending by the government to persons or enterprises opens up dangerous possibilities of waste and favoritism to individuals or enterprises. It invites political and private pressure, or even corruption." Nearly a generation after the Dawes loans, Hoover testified before the Senate: "Corruption in business affects only the pockets of the employer or the owner. Corruption in government affects the pockets of all taxpayers, but far worse, it affects the morals of a people and lowers their respect for government." Putting distance between himself and the scandals at the RFC, Hoover added, "It would appear that the test of public interest has been very little applied in recent years."[48]

The criticism of his role in the scandals stung Jones, who had been a board member and then head of the RFC for thirteen years. Writing to J. William Fulbright, the Democrat from Arkansas who was the chairman of the Senate's RFC subcommittee in 1950, Jones asserted that the agency "should be given a decent burial, lock, stock, and barrel . . . because none of the conditions which prompted the creation of the RFC exist today. . . . Government lending in competition with private business is not a proper function under our free-enterprise system. . . . There is ample credit for all legitimate and justifiable loans." In concluding his letter, Jones reminded Fulbright that "where the sugar is you will always find the flies."[49]

In 1951, after the Fulbright subcommittee found that "outside influence" and "political and personal favoritism" dominated the RFC, Congress reorganized the agency during the Truman administration, replacing the five-member board of directors with a single administrator. The reorganization failed to satisfy Senator Harry F. Byrd, the Democrat of Virginia and chairman of the Joint Committee on the Reduction of Federal Expenditures, who criticized the RFC as "an agency which is being used as a work-shop by get-rich-quick political predators." In 1937, Byrd had been the only member of the Senate who voted against the extension of the RFC, and in 1951 he argued that the Depression-era agency should be abolished:

> The RFC is now so permeated with political favoritism that it should be completely cleaned out. . . . In my judgment . . . it has contributed in a large way to political moral delinquency and has done, and is doing, much to cause the people to lose faith in their government, and the agency should be abolished.

Byrd concluded with clarity: "There is an old saying that we have in the Blue Ridge Mountains of Virginia, that you cannot measure a snake until it is dead, and that is true of the RFC."[50]

The debate about the abolition of the RFC ended when Congress passed the Reconstruction Finance Corporation Liquidation Act, which became law on July 30, 1953. It mandated that "the liquidation of assets and winding up of affairs of the Reconstruction Finance Corporation shall be carried out as expeditiously as possible." Though the RFC's lending powers were terminated in 1953, the Secretary of the Treasury continued to supervise the liquidation of the agency until it was finally dissolved in 1957.[51]

Senator Byrd's comments in 1951, during the Truman administration, would have rung just as true at the time of the Dawes loans, when Hoover was in office: "a nonpolitical liquidation of this agency will disclose many evidences of favoritism, collusion, improper influence, and perhaps criminal practices." When Harry Byrd spoke those words, the assets of the Dawes bank that had been pledged to the RFC in 1932 to secure payment of the long overdue Dawes loans were still in the process of being liquidated.[52]

Notes

1. Busch, *Guilty or Not Guilty?*, 135.

2. Ibid., 131, 135; Taylor, "Losses to the Public in the Insull Collapse," 188–204; McDonald, *Insull*, 308–12; Roger R. Trask, "The Odyssey of Samuel Insull," *Mid-America: An Historical Review* 46 (July 1964): 204.

3. People of the State of Illinois v. Samuel Insull, Sr. and Martin J. Insull, Indictment No. 66635; Transcript of Testimony before the Grand Jury, Corporation Securities Company of Chicago Bankruptcy Indictment, May 29, 31, 1933, United States of

America v. Samuel Insull, et al., No. 27326; Transcript of Proceedings before Hon. James H. Wilkerson Jr. and Jury, United States v. Insull et al., No. 26900, SIP/LU; Articles of Amendment to the Articles of Incorporation of Halsey, Stuart and Company changed to Halsey, Stuart and Company, Inc., filed November 8, 1935, ISOS/ISA; Busch, *Guilty or Not Guilty?*, 132–33; McDonald, *Insull*, 308–12, 322; Trask, "Odyssey of Samuel Insull," 204, 205; Wasik, *The Merchant of Power*, 230.

4. Insull, *Memoirs*, 233–38; Samuel Insull to Gladys Insull, October 6, 1932, SIP/LU; Wasik, *The Merchant of Power*, 205–6.

5. Insull, *Memoirs*, 136–37, 239–46, 254–69; McDonald, *Insull*, 239, 312, 314–17; Busch, *Guilty or Not Guilty?*, 133–34; Trask, "Odyssey of Samuel Insull," 205–11; "The Crime Hunt in Insull's Shattered Empire," 12; "Insulls: Greece Again Asked to Extradite Power Magnate," *Newsweek* 2 (September 2, 1933): 27; "Insull Lives in Athens, Greece," *New Outlook* 162 (October 1933): 56–60; "Condition Aggravated," *Time* 23, no. 9 (February 26, 1934): 18; "Popp & Xeros' Client," *Time* 23, no. 13 (March 26, 1934): 17, 18; "Morocco & Istanbul," *Time*, April 9, 1934, 16, 17; "Receipt Given," *Time*, April 23, 1934, 17; "Old Man Comes Home," *Time*, May 14, 1934, 13; Hayes, *Chicago: Crossroads of American Enterprise*, 274; Stuart, *Twenty Incredible Years*, 505.

6. It was also a sad homecoming for Insull because Adelaide Pierce Insull, the thirty-six-year old wife of Insull's only son, Samuel Insull Jr., had died on February 11, 1934. Besides her husband, she was survived by her son, Samuel Insull III, who was less than three years old. Testimony Taken in the Probate Court of Cook County, March 8, 1934, In the Matter of the Estate of Adelaide P. Insull . . . , Deceased, PCCC; "Insull: Prodigal in Jails and Courts of Former 'Empire.'" *Newsweek* 3, no. 20 (May 19, 1934): 15; "Insull Out," *Time* 23, no. 21 (May 21, 1934): 14; McDonald, *Insull*, 315–18; Trask, "Odyssey of Samuel Insull," 211–15; Wasik, *The Merchant of Power*, 205–14.

7. *Hearing before the Committee on the Judiciary, October 30 to November 4, 1933, March 19 to March 23, 1934,* 394–96, 440–57; Busch, *Guilty or Not Guilty?*, 135–38; "Old Man Comes Home," *Time* 23 (May 14, 1934): 12–13; Stuart, *Twenty Incredible Years*, 112, 119, 131, 140, 147, 150–51, 176, 192, 201, 214, 241, 480, 481, 485; *Chicago Tribune*, October 1, 1948; McDonald, *Insull*, 330–31.

8. Transcript of Testimony before the Grand Jury, Corporation Securities Company of Chicago Bankruptcy Indictment, May 29, 31, 1933, United States of America v. Samuel Insull, et al., No. 27326; Transcript of Proceedings before Hon. James H. Wilkerson Jr. and Jury, United States v. Insull et al., No. 26900, SIP/LU; for more information about Insull's criminal proceedings, see Busch, *Guilty or Not Guilty?*, 127–94; McDonald, *Insull*, 319–33.

9. Owen D. Young to Samuel Insull, November 27, 1934; Young to Samuel Insull Jr., November 27, 1934, ODYP/SLU.

10. Charles A. Munroe to Owen D. Young, April 16, 1935, Young to Munroe, April 19, 1935; Young to Samuel Insull, February 26, 1932, ODYP/SLU; Insull, *Memoirs*, 118, 153, 167, 173.

11. *People of the State of Illinois v. Samuel Insull, Sr. and Martin J. Insull*, Indictment No. 66635, SIP/LU; McDonald, *Insull*, 332–33; Busch, *Guilty or Not Guilty?*, 192–94.

12. Trustee's Report and Account of Collections Made from the Subscribers to the Insull Utility Investments Syndicate Agreement of August 15, 1930, In the Matter of Insull, Son & Co., Inc., Bankrupt, In Bankruptcy No. 52930, December 19, 1939, USDC/NDI.

13. Busch, *Guilty or Not Guilty?*, 192–94; McDonald, *Insull*, 332–33, 339.

14. Claim of the National City Bank of New York, November 15, 1938; Inventory, March 14, 1939, In the Matter of the Estate of Samuel Insull, Deceased, Docket 377, PCCC; McDonald, *Insull*, 289–301.

15. Samuel Insull's grand plan of "making Chicago the musical capital of the world" fared no better than his utilities system. He left the Chicago Civic Opera Company straddled with enormous debt on its forty-two-floor opera house and office building, which had cost $23,385,000 in 1929. Unable to rent enough office space to service the debt, Chicago's opera company went out of business. Insull, *Memoirs*, 105–9; McDonald, *Insull*, 243–44; *Time*, November 4, 1929, 54–56.

16. Upham and Lamke, *Closed and Distressed Banks*, 158–60; *New York Times*, December 5, 1933; Charles G. Dawes, W. G. Sibley, December 1, 1934, CGDC/EHC; Franklin D. Roosevelt to Charles G. Dawes, January 10, 1940; Dawes to Roosevelt, January 17, 1940; memo to the file regarding interviews conducted by Stanley High of the National Broadcasting Company, August 2, 1935, FDRP/FDRL; *New York Times*, January 27, 1932.

17. E. B. Penney to C. G. Dawes, September 20, 1932, CGDP/NUL; Decree, May 1, 1937, *RFC v. Central Republic Trust Company*, USDC/NDI.

18. E. B. Penney to C. G. Dawes, September 20, 1932, CGDP/NUL; Joseph E. Otis to the Stockholders of Central Republic Bank and Trust Company, October 20, 1932, PRCP/UI.

19. Fred Franz to City National Bank and Trust Company, October 20, 1932, PRCP/UI.

20. E. Harold Greist to Philip R. Clarke, October 14, 1932; "The Record of Central Republic Bank and Trust Company," Philip R. Clarke, April 16, 1936, PRCP/UI.

21. Edward Menkin to Philip R. Clarke, November 3, 1932, PRCP/UI.

22. "Central Republic Trust Company . . . Audit Report . . . ," November 20, 1934 to April 15, 1946; "Suggestion of the Appointment of William L. O'Connell, as Receiver of Central Republic Trust Company, a Corporation," November 21, 1934, CCCC; "The Record of Central Republic Bank and Trust Company," by Philip R. Clarke, April 16, 1936, PRCP/UI; *Chicago Tribune*, November 22, 1934; *Chicago American*, September 1, 7, 10, 11, 1934; Stuart, *Twenty Incredible Years*, 121, 163–65, 171, 181–85, 197, 220–21, 334, 483, 488, 494, 498.

23. "Bill of Complaint," November 21, 1934; "Order Appointing Receiver," November 21, 1934, People of the State of Illinois . . . Edward J. Barrett, Auditor of Public Accounts of the State of Illinois v. Central Republic Trust Company, CCCC; D.

B. Griffin to Federal Reserve Bank of Chicago, September 30, 1932, RFC/NA; *Chicago Herald-Examiner*, November 21, 1934; *Chicago Tribune*, November 22, 1934.

24. "Bill of Complaint," November 21, 1934; Proof of Claim of RFC against Central Republic Trust Company, Chicago, Illinois, March 16, 1935, People of the State of Illinois . . . Edward J. Barrett, Auditor of Public Accounts v. Central Republic Trust Company, CCCC.

25. "Motion to Spread of Record Receiver's Discharge and to Dissolve Corporation," "Certificate of Discharge," April 18, 1946, People of the State of Illinois Ex Rel, Edward J. Barrett, Auditor of Public Accounts v. Central Republic Trust Company; Wynnett W. McIlvaine v. City National Bank and Trust Company of Chicago, et al., SCCC; RFC v. Central Republic Trust Company, USDC/NDI; "Statement of Claim of Reconstruction Finance Corporation," in the matter of the estate of George W. Dixon, State of Illinois, County of Cook, November 15, 1938; "Supplemental Petition of RFC, in the matter of the estate of George W. Dixon, deceased," State of Wisconsin, County of Waukesha, April 8, 1942; George D. Kaplan to L. B. Hendricks, April 13, 1942; "Memorandum to the Controller," March 22, 1956; F. E. Wilson to M. O. Hoel, Director, Office of Loan Administration and Liquidation, June 24, November 30, 1955, RFC/NA; *Chicago Tribune*, May 25, 1946.

26. Wilson, *Harvey Couch The Master Builder*, 122–32; Wilson, *Harvey Couch*, 90–93; *Chicago Tribune*, November 20, 1934; "Dawes Stockholders Face 14 Million Loss," clippings in PRCP/UI.

27. *Banking Law, State of Illinois*, Sec. 6, December 2, 1930; C. G. Dawes to John R. Morron, July 15, 1938, CGDP/NUL.

28. Supplemental Answer of Dawes Brothers Inc., RFC v. Central Republic Trust Company, USDC/NDI; Jones, *Fifty Billion Dollars*, 79–81.

29. Hoover, *Memoirs*, 168; Jones, *Fifty Billion Dollars*, 79–81; L. Y. Sherman to Will Calvin, January 29, 1933, LYSP/ALPL.

30. Decree, May 1, 1937, RFC v. Central Republic Trust Company, Equity No. 14189, USDC/NDI; Ralph M. Shaw to Philip R. Clarke, May 3, 1937, PRCP/UI; *Reconstruction Finance Corporation v. Central Republic Trust Company, et al.*, 17 F. Supp. 263 (St. Paul, Minn.: West, 1937); *Reconstruction Finance Corporation v. Central Republic Trust Company, et al.*, 11 F. Supp. 976 (St. Paul, Minn.: West, 1936); Sherman, "Charles G. Dawes," 136–38; Jones, *Fifty Billion Dollars*, 79–81; Timmons, *Portrait of an American*, 321; *New York Times*, August 20, 1914; Williamson, "What is the Relative Value?"

31. "City National Bank and Trust Company of Chicago," Huston Bank Letter, Guy Huston and Company, July 23, 1935, PRCP/UI. Timmons, *Portrait of an American*, 324; Schlesinger, *The Crisis of the Old Order, 1919–1933*, 238; Jones, *Fifty Billion Dollars*, 81; Sherman, "Dawes," 107, 139.

32. "Central Republic Trust Company . . . Audit Report . . . November 20, 1934 to April 15, 1946"; "$8,000,000 Suit Filed against Dawes, Banks," May 15, 1937; "Dawes Bank Officers Resist $8,000,000 Suit of Old Stockholders," n.d., PRCP/UI; Decree of Judge James H. Wilkerson, May 1, 1937, RFC v. Central Republic Trust

Company, Equity No. 14189, USDC/NDI; Wynnett W. McIlvaine v. City National Bank and Trust Company of Chicago, et al., SCCC.

33. Wynnett W. McIlvaine v. City National Bank and Trust Company of Chicago, et al., SCCC.

34. *Chicago Tribune*, June 2, 16, 1938, June 16, 1939.

35. Jones, *Fifty Billion Dollars*, 72, 80; C. C. Ridgely Brown to C. G. Dawes, May 9, 1939; Dawes to Brown, May 17, 1939, CGDP/NUL; C. G. Dawes to O. D. Young, June 11, 1942, ODYP/SLU; Williamson, "What Is the Relative Value?"

36. Central Republic Trust Company, Chicago, Illinois, Partial Recovery Value Report, December 31, 1942, and "Recapitulation, Assets Pledged to Secure Loan to the Central Republic Trust Company, Chicago, Illinois, and the Estimated Recovery Values assigned thereto as of December 31, 1943," RFC/NA; *Moody's . . . Banks— Insurance Companies—Investment Trusts—Real Estate Finance and Credit Companies*, 1947, 318.

37. "Recovery Value of Collateral," as of December 31, 1943; "Total Indebtedness," as of December 31, 1943, RFC/NA.

38. Charles Francis of Houston represented Henry Dawes and the Pure Oil Company. *Proposed Extension of the Reconstruction Finance Corporation, Hearings before the Committee on Banking and Currency, United States Senate, Eightieth Congress, First Session on $80,000,000 Loan to the B. & O. Railroad, Part I, April 10, 11, 29, 30, May 5, 6, 22, and 23, 1947* (Washington, D.C.: Government Printing Office, 1947), 2–7; Records of the Examining Division, Comptroller of the Currency's Office USOCC/WNRC; *Moody's Manual of Investments: Banks, 1947*, 318; Sherman, "Dawes," 139; "Chicago Corp. Buy Big Interest in City National Bk.," a clipping in PRCP/UI; *Chicago Tribune*, August 5, 6, 11, 1936, August 4, October 3, 4, 5, 6, 7, 8, 9, 12, 14, 30, November 2, 4, 5, 10, 11, 12, 14, 16, 17, 18, 20, 23, 25, 30, December 1, 2, 3, 8, 10, 12, 14, 29, 31, 1937, January 5, 11, 14, 15, 21, 23, 26, March 29, 30, 31, April 2, May 26, June 3, July 9, 20, 21, August 5, 6, October 15, 1938, February 4, May 16, 17, June 6, July 28, September 1, 2, November 23, 1939, May 7, 1940; *New York Times*, August 5, 11, November 29, 1936, February 14, August 3, 4, October 3, 4, 5, 15, 16, 17, 22, November 3, 4, 5, 23, 24, 26, December 3, 10, 14, 15, 16, 29, 1937, January 7, 11, 14, 18, 21, 22, 23, 24, 26, February 3, 6, 13, March 27, 29, 31, April 2, 10, May 26, June 3, July 13, August 6, 28, October 15, 1938, April 9, May 16, 17, June 6, July 28, September 1, 2, November 23, 1939, April 14, 1940. For a general discussion of the history of the Pure Oil Company during the 1930s, see Harvey's *History of the Pure Oil Company, 1914 to 1941*, 12, 169–205, 223–53, 261.

39. "Fifteen Years, October 6th 1932—1947"; Gibbs Lyons to Board of Directors, City National Bank and Trust Company, June 27, 1933; "Chicago Corp. Buy Big Interest in City National Bk.," a clipping in PRCP/UI; see *Moody's Manual of Investments: Banks, 1932–47*.

40. Records of the Examining Division, Comptroller of the Currency's Office, USOCC/WNRC.

41. Minutes of Board, June 27, 1932, RFC/NA; Records of the Examining Division, Comptroller of the Currency's Office, USOCC/WNRC; H. M. Dawes to C. G.

Dawes, April 4, 1932 (two telegrams); H. M. Dawes to C. G. Dawes, April 8, 1932, CGDP/NUL.

42. Jones, *Fifty Billion Dollars*, 47–49; Records of the Examining Division, Comptroller of the Currency's Office, USOCC/WNRC; see complaint against Charles G. Dawes filed by Charles W. Butler, Executive Director, Waldorf Group, Philadelphia, Pennsylvania, October 11, 1935, USDJ; Sherman, "Dawes," 117; *Stock Exchange Practices . . . Insull, February 15, 16, and 17, 1933*, 1529–34, 1698; *Callaghan's Illinois Statutes Annotated, 1925–1931 Supplement*, 99, 100; *Callaghan's Illinois Statutes Annotated*, 1:690–92; Williamson, "What Is the Relative Value?"

43. James, *The Growth of Chicago Banks*, 2:1087–90; "Preferred Stock Disbursements," January 6, 1934, RFC/NA; *Reconstruction Finance Corporation v. Central Republic Trust Company* (1937), 268–72; Statement of Assets and Liabilities of Charles G. Dawes, December 2, 1931, CGDP/NUL; *Utility Corporations . . . Federal Trade Commission . . . Monthly Report . . . Middle West*, November 15, 1933, 18–19; *Moody's Manual of Investments: Banks, 1932*, 519, 2768; *1933*, 2011; *1934*, 564; *1935*, 1583; *1938*, 1268; *1939*, 741; Sherman, "Dawes," 121, 123–24; Bertie C. Forbes, *Men Who Are Making America* (New York: B. C. Forbes, 1921), 288; *New York Times*, February 4, 1933; *Chicago Tribune*, February 4, 1933; John Morton Blum, *From the Morgenthau Diaries: Years of Crisis, 1928–1938* (Boston: Houghton Mifflin, 1959), 344–46; Robertson, *The Comptroller and Bank Supervision*, 127; Freidel, *Franklin D. Roosevelt*, 190; Williamson, "What Is the Relative Value?"

44. The First National Bank of Chicago redeemed its preferred stock in July 1936, more than eight years before Jesse Jones redeemed his Houston bank's obligation to the RFC. First National Bank, Chicago, Illinois, Continental Illinois National Bank and Trust Company, Chicago, Illinois, and National Bank of Commerce, Houston, Texas, Card Index to Loans Made to Banks, RFC/NA; Records of the Examining Division, Comptroller of the Currency's Office, USOCC/WNRC; Jesse H. Jones to Melvin A. Traylor, December 10, 1927, August 10, 20, 21, 1932; Traylor to Jones, December 8, 1927; clipping of *Washington Herald*, March 6, 1933, JJP/LC; James, *The Growth of Chicago Banks*, 2:1087–90; Williamson, "What Is the Relative Value?"; Jones, *Fifty Billion Dollars*, 49; Olson, *Saving Capitalism*, 39; Studenski and Krooss, *Financial History of the United States*, 383; Friedman and Schwartz, *A Monetary History of the United States*, 421.

45. Hyo Won Cho, "The Evolution of the Reconstruction Finance Corporation: A Study of the Growth and Death of a Federal Lending Agency" (Ph.D. diss., Ohio State University, 1953), 215–93.

46. *Proposed Extension of the Reconstruction Finance Corporation, Hearings before the Committee on Banking and Currency, United States Senate . . . First Session on $80,000,000 Loan to the B. & O. Railroad*, 205–7; Cho, "The Evolution of the Reconstruction Finance Corporation," 215, 221–22.

47. *Proposed Extension of the Reconstruction Finance Corporation, Hearings before the Committee on Banking and Currency, United States Senate . . . First Session on $80,000,000 Loan to the B. & O. Railroad*, 155, 161; Cho, "The Evolution

of the Reconstruction Finance Corporation," 215, 221–23; Spero, *Reconstruction Finance Corporation Loans to the Railroads*, 33–34.

48. *The Hoover Commission Report on Organization of the Executive Branch of the Government* (New York: McGraw-Hill, 1949), 388–89, 392, 402–3; Cho, "The Evolution of the Reconstruction Finance Corporation," 274–77.

49. *Study of Reconstruction Finance Corporation. Hearings before a Subcommittee of the Committee on Banking and Currency, United States Senate, 81st Congress, 2nd Session, on a Study of the Operations of the Reconstruction Finance Corporation Pursuant To S. Res. 219, 81st Congress, Lending Policy,* June 8, 9, 13, and 15, July 3, 5, and 10, 1950. (Washington, D.C.: Government Printing Office, 1950), 444–46; Cho, "The Evolution of the Reconstruction Finance Corporation," 225–26, 277.

50. *Hearings before the Committee on Banking and Currency, United States Senate, 82nd Congress, First Session on S. 514, S. 515, S. 1116, S. 1123, S. 1329, S. 1376, and S. J. Res. 44, Bills to Amend the Reconstruction Finance Corporation Act, as Amended, and for other Purposes, April 27, 30, May 1, 2, 22 and 23, 1951,* 135; Cho, "The Evolution of the Reconstruction Finance Corporation," 265–72.

51. Cho, "The Evolution of the Reconstruction Finance Corporation," 293; *Guide to the National Archives of the United States*, 580–81.

52. Cho, "The Evolution of the Reconstruction Finance Corporation," 265–72, 293; *Guide to the National Archives of the United States*, 580–81.

Conclusion

"Some bankers whose banks failed in 1932 and 1933 felt they could have weathered the storm if it had not been made public that they were getting help from the RFC. It is doubtful if any of them were right."

—Jesse Jones, 1951[1]

The demise of the Reconstruction Finance Corporation did not signal the end of insider abuse and fraud in the banking industry or the financial manipulation of public companies by get-rich-quick predators. This study reveals that there was far more to the banking crises of the early 1930s than depressed conditions. As such, this study should prompt a reinterpretation of the role of banks in turning a financial crisis into the decade-long Great Depression. It should also provide encouragement to those who believe that there is an urgent need to open the bank regulatory system.

Depositors did not suffered any pain during the savings and loan debacle of the 1980s because the federal government insured their deposits, and Congress bailed out the S&L industry, which cost taxpayers at least $123.8 billion. As a result, the impetus for the kind of sweeping reform that would have opened the entire banking system to much-needed public scrutiny never gained momentum.[2]

Responding to the complicity of the regulators, Henry Gonzalez, the chairman of the House Committee on Banking, Finance and Urban Affairs, stated what had become obvious by 1990: "The savings and loan scandals grew in the dark basements of official government secrecy." A report that the General Accounting Office made to the House banking committee could just as easily be describing what happened in Chicago in 1932 or inside the boardrooms of some of the largest companies and banks in the U.S. during the 1990s and

2000s. It could also apply to the largest financial institutions which played an integral part in the economic meltdown of 2008.[3]

After reviewing examination reports and other regulatory records of twenty-six failed S&Ls, but—again, because of bank secrecy laws—without releasing any specifics, the GAO found that:

> extensive, repeated and blatant violations of laws and regulations characterized the failed thrifts that we reviewed in each and every case. Virtually every one of the thrifts was operating in an unsafe and unsound manner and was exposed to risks far beyond what was prudent. Under the Bank Board's definitions alone, fraud or insider abuse existed at each and every one of the failed thrifts and allegations of criminal misconduct abounded. Economic downturns in some sectors of the economy were beyond management's control and affected all of the thrifts. The failed thrifts, with their illegal and unsafe practices coupled with high-risk investments, were unable to withstand the downturns. On the other hand, many thrifts which were operated prudently withstood the same economic conditions in the same areas. Lastly, despite the fact that examination reports revealed critical problems at the failed thrifts, federal regulators did not always obtain agreements for corrective action. When they obtained them they were in many cases violated, ignored, and in many cases it was years before resolutions were taken. The failed thrifts were not responsive to the concerns of the regulators.[4]

Soon after the S&L crisis, Congress reorganized the regulators and increased their power to the extent that during the speculative mania of the late 1990s and early 2000s, America had in place the most elaborate regulatory system in the world. But Congress failed to provide the key element: a way for the public to hold the bankers accountable. Without this, they were able to continue the plunder in secret. Throughout this period of excess and abuse, the bank regulatory system remained far-reaching despite the Gramm-Leach-Bliley Act of 1999, which repealed one of the most significant reforms of the 1930s: the Glass-Steagall Act's separation of most aspects of commercial and investment banking. J. P. Morgan Chase described the repeal of Glass-Steagall, which facilitated the financing of Enron by allowing the securities and banking subsidiaries of J. P. Morgan Chase to work in concert together, as "financial modernization legislation."[5]

Congress also refused to resolve another glaring weakness of the regulatory system: the revolving door between high-level public officials charged with regulating banking and finance and those that they regulated. Officials at the Federal Reserve, the Office of the Comptroller of the Currency, the Department of the Treasury, and the Securities and Exchange Commission, among others at the federal and state levels, routinely move from the public sector back to the private. And some, again, move back to the public sector.

As a result, compliant regulators and the ongoing lack of public scrutiny resulted in investors losing even more billions of dollars during the Enron era. The nation's leading banks funded yet another cycle of corruption and insider abuse, which was fueled through excessive stock options and equity bonuses for executives of public companies. Alan Greenspan, the chairman of the Federal Reserve, said: "An infectious greed seemed to grip much of our business community."[6]

It must be underscored that the regulators were armed with the power to stop the corrupt practices. As early as 1927, a federal appeals court found that the comptroller of the currency had "almost imperialistic powers." And before the New Deal reforms, in 1932, another federal appeals court complained that regulatory powers at the time were, in its opinion, "too sweeping and imperialistic." The same court upheld those powers, however, conceding that in bestowing them, "unquestionably Congress contemplated the upheaval and cataclysm to which the financial structure is subject, the importance of its stability, and the necessity which exists for action unhampered by technicality in emergency."[7]

TOO BIG TO PROSECUTE

Still, during the Enron scandal, the public remained unaware that banking's regulatory system was not functioning—that it had completely broken down. This remains the untold story of Enron. Where were the regulators when Citigroup and J. P. Morgan Chase were financing Enron's phony special-purpose entities with billions of dollars in elaborately disguised loans? They had front-row seats from which to witness all of the bizarre schemes, along with the power to stop them. They also had a clear mandate to remove the unscrupulous bankers who promoted the loans and ban them from the industry, which they failed to do.

The system of supervision failed miserably in reining in the perpetrators of the Enron fiasco and other stunning business failures. Senator Carl M. Levin (D-Michigan) accurately described Enron's deals as "sham contrivances . . . to make Enron look more financially healthy than it really was, violating accounting standards." He stated that "by concocting elaborate schemes of so-called structured finance with no legitimate business purpose other than tax and accounting manipulation, Citigroup and J. P. Morgan Chase helped Enron deceive the investing public as well as Enron employees and stockholders."[8]

Subsequent annual reports and other Securities and Exchange Commission filings of Citigroup and J. P. Morgan Chase also failed to reveal the controversial Enron transactions. Even after the company filed for bankruptcy, the scant information provided was woefully inadequate and neglected to disclose the details of the questionable transactions, including the identities of the loans that regulators had criticized. Actually, these public filings revealed nothing more than bland general discussions and analyses of the status of their commercial and investment banking operations, along with statistical information about their aggregate loan portfolios.

At the same time, in stark contrast to the uninformative SEC filings—as bankers and their lawyers know—the confidential bank examiners' reports contained detailed and candid narratives criticizing insider deals, bad loans, and other imprudent transactions. Also disclosed in these reports were the names of specific borrowers who engaged in high-risk activities and the ventures in which the banks concentrated their loans. In addition, the correspondence between the regulators and the institutions contained information that is illuminating.[9]

To prevent another Enron, which was remarkably similar to the collapse of the Insull empire, all of this vital information must be shared with the public in a timely manner—before the debt-laden companies file for bankruptcy, which are public proceedings. But under current law, both Citicorp—a subsidiary of Citigroup—and Chase Manhattan Bank—a subsidiary of J. P. Morgan Chase—two of the largest financial institutions in the world, are too big to fail, and as long as they continue to operate, their records will never be released.

Nonetheless, the bankruptcy court's examiner for Enron, Neal Batson—who had access to the secret records—concluded that both banks "had actual knowledge of the wrongful conduct in these transactions." But Batson's report was too little, and much too late. Had the details of these transactions been disclosed on the Internet when the bank examination reports were issued, then securities analysts, debt-rating agencies and other gatekeepers would have been compelled to issue timely alerts about their riskiness and the whole disaster could have been avoided. Bank examiners are still confronted with political interference and offers of employment from those they regulate (the opportunity to go through the revolving door), but they do not face the conflicts of interest, lucrative incentives, and not-so-subtle pressure from partners as the analysts, auditors, investment bankers, and attorneys.[10]

Because of the veil of secrecy surrounding the fraudulent transactions, Enron's bankers escaped prosecution. In agreeing to a settlement of some $300 million as penance—certainly not as fair recompense—for the misdeeds of Citigroup and J. P. Morgan Chase, Manhattan District Attorney Robert M. Morgenthau spared Enron's bankers the ordeal of a criminal prosecution. This was unfortunate, in that such a prosecution would have spotlighted the bankers' complicity in devising fraudulent schemes to hide $8.3 billion in loans through the false reporting of the debt as cash flow from operations. And settling, instead of seeking criminal sanctions for the banks and their officials, saved the careers of submissive regulators who could have stopped the madness but failed to do so.

Although refusing to cooperate with the authorities, J. P. Morgan Chase nevertheless issued an apology to Morgenthau: "We have made mistakes. We cannot undo what has been done, but we can express genuine regret and learn from the past." An e-mail from a Chase senior officer more clearly owns up to the bank's culpability: "WE ARE MAKING DISGUISED LOANS, USU-ALLY BURIED IN COMMODITIES OR EQUITIES DERIVATIVES (AND I'M SURE IN OTHER AREAS). WITH A FEW EXCEPTIONS, THEY ARE UNDERSTOOD TO BE DISGUISED LOANS AND APPROVED AS SUCH." Citigroup's bankers in e-mails among themselves also described in explicit detail how they were "manipulating cash flows" with financing schemes at Enron.[11]

Despite agreeing that his office would not prosecute the banks or their officials for their willful misconduct, Morgenthau added that "there is no place in free and fair markets for players who think they can continue to conduct risky business under a cloud of deception and secrecy." Jacob H. Zamansky, a New York lawyer representing some of the investors, protested the settlement: "The message being sent by the regulators is 'write a big enough check and you can get away with anything.'" Simply put, the big banks, which taxpayers bailed out, are too big to prosecute.[12]

The banking secrets of the 1930s, which are now public records, finally reveal how bankers and businessmen violated their fiduciary duties in a desperate effort to save their personal fortunes. Those records contain many lessons for today, the most important of which is the urgent need to provide transparency in the bank regulatory system. The bank regulatory records should be available to the public through the Internet, so that a depositor or investor has only to type in the name of a bank to have immediate access to its regulatory records.[13]

Fully disclosing reckless financing schemes and dubious loans immediately after bank regulators criticize them would accomplish far more than the Sarbanes-Oxley Act of 2002, which failed to sound the alarm bell before the 2008 collapse. Posting their banks' examination reports on the Internet would have a chilling effect on freewheeling executives who, like the late Kenneth L.

Lay, the head of Enron, and Bernard J. Ebbers, the top official of WorldCom, would breach their fiduciary obligations to their stockholders and creditors in order to enrich themselves. Actually, they manipulated the earnings of the public companies so that they could take advantage of their stock options and other bonus compensation.[14]

During the S&L debacle of the 1980s, a few voices, including this one, called for the dismantling of the antiquated bank secrecy system. Congress failed to act, and America went through the Enron era and the near collapse of the economy in 2008. These calamities could have been prevented by revealing the insider abuse and fraud that the big banks funded and the insane derivative deals that they purchased from their affiliated investment companies.[15]

Unfortunately, the financial meltdown in the fall of 2008 had many of the same characteristics as the other major crises in the banking and financial system. We now know that the 2008 debacle was in large part a failure of regulation of monumental proportions. The comptroller of the currency and state banking officials ignored the degradation of prudential standards in making mortgages and allowed unsafe and unsound practices to continue unabated. The Federal Reserve failed to monitor the behavior of the officials of the major bank holding companies, and the Securities and Exchange Commission similarly failed to deal with clear examples of fraudulent behavior. Exacerbating the problems revealed in 2008 was the woefully inadequate regulation of investment banks, which were at the heart of the collapse in derivative markets. After conducting a bipartisan investigation for two years, the U.S. Senate's Subcommittee on Investigations "found that the crisis was not a natural disaster, but the result of high risk, complex financial products; undisclosed conflicts of interest; and the failure of regulators, the credit rating agencies, and the market itself to rein in the excesses of Wall Street."[16]

The need to dismantle the regulatory system to support free markets has been part of the national mindset since Ronald Reagan. In his first inaugural address, Reagan declared that "government is not the solution [to our current economic problems]. Government is the problem." Supporting such an attitude was the exotic work of academics specializing in banking and finance who propounded elaborate theories about the self-correcting nature of markets. But the free market system cannot function properly without reliable information. Surprisingly, many of the so-called independent academics were on the payroll of the big banks.[17]

The muscular lobbying of the banking and financial industries compromised not only the regulatory agencies but also Congress. As Senator Richard Durbin, Democrat of Illinois, observed in a moment of unusual candor, in April 2009, "the banks—hard to believe in a time when we're facing a banking crisis that many of the banks created—are still the most powerful lobby on Capitol Hill. And they frankly own the place." Durbin's legislation, which would have allowed bankruptcy judges to modify mortgages on primary residences, was defeated by the banking lobby.[18] (During the crisis of 2008 and its aftermath, there were also many examples of the continuing problem of revolving doors. It was remarkable that two recent secretaries of the treasury [Robert Rubin and Henry Paulson] served at the top of Goldman Sachs. Rubin left his post at the Treasury [1995–1999] and became a director and chairman of the executive committee, and then interim chairman of Citigroup. When Rubin arrived, Citigroup was a behemoth in the making, while the New Deal-era Glass-Steagall Act, which had segregated commercial from investment banking, was being repealed. With Rubin's "invisible hand," Citigroup was ready to expand into areas that Glass-Steagall had long prohibited, becoming the largest financial services company in the United States.)

Henry Paulson, the former chairman and chief executive officer of Goldman Sachs, also served as Secretary of the Treasury (2006–2009). After strategic campaign contributions to Clinton, Bush, Obama, Christopher Dodd, the chairman of the Senate banking committee, and Barney Frank, the chairman of the House banking committee, Goldman Sachs enjoyed the good fortune of having Paulson as the Secretary of the Treasury during the financial debacle of September 2008. The bank rescue plan approved by Congress in the throes of the meltdown—after dire warnings from Paulson and chairman of the Federal Reserve Ben Bernanke about the near collapse of the world's financial system—led to a $700 billion line of credit from the American taxpayers. Then, on October 28, 2008, a few days before the presidential election, Paulson's former firm, Goldman Sachs, sold its securities for $10 billion in a private placement to the U.S. Department of the Treasury while Paulson was Secretary of the Treasury. And it was revealed shortly after the election that the major beneficiaries of the Troubled Assets Relief Program, especially American International Group, used taxpayer funds to make good on credit default swaps (insurance policies on derivatives) owed to Goldman Sachs, among others. The details of the deliberations that led to the TARP and its initial beneficiaries remain shrouded in secrecy. But it is now clear that Paulson made decisions as Bush's Treasury secretary that benefited his previous firm, which received an additional $12.9 billion of taxpayer's money from the bailed out AIG, which would not have to be paid back to the U.S. government. He admitted as much in his book, *On the Brink*. In addition, Goldman Sachs's borrowings from the Federal Reserve reached a high of $35.39 billion in October 2008, just before the election of Barack Obama.[19]

Yet the election of Barack Obama failed to release Washington from Wall Street's stranglehold. Indeed, Obama's administration has faced sharp criticism for appointing top economic advisers with cozy connections to Wall Street. Simon Johnson, formerly the chief economist of the International Monetary Fund, has argued that since the 1980s there has been a "quiet coup" with Wall Street insiders capturing the banking and financial policy-making in the White House. Critics have maintained that Johnson's piece in the *Atlantic* was too sensationalist. But I think Johnson understated the crude corruption that exists in the corridors of power in Washington. Few insiders should doubt that since the Reagan and first Bush administrations, despite their S&L debacle, and continuing through the Clinton, second Bush, and Obama administrations, despite their Enron fiasco and financial meltdowns: Wall Street's view of the world dominated banking and financial policy at the highest levels of the government.[20]

During Obama's administration, his key economic advisers included Secretary of the Treasury Timothy Geithner and Lawrence Summers, the head of the President's National Economic Council. The latter served as Treasury secretary at the end of the Clinton administration, where he supported the Gramm-Leach-Bliley legislation of 1999 that ended the restrictions of the 1933 Glass-Steagall Act and made way for the growth of enormous banking operations like Citigroup and Bank of America—two of the nation's most troubled banks. In addition, Summers joined with Rubin, Alan Greenspan, and others to prevent proposals to regulate derivatives, propounding the arguments that markets adequately price risk and are self-correcting.[21]

Geithner, a protégé of Rubin and Summers, moved into his cabinet position after being the president of the Federal Reserve Bank of New York. There he missed the signals that many academics, journalists, and traders perceived of the impending collapse of financial institutions, which were highly leveraged and trading in risky financial products. He failed to use the considerable powers of the New York Federal Reserve to halt the excessive levels of leverage and reckless behavior of the officials of the major banks, and the high-flying investment operations of commercial banks.[22]

Without the shroud of secrecy hanging over the financial regulatory system, the 2008 meltdown should have been a predictable phenomenon. This policy of secrecy, however, continued even after tens of billions of dollars were spent bailing out financial institutions, leaving in place most of the banking officials who participated in the fiasco. And during the Obama administration, like the Clinton and Bush administrations, the top economic advisers were officials who shared the view that the markets functioned more efficiently when regulators operated behind closed doors.

Breathing the rarefied air in the Capitol building and White House, the conflicted policy makers of the Obama administration and well-financed members of Congress worked in concert with their patrons on Wall Street to ensure that sweeping reform to protect the economy from systemic banking crises would not be a part of the Dodd-Frank Act. Despite the growing criticism of the behavior of the officials of the major banks, Obama accepted the unsound policy that they were simply too big to fail. They left the structure of the banking and finance industry as it had developed since the Reagan years but—once again—reorganized the regulators and consolidated consumer regulation in the new consumer watchdog bureau, which will have no bite without real disclosure. Yet, state and federal regulators already had the statutory authority, which was greatly enhanced after the S&L debacle, to protect the public from unscrupulous bankers throughout the 1990s and 2000s. They had the power to remove dishonest, incompetent or reckless bankers and the mandate to seize insolvent banks. Nevertheless, in most instances compliant regulators refused to assert their powers. This regulatory void allowed rogues to operate freely within the banking system.[23]

The reorganization of the regulators will be ineffective because the Obama administration and Congress refused to open the secret vault of the bank regulatory system. So long as financial institutions operate in secret combined with the constant movement of top level officials from the private to the public sector, and vice versa, the public has no assurance that its interest will be served. In fact, it should not expect that its interests will be served. That is the message of this book.

The RFC's loan to Dawes, based on cronyism, corruption, and fraud, was part of a pattern that marked many of Dawes' previous dealings. Even so powerful a figure as Samuel Insull was jettisoned—along with investors and depositors—when the collapse of his utility empire threatened the interests of the private and public sector officials like Dawes who understood how to use political power and public funds to serve their private interests. Dawes and his associate Jesse Jones were experts of the crony banking system, which remains in place to this day, outside of the public's view.

America's bank regulatory system was augmented after the S&L crisis of the 1980s, the Enron debacle of the early 2000s, and the near economic collapse of 2008. But because of the constantly revolving door between the banking industry and the government, fundamental change will never occur without putting a bright spotlight on the misconduct of unscrupulous bankers and their cozy relationships with regulatory officials. Relying on "experts" drawn from the private sector will not solve the current financial crisis. Regulatory transparency and the abolition of bank secrecy is the only way to discipline a banking and financial industry that too often ignores the larger public interest. By making such information publicly available, politicians, journalists, academics, financial analysts, bloggers, and interested citizens can form independent judgments about the problems at their own bank and within the financial system. Using the Internet to eliminate regulatory and banking secrecy is the only way to prevent the next banking crisis.

TOO BIG TO DISCLOSE

As long as a bank survives, the regulatory records of the institution, which government employees prepared at taxpayers' expense, remain confidential. The Obama administration's feeble attempt to reform the financial system failed to achieve regulatory transparency. The failure was due in large part because the administration's top officials viewed the regulatory system from the perspective of the largest banks, ensuring that the same banks that were too big to fail also remain too big to disclose their insider abuse.

During the last three decades, members of Congress, the heads of federal regulatory agencies, and the White House acted as if what was good for the big banks was good for America. Certainly the six largest financial institutions in the United States (Bank of America, J. P. Morgan Chase, Citigroup, Wells Fargo, Goldman Sachs, and Morgan Stanley) have had a major economic impact. Their total assets are equal to almost 63 percent of the country's GDP (about $14.3 trillion in 2009). Not surprisingly, these behemoths have great clout in Washington. These institutions and those tied to them in government have dominated the debate about how to prevent another crisis like the economic meltdown of 2008.[24]

To temper the influence of the banking lobby, the public needs an easily accessible and independent source of information about banking and finance. Such professional information has existed since the formation of the Office of the Comptroller of the Currency in 1863. Now the federal banking regulatory bodies, the Federal Reserve, the Comptroller of the Currency, and the Federal Deposit Insurance Corporation, have professional staffs of auditors and accountants that routinely produce analyses of the operations of the financial institutions. Unfortunately, the reports and opinions of the professional civil servants remain hidden from public view.

Any hope of changing the broken regulatory system depends on real transparency. That is, the availability of independent analyses of banking activity, which are contained within the bank examination reports and other regulatory records. Because of the lack of public accountability, Congress, top federal regulators, and the White House have blithely ignored this treasure trove of financial information. The most valuable lesson learned from the 2008 debacle should be that taxpayers have an absolute right to the timely publication of these analyses and findings. So the federal bank regulatory agencies must be required to post their secret materials on their websites. With this information available, Congress and the White House will be forced to act in the broader public interest.[25]

Regulatory transparency would restore the public's trust. The financial crisis of 2008 demonstrated the dramatic breakdown of the bank regulatory system. Indeed, the system is rigged to favor the private interests of the largest institutions at the expense of the public. Present and past members of Congress and the executive branch have done the bidding for the big banks, refusing to enforce regulations while codifying predatory bank and credit card practices that have savaged ordinary Americans. While weakly enforcing robust regulations, the heads of major regulatory agencies, often following career paths that moved them between high-paying financial sector jobs and public "service," advocated further deregulation. And recent administrations, both Democratic and Republican, have been populated with economic advisers who seem to think primarily of the interests of the big banks.[26]

Opening the secret vault will be difficult. Bank officials will continue to oppose furiously any scrutiny of the way they operate. The biggest banks will also continue to use the enormous influence they have in Washington. During the 1990s and 2000s, members of Congress, sitting on the banking committees, eagerly scooped up campaign funds from bankers. But this is nothing new: the Clinton, Bush, and Obama campaigns took excessive contributions from bankers too, which guaranteed them easy access to the White House.[27]

Meanwhile, the top officials of the major regulatory agencies have refused to advocate real transparency, which would put a bright spotlight on their regulatory lapses. It's not only the revolving door between financial institutions and government appointments that shapes their outlook. Many officials are blinded by ideology. Alan Greenspan was not the only top regulatory official who subscribed to notions of self-correcting, efficient markets. Nor was he alone in holding the naïve belief that professionals like lawyers, accountants, and ratings agencies would never stretch the boundaries of law and traditional practice lest they tarnish their reputations.[28]

My histories of bank failures in Florida during the 1920s and in Chicago during the 1930s showed that most of the professionals employed in state and federal regulatory agencies did their jobs. But the top regulatory officials embargoed the professional opinions of their staffs for political or corrupt reasons. So the public in the 1920s and 1930s never learned which banks were in trouble, why, and for how long—until many of them failed taking with them the savings and investments of ordinary citizens. The suppression of information today among regulatory agencies serves the same purpose as it did decades ago. It allows bankers to engage in risky, reckless behavior, as Louis Brandeis said, "with other people's money."[29]

Washington insiders have no incentive to release the information amassed through the work of professional auditors, accountants, and bank supervisors fulfilling their mandated responsibilities to monitor banks. Still, this is a good moment to advocate transparency. Fostering a tradition of transparency and providing independent information to the public would counter the tendency of regulators to forbear the enforcement of regulations when confronted by political interference. Taxpayer anger about the publicly funded bank bailout offers a unique opportunity to change the cozy way the system operates.[30]

Following the Enron debacle in 2001, Congress passed laws and regulations that supposedly would prevent the abuses that the company engaged in. Subsequent efforts to enforce these regulations failed as the heads of regulatory agencies capitulated on a number of issues. Consequently, the big banks and their financial subsidies created ever more opaque, complex instruments designed to help their clients evade taxes and regulations. They also designed exotic trading strategies like the one that brought fraud charges against Goldman Sachs.[31]

Prior to the financial meltdown of 2008, America had the most elaborate bank regulatory system in the world. Despite eight decades of ever-increasing authority and regulatory agencies, the sheer magnitude of the recent banking crisis proved that the regulatory system, relying exclusively on regulators operating behind closed doors, cannot police the largest financial institutions, which continue to threaten the global economy with a systemic banking collapse. The passage of the Dodd-Frank Wall Street Reform and Consumer Protection Act in July 2010 merely added to the already sweeping regulatory power.[32]

Wall Street and its friends in Congress, the White House, and among the heads of the regulatory agencies will continue to manipulate the system, if previous experience is any guide. Banking and politics have always produced a toxic mix of bankers in snug relationships with leading politicians. It was evident by the end of the nineteenth century and the beginning of the twentieth century as the comptrollers of the currency at the time were involved in monumental self-dealing. An unprecedented growth of banking speculation in the 1920s was followed by the worst economic crisis in American history during the 1930s. In the 1920s, politicians and bankers worked together to further their own narrow interests. As we have seen, in the 1930s it was the Reconstruction Finance Corporation that bailed out bankers with the right political connections among the leaders of both major parties. The same was true during the savings and loan collapse in the 1980s. And now we have the Great Recession caused by reckless speculation, insider abuse, and fraud abetted by top regulatory officials and well-financed members of Congress.[33]

In this moment of anxiety, taxpayers have the power to force openness and accountability in the banking industry. Transparency would strike at the power of the alliance between banks and politicians, and provide the necessary information to make the markets function properly. There is no doubt that releasing the secrets of the banking industry would provide a wrenching adjustment among insiders. But secrecy and the lack of information about the fraud and insider abuse in the financial system led to the meltdown of 2008, which caused the worst recession since the depression in the 1930s. Not addressing this problem now invites financial upheavals in the future.[34]

Notes

1. Jones, *Fifty Billion Dollars*, 82.

2. Teresa Simons, "Banking on Secrecy," *Washington Monthly*, December 1990, 31. Henry N. Pontell and Kitty Calavita, "The Savings and Loan Industry," in *Beyond the Law: Crime in Complex Organizations*, edited by Michael Tonry and Albert J. Reiss Jr. (Chicago: University of Chicago Press, 1993), 18:203–4, 212–13; Raymond B. Vickers, "Sleazy Banking in the '20s and Today," *Wall Street Journal*, May 23, 1989.

3. *Wall Street and the Financial Crisis: Anatomy of a Financial Collapse*, 1–12; *The Financial Crisis Inquiry Report*, xv–xxvii.

4. "Failed Financial Institutions: Reasons, Costs, Remedies and Unresolved Issues," Statement of Frederick D. Wolf before the U.S. House Committee on Banking, Finance and Urban Affairs, United States General Accounting Office Testimony, January 13, 1989, 9, 10, 11, 13, 21, 22, 40.

5. See the Financial Institutions Reform, Recovery, and Enforcement Act of 1989, Public Law No. 101–73, 103 Stat. 183 (1989). For a discussion of the Gramm-Leach-Bliley Act, see Form 10-K of J. P. Morgan Chase & Co., December 31, 2001.

6. John C. Coffee Jr., "Gatekeeper Failure and Reform: The Challenge of Fashioning Relevant Reforms," *Boston University Law Review* 84, no. 2 (April 2004): 302–3. Also see Professor Coffee's "What Caused Enron? A Capsule Social and Economic History of the 1990s," *Cornell Law Review* 89, no. 2 (January 2004): 269–79; and his "Understanding Enron: 'It's about the Gatekeepers, Stupid,'" *Business Lawyer* 57, no. 4 (August 2002): 1403–20.

7. *U.S.N.B. of La Grande v. Pole*, 2 F. Supp. 153, 157 (D. Ore. 1932); *Liberty National Bank of South Carolina at Columbia v. McIntosh*, 16 F. 2d 906; White, *Teaching Materials on Banking Law*, 65–67, 868–73.

8. *Houston Chronicle*, December 10, 2002; *Los Angeles Times*, July 28, 2003; *New York Times*, August 1, 2003; Raymond B. Vickers, "Bank Secrecy Should Be Ended—This Would Make the Financial System Safer," *The Long Term View: Secrecy Is Everywhere* 6, no. 1 (Massachusetts School of Law at Andover, Fall 2003): 5–11.

9. See the Form 10-K and 2001 Annual Report of J. P. Morgan Chase & Co.; and J. P. Morgan Chase's Form 10-Q for the third quarter ending September 30, 2002; and its SEC Form 8-K, January 2, 2003; "List of Creditors Holding 20 Largest Unsecured Claims," United States Bankruptcy Court Southern District of New York, In re Enron Corp. Debtor, December 2, 2001. See the Form 10-K and 2001 Annual Report of Citigroup Inc. and its subsidiaries, and Form 10-Q for the third quarter ending September 30, 2002; Testimony of Robert Roach, Chief Investigator, Permanent Subcommittee on Investigations, "The Role of the Financial Institutions in Enron's Collapse," July 23, 2002. See also Paul M. Horvitz, "Commercial Bank Financial Reporting and Disclosure," *Journal of Contemporary Business* 6, no. 3 (Summer 1977): 60–75; Michael R. Rice, "SEC Urged to Go Slow on Problem Loan Disclosure," *Bankers Monthly* 92, no. 6 (June 15, 1975): 26, 31.

10. For a general discussion of the role of gatekeepers, including corporate and securities attorneys, see John C. Coffee Jr., "The Attorney as Gatekeeper: An Agenda for the SEC," *Columbia Law Review* 103, no. 5 (June 2003): 1293–1316; *New York Times*, August 1, 2003.

11. The capitalization was in the original e-mail. News Release, District Attorney, New York County, July 28, 2003; United States Securities and Exchange Commission, Plaintiff, v. J. P. Morgan Chase & Co., Defendant, U. S. District Court, Southern District of Texas, Houston Division, July 2003; United States of America before the Securities and Exchange Commission, In the Matter of Citigroup, Inc., Respondent, Order Instituting a Public Administrative Proceeding Pursuant to Section 21C of the Securities Exchange Act of 1934, Making Findings, and Imposing a Cease-and-Desist Order and Other Relief, July 2003.

12. News Release, District Attorney, New York County, July 28, 2003; "Enron's Bankers: A Great Prison Escape. As Citi and J. P. Morgan settled up, new evidence underscored their roles in the dirty dealing. So why isn't jail time an option?" *Business Week Online*, July 31, 2003.

13. *Guide to the National Archives of the United States*, 161.

14. "SEC Charges Kenneth L. Lay, Enron's Former Chairman and Chief Executive Officer, with Fraud and Insider Trading," press release of the U.S. Securities and Exchange Commission, July 8, 2004, www.sec.gov/news/press/2004–94.htm; United States of America v. Bernard J. Ebbers, Defendant, Indictment,S302Cr.1144(BSJ), news.findlaw.com/hdocs/docs/worldcom/usebbers504ind3s.pdf; John C. Coffee Jr., "A Theory of Corporate Scandals: Why the USA and Europe Differ," *Oxford Review of Economic Policy* 21, no. 2 (2005): 198–99. For a discussion of the Sarbanes-Oxley Act, see Coffee, "Gatekeeper Failure and Reform," 333–45. Also see the *Public Company Accounting Reform and Investor Protection Act of 2002*, otherwise known

as the Sarbanes-Oxley Act, 107 Public Law No. 204, 116 Stat. 745 (2002), 15 U.S.C. Section 7201; *The Financial Crisis Inquiry Report*, xv–xxviii.

15. Vickers, *Panic in Paradise*, 2–4, 219–20; Vickers, "Sleazy Banking in the '20s and Today"; Raymond B. Vickers, "Open the Vault: The Urgent Need to Abolish Bank Secrecy," *Business Library Review, An International Journal*, February 1996, 1–7; Vickers, "Bank Secrecy Should Be Ended"; Simons, "Banking on Secrecy," 31–37; Adams, *The Big Fix*, 279; *The Financial Crisis Inquiry Report*, xv–xxviii.

16. *Wall Street and the Financial Crisis: Anatomy of a Financial Collapse*, 1.

17. Cooper, *The Origin of Financial Crises*; David O. Whitten, review of *Panic in Paradise: Florida's Banking Crash of 1926*, *Business Library Review, An International Journal*, February 1996, 7–11; *The Financial Crisis Inquiry Report*, xv–xxviii.

18. Adam Doster, "Durbin on Congress: 'Banks Frankly Own the Place,'" April 29, 2009, Progress Illinois, www.progressillinois.com.

19. See Henry M. Paulson, Jr., *On the Brink: Inside the Race to Stop the Collapse of the Global Financial System* (New York: Business Plus, 2010), 224, 225, 258, 268, 276, 277, 359, 362–68; "AIG Payments to Banks Stir Outrage," Reuters, March 16, 2009; Simon Johnson, "The Quiet Coup," *Atlantic Magazine*, May 2009; "Goldman Sach's Emergency Loans from Fed Surpassed $24 Billion Amid Crisis," December 1, 2010.

20. Johnson, "The Quiet Coup."

21. See Rick Schmitt, "Prophet and Loss," *Stanford Magazine*, March/April 2009; *The Financial Crisis Inquiry Report*, 47–49.

22. For a summary of the criticisms see Editorial, "Questions for Mr. Geithner," *New York Times*, December 14, 2008.

23. Gretchen Morgenson, "Too Big to Fail, or Too Big to Handle?" *New York Times*, Sunday Business, June 21, 2009, 1–2; *The Financial Crisis Inquiry Report*, xv–xxviii.

24. Robert L. Borosage, "The Big Bank Lobby: Too Big to Bear?" Huffington Post.com, May 11, 2010; Kevin Connor, *Big Bank Takeover: How Too-Big-to-Fail's Army of Lobbyists Has Captured Washington*, Campaign for America's Future, www.ourfuture.org; David Cho, "Banks 'Too Big to Fail' Have Grown Even Bigger; Behemoths Born of the Bailout Reduce Consumer Choice, Tempt Corporate Moral Hazard," *Washington Post*, August 28, 2009; Sewell Chan, "On Hill, Geithner Makes the Case for a Bank Tax," *New York Times*, May 5, 2010; National Information Center List of Top 50 Bank Holding Companies as of 3/31/2010, www.ffiec.gov; Peter Boone and Simon Johnson, "Shooting Banks: Obama's Impotent Assault on Wall Street," *New Republic*, February 24, 2010; "Six Largest Banks Getting Bigger, Brown Said," April 25, 2010, www.politifact.com; Bureau of Economic Analysis of the U.S. Department of Commerce, Table 1.1.5 Gross Domestic Product, last revised April 30, 2010, www.bea.gov; *World Factbook*, Chart—Country Comparison: GDP, www.cia.gov.

25. Daniel Roth, "Road Map for Financial Recovery: Radical Transparency Now!" *Wired*, February 23, 2009; Steven Sloan, "Stress Tests Touch Off Debate on Disclosure," *American Banker*, April 30, 2009; Steven Sloan, "Going Public with Camels Ratings Could Be Next Step," *American Banker*, April 30, 2009; Steven Sloan, "Fed's Tough Transparency Talk Doesn't Apply on Pay," *American Banker*, November 2,

2009; Joe Adler, "Wamu Policing Slammed, Levin Blames OTS Execs," *American Banker*, April 16, 2010; Sandy B. Lewis and William D. Cohan, "The Economy Is Still at the Brink," *New York Times*, June 7, 2009; Paul Krugman, "Bubbles and the Banks," *New York Times*, January 8, 2010; Henry Paulson, "How to Watch the Banks," *New York Times*, February 16, 2010; Lauren Silva Laughlin and Richard Beales, "For Public Trust, Try Disclosure," *New York Times*, June 5, 2009; "Don't Blame the New Deal," *New York Times*, September 28, 2008; Gretchen Morgenson and Don Van Natta Jr., "Even in Crisis, Banks Dig In for Battle against Regulation," *New York Times*, June 1, 2009; Julie Creswell and Ben White, "The Guys from 'Government Sachs,'" *New York Times*, October 19, 2008; "FOIA and the Fed: Do We Have a Right to Know the Central Bank's Inner Workings?" *Washington Post*, October 22, 2009; Neil Irwin, "Bernanke Seeks to Preserve Fed Power; Common Ground Sought with Lawmakers on Oversight, Transparency," *Washington Post*, February 25, 2010; Neil Irwin, "Senate Bill Leaves Fed at the Center of U.S. Oversight; Central Bank Faces an Audit but Overhaul May Widen Its Scope," *Washington Post*, May 17, 2010; Neil Irwin, "At N.Y. Fed, Blending In Is Part of the Job; Some Fear Wall Street Too Heavily Influences the Financial Enforcer," *Washington Post*, July 20, 2009; J. D. Foster, "Transparency and Accountability at the Federal Reserve," Heritage Foundation, November 20, 2009; "Levin-Kaufman Package of Amendments Introduced to Stop Wall Street Abuses," information released by Senator Ted Kaufman, May 11, 2010; David Lazarus, "Delays in Reform Hasten Next Crisis," *Los Angeles Times*, April 23, 2010; Michael Beckel, "Campaign Cash from Wall Street Favored Representatives Who Opposed Finance Reform Bill," Center for Responsive Politics, OpenSecrets blog, December 12, 2009; Michael Beckel, "Senators Who Opposed Financial Reform Got More Cash on Average from Wall Street Interests," Center for Responsive Politics, OpenSecrets blog, May 24, 2010; Jim McElhatton and Jennifer Haberkorn, "Failed Firms' Leaders Gave Big to Politicians," *Washington Times*, September 19, 2008.

26. Greg Gordon, "Goldman's Connections to White House Raise Eyebrows," *McClatchy-Tribune News Service*, April 21, 2010; Borosage, "The Big Bank Lobby: Too Big to Bear?"; Connor, *Big Bank Takeover*; Boone and Johnson, "Shooting Banks."

27. Borosage, "The Big Bank Lobby: Too Big to Bear?"; Robert L. Borosage, "Dick Durbin: Banks 'Frankly Own the Place,'" Huffington Post.com, April 29, 2009; Connor, *Big Bank Takeover*; Morgenson and Van Natta, Jr., "Even in Crisis, Banks Dig in for Battle Against Regulation," June 1, 2009; Binyamin Appelbaum and Eric Lichtblau, "Banks Lobby to Rid Finance Bill of Ban on Trading in Derivatives," *New York Times,* May 10, 2010; David M. Herszenhorn, "Bill Passed in Senate Broadly Expands Oversight of Wall Street," *New York Times*, May 20, 2010; Boone and Johnson, "Shooting Banks"; Lindsay Renick Mayer, "Commercial Banks Hope for Return on Investment in Congress," Center for Responsive Politics, OpenSecrets blog, www.opensecrets.org, November 16, 2009; Beckel, "Campaign Cash from Wall Street Favored Representatives Who Opposed Finance Reform Bill"; Beckel, "Senators Who Opposed Financial Reform Got More Cash on Average from Wall Street Interests."

28. Neil Irwin and Amit R. Paley, "Greenspan Says He Was Wrong on Regulation; Lawmakers Blast Former Fed Chairman," *Washington Post*, October 24, 2008; David Cho, "A Conversion in 'This Storm,'" *Washington Post*, November 18, 2008; Jim Puzzanghera, "Financial Crisis; Greenspan Defends Fed's Actions; The Former Chairman Responds to Criticism That the Agency Failed to Stop the Housing Bubble," *Los Angeles Times*, April 8, 2010.

29. Vickers, *Panic in Paradise*; Vickers, "Sleazy Banking in the '20s and Today"; Brandeis, *Other People's Money and How the Bankers Use It*.

30. Neil Irwin, "Bernanke Jabs Back at Fed's Critics in Congress; Lawmakers More Vocal about Rescue Program as Recession Persists," *Washington Post*, July 22, 2009; Neil Irwin, "Bernanke Seeks to Preserve Fed Power; Common Ground Sought with Lawmakers on Oversight, Transparency," *Washington Post*, February 25, 2010; Edward Simpson Prescott and Stephen Slivinski, "Viewpoint: A Case against Disclosing Camels Ratings," *American Banker*, May 29, 2009; Cheyenne Hopkins, "'Too Big to Fail' Proves Too Difficult to Destroy; Plans May Soften the Blow of Failures, but Not Fix the Problem," *American Banker*, February 10, 2010; Stacy Kaper, "Frank Seeking Compromise on Fed Disclosure," *American Banker*, September 28, 2009; Morgenson and Van Natta Jr., "Even in Crisis, Banks Dig In for Battle against Regulation," *New York Times*, June 1, 2009; Morgenson, "The Cost of Saving These Whales," *New York Times*, October 4, 2009; Sewell Chan, "Financial Debate Renews Scrutiny on Size of Banks," *New York Times*, April 21, 2010; David M. Herszenhorn, "Bid to Shrink Big Banks Falls Short," *New York Times*, May 7, 2010; Jim Puzzanghera, "Financial Meltdown; Banks May Face Levies for Bailouts; Obama Wants to Make Dozens of Big Financial Firms, Even Some That Didn't Get Aid, Cover Possible TARP Losses," *Los Angeles Times*, January 14, 2010; Borosage, "The Big Bank Lobby: Too Big to Bear?"; Foster, "Transparency and Accountability at the Federal Reserve"; Stephen Dinan, "Senate Calls for Audit of Three Years of Fed Deals: Full Policy Will Stay Behind 'Closed Doors,'" *Washington Times*, May 12, 2010; Boone and Johnson, "Shooting Banks."

31. Carrie Johnson, "Businesses Prepare to Mount a Concerted Attack on Regulation," *Washington Post*, March 12, 2007; Ronald D. Orol, "House Approves Sweeping, Post-Crisis Bank Reform," *McClatchy-Tribune News Service*, December 11, 2009; Peter J. Henning, "In Lehman's Demise, Some Shades of Enron," *New York Times*, DealBook blog, www.dealbook.blogs.nytimes.com, March 12, 2010; Susan P. Koniak, George M. Cohen, David A. Dana, and Thomas Ross, "How Washington Abetted the Bank Job," *New York Times*, April 4, 2010; "Investors Beware," *New York Times*, November 7, 2009.

32. *The Financial Crisis Inquiry Report*, xv–xxviii; Vickers, *Panic in Paradise*, 1–2.

33. Lindsay Renick Mayer, "Congressmen Hear from TARP Recipients Who Funded Their Campaigns," Center for Responsive Politics, OpenSecrets blog, www.opensecrets.org, February 10, 2009; Lindsay Renick Mayer, "Commercial Banks Lobby Federal Government to Save Billions on Derivatives," September 4, 2009; Michael Beckel, "Down but Not Quite Out: An Examination of Insurance Giant AIG's

Waning Clout," Center for Responsive Politics, OpenSecrets blog, www.opensecrets. org, December 3, 2009; Cassandra LaRussa and Larry Makinson, "Congressional Inquisitors Also Beneficiaries of Firm's Financial Largesse," Center for Responsive Politics, OpenSecrets blog, www.opensecrets.org, April 28, 2010; "Cashing In," Public Citizen, www.citizen.org, November 19, 2009; Timothy Curry and Lynn Shibut, "The Cost of the Savings and Loan Crisis: Truth and Consequences," *FDIC Banking Review* 13, no. 2 (Fall 2000); Ellen Simon, "Helium for the Credit Bubble: Regulators' Absence," *Associated Press*, September 22, 2008; "Don't Blame the New Deal," *New York Times*, September 28, 2008; Floyd Norris, "Accountants Misled Us into Crisis," *New York Times*, September 11, 2009; Catherine Rampell, "Lax Oversight Caused Crisis, Bernanke Says," *New York Times*, January 4, 2010; "Sen. Carl Levin Opening Statement: PSI Hearing on Wall Street and the Financial Crisis: The Role of Bank Regulators," *Congressional Documents and Publications*, April 16, 2010; Puzzanghera, "Financial Crisis; Greenspan Defends Fed's Actions; The Former Chairman Responds to Criticism That the Agency Failed to Stop the Housing Bubble"; Lazarus, "Delays in Reform Hasten Next Crisis."

34. Lazarus, "Delays in Reform Hasten Next Crisis"; *The Financial Crisis Inquiry Report*, xv–xxviii; *Wall Street and the Financial Crisis: Anatomy of a Financial Collapse*, 1–12.

Bibliographical Essay

Since the conclusions of this study clash with previous studies of the bank failures of the Great Depression, it seems instructive to look closely at the relevant works. Using records not examined comprehensively before, I determined that the bank failures during the Chicago panic of 1932 were caused by massive fraud and insider abuse. Without using primary source materials, an accurate interpretation of the bank failures of the 1930s is impossible.

Jesse Jones and Charles Dawes were concerned about how historians would view them, so they collaborated on telling the same story about the bailout. Toward this end, they both hired Bascom N. Timmons, the longtime Washington correspondent for the *Houston Chronicle*, which Jones owned, to write their biographies. Predictably, Timmons wrote two sympathetic accounts of Dawes and Jones: *Portrait of an American: Charles G. Dawes* and *Jesse H. Jones: The Man and the Statesman*. Timmons had also received loans from Henry Dawes while he was writing the biography of Charles. Despite their obvious bias, both books have had a significant influence on a generation of historians reviewing the business practices of the two men.[1]

Dawes also wrote a number of one-sided accounts about his experiences in government, and Jones published a less than candid memoir about his years at the Reconstruction Finance Corporation. Jones ventured that "of all the hundreds of thousands of transactions handled by the RFC and its subsidiaries, the one which stirred up the most and longest public interest and evoked the keenest controversy in Congress and out was the so-called Dawes loan." Though a staunch advocate of the Dawes bailout, Jones admitted that "probably twenty million depositors in other banks throughout the country suffered a greater loss on their accounts in closed banks than they would have suffered had their banks not remained open too long, thus allowing the frightened or 'smart' money to skip out, leaving unsuspecting and more loyal depositors to hold the bag." Yet Jones remained loyal to Dawes and defended the bailout for the rest of his life. For instance, in 1942 Jones was privately saying that "93% of the loan had been paid, and the remaining collateral would liquidate the balance with a substantial amount for interest." Jones's statements contradicted his own staff reports, which showed that the Dawes bank still owed $45,331,464 to the RFC at the end of 1941, and $45,348,872 as of December 31, 1942.[2]

In *The Banking Panics of the Great Depression* (1996), Elmus Wicker recognized the Chicago banking crisis as one of five significant panics of the Great Depression. Milton Friedman and Anna Jacobson Schwartz identified only four panics in their 1963 book, *A Monetary History of the United States, 1867–1960*. Wicker observed that Friedman and Schwartz "did not identify the June–July episode [the Chicago panic] as one of the banking crises of the Great Depression. No mention is even made of it!" Neither Wicker nor Friedman and Schwartz reviewed the federal banking records or the state liquidation and litigation records that are used in this book. The national bank records were sealed at the Washington National Records Center and the National Archives when Friedman and Schwartz were doing their research, but Wicker could have used them if he had sought access from the comptroller of the currency's office. The state liquidation and litigation records have been available at the Cook County Courthouse since the state banks failed.[3]

Without using the federal or state banking records, Wicker was only able to hint that the Dawes loan was issued because the RFC directors gave preferential treatment to their former colleague. He pointed to the RFC's denial of large loans to two Detroit banks during the panic of 1933, even when the RFC directors recognized that their refusal to issue the loans would have a devastating impact on the national banking situation. As Wicker queried: "We shall have to ask what was so different about the banking difficulties in Detroit and those in Chicago that warranted discriminatory treatment?"[4]

Because he did not review the assets pledged to secure the RFC's loans to the Dawes bank, Wicker could not determine if the loans should have been made. So he only raised the question about the appearance of impropriety. The only reference that Wicker used in his discussion of the Dawes loan was Cyril James's 1938 book, *The Growth of Chicago Banks*. Quoting from James, Wicker indicated that the Central Republic Bank was in trouble because of the "hysterical fear and anxiety" of its depositors. I doubt Wicker would have reached this conclusion had he reviewed the liquidation and litigation records of the bank in the Cook County Courthouse, and the comptroller of the currency's records of the National Bank of the Republic, whose millions of dollars of worthless assets were assumed by the Dawes bank in

1931. Wicker revealed his dependence on newspaper articles by stating that he did not know the reasons for the bank failures because neither the *Chicago Tribune* nor the *Commercial and Financial Chronicle* reported "the reasons for closing other than action of the Board of Directors, which may mean almost anything." Wicker described his methodology as "an extensive search . . . of old newspaper files" in Chicago and other cities. As he pointed out, "Granted that the information available may leave something to be desired, the best that we can do is to strive to get the story straight even if there are some significant details still missing." Although Wicker's book is useful, it does not explain why the individual banks failed.[5]

Another example of a recognized work based on flawed data is the article first presented in 1994 and then revised in 1997 by Charles W. Calomiris and Joseph R. Mason, titled "Contagion and Bank Failures during the Great Depression: The June 1932 Chicago Banking Panic." Though Calomiris and Mason's work is better documented than Wicker's book, the documentation is woefully inadequate. They relied on balance sheets appearing in call reports, reports of condition, and the financial statements issued by the state and national banks of Chicago to determine the soundness of the banks that either failed or survived the panic. These included the fraudulent balance sheets of Dawes's Central Republic Bank and the failed state banks. Published bank call reports listed a few details such as the aggregate amount of loans and other assets, the liabilities, and the purported capital of the banks. If examiners classified assets (such as the loans to Insull's entities) as bad debts or complete losses, the bankers usually failed to report the reduced market values of the loans or to charge them off the books of the banks. As Friedman and Schwartz stated, "The recorded capital figures were widely recognized as overstating the available capital, because assets were being carried on the books at a value higher than their market value." Edward Barrett, the banking commissioner of Illinois, stated in his petition of receivership for the Dawes bank that its assets "as carried on [its] books . . . were and are erroneous and did not, and do not, correctly reflect the true value thereof."[6]

Calomiris and Mason erroneously concluded that the Dawes bank was one of the "panic survivors" when, in fact, it ceased conducting a banking business on October 6, 1932. This conclusion affected their entire study because they divided most of their charts into failed banks and survivor banks. They did not even conclude that the Dawes bank was one of the "nonpanic failures." Moreover, Calomiris and Mason made the erroneous statement that the "Central Republic was a solvent bank saved from failure by the collective intervention of other Loop banks." They wrote that the price of the Dawes bank's stock "rebounded rapidly" after June 27, 1932. But the publicly traded stock of the Central Republic Bank ceased trading after October 6, 1932. And they said that "once the crisis passed, Central Republic saw its deposit out-flows cease." Actually, Central Republic Bank had deposits of $112,308,320 on June 30, 1932, but they had fallen to $72,977,441 by October 6, 1932, when its deposits were assumed by Dawes's new bank, City National Bank and Trust Company.[7]

To their credit, Calomiris and Mason discovered "the wealth of [comp-troller of the currency's office] file material" and they used records of eight of the failed banks in their 1997 article. After reviewing these records, they concluded, "In every case for which we have records, the bank examiners had indicated extreme problems at the bank at least as early as the end of April 1932." They also acknowledged the financial reporting problems dis-cussed earlier when they stated, "In many cases, bank fraud and accounting irregularities explain why banks that failed during the panic appear stronger statistically." They do not indicate, however, why they did not look beyond the regulatory records of eight of the failed national banks. Additionally, they did not review the receivership and litigation records of the failed state banks. My view of the condition of the Dawes bank and the propriety of the RFC's loans also differs from their conclusions because my research included the extensive records of the RFC. The authors made the unsupported statement that "RFC liquidity support for the Chicago banks [including the Dawes bank]—like all RFC lending during this period—was fully collateralized by very high-quality, liquid assets." No documentation was provided to support this incorrect statement; Calomiris and Mason were merely reciting what federal law required and therefore should have been the case. Indeed, their failure to review and use all of the available public records made it impossible for them to know the value of the collateral securing the RFC loans or the condition of the banks receiving the loans. So they were unable to determine the real causes of the bank failures that occurred during the last two weeks of June 1932.[8]

Richard H. Keehn and Gene Smiley argued for the need to keep a tight veil of secrecy around the banking industry in two papers appearing in *Essays in Economic and Business History* in 1988 and 1993. The examination and liquidation records of national banks and the RFC's individual loan files were available when Keehn and Smiley wrote their articles. And the pleadings and other litigation and receivership records of failed state banks were available in the county courthouses where the banks had been located. Yet the sources that Keehn and Smiley used for their studies were the annual reports of state banking departments and correspondence between them and state regulators when the annual reports had been destroyed or lost, the comptroller of the currency's annual reports, and the RFC's monthly reports listing the names of loan recipients. These records were used to "compare the date of public disclosure of RFC borrowing with individual bank failure dates," which they argued showed "that a significant number of banks probably were harmed by publication of the loan lists." Based on this scant information, they concluded that "the impact of publication of the names of RFC bank borrowers was an important factor contributing to the rise in bank failures and the downturn in economic activity."[9]

Keehn and Smiley also relied on Lawrence Sullivan's 1936 book *Prelude to Panic: The Story of the Bank Holiday.* Keehn and Smiley quote Sullivan's statement that "the R.F.C. publicity closed several hundred banks which, without the added pressures of 'publicity runs' might have weathered the storm." But Sullivan made a contradictory statement on the same page: "The historical evidence now is clear that there was but one immediate and decisive national impulse behind the bank panic—steadily mounting fears that Mr. Roosevelt, at election day 1932, held at least an open mind on the questions of gold suspension and inflation." For "similar views" about the dangers of publicity, Keehn and Smiley refer the reader to Friedman and Schwartz's *A Monetary History of the United States* and Lester V. Chandler's *American Monetary Policy: 1928–1941*, both of which were published before the release of the federal banking records. Friedman and Schwartz cite Hoover's memoirs as their authority for the evils of the limited disclosure clause naming the banks that received RFC loans. On the other hand, Chandler cited no authority and simply stated, "Borrowings from the RFC might have been larger and more helpful if that agency had not been forced to disclose the names of its borrowers."[10]

Taking a more scholarly approach and sharing a much different viewpoint, Cyril B. Upham and Edwin Lamke observed in 1934:

> It has been alleged that the publication of the names of banks borrowing from the RFC caused depositors in these institutions to lose confidence. This allegation is not substantiated by the record of failures. Names of RFC borrowers were made public for the first time in the latter part of August 1932, and there were fewer failures in September than in any previous month since March. In October and November the number was but slightly higher than in August. Depositors had a right to know if their institution was borrowing, and they would have known it from the next statement in any event.[11]

Merely comparing the date of publication (January 25, 1933, with respect to the RFC loans made to the Chicago banks that failed in June 1932) with the date of failure does not prove that a particular bank failed because of disclosure that it had received a loan from the RFC. And Keehn and Smiley conceded that the Chicago banks failed "before the RFC loan lists were published, so publicity could not have been a major cause of failure in those cases." One must study each bank failure on an individual basis. If a bank was weak from bad loans and insider abuse then it would be further weakened when it assumed debt from the RFC. If Keehn and Smiley had reviewed all of the available public records relating to the individual bank failures, they could have determined why each bank failed. This is a time-consuming process that cannot be short-circuited.[12]

In 1977, James S. Olson wrote, in *Herbert Hoover and the Reconstruction Finance Corporation, 1931–1933*, "Hoover faced a manifestly simple choice: either save the [Dawes] Central Republic Bank or preside over the destruction of the United States banking system." He added that "the unprecedented loan postponed the national banking disaster." He then described Charles Dawes, whom Hoover had appointed as president of the RFC, as "an internationally prominent man" who "brought to the agency valuable financial experience and international prestige."[13]

Olson's books, including *Saving Capitalism: The Reconstruction Finance Corporation and the New Deal, 1933–1940*, have been considered the definitive works on the subject. Nevertheless, I disagree sharply with his conclusions. When he wrote those words in 1977, the records of the comptroller of the currency's examining division were still sealed. The receivership records of Chicago's state banks, including the Dawes bank, were available to the public, however. And in Olson's second book, which was written well after the comptroller of the currency's regulatory records had become legally available in 1982, Olson still maintained that the RFC had no choice but to issue $90 million to the Dawes bank "to prevent a massive banking panic in the Midwest."[14]

Olson also made the erroneous statement that the Dawes loans were "financially justifiable," which, as we have seen, is simply not supported by the facts. After reviewing the Dawes loans strictly on their merits, and relying on public records rather than attempting to place them in some economic or statistical context to determine if they served a public purpose, it can be said without a credible challenge that the RFC was used in the case of the Dawes bailout as a patronage system to dispense a political favor, not as a tool for "saving capitalism." Olson also neglected to mention in his books that the RFC was abolished because of criticisms of "political and personal favoritism."[15]

Olson's study of Jesse Jones also suffered from a lack of primary source materials. Had he reviewed the banking and bankruptcy records at the National Archives, I doubt he would have concluded that Jones "nurtured an incorruptible sense of personal ethics." He might not have concluded that

Jones "knew how to handle people and money." What the evidence reveals is, rather, that Jones knew how to manipulate the system and misuse other people's money. Further demonstrating a naïveté about his subject, Olson wrote that "Jones was passionately committed to the efficacy of state capitalism" and that Jones believed that "the federal government had the ability and the responsibility to rescue capitalism." Though Olson listed in his bibliography the Charles Dawes papers at Northwestern and the Jones papers at the Library of Congress, which show otherwise, he stated that Jones "could barely stand Eugene Meyer and Charles Dawes." Jones did get into a shoving match with Meyer after the *Washington Post*, which Meyer owned, published an editorial critical of Jones in 1942. But throughout both of their lifetimes, Jones regarded Dawes as a close friend. Their friendship was evident when they served together on the RFC board and throughout the 1930s and early 1940s when Jones was head of the RFC, the agency still liquidating the Dawes loan, which had been in default since 1932.[16]

My view of Jesse Jones is also more critical than Walter L. Buenger's, though his work has been helpful despite our divergent views. My opinion of Jones began to change when I discovered his $350,000 undocumented loan from Melvin Traylor's bank, which had been listed among the comptroller of the currency's records. Buenger did not use those records during his study of Jones's business practices. The shadiness of Jones's business practices became clearer when I reviewed the bankruptcy records of a number of his enterprises located in the National Archives branch in Fort Worth, which Buenger also did not use.[17]

In *Freedom from Fear*, which won the 2000 Pulitzer Prize for history, David Kennedy paints two different portraits of Herbert Hoover. At one point he quotes the columnist Walter Lippman, who said, "in the realm of unreason [Hoover was], for a statesman, an exceptionally thin-skinned and easily bewildered man." But later Kennedy added that Hoover "frequently dazzled visitors with his detailed knowledge and expert understanding of American business." He quoted Hoover's secretary, Theodore Joslin, who said that his boss had "a mathematical brain. Let banking officials, for instance, come into his office and he would rattle off the number of banks in the country, list their liabilities and assets, describe the trend of fiscal affairs, and go into liquidity, or lack of it, of individual institutions, all from memory." Although well written and well organized, Kennedy's book relies on secondary sources and adds little to what is already known about Hoover. And he does not even mention the Dawes loans.[18]

In *Networks of Power: Electrification in Western Society, 1880–1930*, Thomas P. Hughes cautions that Insull looms large in the history of Chicago's electric industry and was a "pivotal figure" for four decades, but this did not mean he should be taken for "a great man." I agree with Hughes on this point but part from him with his reliance on Forrest McDonald's sympathetic 1962 book, *Insull*, which was published two decades before the release of the banking records. Hughes, gave weight to McDonald's interview with Insull's son about a conversation he supposedly had with the prosecutor during the mail fraud trial. According to the "favorable hearsay," the prosecutor and the defendant were standing next to each other at adjoining stalls in the men's room of the federal courthouse. The prosecutor purportedly said to Junior: "Say, you fellows were legitimate businessmen."

I found Harold L. Platt's *The Electric City: Energy and the Growth of the Chicago Area, 1880–1930* to be less dependent on McDonald's work and thus a more reliable source. It makes use of the records of the Commonwealth Edison Company and other Insull entities. Platt, a history professor at Loyola University of Chicago, where the Insull papers are located, based his conclusions on primary source documents.[19]

A colorful and entertaining read, John F. Wasik's 2006 book about Insull, *The Merchant of Power: Samuel Insull, Thomas Edison, and the Creation of the Modern Metropolis*, again relies far too heavily on McDonald's biography, which, he acknowledges, was "a prime source." Though Wasik also relied on Platt's work, he sometimes pulled more punches than McDonald. In addition, Wasik's scant research on the financial entanglements of Insull and his companies also affected the tone of his narrative. Wasik did not review the state bank receivership records or the national bank examination reports, and he failed to discuss Insull's intimate relationships with Melvin Traylor and the Reynolds brothers and the calamity that the Insull loans caused at their banks.

It is illuminating to look at the three accounts of Insull's transaction with the Gray Wolves of the Chicago city council. Platt provides evidence that Insull paid $170,000 to the corrupt politicians, while McDonald, relying on a conversation with Insull Jr., put the payment at $50,000. Even though both books were written long before Wasik's book, Wasik wrote: "Insull still would not pay the bribe. . . . Insull had gained the upper hand and the Gray Wolves backed off." Insull's transaction with the Gray Wolves should be at the center of the debate about Insull's business ethics, nevertheless Wasik failed to explain why his account was so different than Platt's and McDonald's.[20]

During the mid-1950s, Forrest McDonald worked as the executive secretary for the American History Research Center, which was affiliated with the State Historical Society of Wisconsin. McDonald wrote in his memoir: "While I was working at the Center—actually, I was the Center." McDonald spent much of his time engaged in fund-raising activities because the Center was beset with financial problems. As a consequence, McDonald developed a far-too-cozy relationship with Samuel Insull Jr., resulting in a questionable arrangement that made the young historian, a student of the 18th century who had been awarded his Ph.D. less than a year earlier, the official biographer of Samuel Insull, one of the business titans of the early 20th century whose empire was so complicated that it even confused Insull. (McDonald described the collapse of Insull's empire as "the biggest business failure in the history of the world.") As part of the written contract, McDonald would become the first historian to be granted access to the papers of Samuel Insull. But in a side agreement, Junior would give to the Center the same amount of money as McDonald's salary. No doubt, it was a coup for McDonald, who later wrote that he had "longed to study [Samuel Insull's] personal and corporate records and to write his biography . . . and began to connive to gain access to the necessary documents."[21]

According to the contract between Insull Jr., Samuel Insull III, and the Center, which was later assigned to the University of Chicago Press, the Insulls were granted control over the use of the materials in the book for any productions to appear on television, radio, or in a movie. Though the contract contained a so-called academic freedom clause giving McDonald the "final decision," its language, as well as a stringent reservation of rights clause that allowed Junior to criticize the manuscript prior to publication, appeared to have a chilling effect on McDonald's independence. The contract was unusual in another disturbing respect. After working with McDonald during the research and writing of his book about the Wisconsin utilities industry, Junior had become very comfortable with the fledgling historian but he was concerned about a less friendly successor author if McDonald did not complete the work. So the contract provided that the Insulls would have veto power over McDonald's successor. This provision went so far as to say that if the two Insulls died, then approval of a new author would be by someone designated in the last will and testament of Insull Jr.[22]

In 1962, before the publication of *Insull*, Junior began to assert his control over the television rights of his father's biography. When he learned that the Chicago Educational TV Association was planning a special program about his father, titled *The Day the Sky Fell*, Junior wrote an aggressive letter to the executive director of the association warning him that the proposed program would probably infringe on the copyrights of his father's memoirs, which he owned, and McDonald's work about his father, which he controlled. In closing, Junior said that he was concerned about sensational and distorted television reporting, and he recommended that members of the media contact and listen to McDonald, an "informed and objective source." Insull Jr. sent copies of the letter to his Chicago law firm, McDonald, the assistant director of the University of Chicago Press, and the reporter of the *Chicago Sun-Times*, who had written the article about the upcoming television program. Junior also sent similar letters to the four local television stations and their affiliated networks. Needless to say, his letters were quite extraordinary, yet the University of Chicago Press published the Insull biography the next year without modifying this part of the contract with Insull Jr.[23]

In fairness to the press, its staff may have been intimidated by Insull Jr., whose legal prowess was well known to them. Junior's Chicago law firm, Quinn, Riordan, Jacobs and Barry, prepared the contracts and amendments between Insull Jr., McDonald, the Center, and the University of Chicago Press relating to the publication of *Insull* and *We the People*, and the law firm was sometimes copied on correspondence that Junior sent to the press. In 1960, an accounting dispute erupted between the University of Chicago Press and Insull Jr. when Junior, who then owned half of the rights to McDonald's *We the People*, claimed that he had not received a royalty statement in eighteen months. On Junior's behalf, McDonald intervened with Carroll G. Bowen, the assistant director of the press, demanding to know, "What the hell is wrong with your accounting department, daddy-o?" McDonald then warned Bowen about Junior, "He's a dear sweet lovely guy and all that, but he's just temperamental enough to do something wild like start a suit against the university for embezzlement or something, so for god's sake raise hell with the accounting dept., will you?" Bowen wrote Insull Jr. "a mollifying letter" stating that the press had paid him $1,069.23 on August 15, 1959, and that he would be receiving $1,286.46 on August 15, 1960. Bowen also told McDonald that Junior was wrong, but the point had been made. Junior underscored his litigiousness in 1962—before *Insull* was published—when he sent a letter to Bowen and copied it to McDonald, which reminded them that "two or three years ago when I filed some libel suits" (about statements written about his father), a Texas newspaper ran "a major front-page headline" about the lawsuits.[24]

The University of Chicago Press received two highly critical reviews from independent referees about McDonald's manuscript prior to its publication. William Miller, one of the scholarly referees, hoped that McDonald would revise the manuscript "to mitigate the sycophantic tone. Needless and futile." And Miller wrote, "This manuscript is obviously an apologia of Samuel Insull and his work. . . . Much of [McDonald's] research has been conducted by means of interviews; and given the sycophantic tone of much of the book, it is easy for the reader to suppose that much of the interviewing unearthed only favorable hearsay." Miller recommended that the book be published, but he stated, "It would be a better book with fewer purple passages about its central figure and his sterling character."[25]

Stanley A. Kaplan, a preeminent corporate and securities law professor at the University of Chicago, and an independent referee who reviewed the manuscript, concluded that McDonald had become "a hero worshiper of Mr. Insull." Kaplan wrote to the University of Chicago Press prior to its publication of *Insull*, "[McDonald] portrays things in black and white and presents Mr. Insull's conduct as that of a paragon of virtue and presents the conduct of his opponents as if they were a piratical crowd of looters and scoundrels." Kaplan, who was an expert on insider trading and other conflict-of-interest issues affecting corporate boards of directors, harshly criticized McDonald's description of "the Morgan 'raid' against Insull" as an oversimplification because "the position of Insull was something less than wholly right and the position of the Morgan group was something less than wholly wrong." Kaplan stated that McDonald had failed to present "sufficient evidence to support such a position or to compel the reader to accept his broad generalizations." The respected law professor concluded that McDonald's "description of legal and financial matters, in many instances, struck me as over-simplified, over-positive or superficial."[26]

Unfortunately, the tone remained unchanged when the book was published. McDonald asserted that Morgan and the other New York banks were able to bring the great man down by "simply changing the accounting system." McDonald suggested that the New York bankers made a point of depicting Insull as a scoundrel as part of their scheme to seize control of his companies. Though they held as collateral enough shares to control Insull's companies, in 1932 "corporate rape had ceased to be fashionable." In McDonald's view, the bankers had to "reverse the facts and cast themselves in the role of man on a white horse, rescuing the widows and orphans from the clutches of a scoundrel." By forcing Insull to hire Arthur Andersen and Company "to supervise all expenditures by the Insull companies and maintain the status quo of all creditors . . . and incidentally to report any 'improper transactions' they might turn up," the bankers shifted the focus and put Insull in "handcuffs." Supposedly, Morgan and the other New York banks took this action to block Insull from pulling off the kind of "miracle" he had managed to pull off in the past through his ability to "juggle" the books. Again, according to McDonald, the new auditors, who were somehow the tools of the New York banks, eliminated Insull's retirement reserve depreciation system and replaced it with the straight-line depreciation system used in industrial accounting, so that "by a stroke of the pen, Middle West became insolvent." Furthermore, McDonald claimed, by extending the system backward, "Middle West became retroactively insolvent, never having earned any money, and thus nothing but a worthless pile of paper that had been kept alive only by continuous impairment of capital, disguised by improper bookkeeping."

McDonald's assertion that Andersen participated in a grand conspiracy to destroy Insull was frivolous, but his description of the insolvent condition of Middle West was correct. Andersen was never the tool of the New York banks that McDonald described. Rather than being forced by the New York banks to hire Andersen, as McDonald would have it, Insull himself hired Andersen in an attempt to persuade the New York banks to extend their loans, which would have helped him to avoid bankruptcy. McDonald also spectacularly understated the debt burden of Middle West, writing that "for the want of ten million dollars, a billion and half dollar corporation went under." In fact, the company had total short-term debt of $600 million, plus the additional $40 million of debt that began maturing annually for four years, beginning on June 1, 1932. Another $27 million in bank loans was on a demand basis. McDonald was correct in averring that the bankers did not have "clean hands" because their banks were "overly and illegally extended." Insull and his family were also culprits, however, because they violated their fiduciary obligations to their stockholders, bondholders, and other creditors through the reckless pledging of all of the assets that they controlled to the banks in a desperate attempt to maintain personal control of the utility system and its holding companies.[27]

Still troubling were the behind-the-scenes machinations between McDonald and Insull Jr., which were revealed in McDonald's memoir and in the files of the University of Chicago Press. In 2004, the University Press of Kansas published McDonald's *Recovering the Past: A Historian's Memoir*. In it he revealed dubious details about his personal relationship with Junior. McDonald admitted that "money problems continued to plague the Center," and he revealed that he was also facing serious personal and financial problems when he was working on *Insull*. (McDonald also confirmed that his personal and financial problems did not end when he accepted a position as an associate professor at Brown University in 1959.) So the Center and McDonald "resorted to a desperate move"; McDonald negotiated yet another deal with Insull Jr., who had a "direct concern" about "the solvency of the Center," to bail them out.[28]

After becoming the executive secretary of the Center, McDonald transferred his rights in his manuscript, *We the People*, to the Center. Since McDonald and the Center were having difficulties paying their expenses, McDonald negotiated the sale of a 50 percent interest in the forthcoming book to the University of Chicago Press for $5,000. McDonald then arranged to sell the Center's rights to the other half of the book to Insull Jr. In 1958, four years before the publication of McDonald's biography of his father, Insull Jr. paid $5,000 to the Center (a sum worth about $37,100 in today's dollars). Though McDonald disclosed selected parts of the contract with

Insull Jr. relating to the biography of his father, he failed to reveal that Insull Jr. had a financial stake in McDonald's *We the People*, which the University of Chicago Press also published just before the publication of *Insull*. Had McDonald's friendly relationship with Insull Jr. been fully disclosed, reviewers would surely have questioned McDonald's bias and the propriety of the financial relationships.[29]

In a 1958 review of McDonald's *Let There Be Light: The Electric Utility Industry in Wisconsin, 1881–1955*, the historian Louis C. Hunter leveled a scathing criticism of McDonald's ties to the utilities industry. Hunter wrote, "Dr. McDonald fails to give the public aspect the amount of attention its importance demands, and his study is strongly biased in favor of the industry whose constructive achievements he rightly admires." Hunter noted that McDonald had given little attention to the regulatory reform movements aimed at the utilities industry during the Progressive Era and the 1920s, saying instead that the industry had been subjected to adverse legislation resulting from "bad public relations." Hunter pulled no punches when he questioned McDonald's impartiality:

> It is the historian's function to remove the distortions produced by the heat of public controversy. To accomplish this demands from the researcher the most scrupulous impartiality and an unceasing effort to attain and maintain objectivity. He must establish for himself a position of careful aloofness from all parties to the controversy. This [McDonald] has not succeeded in doing, and for understandable reasons. As the preface informs us, not only was this study financed by the Wisconsin Utilities Association, through a grant to the State Historical Society of Wisconsin, but [McDonald] was assisted in many ways by a historical committee consisting of representatives of nine major power companies.[30]

Though McDonald would later admit the obvious—"I was on friendly terms with the electric utility industry"—Clifford L. Lord, the director of the State Historical Society, defended McDonald, the Society, and the Center. Lord admitted that the Wisconsin Utilities Association had given enough money to the State Historical Society so that it could hire McDonald to write a history of the utilities industry in the state. But Lord stated that "no strings are attached in any way" and that "other reputable educational institutions" had done the same thing. Because "the book was obviously controversial," Lord's organization had chosen three referees to review McDonald's manuscript (after it had been written and years after he had been hired), who could be regarded as "hostile witnesses." In defiance, Lord pledged to continue the questionable practice in the future. Lord asked "what further safeguards to scholarly responsibilities" Hunter would recommend. Hunter answered, calling for full disclosure about any financial arrangements from a sponsoring organization at the beginning of any books written with such assistance. And he quoted the advice given by a "distinguished scholar" to another educational association when it considered just such a financing arrangement with a sponsor, "I wouldn't touch it with a ten-foot pole."[31]

The historian Roy N. Lokken agreed that McDonald was biased. In his review of *Let There Be Light*, Lokken wrote, "the fact that McDonald carefully selected his source materials so that favorable light would be cast on only one side of the story is clearly evident throughout *Let There Be Light*." Lokken also pointed out that "the expenses of the research were paid for by the Wisconsin Utilities Association, a special-interest group consisting of Wisconsin utility companies." Commenting on the treatment of Insull in *Let There Be Light*, four years before *Insull* was published, the senior scholar noted that "McDonald's one-sided research also distorted his interpretation of the controversies" surrounding the regulation and ownership of public utilities during the 1920s. "In fact, [McDonald] places Senator Norris in a very bad light, while exonerating Insull in every way."[32]

The propriety of the financial support provided by the industry-sponsored Wisconsin Utilities Association, which in turn funded McDonald's salary and expenses through a grant to the State Historical Society, sparked allegations of fraud and embezzlement against McDonald within the Society. McDonald had been hired to write the history of the Wisconsin utilities industry in June 1953. He conceded that "the arrangement was comfortable" and that he had a good relationship with the industry committee formed to work with him "despite my total ignorance of the subject." Fearing that the allegations "could have destroyed [his] career," McDonald once again turned to Insull Jr., who dispatched Abner Stilwell to defend McDonald at the annual meeting of the State Historical Society. (Stilwell had been the vice president of Continental Illinois Bank, which was by far the largest creditor of the Insull entities, with outstanding loans of nearly $60 million. Stilwell's personal company, Stilwell & Co., had also been a stockholder of the Dawes bank. Both the Continental Illinois Bank and Dawes's Central Republic Bank continued to fund the Insull family even after their companies collapsed.) McDonald survived the attack and the University of Chicago Press published both *We the People* and *Insull*. The probate records of Insull Jr. indicated that his arrangement with the University of Chicago Press continued for at least the next twenty-five years, when his estate received a royalty payment from the University of Chicago Press on June 17, 1983.[33]

McDonald, whose work has been accepted as the authority on Insull by a generation of historians, often contradicts himself when discussing Insull's business ethics. On the one hand, he implies that Insull was a man who was effective in arranging "personal, extralegal arrangements" with corrupt city commissioners before electric franchises were awarded. On the other hand, McDonald states that Insull was "incorruptible." McDonald emphasizes that a Chicago jury acquitted Insull of mail fraud and embezzlement charges. Insull may not have been guilty of mail fraud or embezzlement, but it is certain that he improperly influenced some of Chicago's leading bankers into violating one of the core principles of state and federal banking laws designed to prevent dangerous concentrations of credit. Chicago's banks made loans of more than $150 million to borrowers securing their loans with Insull securities or to Insull's entities. The insider abuse by Insull and his bankers not only led to the collapse of his empire but also was a primary cause of the Chicago banking panic of June 1932. McDonald completely ignored this basic fact.[34]

The issue of bias and the appearance of impropriety remain serious problems for the history profession, especially in the area of banking and business history, where historians are routinely retained to write the history of a company, bank, or industry in a particular state. And the influence of the banking industry, combined with a secret regulatory system, make the writing of a history of banking all the more difficult. Finally, it is time to eliminate the code of secrecy that separates the public from the truth about its banking industry.

Notes

1. Bascom Timmons also wrote *Garner of Texas*. Timmons, *Jesse H. Jones*, 164, 165; Timmons, *Portrait of an American*; Records of the Examining Division, Comptroller of the Currency's Office, USOCC/WNRC. For an example of a historian's account being heavily influenced by Timmons's biographies, see Buenger, "Between Community and Corporation," 482.

2. Jones, *Fifty Billion Dollars*, 72, 80.

3. Wicker, *The Banking Panics of the Great Depression*, 17, 112. Wicker's book was first published by Cambridge University Press in 1996. Friedman and Schwartz, *A Monetary History of the United States*; Vickers, *Panic in Paradise*, xi, 1, 5.

4. Wicker, *The Banking Panics of the Great Depression*, 17, 110–14.

5. Wicker, *The Banking Panics of the Great Depression*, xvii, 17, 110–14; James, *The Growth of Chicago Banks*, 2:1034, 1195.

6. In 1994, Calomiris and Mason had published a similar article under the same title: Charles W. Calomiris and Joseph R. Mason, "Contagion and Bank Failures during the Great Depression: The June 1932 Chicago Banking Panic" (Working Paper No. 4934, National Bureau of Economic Research, Inc., November 1994), 1–25, including abstract, figures, tables, and notes; Calomiris and Mason, "Contagion and Bank Failures during the Great Depression: The June 1932 Chicago Banking Panic," 863–83; Friedman and Schwartz, *A Monetary History of the United Sates*,

330; "Fifteen Years, October 6th 1932—1947," PRCP/UI; "Bill of Complaint, People of the State of Illinois . . . v. Central Republic Trust Company . . . ," November 21, 1934, CCCC.

7. Calomiris and Mason, "Contagion and Bank Failures during the Great Depression" (1994), 1–25; Calomiris and Mason, "Contagion and Bank Failures during the Great Depression" (1997), 863–83.

8. Calomiris and Mason, "Contagion and Bank Failures during the Great Depression" (1997), 863–83.

9. Keehn and Smiley, "U.S. Bank Failures, 1932–1933: A Provisional Analysis," 136–56; Friedman and Schwartz, *A Monetary History of the United Sates*, 325; Butkiewicz, "The Impact of a Lender of Last Resort during the Great Depression," 197–201, 207–10, 214.

10. Lawrence Sullivan, *Prelude to Panic: The Story of the Bank Holiday* (Washington, D.C.: Statesman Press, 1936), 45–54; Friedman and Schwartz, *A Monetary History of the United Sates*, 325; Lester V. Chandler, *American Monetary Policy: 1928–1941* (New York: Harper and Row, 1971), 209; Hoover, *Memoirs,* 110–11.

11. Upham and Lamke, *Closed and Distressed Banks*, 155–56.

12. Keehn and Smiley, "U.S. Bank Failures, 1932–1933: A Provisional Analysis," 136–56; Keehn and Smiley, "U.S. Bank Failures, 1932–1933: Additional Evidence on Regional Patterns, Timing, and the Role of the Reconstruction Finance Corporation," 131–39; Vickers, *Panic in Paradise*, xi–xiv; Guglielmo, "Illinois State Bank Failures in the Great Depression," 44–62.

13. Olson, *Herbert Hoover and the Reconstruction Finance Corporation*, 40, 58, 59.

14. Olson, *Saving Capitalism*, 17–18; George Sternlieb and David Listokin, eds., *New Tools for Economic Development: The Enterprise Zone, Development Bank, and RFC* (Piscataway, N.J.: Rutgers University Press, 1981).

15. Olson, *Hoover and the Reconstruction Finance Corporation*, 59.

16. See "Czar: Jesse Jones and His Empire," chapter 3 in Olson's *Saving Capitalism*, 42–62.

17. See Buenger, "Between Community and Corporation"; Buenger and Pratt, *But Also Good Business*; Records of the Examining Division, Comptroller of the Currency's Office, USOCC/WNRC.

18. Kennedy, *Freedom from Fear*, 50, 94, 95; Joslin, *Hoover Off the Record*, 17.

19. McDonald, *Insull*, 331; see William Miller's criticisms about McDonald's "sycophantic tone" and his use of "favorable hearsay" in William Miller to John H. Kendrick, April 24, 1962; "Report on Forrest McDonald's Biography of Insull" by William Miller, April 24, 1962; Miller to Kendrick, May 8, 1962, UCPC/UCL; Hughes, *Networks of Power*, 201, 203–4; Platt, *The Electric City*.

20. Platt, *Electric City*, 81–82, 132–35, 313; McDonald, *Insull*, 81–89; Wasik, *The Merchant of Power*, 77–78, 249–50.

21. Agreement between Samuel Insull Jr., Samuel Insull III, and American History Research Center, July 9, 1956, UCPC/UCL; McDonald, *Recovering the Past*, 64, 74, 77, 78, 82.

22. When the American History Research Center assigned its rights to publish *Insull* under the contract with Samuel Insull Jr. to the University of Chicago Press, the press required the deletion of paragraph 6, which provided that if the book was successful then its surplus royalties—in the "sole discretion" of the Center—would be distributed to McDonald and "The Samuel and Margaret Insull Memorial Fund." Agreement between Samuel Insull Jr., Samuel Insull III, and American History Research Center, Inc., July 9, 1956, UCPC/UCL. McDonald, *Recovering the Past*, 74, 77, 78, 82; McDonald, *Insull*, xi.

23. Samuel Insull Jr. to John W. Taylor, April 20, 1961, UCPC/UCL.

24. Samuel Insull Jr. to Joseph O. Kostner, January 16, 1959; Forrest McDonald to Carroll G. Bowen, July 18, 1960; Bowen to Samuel Insull Jr., July 27, 1960; Bowen to McDonald, July 27, 1960; Insull Jr. to Bowen, with enclosure, April 24, 1962, UCPC/UCL.

25. William Miller to John H. Kendrick, April 24, 1962; "Report on Forrest McDonald's Biography of Insull" by William Miller, April 24, 1962; Miller to Kendrick, May 8, 1962, UCPC/UCL.

26. Stanley A. Kaplan, Review of "The Fall of the House of Insull" by Forrest McDonald, April 4, 1962, UCPC/UCL.

27. *Chicago Tribune*, April 7, 8, 14, June 1, 1932; Wade Calvert, "The Hand of Morgan in the Insull Case: Trying to Control the Nation's Utilities," *Current Opinion* 172 (June 1933); Taylor, "Losses to the Public in the Insull Collapse," 195–97; Insull, *Memoirs*, 96; McDonald, *Insull*, 289–301; Stanley A. Kaplan, Review of "The Fall of the House of Insull" by Forrest McDonald, April 4, 1962, UCPC/UCL.

28. McDonald, *Recovering the Past*, 82–86, 90, 93–96; Forrest McDonald to Roger Shugg, July 7, 1958; Carroll C. Bowen to McDonald, August 16, 1961; McDonald to Bowen, August 18, 1961, UCPC/UCL.

29. McDonald, *Recovering the Past*, 78, 82.

30. Louis C. Hunter, a review of *Let There Be Light: The Electric Utility Industry in Wisconsin, 1881–1955*, by Forrest McDonald, *Mississippi Valley Historical Review*, 45, no. 1 (June 1958): 158–60; Forrest McDonald, *Let There Be Light: The Electric Utility Industry in Wisconsin, 1881–1955* (Madison: American History Research Center, 1957): v–viii.

31. McDonald, *Recovering the Past*, 66; Clifford L. Lord to the Managing Editor; and Louis C. Hunter to the Managing Editor, "Communications," *Mississippi Valley Historical Review*, 45, no. 3 (Dec. 1958): 563–65.

32. Roy N. Lokken, "McDonald's Theory of History: A Critique," *Wisconsin Magazine of History* 41, no. 4 (Summer 1958): 264–69.

33. McDonald, *Recovering the Past*, 62–64, 70, 82–84; Executor's First and Final Account, February 26, 1985, In the Matter of the Estate of Samuel Insull Jr., Deceased, CCKC.

34. Records of the Examining Division, Comptroller of the Currency's Office, USOCC/WNRC; McDonald, *Insull*, 30; James, *The Growth of Chicago Banks*, 1030.

Abbreviations Used in the Notes

ALPL	Abraham Lincoln Presidential Library, Springfield, Illinois.
BBP/PU	Bernard Baruch Papers, Seeley G. Mudd Manuscript Library, Princeton University, Princeton, New Jersey.
CCCC	Circuit Court of Cook County, In Chancery, Cook County Courthouse, Chicago, Illinois.
CCDC	County Court, City and County of Denver, Colorado.
CCKC	Circuit Court of Kane County, Kane County Probate Division, Geneva, Illinois.
CGDC/EHC	Charles G. Dawes Collection, Evanston History Center, Evanston, Illinois.
CGDP/NUL	Charles G. Dawes Papers, Special Collections, Northwestern University Library, Evanston, Illinois.
CHM	Archives of the Chicago History Museum, Chicago, Illinois.
CrCCC	Criminal Court of Cook County, Cook County Courthouse, Chicago, Illinois.
DRRP/CHM	Donald R. Richberg Papers, Chicago History Museum, Chicago Illinois.
EMP/LC	Eugene Meyer Papers, Library of Congress, Washington, D.C.
EOKP/LU	E. Ogden Ketting Papers, Loyola University Chicago Archives, Chicago, Illinois.
FDRP/FDRL	Franklin D. Roosevelt Papers, Franklin D. Roosevelt Presidential Library, Hyde Park, New York.

GLHP/CU   George Leslie Harrison Papers, Columbia University,
                Rare Book and Manuscript Library, New York, New York.

HHP/HHPL   Herbert Hoover Papers, Herbert Hoover Presidential
                Library, West Branch, Iowa.

IAPA/ISA   Illinois Auditor of Public Accounts and Commissioner of
                Banks and Trust Companies, Record Group 409, Illinois
                State Archives, Springfield, Illinois.

ISEP/NA   Investigation of Stock Exchange Practices, U.S. Senate
                Banking and Currency Committee, Record Group Sen.
                73A-F3, National Archives, Washington, D.C.

ISOS/ISA   Illinois Secretary of State, Record Group 103, Illinois State
                Archives, Springfield, Illinois.

JHJ/CCHC   Jesse Holman Jones Probate Records, County Court of
                Harris County, Texas, Houston, Texas.

JJP/LC   Jesse H. Jones Papers, Library of Congress, Washington,
                D.C.

JJC/UT   Jesse H. Jones Collection, Center for American History,
                University of Texas, Austin, Texas.

LYSP/ALPL   Lawrence Y. Sherman Papers, Abraham Lincoln
                Presidential Library, Springfield, Illinois.

MGJ/CCHC   Mary Gibbs Jones Probate Records, County Court of
                Harris County, Texas, Houston, Texas.

ODYP/SLU   Owen D. Young Papers, St. Lawrence University Libraries
                Special Collections, Canton, New York.

PCCC   Probate Court of Cook County, Cook County Courthouse,
                Chicago, Illinois.

PRCP/UI   Philip R. Clarke Papers, Department of Special
                Collections, Library of University of Illinois at Chicago,
                Illinois.

RFC/NA   Reconstruction Finance Corporation Records, Record
                Group 234, National Archives at College Park, College
                Park, Maryland.

SCCC   Superior Court of Cook County, Cook County Courthouse,
                Chicago, Illinois.

SIP/LU   Samuel Insull Papers, Loyola University Chicago
                Archives, Chicago, Illinois.

UCPC/UCL	University of Chicago Press Collection, Special Collections Research Center, University of Chicago Library, Chicago, Illinois.
USDC/NDI	U.S. District Court Records, Record Group 21, Northern District of Illinois, National Archives and Records Administration, Chicago, Illinois.
USDC/SDT	U.S. District Court Records, Record Group 21, Southern District of Texas, Houston, Equity Case Files 1907–1938, National Archives and Records Administration, Fort Worth, Texas.
USDJ	U.S. Department of Justice, Record Group 60, National Archives at College Park, College Park, Maryland.
USOCC/NA	U.S. Office of the Comptroller of the Currency, Record Group 101, Records of the Division of Insolvent National Banks, 1863–1950, National Archives at College Park, College Park, Maryland.
USOCC/WNRC	U.S. Office of the Comptroller of the Currency, Record Group 101, Records of the Examining Division, 1863–1935. National Archives at College Park, College Park, Maryland.
USS/NA	Records of the United States Senate, Record Group 46, National Archives Building, Washington, D.C.
WMP/UU	Wilson McCarthy Papers, Marriott Library, Special Collections, University of Utah, Salt Lake City.

Select Bibliography

GOVERNMENT DOCUMENTS AND PUBLICATIONS

Abraham Lincoln Presidential Library, Springfield, Illinois.

Annual Report of the Comptroller of the Currency. U.S. Treasury Department. Washington, D.C.: Government Printing Office, 1920–35, 1968.

Annual Report of the Federal Reserve Board. Washington, D.C.: Government Printing Office, 1920–35.

Annual Report of the Interstate Commerce Commission. Washington, D.C.: Government Printing Office, 1932–44.

Bank Failure: An Evaluation of the Factors Contributing to the Failure of National Banks. Washington, D.C.: Office of the Comptroller of the Currency, June 1988.

Banking Law State of Illinois. Auditor's Edition. Edward J. Barrett, Auditor of Public Accounts, December 2, 1930.

Callaghan's Illinois Statutes Annotated, 1932–1935 Supplement. Chicago: Callaghan and Company, 1935.

Callaghan's Illinois Statutes Annotated, 1925–1931 Supplement. Chicago: Callaghan and Company, 1931.

Circular No. 1 of the Reconstruction Finance Corporation, Information for Banks and Other Financial Institutions Desiring to Apply for Loans under the Reconstruction Finance Corporations Act, February 1932. Washington, D.C.: Government Printing Office, 1932.

Circuit Court of Cook County Records. Chicago, Illinois.

The Code of the Laws of the United States of America, December 7, 1925–July 16, 1932. Washington, D.C.: Government Printing Office, 1926–33.

Creation of a Reconstruction Finance Corporation. Hearings before a Subcommittee of the Committee on Banking and Currency, U.S. Senate, 72nd Cong., 1st sess., December 18, 19, 21, 22, 1931.

The Currency. U.S. Senate Document No. 161. 63rd Cong., 1st sess., 1913.

"Failed Financial Institutions: Reasons, Costs, Remedies and Unresolved Issues." Statement of Frederick D. Wolf before the U.S. House Committee on Banking, Finance and Urban Affairs. U.S. General Accounting Office Testimony, January 13, 1989.

Federal Reserve Bulletin. 1920–35. Washington, D.C.: Government Printing Office, 1920–35.

Financial Crisis Inquiry Commission. *The Financial Crisis Inquiry Report*. Washington, D.C.: Government Printing Office, January 2011.

Financial Institutions Reform, Recovery, and Enforcement Act of 1989, Public Law No. 101–73, 103 Stat. 183 (1989).

Former Reconstruction Finance Corporation Properties. Hearings before a Subcommittee of the Committee on Government Operations, House of Representatives, 91st Cong., 1st Session, H.R. 4599, October 29 and December 9, 1969.

Guide to the National Archives of the United States. Washington, D.C.: National Archives and Records Administration, 1987.

Hearings before the Committee on Banking and Currency, United States Senate, 82nd Congress, 1st Session on S. 514, S. 515, S. 1116, S. 1123, S. 1329, S. 1376, and S. J. Res. 44, Bills to Amend the Reconstruction Finance Corporation Act, as Amended, and for Other Purposes. April 27, 30, May 1, 2, 22 and 23, 1951. Washington, D.C.: Government Printing Office, 1951.

Hearing before the Committee on the Judiciary, House of Representatives, 73rd Congress, 1st Session on Receivership and Bankruptcy Investigation, October 30 to November 4, 1933, March 19 to March 23, 1934, House of Representatives Subcommittee Investigating Receiverships and Bankruptcies, Chicago, Illinois. Washington, D.C.: Government Printing Office, 1934.

Hearing before the Committee on the Judiciary, House of Representatives, 73rd Congress, 2nd Session on Receivership and Bankruptcy Investigation, April 21, 1934, May 2, 1934, House of Representatives Subcommittee Investigating Receiverships and Bankruptcies, Chicago, Illinois, Part 2. Washington, D.C.: Government Printing Office, 1934.

Illinois Auditor of Public Accounts and Commissioner of Banks and Trust Companies, Record Group 409, Illinois State Archives, Springfield, Illinois.

Illinois Secretary of State, Record Group 103, Illinois State Archives, Springfield, Illinois.

Letter from the Comptroller General of the United States Transmitting Report on the Audit of Reconstruction Finance Corporation and Affiliated Corporations, the RFC Mortgage Company, and Federal National Mortgage Association for the Fiscal Year ended June 30, 1945. Washington, D.C.: Government Printing Office, 1947.

"List of Creditors Holding 20 Largest Unsecured Claims," United States Bankruptcy Court, Southern District of New York, In re Enron Corp. Debtor, December 2, 2001.

The National Bank Act as Amended and Other Laws Relating to National Banks. Washington, D.C.: Government Printing Office, 1920–35.

Proposed Extension of the Reconstruction Finance Corporation, Hearings before the Committee on Banking and Currency, United States Senate, 80th Congress, 1st Session on $80,000,000 Loan to the B. & O. Railroad, Part I, April 10, 11, 29, 30, May 5, 6, 22, and 23, 1947. Washington, D.C.: Government Printing Office, 1947.

Public Company Accounting Reform and Investor Protection Act of 2002, 107 Public Law No. 204, 116 Stat. 745 (2002), 15 U.S.C. Section 7201.

Reconstruction Finance Corporation Act. H.R. 7360, 72nd Cong., 1st sess., January 21, 1932.

Reconstruction Finance Corporation Act as Amended and Provisions of the Emergency Relief and Construction Act of 1932 Pertaining to Reconstruction Finance Corporation, July 21, 1932. Washington, D.C.: Government Printing Office, 1932.

Reconstruction Finance Corporation v. Central Republic Trust Company, et al. 11 Federal Supplement 976. St. Paul, Minn.: West, 1936.

Reconstruction Finance Corporation v. Central Republic Trust Company, et al. 17 Federal Supplement 263. St. Paul, Minn.: West, 1937.

Reconstruction Finance Corporation Seven-Year Report to the President and the Congress of the United States, February 2, 1932 to February 2, 1939, by Jesse H. Jones, Chairman.

Records of the Reconstruction Finance Corporation, Record Group 234, National Archives at College Park, College Park, Maryland.

Report to the Committee on the Judiciary, House of Representatives, 73rd Congress, 2nd Session, on Receivership and Bankruptcy Investigation by the Subcommittee of the Committee of the Judiciary of the House of Representatives Investigating Receiverships and Bankruptcies at Chicago, Illinois. Washington, D.C.: Government Printing Office, 1934.

Report to the President of the United States by the Director of the Bureau of Budget. Washington, D.C.: Government Printing Office, 1922.

Reports of Cases at Law and in Chancery Argued and Determined in the Supreme Court of Illinois, vol. 278, 1917, John F. Golden et al. Appellants, v. John A. Cervenka et al. Appellees; William C. Niblack, Appellant v. John F. Golden et al. Appellees, 409–64.

Reports of Cases at Law and in Chancery Argued and Determined in the Supreme Court of Illinois, vol. 293, June 1920, The People of the State of Illinois, Defendant in Error, v. Charles B. Munday, Plaintiff in Error, Receiver's First Report and Account Current, June 2, 1915, 191–210.

Reports of Cases at Law and in Chancery Argued and Determined in the Supreme Court of Illinois, vol. 312, 1924, The Chicago Title and Trust Company, Receiver, Appellant, v. The Central Trust Company of Illinois, Appellee—The Chicago Title and Trust Company, Appellee, v. The Central Trust Company, Appellant, 396–519.

Reports of Cases Determined in the Appellate Courts of Illinois, vol. 224, 1922, The Chicago Title and Trust Company, Receiver of LaSalle Street Trust and Savings

Bank, Cross-complainant and Appellant, v. Central Trust Company of Illinois, Cross-defendant and Appellee, 475–505.

Statement by Charles G. Dawes before the Committee on Ways and Means, House of Representatives, April 21, 1932, Information Division, Speeches and Statements by Key Personnel, 1932–54. Records of the Reconstruction Finance Corporation, Record Group 234, National Archives at College Park, College Park, Maryland.

Statement Showing Total Resources and Liabilities of Illinois State Banks, June 30, 1932, compiled by Oscar Nelson, Auditor of Public Accounts. Springfield: Journal Printing Company, 1932.

Stock Exchange Practices. Hearings before a Subcommittee of the Committee on Banking and Currency, United States Senate, 72nd Congress, 2nd Session, On S. Res. 84 and S. Res. 239, Resolutions to Thoroughly Investigate Practices of Stock Exchanges with Respect to the Buying and Selling and the Borrowing and Lending of Listed Securities the Values of Such Securities and the Effects of Such Practices. Part 5 (Insull), February 15, 16, and 17, 1933. Washington, D.C.: Government Printing Office, 1933.

Stock Exchange Practices. Report of the Committee on Banking and Currency, 73rd Congress, 2nd Session, Report No. 1455, June 6, 1934. Washington, D.C.: Government Printing Office, 1934.

Study of Reconstruction Finance Corporation. Hearings before a Subcommittee of the Committee on Banking and Currency, United States Senate, 81st Congress, 2nd Session, on a Study of the Operations of the Reconstruction Finance Corporation Pursuant To S. Res. 219, 81st Congress, Lending Policy, June 8, 9, 13, and 15, July 3, 5, and 10, 1950. Washington, D.C.: Government Printing Office, 1950.

Superior Court of Cook County Records. Chicago, Illinois.

Testimony of Robert Roach, Chief Investigator, Permanent Subcommittee on Investigations, "The Role of the Financial Institutions in Enron's Collapse," July 23, 2002.

Texas Department of Banking, *Bank History National Banks*, 60, 69, 101, *www.banking.state.tx.us/pubs/nbs.pdf.*

Texas Secretary of State Records. Texas State Library and Archives, Austin, Texas.

U.S. Department of Justice Records, Record Group 60, National Archives Building, Washington, D.C.

U.S. District Court Records. Record Group 21, Northern District of Illinois, National Archives and Records Administration, Great Lakes Region, Chicago, Illinois.

U.S. District Court Records. Record Group 21, Southern District of Florida, 1828–1943, National Archives and Records Administration, Southeast Region, Atlanta, Georgia.

U.S. District Court Records, Record Group 21, Southern District of Texas, Houston, Equity Case Files 1907–1938, National Archives and Records Administration, Southwest Region, Fort Worth, Texas.

U.S.N.B. of La Grande v. Pole. 2 F. Supp. 153, 157 (D. Ore. 1932).

U.S. Office of the Comptroller of the Currency. Record Group 101, Records of the Division of Insolvent National Banks, 1863–1950. National Archives at College Park, College Park, Maryland.

U.S. Office of the Comptroller of the Currency. Record Group 101, Records of the Examining Division, 1863–1935. National Archives at College Park, College Park, Maryland.

U.S. Reconstruction Finance Corporation. *Quarterly Report*, 1932–35. Washington, D.C.: Government Printing Office, 1932–35.

Utility Corporations, Letter from the Chairman of the Federal Trade Commission Transmitting, in Response to Senate Resolution No. 83, 70th Congress, a Monthly Report on the Electric Power and Gas Utilities Inquiry, Middle West Utilities Co. and Subsidiaries, December 16, 1931. Washington, D.C.: Government Printing Office, 1932.

Utility Corporations, Letter from the Chairman of the Federal Trade Commission Transmitting, in Response to Senate Resolution No. 83, 70th Congress, a Monthly Report on the Electric Power and Gas Utilities Inquiry, No. 59, Middle West Utilities Co. and Subsidiaries, November 15, 1933. Washington, D.C.: Government Printing Office, 1934.

Utility Corporations, Letter from the Chairman of the Federal Trade Commission Transmitting, in Response to Senate Resolution No. 83, 70th Congress, a Monthly Report on the Electric Power and Gas Utilities Inquiry, No. 67, Corporations Securities Co. of Chicago, July 18, 1934. Washington, D.C.: Government Printing Office, 1935.

Wall Street and the Financial Crisis: Anatomy of a Financial Collapse, Majority and Minority Staff Report, Permanent Subcommittee on Investigations, U.S. Senate, April 13, 2011, www.hsgac.senate.gov.

MANUSCRIPT COLLECTIONS

Baruch, Bernard, Papers. Seeley G. Mudd Manuscript Library, Princeton University, Princeton, New Jersey.

Clarke, Philip R., Papers. Department of Special Collections, Library of University of Illinois at Chicago, Illinois.

Dawes, Charles G., Collection. Evanston History Center, Evanston, Illinois.

Dawes, Charles G., Papers. Special Collections Department, Northwestern University Library, Evanston, Illinois.

Harrison, George Leslie, Papers. Columbia University, Rare Book and Manuscript Library, New York, New York.

Hoover, Herbert, Holdings, 1874–1964. Hoover Institution Archives, Stanford University, Stanford, California.

Hoover, Herbert, Papers. Herbert Hoover Presidential Library, West Branch, Iowa.

Insull, Samuel, Papers, Loyola University Chicago Archives, Chicago, Illinois.

Jones, Jesse H., Papers. Library of Congress, Washington, D.C.

Jones, Jesse Holman, Papers. Center for American History, University of Texas, Austin, Texas.

Ketting, E. Ogden, Papers. Loyola University Chicago Archives, Chicago, Illinois.

McCarthy, Wilson, Papers. Marriott Library, Special Collections, University of Utah, Salt Lake City.

Meyer, Eugene, Papers. Library of Congress, Washington, D.C.

Richberg, Donald R., Papers. Chicago History Museum, Chicago Illinois.

Roosevelt, Franklin D., Papers. Franklin D. Roosevelt Presidential Library. Hyde Park, New York.

Sherman, Lawrence Y., Papers. Abraham Lincoln Presidential Library, Springfield, Illinois.

Young, Owen D., Papers. Special Collections and Archives, St. Lawrence University Libraries, Canton, New York.

ARTICLES, THESES, DISSERTATIONS, BOOKS, FILMS AND UNPUBLISHED MANUSCRIPTS

Acheson, Sam Hanna. *Joe Bailey: The Last Democrat*. New York: Macmillan, 1932.

Ackerman, Carl W. *Dawes—the Doer!* New York: ERA Publications, 1924.

Adams, James Ring. *The Big Fix: Inside the S&L Scandal*. New York: Wiley, 1990.

Adler, Joe. "Wamu Policing Slammed, Levin Blames OTS Execs." *American Banker*, April 16, 2010.

Ahamed, Liaquat. *Lords of Finance: The Bankers Who Broke the World*. New York: Penguin Press, 2008.

Allen, Frederick Lewis. *The Big Change: America Transforms Itself, 1900–1950*. New York: Harper and Brothers, 1952.

———. *Only Yesterday: An Informal History of the Nineteen-Twenties*. New York: Harper and Brothers, 1931.

———. *Since Yesterday*. New York: Harper and Brothers, 1940.

Alston, Lee J., Wayne A. Grove, and David C. Wheelock. "Why Do Banks Fail? Evidence from the 1920s." *Explorations in Economic History* 31 (1994): 409–31.

Anti-Depression Legislation: A Study of the Acts, Corporations, and Trends Growing Out of the "Battle with Depression." New York: American Institute of Banking, 1933.

Applegate, Ester Matthews. "The Reconstruction Finance Corporation." Master's thesis, University of Washington, 1932.

Bailey, Richard. "Morris Sheppard." *Profiles in Power: Twentieth-Century Texans in Washington*. Edited by Kenneth E. Hendrickson Jr., Michael L. Collins, and Patrick Cox, 27–40. Austin: University of Texas Press, 2004.

Baruch, Bernard M. *Baruch: The Public Years*. New York: Holt, Rinehart and Winston, 1960.

Batra, Ravi. *The Great Depression of 1990*. New York: Simon & Schuster, 1987.

Bergreen, Laurence. *Capone: The Man and the Era*. New York: Simon & Schuster, 1994.

Bernanke, Ben S. *Essays on the Great Depression*. Princeton, N.J.: Princeton University Press, 2000.

Biographical Directory of the American Congress: 1774–1961. Washington, D.C.: Government Printing Office, 1961.

Blackford, Mansel G., and K. Austin Kerr. *Business Enterprise in American History*. Boston: Houghton Mifflin, 1986.

Blegen, Theodore C. *Minnesota: A History of the State*. St. Paul: University of Minnesota Press, 1975.

Bliven, Bruce. "Charles G. Dawes, Super-Salesman." *New Republic*, January 25, 1928, 263–67.

Blum, John Morton. *From the Morgenthau Diaries: Years of Crisis, 1928–1938*. Boston: Houghton Mifflin, 1959.

Boller, Paul F., Jr. *Presidential Campaigns*. New York: Oxford University Press, 1985.

Boone, Peter, and Simon Johnson. "Shooting Banks: Obama's Impotent Assault on Wall Street." *New Republic*, February 24, 2010.

Borosage, Robert L. "The Big Bank Lobby: Too Big to Bear?" Huffington Post.com, May 11, 2010.

Bowers, Claude G. *Beveridge and the Progressive Era*. New York: Literary Guild, 1932.

Brandeis, Louis D. *Letters of Louis D. Brandeis*. Edited by Melvin I. Urofsky and David W. Levy. Albany: State University of New York Press, 1971.

———. *Other People's Money and How the Bankers Use It*. New York: Frederick A. Stokes, 1914; reprinted, 1932.

———. *Other People's Money and How the Bankers Use It*. Edited by Melvin I. Urofsky. Boston: Bedford Books of St. Martin's Press, 1995.

Brinkley, Douglas. *The Quiet World: Saving Alaska's Wilderness Kingdom, 1879–1960*. New York: Harper Collins, 2011.

Brown, Norman D. *Hood, Bonnet, and Little Brown Jug: Texas Politics, 1921–1928*. College Station: Texas A&M University Press, 1984.

Bryce, Robert. *Pipe Dreams: Greed, Ego, and the Death of Enron*. New York: Public Affairs, 2002.

Buenger, Walter L. "Between Community and Corporation: The Southern Roots of Jesse H. Jones and the Reconstruction Finance Corporation." *Journal of Southern History* 56 (August 1990): 481–510.

———. "Jesse Jones." *Profiles in Power: Twentieth-Century Texans in Washington*. Edited by Kenneth E. Hendrickson Jr., Michael L. Collins, and Patrick Cox, 66–84. Austin: University of Texas Press, 2004.

Buenger, Walter L., and Joseph A. Pratt. *But Also Good Business: Texas Commerce Banks and the Financing of Houston and Texas, 1886–1986*. College Station: Texas A&M University Press, 1986.

Bukowski, Douglas. *Big Bill Thompson, Chicago, and the Politics of Image*. Urbana: University of Illinois Press, 1998.

Burner, David. *Herbert Hoover: A Public Life*. New York: Alfred A. Knopf, 1979.

Burns, Helen M. *The American Banking Community and New Deal Banking Reforms, 1933–1935*. Westport, Conn.: Greenwood Press, 1974.

Burns, James MacGregor. *Roosevelt: The Lion and the Fox*. New York: Harcourt, Brace and World, 1956.

Busch, Francis X. *Guilty or Not Guilty?* Indianapolis: Bobbs-Merrill, 1952.

Butkiewicz, James L. "The Impact of a Lender of Last Resort during the Great Depression: The Case of the Reconstruction Finance Corporation." *Explorations in Economic History* 32 (1995): 197–216.

Calomiris, Charles W., and Joseph R. Mason. "Contagion and Bank Failures during the Great Depression: The June 1932 Chicago Banking Panic." *American Economic Review* 87, no. 5 (December 1997): 863–83.

———. "Contagion and Bank Failures during the Great Depression: The June 1932 Chicago Banking Panic." Working Paper No. 4934, National Bureau of Economic Research, Inc. (November 1994).

Calvert, Wade. "The Hand of Morgan in the Insull Case: Trying to Control the Nation's Utilities." *Current Opinion* 172 (June 1933).

Carosso, Vincent P. *Investment Banking in America: A History*. Cambridge, Mass.: Harvard University Press, 1970.

———. *The Morgans: Private International Bankers, 1854–1913*. Cambridge, Mass.: Harvard University Press, 1987.

———. "The Wall Street Money Trust from Pujo through Medina." *Business History Review* 47 (Winter 1973): 421–37.

Cartinhour, Gaines Thomson. *Branch, Group and Chain Banking*. New York: Macmillan, 1931.

Case, Josephine Young, and Everett Needham Case. *Owen D. Young and American Enterprise: A Biography*. Boston: David R. Godine, 1982.

Chandler, Lester V. *America's Greatest Depression, 1929–1941*. New York: Harper and Row, 1970.

———. *American Monetary Policy: 1928–1941*. New York: Harper and Row, 1971.

Charlton, Joseph William. "The History of Banking in Illinois since 1863." Ph.D. diss., University of Chicago, 1938.

Cho, Hyo Won. "The Evolution of the Functions of the Reconstruction Finance Corporation: A Study of the Growth and Death of a Federal Lending Agency." Ph.D. diss., Ohio State University, 1953.

Cockrell, Monroe F. "Banking in Chicago: 1929–1935, Deep Depression Years." Manuscript, Chicago, Illinois, May 1948.

Coffee, John C. Jr. "The Attorney as Gatekeeper: An Agenda for the SEC." *Columbia Law Review* 103, no. 5 (June 2003): 1293–1316.

———. "Gatekeeper Failure and Reform: The Challenge of Fashioning Relevant Reforms." *Boston University Law Review* 84, no. 2 (April 2004): 301–64.

———. *Gatekeepers: The Role of the Professions in Corporate Governance.* Clarendon Lectures in Management Studies. New York: Oxford University Press, 2006.

———. "A Theory of Corporate Scandals: Why the USA and Europe Differ." *Oxford Review of Economic Policy* 21, no. 2 (2005): 198–211.

———. "Understanding Enron: 'It's about the Gatekeepers, Stupid.'" *Business Lawyer* 57, no. 4 (August 2002): 1403–20.

———. "What Caused Enron? A Capsule Social and Economic History of the 1990s." *Cornell Law Review* 89, no. 2 (January 2004): 269–309.

Coit, Margaret L. *Mr. Baruch.* Boston: Houghton Mifflin, 1957.

Collins, Frederick L. "A Woman Whose Dream Came True." *Delineator* 3 (October 1927): 12, 131–33.

Connally, Tom, and Alfred Steinberg. *My Name Is Tom Connally.* New York: Thomas Y. Crowell, 1954.

Connor, Kevin. *Big Bank Takeover: How Too-Big-to-Fail's Army of Lobbyists Has Captured Washington*, Campaign for America's Future, www.ourfuture.org.

Coolidge, Calvin. *Autobiography of Calvin Coolidge.* New York: Cosmopolitan Book Corporation, 1929.

———. *The Price of Freedom: Speeches and Addresses.* New York: Scribner, 1924.

Cooper, George. *The Origin of Financial Crises: Central Banks, Credit Bubbles, and the Efficient Market Fallacy.* New York: Vintage Books, 2008.

Cox, Patrick. "John Nance Garner." *Profiles in Power: Twentieth-Century Texans in Washington.* Edited by Kenneth E. Hendrickson Jr., Michael L. Collins, and Patrick Cox, 41–63. Austin: University of Texas Press, 2004.

Creswell, Julie, and Ben White. "The Guys from 'Government Sachs.'" *New York Times*, October 19, 2008.

"The Crime Hunt in Insull's Shattered Empire," *Literary Digest,* October 15, 1932, 12–13.

Critchlow, Donald T., and Ellis W. Hawley, eds. *Federal Social Policy: The Historical Dimension.* University Park: Pennsylvania State University Press, 1988.

Cruver, Brian. *Anatomy of Greed: The Unshredded Truth from an Enron Insider.* New York: Carroll & Graf, 2002.

Cudahy, Richard D., and William D. Henderson. "From Insull to Enron: Corporate (Re)Regulation after the Rise and Fall of Two Energy Icons." *Energy Law Journal* 26, no. 1 (2005): 35–110.

Curry, Timothy, and Lynn Shibut. "The Cost of the Savings and Loan Crisis: Truth and Consequences." *FDIC Banking Review* 13, no. 2 (Fall 2000).

Dana, Julian. *A. P. Giannini: Giant in the West.* New York: Prentice-Hall, 1947.

Daniels, Jonathan. *Ordeal of Ambition: Jefferson, Hamilton, Burr.* Garden City, N.Y.: Doubleday, 1970.

Dawes, Charles G. *The Banking System of the United States and Its Relation to the Money and Business of the Country.* Chicago: Rand, McNally, 1894.

———. *Essays and Speeches.* Boston: Houghton Mifflin, 1915.

———. *The First Year of the Budget of the United States*. New York: Harper and Brothers, 1923.

———. *Journal as Ambassador to Great Britain*. New York: Macmillan, 1939.

———. *A Journal of the Great War*. Boston: Houghton Mifflin, 1921.

———. *A Journal of the McKinley Years*. Chicago: Lakeside Press, R. R. Donnelley & Sons, 1950.

———. *Notes as Vice President, 1928–1929*. Boston: Little, Brown, 1935.

Dawes, Rufus R. *Service with the Sixth Wisconsin Volunteers*. Marietta, Ohio: E. R. Alderman and Sons, 1890.

Degler, Carl N. "The Ordeal of Herbert Hoover." *Yale Review* 52 (June 1963): 563–83.

"Developments in President Hoover's Program to Stabilize Credit." *Congressional Digest* 10, no. 12 (December 1931): 300.

Dodge, Mark M., ed. *Herbert Hoover and the Historians*. West Branch, Iowa: Herbert Hoover Presidential Library Association, 1989.

"Don't Blame the New Deal." *New York Times*, September 28, 2008.

Doti, Lynne Pierson. "Nationwide Branching: Some Lessons from California." *Essays in Economic and Business History: Selected Papers from the Economic and Business Historical Society*. Edited by Edwin J. Perkins, 6:141–60. Los Angeles: History Department, University of Southern California, 1988.

Doti, Lynne Pierson, and Larry Schweikart. *Banking in the American West: From the Gold Rush to Deregulation*. Norman: University of Oklahoma Press, 1991.

———. *California Bankers, 1848–1993*. Needham Heights, Mass.: Ginn Press, 1994.

Dunne, Edward F. *Illinois: The Heart of the Nation*. 5 Vols. Chicago: Lewis Publishing Company, 1933.

Ebersole, J. Franklin. "One Year of the Reconstruction Finance Corporation." *Quarterly Journal of Economics* 47 (May 1933): 464–92.

Eichengreen, Barry. *Golden Fetters: The Gold Standard and the Great Depression, 1919–1939*. New York: Oxford University Press, 1992.

Elliott, A. Larry, and Richard J. Schroth. *How Companies Lie: Why Enron IS Just the Tip of the Iceberg*. New York: Crown Business, 2002.

Enron: The Smartest Guys in the Room. Documentary film directed by Alex Gibney. Released on April 22, 2005.

Esbitt, Milton. "Bank Portfolios and Bank Failures during the Great Depression: Chicago." *Journal of Economic History* 46 (June 1986): 455–62.

"Extent of Federal Supervision of Banking Today." *Congressional Digest* 10, no. 12 (December 1931): 293–95.

Farr, Finis. *Chicago: A Personal History of America's Most American City*. New Rochelle, N.Y.: Arlington House, 1973.

Faulkner, Harold U. *From Versailles to the New Deal*. New Haven, Conn.: Yale University Press, 1950.

Fausold, Martin L. *The Presidency of Herbert C. Hoover*. Lawrence: University Press of Kansas, 1985.

Feagin, Joe R. *Free Enterprise City: Houston in Political-Economic Perspective*. New Brunswick, N.J.: Rutgers University Press, 1988.

Fearon, Peter. *War, Prosperity and Depression: The U.S. Economy 1917–45*. Lawrence: University Press of Kansas, 1987.

Flynn, John T. "Inside the R.F.C.: An Adventure in Secrecy." *Harper's Magazine*, January 1933, 161–69.

———. *The Roosevelt Myth*. New York: Devin-Adair, 1956.

"FOIA and the Fed: Do We Have a Right to Know the Central Bank's Inner Workings?" *Washington Post*, October 22, 2009.

Forbes, Bertie C. *Men Who Are Making America*. New York: B. C. Forbes, 1921.

Foster, J. D. "Transparency and Accountability at the Federal Reserve." Heritage Foundation, November 20, 2009.

Fox, Loren. *Enron: The Rise and Fall*. Hoboken, N.J.: John Wiley & Sons, 2003.

Freidel, Frank. "Election of 1932." *History of American Presidential Elections, 1789–1968*. Edited by Arthur M. Schlesinger Jr., 3:2707–39. New York: Chelsea House Publishers and McGraw-Hill, 1971.

———. *Franklin D. Roosevelt*. Boston: Little, Brown, 1952.

———. *Franklin D. Roosevelt: A Rendezvous with Destiny*. Boston: Little, Brown, 1990.

Friedman, Milton, and Anna Jacobson Schwartz. *A Monetary History of the United States: 1867–1960*. Princeton, N.J.: Princeton University Press, 1963.

———. *The Great Contraction, 1929–1933*. Princeton, N.J.: Princeton University Press, 1965.

Galbraith, John Kenneth. *Economics in Perspective: A Critical History*. Boston: Houghton Mifflin, 1987.

———. *The Great Crash, 1929*. Boston: Houghton Mifflin, 1972.

Garrett, Garet. "Why Some Banks Fail and Others Don't." *Saturday Evening Post*, May 20, 1933, 3–5, 67–70, 72.

Goedeken, Edward Adolph. "Charles G. Dawes in War and Peace, 1917–1922." Ph.D. diss., University of Kansas, 1984.

Goff, John S. *Robert Todd Lincoln: A Man in his Own Right*. Norman: University of Oklahoma Press, 1969.

Robert Todd Lincoln: A Man in his Own Right. Manchester, Vermont: Friends of Hildene, Inc., 2005.

Gordon, Greg. "Goldman's Connections to White House Raise Eyebrows." *McClatchy-Tribune News Service*, April 21, 2010.

Gordon, John Steele. "Understanding the S&L Mess." *American Heritage* 42 (February–March 1991): 49–51, 54, 56, 58–60, 62–63, 65–66, 68.

Gottfried, Alex. *Boss Cermak of Chicago: A Study of Political Leadership*. Seattle: University of Washington Press, 1962.

Green, Paul M., and Melvin G. Holli, eds. *The Mayors: The Chicago Political Tradition*. Carbondale: Southern Illinois University Press, 1987.

Guglielmo, Mark Anthony. "Illinois State Bank Failures in the Great Depression." Ph.D. diss., University of Chicago, 1998.

Hair, William Ivy. *The Kingfish and His Realm: The Life and Times of Huey P. Long.* Baton Rouge: Louisiana State University Press, 1991.

Harvey, Arlington C. *History of the Pure Oil Company, 1914 to 1941.* Chicago, 1941.

Hawley, Ellis W. *The Great War and the Search for a Modern Order: A History of the American People and Their Institutions, 1917–1933.* New York: St. Martin's Press, 1979.

———, ed. *Herbert Hoover as Secretary of Commerce: Studies in New Era Thought and Practice.* Iowa City: University of Iowa Press, 1981.

———. *The New Deal and the Problem of Monopoly: A Study in Economic Ambivalence.* Princeton, N.J.: Princeton University Press, 1966.

Hayes, Dorsha B. *Chicago: Crossroads of American Enterprise.* New York: Julian Messner, 1944.

Hession, Charles H., and Hyman Sandy. *Ascent to Affluence: A History of American Economic Development.* Boston: Allyn and Bacon, 1969.

Hicks, John D. *Republican Ascendancy, 1921–1933.* New York: Harper & Row, 1960.

Hildebrant, Donald Victor. "The Reconstruction Finance Corporation." Master's thesis, Ohio State University, 1951.

Hilderbrand, Robert C. "Edward M. House." *Profiles in Power: Twentieth-Century Texans in Washington.* Edited by Kenneth E. Hendrickson Jr., Michael L. Collins, and Patrick Cox, 1–25. Austin: University of Texas Press, 2004.

History of the Pure Oil Company, Vol. 2. Chicago, 1953.

Hoffman, Dennis E. *Scarface Al and the Crime Crusaders: Chicago's Private War Against Capone.* Carbondale: Southern Illinois University Press, 1993.

Hofstadter, Richard. *The American Political Tradition and the Men Who Made It.* New York: Knopf, 1970.

———. *The Paranoid Style in American Politics.* New York: Knopf, 1966.

Holcomb, Bob Charles. "Senator Joe Bailey: Two Decades of Controversy." Ph.D. diss., Texas Technological College, 1968.

The Hoover Commission Report on Organization of the Executive Branch of the Government. New York: McGraw-Hill, 1949.

Hoover, Herbert. *The Memoirs of Herbert Hoover: The Great Depression, 1929–1941.* New York: Macmillan, 1952.

Hoover, Herbert, and Calvin Coolidge. *Campaign Speeches of 1932.* New York: Doubleday, Doran, 1933.

Hoover, Irwin Hood. *Forty-Two Years in the White House.* Boston: Houghton Mifflin, 1934.

Horvitz, Paul M. "Commercial Bank Financial Reporting and Disclosure." *Journal of Contemporary Business* 6, no. 3 (Summer 1977): 60–75.

———. "Financial Disclosure: Is More Always Better?" *Journal of Retail Banking Services* 18, no. 4 (Winter 1996): 57–61.

Houston. Writers' Program of the Work Projects Administration in Texas. Houston: Anson Jones Press, 1942.

Hoyt, Homer. *One Hundred Years of Land Values in Chicago: The Relationship of the Growth of Chicago to the Rise of Its Land Values, 1830–1933*. Washington, D.C.: Beard Books, 2000.

Hubbard, R. Glenn, ed. *Financial Markets and Financial Crises*. Chicago: University of Chicago Press, 1991.

Hughes, Thomas P. "The Electrification of America: The System Builders." *Technology and Culture* 20 (January 1979): 124–61.

———. *Networks of Power: Electrification in Western Society, 1880–1930*. Baltimore: Johns Hopkins University Press, 1983.

Hunter, Louis C. Review of *Let There Be Light: The Electric Utility Industry in Wisconsin, 1881–1955* by Forrest McDonald. *Mississippi Valley Historical Review* 45, no. 1 (June 1958): 158–60.

Huston, Francis Murray. *Financing an Empire: History of Banking in Illinois*, Vol. 2. Chicago: S. J. Clarke Publishing, 1926.

Hutchinson, William Thomas. *Lowden of Illinois: The Life of Frank O. Lowden*. Chicago: University of Chicago Press, 1957.

Huthmacher, J. Joseph, and Warren I. Susman. *Herbert Hoover and the Crisis of American Capitalism*. Cambridge, Mass.: Schenkman Publishing, 1973.

Inside Job. Documentary film directed by Charles Ferguson. Released on October 8, 2010.

"Insull: Prodigal in Jails and Courts of Former 'Empire.'" *Newsweek* 3, no. 20 (May 19, 1934): 15.

Insull, Samuel. *The Memoirs of Samuel Insull*. Polo, Ill.: Transportation Trails, 1992.

Irwin, Neil. "At N.Y. Fed, Blending In Is Part of the Job; Some Fear Wall Street Too Heavily Influences the Financial Enforcer." *Washington Post*, July 20, 2009.

———. "Bernanke Seeks to Preserve Fed Power; Common Ground Sought with Lawmakers on Oversight, Transparency." *Washington Post*, February 25, 2010.

———. "Senate Bill Leaves Fed at the Center of U.S. Oversight; Central Bank Faces an Audit but Overhaul May Widen Its Scope." *Washington Post*, May 17, 2010.

Irwin, Neil, and Amit R. Paley. "Greenspan Says He Was Wrong on Regulation; Lawmakers Blast Former Fed Chairman." *Washington Post*, October 24, 2008.

James, F. Cyril. *The Growth of Chicago Banks*, Vols. 1 and 2. New York: Harper and Brothers, 1938.

James, Marquis, and Bessie Rowland James. *Biography of a Bank: The Story of Bank of America N.T. and S.A.* New York: Harper and Brothers, 1954.

Jenkins, Roy. *Franklin Delano Roosevelt*. New York: Henry Holt and Company, 2003.

Johnson, Simon. "The Quiet Coup." *Atlantic*, May 2009.

Johnston, Marguerite. *Houston: The Unknown City, 1836–1946*. College Station: Texas A&M University Press, 1991.

Jones, Jesse H., with Edward Angly. *Fifty Billion Dollars: My Thirteen Years with the RFC (1932–1945)*. New York: Macmillan, 1951.

Josephson, Matthew. *Edison*. New York: McGraw-Hill, 1959.

Joslin, Theodore G. *Hoover Off the Record*. Garden City, N.Y.: Doubleday, Doran & Company, 1934.

Keehn, Richard H., and Gene Smiley. "U.S. Bank Failures, 1932–1933: A Provisional Analysis." *Essays in Economic and Business History* 6 (1988): 136–56.

———. "U.S. Bank Failures, 1932–1933: Additional Evidence on Regional Patterns, Timing, and the Role of the Reconstruction Finance Corporation." *Essays in Economic and Business History* 11 (1993): 131–42.

Kennedy, David M. *Freedom from Fear: The American People in Depression and War, 1929–1945*. New York: Oxford University Press, 1999.

Kennedy, Susan Estabrook. *The Banking Crisis of 1933*. Lexington: University Press of Kentucky, 1973.

Klein, Maury. *Rainbow's End: The Crash of 1929*. New York: Oxford University Press, 2001.

Krugman, Paul. "Bubbles and the Banks." *New York Times*, January 8, 2010.

Lass, William E. *Minnesota: A History*. New York: W. W. Norton, 1998.

Laughlin, Lauren Silva, and Richard Beales. "For Public Trust, Try Disclosure." *New York Times*, June 5, 2009.

Lazarus, David. "Delays in Reform Hasten Next Crisis." *Los Angeles Times*, April 23, 2010.

Leach, Paul Roscoe. *That Man Dawes*. Chicago: Reilly & Lee, 1930.

Leuchtenburg, William E. *The Perils of Prosperity, 1914–32*. Chicago: University of Chicago Press, 1958.

Levine, Lawrence W. *Defender of the Faith, William Jennings Bryan: The Last Decade, 1915–1925*. New York: Oxford University Press, 1965.

Lewis, Sandy B., and William D. Cohan. "The Economy Is Still at the Brink." *New York Times*, June 7, 2009.

Lokken, Roy N. "McDonald's Theory of History: A Critique." *Wisconsin Magazine of History* 41, no. 4 (Summer 1958): 264–69.

Long, Huey P. *Every Man a King: The Autobiography of Huey P. Long*. Cambridge, Mass.: Da Capo Press, 1996.

"The Loss of Owen D. Young," *Nation*, January 4, 1933, 4.

Lubell, Samuel. "The House That Jesse Built." *Saturday Evening Post*, December 7, 1940, 29, 107, 108, 110, 112, 115, 116.

———. "New Deal's J. P. Morgan." *Saturday Evening Post*, November 30, 1940, 9–11, 88–90, 92.

Lyons, Eugene. *The Herbert Hoover Story*. Washington, D.C.: Human Events, 1959.

The Martindale-Hubbell Law Directory. New York: Martindale-Hubbell Law Directory, yearly.

Mason, Alpheus Thomas. *Brandeis: A Free Man's Life*. New York: Viking Press, 1946.

Mason, Joseph Russell. "The Determinants and Effects of Reconstruction Finance Corporation Assistance to Banks during the Great Depression." Ph.D. diss., University of Illinois, 1996.

———. "Do Lender of Last Resort Policies Matter? The Effects of Reconstruction Finance Corporation Assistance to Banks during the Great Depression." *Journal of Financial Services Research* 20 (2001): 1, 77–95.

Masters, Edgar Lee. *The Tale of Chicago*. New York: G. P. Putnam's Sons, 1933.

McComb, David G. *Houston: The Bayou City*. Austin: University of Texas Press, 1969.

McCraw, Thomas K. *The Prophets of Regulation*. Cambridge, Mass.: Harvard University Press, 1984.

McCusker, John J. *How Much Is That in Real Money? A Historical Commodity Price Index for Use as a Deflator of Money Values in the Economy of the United States*. Worcester, Mass.: American Antiquarian Society, 2001.

McDonald, Forrest. *Insull*. Chicago: University of Chicago Press, 1962.

———. *Let There Be Light: The Electric Utility Industry in Wisconsin, 1881–1955*. Madison, Wisc.: American History Research Center, 1957.

———. *Recovering the Past: A Historian's Memoir*. Lawrence: University Press of Kansas, 2004.

———. "Samuel Insull and the Movement for State Utility Regulatory Commissions." *Business History Review* 32, no. 3 (Autumn 1958): 241–54.

McElhatton, Jim, and Jennifer Haberkorn. "Failed Firms' Leaders Gave Big to Politicians." *Washington Times*, September 19, 2008.

McGee, Dorothy Horton. *Herbert Hoover: Engineer, Humanitarian, Statesman*. New York: Dodd, Mead & Company, 1959.

"Melvin A. Traylor: Homespun American," Traylor for President Club, Fort Worth, Texas, February 19, 1932, University of Texas, Austin, Texas.

Meyer, Eugene. "From Laissez Faire with William Graham Sumner to the RFC." *Public Policy*. Edited by Carl J. Friedrich and J. Kenneth Galbraith, 3–27. Cambridge, Mass.: Harvard University, 1954.

Mills, Ogden L. *The Seventeen Million*. New York: MacMillan, 1937.

Mills, D. Quinn. *Buy, Lie, and Sell High: How Investors Lost Out on Enron and the Internet Bubble*. Upper Saddle River, N.J.: Financial Times Prentice Hall, 2002.

Mitau, G. Theodore. *Politics in Minnesota*. Minneapolis: University of Minnesota Press, 1960.

Mitchell, Broadus. *Depression Decade: From New Era through New Deal, 1929–1941*. New York: Holt, Rinehart, 1947.

Moody's Manual of Investments, American and Foreign: Banks—Insurance Companies—Investment Trusts—Real Estate Finance and Credit Companies. New York: Moody's Investors Service, yearly.

Moody's Manual of Investments, American and Foreign: Industrial Securities, 1931. New York: Moody's Investors Service, 1931.

Moody's Manual of Investments, American and Foreign: Public Utility Securities, 1932. New York: Moody's Investors Service, 1932.

Moos, Malcolm Charles. *The Republicans: A History of Their Party*. New York, Random House, 1956.

Morgenson, Gretchen. "Too Big to Fail, or Too Big to Handle?" *New York Times*, Sunday Business, June 21, 2009, 1–2.

Morgenson, Gretchen, and Don Van Natta Jr. "Even in Crisis, Banks Dig In for Battle against Regulation." *New York Times*, June 1, 2009.

Morison, Samuel Eliot. *The Oxford History of the American People*. New York: Oxford University Press, 1965.

Morris, Dan, and Inez Morris. *Who Was Who in American Politics*. New York: Hawthorn Books, 1974.

Myers, William Starr, ed. *The State Papers and Other Public Writings of Herbert Hoover*. 2 Vols. New York: Doubleday, Doran, 1934.

Nash, Gerald D. "Herbert Hoover and the Origins of the Reconstruction Finance Corporation." *Mississippi Valley Historical Review* 46 (December 1959): 455–68.

Neville, Howard Ralph. "An Historical Study of the Collapse of Banking in Detroit, 1929–1933." Ph.D. diss., Michigan State University, 1956.

Official Report of the Proceedings of the Eighteenth Republican National Convention Held in Cleveland, Ohio, June 10, 11, and 12, 1924, Resulting in the Nomination of Calvin Coolidge, of Massachusetts for President and the Nomination of Charles G. Dawes, of Illinois for Vice-President. New York: Tenny Press, 1924.

Olasky, Marvin N. "Hornswoggled!" *Reason* 17 (February 1986): 29.

Olson, James S. "The End of Voluntarism: Herbert Hoover and the National Credit Corporation." *Annals of Iowa* 41 (Fall 1972): 1104–13.

———. "From Depression to Defense: The Reconstruction Finance Corporation, 1932–1940." Ph.D. diss., State University of New York at Stony Brook, 1972.

———. "Harvey C. Couch and the Reconstruction Finance Corporation." *Arkansas Historical Quarterly* 32 (Autumn 1973): 217–25.

———. *Herbert Hoover and the Reconstruction Finance Corporation, 1931–1933*. Ames: Iowa State University Press, 1977.

———. "Herbert Hoover and 'War' on the Depression." *Palimpsest* 54 (July–August 1973): 26–31.

———. *Saving Capitalism: The Reconstruction Finance Corporation and the New Deal, 1933–1940*. Princeton, N.J.: Princeton University Press, 1988.

Palyi, Melchior. *The Chicago Credit Market*. New York: Arno Press, 1975.

Pancake, John S. *Thomas Jefferson and Alexander Hamilton*. Woodbury, N.Y.: Barron's Educational Series, 1974.

Paulson, Henry. "How to Watch the Banks." *New York Times*, February 16, 2010.

Paulson, Henry M., Jr. *On the Brink: Inside the Race to Stop the Collapse of the Global Financial System*. New York: Business Plus, 2010.

Pecora, Ferdinand. *Wall Street under Oath*. New York: Simon & Schuster, 1939.

Peel, Roy V., and Thomas C. Donnelly. *The 1932 Campaign: An Analysis*. New York: Farrar and Rinehart, 1935.

Pixton, John E., Jr. "The Early Career of Charles G. Dawes." Ph.D. diss., University of Chicago, 1952.

Platt, Harold L. "The Cost of Energy: Technological Change, Rate Structures, and Public Policy in Chicago, 1880–1920." *Urban Studies* 26 (February 1989): 32–44.

———. *The Electric City: Energy and the Growth of the Chicago Area, 1880–1930.* Chicago: University of Chicago Press, 1991.

Pole, J. W. "The Need for New Federal Banking Legislation: Proposed Remedies Discussed." *Congressional Digest* 10, no. 12 (December 1931): 297.

Pontell, Henry N., and Kitty Calavita. "The Savings and Loan Industry." *Beyond the Law: Crime in Complex Organizations.* Edited by Michael Tonry and Albert J. Reiss Jr., 18:203–46. Chicago: University of Chicago Press, 1993.

Poor's Register of Directors of the United States and Canada, 1929. New York: Poor's Publishing Company, 1929.

Pumphrey, Preston V. "New SEC Disclosure Rules Are Necessary." *Bankers Monthly* 92, no. 8 (August 15, 1975): 35–36.

Pusey, Merlo J. *Eugene Meyer.* New York: Alfred A. Knopf, 1974.

Remini, Robert V. *Andrew Jackson.* New York: Harper & Row, 1966.

"Report of the President of A Century of Progress to the Board of Trustees," March 14, 1936, Library of Congress, Washington, D.C.

Restoring Confidence in the U.S. Capital Markets: A Call for Financial Services Regulatory Modernization. Center for Capital Markets Competitiveness, U.S. Chamber of Commerce, Washington, D.C., March 11, 2009.

Rice, R. Michael. "SEC Urged to Go Slow on Problem Loan Disclosure." *Bankers Monthly* 92, no. 6 (June 15, 1975): 26, 31.

Richardson, Rupert N., Adrian N. Anderson, and Ernest Wallace. *Texas: The Lone Star State.* Upper Saddle River, N.J.: Prentice Hall, 1997.

Richberg, Donald R. "De-Bunking Mr. Dawes." *New Republic,* July 9, 1924, 180–82.

Robertson, Ross M. *The Comptroller and Bank Supervision: A Historical Appraisal.* Washington, D.C.: Office of the Comptroller of the Currency, 1968.

Robinson, Edgar Eugene, and Vaughn Davis Bornet. *Herbert Hoover, President of the United States.* Stanford, Calif.: Hoover Institution Press, 1975.

Roosevelt, Franklin D. *The Public Papers and Addresses of Franklin D. Roosevelt.* Edited by Samuel Rosenman. 5 Vols. New York: Random House, 1938.

Rosen, Elliot A. *Hoover, Roosevelt, and the Brains Trust: From Depression to New Deal.* New York: Columbia University Press, 1977.

Roth, Daniel. "Road Map for Financial Recovery: Radical Transparency Now!" *Wired,* February 23, 2009.

Rothbard, Murray N. *America's Great Depression.* Kansas City: Sheed and Ward, 1975.

Rufus Cutler Dawes, 1867–1940. Chicago: A Century of Progress, 1940.

"Samuel Insull." *Time,* November 4, 1929, 54.

"Samuel Insull: The Collapse." *New Republic,* October 5, 1932, 202.

"Samuel Insull: The Rise to Power." *New Republic,* September 21, 1932, 142–44.

Schlesinger, Arthur M., Jr. *The Age of Jackson.* Boston: Little, Brown, 1950.

———. *The Crisis of the Old Order, 1919–1933,* Vol. 1, of *The Age of Roosevelt.* Boston: Houghton Mifflin, 1957.

———. *The Politics of Upheaval*, Vol. 3 of *1935–1936, The Age of Roosevelt*. Boston: Houghton Mifflin, 1960.

Schmelzer, Janet. "Tom Connally." In *Profiles in Power: Twentieth-Century Texans in Washington*. Edited by Kenneth E. Hendrickson Jr., Michael L. Collins, and Patrick Cox, 85–103. Austin: University of Texas Press, 2004.

Schmidt, John R. *"The Mayor Who Cleaned Up Chicago": A Political Biography of William E. Dever*. Dekalb: Northern Illinois University Press, 1989.

Schmitt, Rick. "Prophet and Loss." *Stanford Magazine,* March/April 2009.

Schuker, Stephen A. "The Candidacy That Never Was: Owen D. Young and the Presidential Election of 1932." *Statesmen Who Were Never President*. Edited by Kenneth W. Thompson, 2:125–44. Miller Center Series on Statesmen Defeated for President. Lanham, Md.: University Press of America, 1996.

Schwarz, Jordan Abraham. "The Politics of Fear: Congress and the Depression during the Hoover Administration." Ph.D. diss., Columbia University, 1967.

Sherman, Richard Garrett. "Charles G. Dawes: An Entrepreneurial Biography, 1865–1951." Ph.D. diss., University of Iowa, 1960.

Shriver, Phillip R. "A Hoover Vignette." *Ohio History* 91 (1982): 74–82.

Simons, Teresa. "Banking on Secrecy." *Washington Monthly*, December 1990, 31–37.

Smith, Rixey, and Norman Beasley. *Carter Glass: A Biography*. New York: Longmans, Green, 1939.

Sloan, Steven "Fed's Tough Transparency Talk Doesn't Apply on Pay." *American Banker*, November 2, 2009.

———. "Stress Tests Touch Off Debate on Disclosure." *American Banker*, April 30, 2009.

Sobel, Robert. *Herbert Hoover at the Onset of the Great Depression, 1929–1930*. Philadelphia: J. B. Lippincott Company, 1975.

Sonnichsen, C. L., and M. G. McKinney. *The State National since 1881: The Pioneer Bank of El Paso*. El Paso: Texas Western Press, 1971.

Sortland, Robert A. "Charles G. Dawes: Businessman in Politics." Master's thesis, Heidelberg College, 1957.

Soule, George. *Prosperity Decade: From War to Depression, 1917–1929*. New York: Rinehart, 1947.

Spero, Herbert. *Reconstruction Finance Corporation Loans to the Railroads: 1932–1937*. Boston: Bankers Publishing Company, 1939.

Spratt, John S. "Banking Phobia in Texas." *Southwest Review* 60 (Autumn 1975): 341–54

"A Stab in the Dark." *Independent* 113 (September 13, 1924): 145–46.

Sternlieb, George, and David Listokin, eds. *New Tools for Economic Development: The Enterprise Zone, Development Bank, and RFC*. Piscataway, N.J.: Rutgers University Press, 1981.

Stone, George P. "Samuel Insull Is Chicago's Biggest Boss." *New York Times Magazine*, August 15, 1926.

Stuart, William H. *The Twenty Incredible Years*. Chicago: M. A. Donohue, 1935.

Studenski, Paul, and Herman E. Krooss. *Financial History of the United States*. New York: McGraw-Hill, 1963.

Sullivan, Lawrence. *Prelude to Panic: The Story of the Bank Holiday*. Washington, D.C.: Statesman Press, 1936.

Sullivan, Mark. *Our Times: The Twenties*, Vol. 6. New York: Charles Scribner's Sons, 1935.

Tarbell, Ida M. *Owen D. Young: A New Type of Industrial Leader*. New York: Macmillan, 1932.

Tarr, Joel A. "J. R. Walsh of Chicago: A Case Study in Banking and Politics, 1881–1905." *Business History Review* 40, no. 4 (Winter 1966): 451–66.

———. *A Study in Boss Politics: William Lorimer of Chicago*. Urbana: University of Illinois Press, 1971.

Tate, Alfred O. *Edison's Open Door*. New York: E. P. Dutton, 1938.

Taylor, Arthur R. "Losses to the Public in the Insull Collapse, 1932–1946." *Business History Review* 36 (Summer 1962): 188–204.

Thomas, Norman. "Owen D. Young and Samuel Insull." *Nation*, January 11, 1933, 35–37.

Thomas, R. G. "Concentration in Banking Control through Interlocking Directorates as Typified by Chicago Banks." *Journal of Business of the University of Chicago* 6, no. 1 (January 1933): 1–14.

Thomas, Rollin G. *The Development of State Banks in Chicago*. New York: Arno Press, 1980.

Thompson, Carl D. *Confessions of the Power Trust*. New York: E. P. Dutton, 1932.

Thompson, Roger. "'Too Big to Fail': Reining in Large Financial Firms." Harvard Business School Working Knowledge, June 22, 2009, http:/hbswk.hbs.edu/item/6230.html.

Thompson, W. Ernest. "Melvin A. Traylor, 1878–1934." *Southwestern Historical Quarterly* 67 (October 1963): 226–34.

Timmons, Bascom N. *Garner of Texas: A Personal History*. New York: Harper and Brothers, 1948.

———. *Jesse H. Jones: The Man and the Statesman*. New York: Henry Holt, 1956.

———. *Portrait of an American: Charles G. Dawes*. New York: Henry Holt, 1953.

Todd, Walker F. "Lessons of the Past and Prospects for the Future in Lender of Last Resort Theory." Working Paper 8805, Federal Reserve Bank of Cleveland, August 1988.

Trask, Roger R. "The Odyssey of Samuel Insull." *Mid-America: An Historical Review* 46 (July 1964): 204–15.

Upham, Cyril B., and Edwin Lamke. *Closed and Distressed Banks: A Study in Public Administration*. Washington, D.C.: Brookings Institution Press, 1934.

Vickers, Raymond B. "Bank Secrecy Should Be Ended—This Would Make the Financial System Safer." *The Long Term View: Secrecy Is Everywhere* 6, no. 1 (Massachusetts School of Law at Andover, Fall 2003): 5–11.

———. *Panic in Paradise: Florida's Banking Crash of 1926*. Tuscaloosa: University of Alabama Press, 1994.

———. "Sleazy Banking in the '20s and Today." *Wall Street Journal*, May 23, 1989.

———. "Open the Vault: The Urgent Need to Abolish Bank Secrecy." *Business Library Review: An International Journal*, February 1996, 1–7.

Vietor, Richard H. K. *Contrived Competition: Regulation and Deregulation in America*. Cambridge, Mass: Belknap Press, 1994.

Wagenknecht, Edward. *Chicago*. Norman: University of Oklahoma Press, 1964.

Wasik, John F. *The Merchant of Power: Samuel Insull, Thomas Edison, and the Creation of the Modern Metropolis*. New York: Palgrave Macmillan, 2006.

Wead, Doug. *All the Presidents' Children: Triumph and Tragedy in the Lives of America's First Families*. New York: Atria Books, 2003.

Weller, Cecil Edward, Jr. *Joe T. Robinson: Always a Loyal Democrat*. Fayetteville: University of Arkansas Press, 1998.

Whisenhunt, Donald W., ed. *The Depression in the Southwest*. Port Washington, N.Y.: Kennikat Press, 1980.

White, James J. *Teaching Materials on Banking Law*. St. Paul, Minn.: West, 1976.

White, Lawrence J. *The S&L Debacle: Public Policy Lessons for Bank and Thrift Regulation*. New York: Oxford University Press, 1991.

White, Trentwell M. *Famous Leaders of Industry*. Boston: L. C. Page, 1931.

White, William Allen. *Calvin Coolidge: The Man Who Is President*. New York: Macmillan, 1925.

———. *A Puritan in Babylon: The Story of Calvin Coolidge*. New York: Macmillan, 1938.

Whitten, David O. Review of *Panic in Paradise: Florida's Banking Crash of 1926*, *Business Library Review: An International Journal,* February 1996, 7–11.

Who's Who in America. Edited by Albert Nelson Marquis. Chicago: A. N. Marquis Company, 1932.

Who's Who in Chicago and Vicinity: The Book of Chicagoans, 1931. Edited by Albert Nelson Marquis. Chicago: A. N. Marquis Company, 1931.

Who's Who in Finance, Banking and Insurance: A Biographical Dictionary of Contemporary Bankers, Capitalists and Others Engaged in Financial Activities in the United States and Canada. Vol. Edited by John William Leonard. New York: Joseph & Sefton, 1911.

Wicker, Elmus. *The Banking Panics of the Great Depression*. New York: Cambridge University Press, 2000.

Wilbur, Ray Lyman, and Arthur Mastick Hyde. *The Hoover Policies*. New York: Charles Scribner's Sons, 1937.

Williams, T. Harry. *Huey Long*. New York: Vintage Books, 1981.

Williamson, Samuel H. "What Is the Relative Value? Seven Ways to Compute the Relative Value of a U.S. Dollar Amount, 1774 to Present," Measuring Worth, April 2010, www.measuringworth.com/uscompare.

Wilson, Stephen. *Harvey Couch: An Entrepreneur Brings Electricity to Arkansas*. Little Rock: August House, 1986.

Wilson, Walter H. *To the Honorable Charles G. Dawes, Altogether the Ablest, Kindest and Best Man I Have Known*. Chicago: Lakeside Press, R. R. Donnelley & Sons, 1928.

Wilson, Winston P. *Harvey Couch: The Master Builder*. Nashville: Broadman Press, 1947.

Wilson, Woodrow. *The New Freedom*. Englewood Cliffs, N.J.: Prentice-Hall, 1961.

_____. *Woodrow Wilson Papers*. Edited by Arthur S. Link. Princeton, N.J.: Princeton University Press, 1966.

Young, Owen D., and Gerard Swope. *Selected Addresses of Owen D. Young and Gerard Swope*. New York: General Electric Company, 1930.

Index

A. O. Slaughter and Company, 74
Adams State Bank of Chicago, 160, 177n54
AIG. *See* American International Group
Akron Gas Light Company, 26
Albers, Charles H., 149
Allen, Lawrence, 71
Allen and Dalby law firm, 71
Alliance National Bank, 142–43, 177n54
American Bankers Association, 35, 194
American Exchange National Bank of Lincoln, Nebraska, 26
American History Research Center, 292–93, 296–97, 301n22
American International Group (AIG), xix, 273
American Monetary Policy: 1928-1941 (Chandler), 289
American Power and Light Company, 49
American Red Cross, 24, 99–101
Andersen, Arthur, xvii, 64–65
Andrews, Rodney D., 165–66
antitrust violations, 254
Arthur, Chester, 5
Arthur Andersen and Company, xvii, 64–65, 295

Atlantic, 274
Austin State Bank of Chicago, 162, 173

Bacchus, L. L., 19–20
bailouts, 73, 116, 123; Dawes bank and, x, 87–88, 92, 97, 117, 121, 125–26, 140, 141, 182–200, 205; federal program, 163–64; Giannini and, 182–83; Insull, Samuel Jr., and utility entities, xi; Jones, Jesse H. real estate and, xi; Jones bank and, 92
Bain, John, 146, 159; fraud, 159; unsecured loans, 165, 167
Bain, John H., 159
Bain, Robert A., 159
Bain banks, 146, 159, 167, 171
Baker, Fentress and Company, 74
Baker, James A., 100, 130n31
Baltimore and Ohio Railroad Company, 239, 257-58
bank closings, 28, 155, 164, 177n54; bank regulators and, 277; Central Republic Bank and Trust Company of Chicago, 230; epidemic of, xii–xiii; fraud and, 288; Jones, Jesse H., and, 267; LaSalle Street National Bank, 8, 19–20, 20; Peoples National

Bank and Trust Company and, 159–60
Bankers Mortgage Company, 97, 117–19
bank holiday of 1933, 96, 98, 289
banking, xii, 257, 267, 286; code violations and, 11; Dawes, Charles, G. abuses and, 16, 20–21; fraud and, 18, 28, 98, 125, 267; lobby and, 276; Lorimer abuses and, 16–17; role in Great Depression and, 267; secrecy and, 268; Senate Committee on Banking and Currency and, 48, 257; too big to disclose and, 276–79; too big to prosecute and, 269–76
Banking-in-the-Sunshine bill, xii
The Banking Panics of the Great Depression (Wicker), 286-87
Bank of America, 95, 119, 190, 208n25, 276; enormity of, 274; Reynolds, Arthur, at, 256–57; RFC loans to, 120–22, 124–26, 182–83
Bank of England, 88
Bank of Italy Mortgage Company, 121, 182
bank panics, 239, 287; Dawes bank and insider abuse, 154–71; of Great Depression, 286–87; Insull, Samuel, Sr., and, 47–58; LaSalle Street National Bank and, 19–20, *20*; Panic of 1893, 6, 19, 233; Panic of 1907, 100, 233
bank regulators, x, 228; bodies of, 276; compliant and, 268; confidentiality and, xiii, xv, 275; economic meltdown of 2008 and, xviii–xix, 278; Enron financial crisis and, 278; fiduciary duties of, xviii; flaws of, xvi; public trust and, 277; records, 271; regulatory transparency of, xii, xv–xvi, 277, 279
bankruptcies, xvii; Corporation Securities Company and, 50–51, 56, 60, 66, 72, 75, 240; Dawes, Charles Cutler and, 65, 141; fraud and,

241, 243, 258; Houston Properties Corporation and, 107; IUI, 49–51, 60, 63, 66, 73, 76, 240; Jones, Jesse H., 111–12; Middle West Utilities Company and, 50–51, 240; Midland Utilities Company and, 240
Barrett, Edward J., 74, 154, 161, 248–49, 287
Baruch, Bernard, 95, 101, 215, *216*, 257; City National Bank and, 218; Jones, Jesse H., and, 217; new Dawes bank plan and, 215–19, 231
Batten, Barton, Durstine and Osborn Corporation, 231–32
Beale, William G., 9, 13
Bernanke, Ben, 273
Bestor, H. Paul, 92, 95
Birney, F. O., 156
Black Thursday, 54
Bogue, Morton G., 189–91; new Dawes bank plan and, 221, 224–27
Bowen, Carroll G., 294
Bowmanville National Bank, 157–59
Boyd, Darrell S., 227
Brady, James J., 18–19
Brandeis, Louis D., xiv, xix, 278
Brennen, George E., 14
Brookhart, Smith W., 1, 24
Brown, Edward, 64, 68, 74, 104, 187; new Dawes bank plan and, 222
Brundage, Edward J., 242
Bryan, William Jennings, 26
Buckner, Mortimer, 89
Budd, Britton I., 140
Buenger, Walter L., 291
Burgess, W. Randolph, 185–87
Bush, George H. W., 274
Bush, George W., xix, 273, 275; campaign contributions and, 277
Buss, Ralph, 190, 193, 203–4
Butler, George A., 107, *108*, 111–13, 134n66; Jones bank director, 118; as real estate trustee, 114
Byrd, Harry F., 259

C. A. Mosso Laboratories, 247
Calomiris, Charles W., 287–88
Capone, Al, ix, 242
Carlstrom, Oscar E., 148
Castle, Charles Sumner, 143, 162, 172n12
Central Hanover Bank and Trust Company of New York, 49, 63, 65, 76
Central Illinois Securities Corporation, 231
Central Manufacturing District Bank, 168–69
Central Republic Bank and Trust Company of Chicago, x, 40n28, *51*, 67, 71, 83n45, 118, 139–41, 145, 153, 156-57, 163, 197; assets of, 226, 249, 273; capital of, 56–57; closing of, 230; depositors and, 155; deposits and, 195, 228, 288; examination of, 203; fraudulent balance sheets and, 287; hopeless condition of, 219, 232; hysterical fear and anxiety and, 286; loans and, 84n58, 195, 228; name change and, 144; receivership representation and, 72; retirement announcement and, 231–33; stockholders and, 246, 249–50, 255
Central Republic Company, 229, 231
Central Trust Company of Illinois, 18, 22, 24, 27, 29–30, 40n28, 51-52; name change of, 144; total deposits and, 145
Cermak, Anton J., 34, 164, 184, 199, 249
Chamberlain, Austen, 23
Chamber of Commerce, U.S., xi, 33
Chandler, Lester V., 289
Charles G. Hiney and Company, 110
Chase Manhattan Bank, xvii, 270
Chase National Bank, 76, 142
Chicago, North Shore and Milwaukee Railroad Company, 31, 140
Chicago Civic Opera Company, 9–10, 261n15

Chicago Clearing House, 146
Chicago Daily News, 115
Chicago Edison Company, 5–8, 33
Chicago Evening Post, 146
Chicago Gold Coast, 9–10
Chicago National Bank, 25–26, *28*
Chicago Railways Company, 7–8
Chicago Rapid Transit Company, 31, 140
Chicago Southern Railway Company, 28
Chicago Stock Exchange, 51
Chicago Tribune, 66–69, 72, 145
Chicago World's Fair of 1933, 29–31, 160, 233, 246
Chickasha Gas and Electric Company, 27
Citicorp, xvii, 270
Citigroup, xix, 273; enormity of, 274, 276; Enron financial crisis and, 269–71
Citizens State Bank of Melrose Park, 156
City National Bank: advertising and, 231; Baruch and, 218; chairman and, 220; deposits of, 288; liabilities of, 225; opening of, 154, 213, 230, 245; paying for good will for, 224, 252; profits and, 232–33, 254; stocks and, 251
Clapp, Moses E., 1, 24
Clarke, Harley L., 223
Clarke, Philip, 79, 144–46, 160, 192; on Dawes bank insolvency, 196–97, 200–201, 203; new Dawes bank plan and, 220, 222–24, 230; salary, 232
Clay, Cassius M., 258
Clinch, R. Floyd, 30, 52
Clinton, Bill, xi, xix, 273–74; campaign contributions and, 277
Coffee, John C., xvii
Coffin, Charles A., 7, 38n11
Commercial National Bank and Trust Company, 76

Commonwealth Edison Company, 7, 9, 12–13, 31; debt of, 72; indictment and, 240; shares of, 60–61, 76, 78; stock collapse and, 73; stockholders of, 62–63; survival of, 66–67

Commonwealth Electric Company, 6–7

Comptroller of the currency, 140, 143, 232, 276; Dawes, Charles G., as, 2, 11, 15, 25–26, 222, 230; Dawes, Henry, as, 23; formation of, 276; imperialistic powers of, 268; office of, 161, 223, 254, 286; Pole as, 150, 157; records of, 290–91; reports and, 150, 288; standards, of, 272; warnings to, 148

Consumer Financial Protection Bureau, xii

Continental and Commercial National Bank of Chicago, 13

Continental and Commercial Trust and Savings Bank, 13

Continental Illinois Bank and Trust Company, 10, 13, 34, 52, 55, 64, 68, 78–79, 146, 166, 186–87; depositors of alarmed, 155; false financial statements of, 245; indictment and, 156, 240; loans from, 53–54, 61, 70, 74, 81n13, 89, 142, 192, 256

Continental Shares, Inc., 58

Cooke, George A., 74–75

Cooke, Sullivan and Ricks law firm, 74

Cooksey, George, 96–97, 188–90

Coolidge, Calvin, x, *3*, 23, 25, 95–96, 102; campaign of, 25; receivership candidate and, 75

Corporation Securities Company, 32; bankruptcy, 50–51, 60, 73, 76, 240; debt and, 48, 72; formation of, 60; loans to, 49, 56, 77; receivership of, 72, 74; shares of, 53; stock collapse of, 73; stockholders and, 62

Cosmopolitan State Bank of Chicago, 161–62

Couch, Harvey C., 88, 90, 128n10; Dawes, Charles G., and, 183, 250;

McCarthy, Wilson, and, 94–95; new Dawes bank plan and, 215, 228–29; on RFC board, 90–92, 221

Courtney, Thomas J., 155

Cowles, Gardner, 223

Cullom, Shelby M., 27

Cummings, Homer S., 199

Daley, Richard M., xi–xii

Daley, William M., xi

Davidson, T. Whitfield, 110

Davis, John W., 25, 101–2

Dawes, Berman G., 29

Dawes, Charles Cutler, 65, 141

Dawes, Charles G., x, 1, *3*, *51*, *56*, *218*; banking abuses and, 16, 20–21; Chicago World's Fair of 1933 and, 29–31; class action suit against, 252–53; collusion by, 23–25; comptroller of the currency and, 2, 11, 15, 25–26, 222, 230; Couch and, 183, 250; credibility of, 255; crony banking and, 275; Dawes bank bailout demand and, 182–200; Distinguished Service Medal and, 22; ethical standards of, xvi–xvii; European reconstruction and, 204; fraud and, 34, 253; as ambassador to Great Britain, 29–30, 141; high finance manipulation and, 247; Hoover and, 87–88; Insull, Samuel, Sr., connections to, 11, 25–29; irascibility of, 30; Jones, Jesse H., on, 183, 286; Lorimer and, 15–16, 18; new Dawes bank plan and, 214–33; Nobel Peace Prize and, 3, 23; organizational and diplomatic skills of, 2–3; Pershing and, 22; political abuses and, 15; profile of, 14–25; promoting self interests of, 90–91; Republican Party titan and, 23; rescuing family fortune and, 239; resignation from RFC, 124, 139, 181, 229; as RFC head, 3, 47, 87, 90, 92, 290; RFC lawsuit and, 250–51;

Roosevelt, Franklin, and, 245–46;
Sherman friendship and, 21–23;
testimony on RFC loan policies,
122–23; on veteran payments,
123–24; as Vice President, 25; Vice
President candidate and, 23–24;
Walsh and, 25–28; as playing the
Young card, 30–31, 204, 213–24,
250. *See also* Central Republic Bank
and Trust Company of Chicago; City
National Bank; Dawes bank; new
Dawes bank plan

Dawes, Henry, 22–23, 29, 31, *56*, 65,
143; antitrust charges and, 254;
comptroller of the currency and,
23; Dawes bank control of, 139;
negligence and, 58; new Dawes bank
plan and, 213, 221–22; on Otte, 160

Dawes, Rufus, 22–23, 25, *56*, 65;
Chicago World's Fair of 1933 and,
29–31; Dawes bank control and,
139; financial straits of, 140–41;
negligence of, 58; receivership
candidate and, 75

Dawes, Rufus R., 14

Dawes, William R., 21, *56*; Dawes bank
control and, 139; loan defaults of,
141; negligence of, 58

Dawes bank, x, xv, xxin4, 9, 24;
banking code violations and, 11;
bank panics and, 154–71; Chicago,
North Shore and Milwaukee Railroad
Company loan and, 140; Clarke,
Philip, on insolvency and, 196–97,
200–201, 203; control of, 139; daily
operations of, 56; Dawes, Charles
G., bailout demand and, 182–200;
Dawes, Henry, control and, 139;
Dawes, Rufus, control of, 139;
Dawes, William R., control of, 139;
debt and, 253; deposits, 181–82;
false financial statements and, 245;
flawed process and, 200–206; fraud
and, 255; German notes and, 204–5;
Hoover and, 67, 125–26, 187, 189,
198, 200–202; Jones, Jesse H., and,
190–91, 193, 200; liquidation of,
143, 248; loans to, 18–21, 53, 55, 67,
70; McCarthy, Wilson, and, 191–92;
Meyer and, 189–92, 194; Mills and,
1864, 190, 192, 194; National Bank
of the Republic merger and, 143–51,
232; non-panic failure of, 287; Otis
and, 74, 140–41; Pole as fan of, 151;
portfolio speculation and, 57; profits
and, 255; receivership of, 248–49,
253; RFC bailout of, x, 87–88, 92,
97, 117, 121, 125–26, 140, 141,
182–200, 205; RFC loans to, 87–88,
121, 141; stockholders and, 34,
247–48, 298; Traylor and, 186–87,
189, 200, 205; Walsh and, 27–28.
See also Central Republic Bank and
Trust Company of Chicago; City
National Bank; new Dawes bank
plan

Dawes bank: insider abuse and, 51, 105;
indictments and, 151–54; liquidation
records of, 142; National Bank of the
Republic merger and, 143–51, 232;
overview of, 139–43; panic strikes
at, 154–71

Dawes Brothers, Inc., 140, 153, 225,
230; stockholders, 250–52

Dawes Committee, 204

Dawes Lumber Company, 14

Dawes Plan, 23, 123, 186, 204

The Day the Sky Fell, 293

debts: Commonwealth Edison Company
and, 72; Corporation Securities
Company and, 48, 72; Dawes bank
and, 253; Insull, Martin and, 79;
Insull, Samuel, Jr., and, 79; Insull,
Samuel, Sr., and, 8–9, 11, 79; Middle
West Utilities Company and, 61;
Public Service Company of Northern
Illinois and, 72

Democratic Party, 90; conservative
faction of, 214; contributors to, 216;
fund-raising of, 103; Jones, Jesse H.,

in, 102–3; leaders and, 87; southern
wing of, 91
Denver and Rio Grande Western
Railroad Company (D&RGW), 92–94
Denver and Salt Lake Railway
Company (D&SL), 92, 94
Dewey, Thomas E., 253
Dodd, Christopher, 273
Dodd-Frank Wall Street Reform and
Consumer Protection Act, 275, 278
Douglas, William O., 254
D&RGW. *See* Denver and Rio Grande
Western Railroad Company
Drovers National Bank, 143
D&SL. *See* Denver and Salt Lake
Railway Company
Durbin, Richard, 272–73

Eaton, Cyrus S., 58–62, 66
Ebbers, Bernard J., 271
Ebersole, Franklin, 121, 126
economic meltdown of 2008, xvi, 268,
272–73, 275; bank regulators and,
xviii–xix, 278; conflict-of-interest
and, xi
Edison, Thomas A., 243; on Chicago
electricity, 6; Insull, Samuel, Sr.,
with, 4–6
Efficient market theory, xviii, 277
electricity, 1, 291–92, 297, 298;
Chickasha Gas and Electric
Company and, 27; Commonwealth
Electric Company and, 6–7;
Edison on Chicago and, 6; Insull,
Samuel, Sr., and, 239; as luxury,
8; Metropolitan Gas and Electric
Company and, 29, 153; National
Electric Light Association and, 6, 7;
North Shore Electric Company and,
26; Union Gas and Electric Company
and, 29, 153; Waukegan Electric
Light Company and, 154; Western
United Gas and Electric Company
and, 31; Westinghouse Electric and

Manufacturing Company and, 7–8.
See also General Electric Company
*The Electric City: Energy and the
Growth of the Chicago Area* (Platt),
292
embezzlement, 240, 298; convictions
and, 156; Insull, Samuel, Sr., and,
240, 243–44, 299; Karel and, 167,
170–71; Standard National Bank
and, 163
Emergency Banking Act of 1933, 257
emperor of Chicago, 2, 4
Enron financial crisis, xi, 274–75; bank
regulators and, 278; Citigroup and,
269–71; fraud in, xvi–xvii; J. P.
Morgan Chase & Co. and, 268–71
Equitable Trust Company, 28
Ericson, Melvin B., 153
Esdohr, Fred H., 165–66
*Essays in Economic and Business
History*, 288
Ettelson, Samuel A., 75–76
Evans, Evan Alfred, 59
Exchange State Bank, 156

Fardy, James F., 252
Farley, James A., 214
Farm Credit Corporation, 95
Federal Deposit Insurance Corporation,
26, 276
Federal Reserve Bank of Chicago, 79,
158, 187, 226
Federal Reserve Bank of New York, 88,
187, 274
Federal Reserve Bank of San Francisco,
119
Federal Reserve Board, 35, 95, 185,
268, 273, 276
Federal Reserve System, 26, 88, 272
Federal Trade Commission, 34
Fentress, Calvin, 74
Fidelity Securities Corporation, 112
Field, Marshall, 5
Field, Stanley, 64, 78; indictment, 240

Fifty Billion Dollars: My Thirteen Years with RFC 1932-1945 (Jones, J. H.), 188

financial activism, 54–55

Financial Crisis Inquiry Commission, xix

First American National Bank and Trust Company of Berwyn, 150, 167, 170–71, 177n54

First Englewood State Bank of Chicago, 162, 173, 177n54

First National Bank of Chicago, 30, 34-36, 71, 104; depositors and, 155; false financial statements of, 245; Foreman bank acquisition and, 146; fraudulent financial statements of, 72; frozen assets of, 56; Jones, Jesse H. loans and, 117–18; loans from, 51, 55–56, 61, 74, 77, 117–18; RFC loans to, 142–43

First Union Trust and Savings Bank, 35, 146

Fisher, Boyden, Bell, Boyd, and Marshall law firm, 227

Fisher, W. Merle, 159

Fisher, Walter T., 227

Fletcher, Duncan U., 116–17

Flexner, Washington, 53, 69–70

Flower, Alexander, 156

Foreman State National Bank, 145, 173n15

Foreman State Trust and Savings Bank, 146, 173n15

Frank, Barney, 273

Frankfurter, Felix, xiv–xv

Franz, Fred, 247

fraud, ix–x, 164, 285, 290; audits and, 156; Bain, John and, 159; bank closings and, 288; banking and, 18, 28, 98, 125, 267; bankruptcy and, 241, 243, 258; Dawes, Charles G. and, 34, 253; Dawes bank, 255; in Enron financial crisis, xvi–xvii; First National Bank of Chicago statements and, 72; Goldman Sachs and, 278; insiders and, xvii, 16; Lorimer and, 18, 21; mail and, 243, 251, 292, 299; National Bank of the Republic and, 151; Peoples National Bank and Trust Company and, 163; RFC and, 275; trials and, 154

Freedom from Fear (Kennedy), 291

Friedman, Milton, 286, 289

Fulbright, J. William, 258

Galbraith, John Kenneth, 51

Galligan, John J., 217

GAO. *See* General Accounting Office

Garfield, James, 5

Garner, John Nance, 90, 96, 118, 214; Jones and, 101

Garrett, Ida, 110

Gatz, Frank J., 156

GE. *See* General Electric Company

Geithner, Timothy, 274

General Accounting Office (GAO), 268–69

General Electric Company (GE), 5, 33, 35, 48, 79, 231; loans from, 49, 52–53

Geyer, Norman O., 153–54

Giannini, Amadeo P., 95, 119, 121, 124–26, 206n5, 208n25, 256; McAdoo and, 257; RFC bailout and, 182–83

Gilbert, S. Parker, 186

Glass-Steagall Act, 268, 273, 274

Goldman Sachs, xi, xix, 273, 276; fraud, 278

Gonzalez, Henry, 267

Gramm-Leach-Bliley Act of 1999, 268, 274, 279n5

Gray Wolves, 6, 292

Great Depression, ix, xvi, 253; banking's role in, 267; bank panics and, 286–87; deepening of, 60; fall of Insull, Samuel, Sr., and, 73; as temporary, 55

Great Recession, 278–79
Green, Dwight H., 240–41
Greenebaum, James E., 105
Greenebaum, Moses Ernest, 105
Greenebaum Sons Investment
    Company, 105
Greenspan, Alan, xix, 269, 274;
    ideology of, 277
Greist, Harold, 247
Grigg, Emma, 107–8
The Growth of Chicago Banks (James),
    286
Guaranty Trust Company, 76
Guardian Trust Company of Cleveland,
    96, 98
Guy Huston and Company, 251

Halsey, Stuart and Company, 74, 240
Hamilton National Bank of Knoxville,
    221
Harding, Warren G., 2, *13*, 22–23, 25,
    242
Harrington, Cornelius J., 162
Harrison, Benjamin, 5
Harrison, George L., 88, 185–87
Harris Trust and Savings Bank of
    Chicago, 64, 66, 146, 193
Heinzelman, Karl J., 156
*Herbert Hoover and the Reconstruction
    Finance Corporation 1931-1933*
    (Olson), 290
Heyne, Fred, 107, 111, 115–16, 118
Hildene, 11–12
Hitler, Adolf, 204
Hogg, William Clifford, 103
Home Savings Bank, 28
Hoover, Herbert, x, xv, 3, 29, 31, 33,
    125, 290; big banks and, 120–26;
    Dawes, Charles G. and, 87–88;
    Dawes bank and, 67, 125–26,
    187, 189, 198, 200–202; financial
    activism of, 54–55; Jones, Jesse H.
    and, 99; mathematical brain of, 291;
    reelection of, 90, 120, 184, 229,

255; RFC and, 88–90, 95–96, 121,
    198–99, 258; secrecy and, 121
Hoover Commission on Organization
    of the Executive Branch of the
    Government, 258
Houdaille-Hershey Corporation, 153
House, Edward, 99, 100, 134n71
House, Thomas William, Jr., 100
House Committee on Banking, Finance
    and Urban Affairs, 267
Houston Chronicle, 100, 118, 285
Houston Post, 100
Houston Post Company, 117
Houston Post-Dispatch, 100
Houston Properties Corporation, 103–6,
    110; bankruptcy and, 107; common
    stock of, 111
Huggins, Kayser, and Liddel law firm,
    118
Huggins, W. O., 118
Hughes, Charles Evans, 23
Hughes, Thomas P., 291–92
Hungarian Central Mutual Credit
    Institute of Budapest, 205
Hunter, Louis C., 297–98
Hurd, Harry B., 221–22
Hurley, Edward N., 71, 160

Igoe, Michael L., 244, 248–49
Igoe and Flaherty law firm, 248
Illinois Bankers Association, 35
Illinois Louisiana Land Company, 21
Illinois Southern Railway Company, 28
Insull (McDonald), 292–95, 298
Insull, Adelaide Pierce, 260n6
Insull, Gladys, 10, 60, 241
Insull, Martin, 32, 53, 60, 69; debt, 79;
    indictment, 240; loan defaults, 70;
    mismanagement by, 76; state charges
    dismissed, 244
Insull, Samuel, III, 293
Insull, Samuel, Jr., 10, 31–32, 48, 55,
    187; debt, 79; family papers and,
    293; on family success, 239; federal

charge acquittal of, 243; financing deals and, 50; indictment of, 240; loans to, 53–54; McDonald deals and, 296–97; television rights and, 293–94; as vice chairman, 74–75

Insull, Samuel, Sr., ix–x, 2, 195; Chicago influence, 1, 9–11; Chicago World's Fair of 1933 and, 29–31; Dawes, Charles G. connections of, 11, 25–29; death of, 244; debt of, 8–9, 11; with Edison, 4–6; electricity and, 239; embezzlement charge of, 240, 243–44, 298; emperor of Chicago, 2, 4; empire loss and, 239, 244–45; ethical standards of, xvi–xvii; extradition and, 241; extralegal deals and, 5; acquittal of federal charges, 243; federal trial of, 242–41; as fugitive, 49–50, 155, 240–45; Gray Wolves bribe and, 6; indictment of, 240; insider syndicates and, 33–34, 51–52, 75; Lincoln and, 11–13; McDonald hero worship of, 295; 1926 Illinois senatorial campaign and, 13–14; as opera patron, 10; profile of, 4–14; public image as, 11; as Samuel Insult, 76; secret syndicate list of, 240; speculation and, 231; state charges dismissed against, 244; Swope and, 48–49; Traylor and, 48–51, 77–78; utility holding companies and, xi, 1, 4, 6–8, 29, 59–60; Walsh and, 26–28; Waukegan Electric Light Company and, 154; Westinghouse Electric and Manufacturing Company threatened and, 7–8; Young and, 30–33, 48–50, 59, 63–64, 67–68, 79, 83n49

Insull, Samuel, Sr., bank loans of, 53–55, 59, 228; customer ownership program and, 62; debt, 79; Eaton control battle and, 58–62, 66; financial collapse of, 58–79; Great Depression blamed on, 73; insider

abuse and, 65; insurance loans proposed and, 67, 83n45; as national indicator, 47; New York banks and, 64–65, 68, 76–77; prelude to panic, 47–58; public hearings and, 59; receivership and, 71–75; reckless expansion and paralysis of action, 69; resignation and, 53, 78–79; state law violations and, 57–58; stock sales and, 52

Insull Son and Company, Inc., 53, 244

Insull Utility Investments (IUI), 32–34; bankruptcy and, 49–51, 60, 63, 66, 73, 76, 240; bonds and, 169; crash of, 35–36; formation of, 59–60; loans to, 48–49, 56, 77; real value losses of, 53, 81n12; receivership and, 68, 72, 74; stock collapse and, 73; stockholders and, 62; stock value and, 52–53, 74; Traylor share purchase of, 72

International Monetary Fund, 274

Irving Trust Company, 63

Isham, Lincoln and Beale law firm, 13, 70, 75–76, 240

IUI. *See* Insull Utility Investments

J. P. Morgan Chase & Co., xi, 65, 141, 268, 276; Enron financial crisis and, 269–71

James, Cyril F., 197, 286

Jefferson Park National Bank, 165–67

Jesse H. Jones: The Man and the Statesman (Timmons), 285

Jesse H. Jones Company, 105, 111–12

Johnson, Simon, 274

Joint Committee on the Reduction of Federal Expenditures, 259

Jones, Jesse H., x, 87–88, *93*, *108*, *246*; ambition of, 100; at American Red Cross, 99–101; on bank closings, 267; bankruptcy of his entities and, 111–12; Baruch and, 217; bond transactions of, 103–7, 109–10,

112–15; cabinet consideration of, 134n71; conflict-of-interest of, 118, 188–89; crony banking and, 275; on Dawes, Charles G., 183, 286; Dawes bank and, 190–91, 193, 200; defending RFC and, 258; in Democratic Party, 102–3; ego, 110; as fall guy, 184; First National Bank of Chicago loans and, 116–20; Garner and, 101; Hoover and, 99; manipulation by, 290; McCarthy, Wilson and, 92, 94; as Mr. Houston, 99; net worth of, 105; new Dawes bank plan and, 224–33; New York City developments and, 104; political influence of, 112; presidential aspirations of, 103; problems shielded by, 112; promoting self interests of, 90–91; real estate bailout and, xi; on RFC board, xv, 90–92, 221; as RFC head, xv, 99–120, 249, 253; RFC loans and, 116–17, 119–20; on RFC procedures, 202–3; shady business practices of, 291; suppressing list of loans and, 97; Traylor and, 104, 117, 257
Jones, John, 110–11, 115–16, 118
Jones, Mary Gibbs, 107, 110
Jones bank, 116, 134n70; bailout of, 92; Butler as director of, 118; RFC stock purchase of, 119–20, 135n80
Joslin, Theodore, 291

Karel, Francis, 167, 170–71
Kaspar-American State Bank, 168
Kayser, Paul, 118
Keehn, Richard H., 288–90
Kennedy, David M., 33, 291
Kerner, Otto, 249
Kiley, Roger J., 162
King, Lee A., 156
King, William H., 91
Klein, Maury, xxiiin, 18
Knox, John, 244

La Follette, Robert M., 24–25
Lamar Hotel, 103, 110
Lamar Properties, Inc., 110
Lamke, Edwin, 289
Lamont, Thomas W., 186
Langgruth, Elmer, 156
Laramie State Bank, 156
LaSalle Street National Bank, 16; closing panic, 19–20, *20*; phony loans, 19
lawsuits, 245–49; Dawes, Charles G., class action, 252–53; Dawes, Charles G., RFC, 250–51. *See also* Dawes bank; trials
Lay, Kenneth L., 271
Leavell, James L., 64, 187
Lee, S. G., 78
Lehman Brothers, xix
Let There Be Light: The Electric Utility Industry in Wisconsin 1881-1955 (McDonald), 297–98
Levin, Carl M., 269
Levitt, Arthur, xix
Lewis, James Hamilton, 164
Leyburn, Aldred P., 148–49, 161, 163, 166
Lincoln, Robert Todd, 5, 9, *13*; Insull, Samuel, Sr., and, 11–13
Lincoln Printing Company, 69–70
Lincoln Trust and Savings Bank of Chicago, 249
Lindley, Walter C., 70–71, 74, 76–77
liquidation: Dawes bank, 142, 248; Peoples National Bank and Trust Company, 256
loans: Central Republic Bank and Trust Company of Chicago and, 195, 228; from Continental Illinois Bank and Trust Company, 53–54, 61, 74, 255; to Corporation Securities Company, 49, 56, 77; Dawes, William R., defaults on, 141; Dawes bank and, 18–21, 53, 55, 67, 70; from First National Bank of Chicago, 51,

55–56, 61, 74, 77, 117–18; from
GE, 49, 52–53; Insull, Samuel, Jr.,
and, 53–54; Insull, Samuel, Sr.,
and, 53–55, 59, 228; insurance and,
67, 83n45; to IUI, 48–49, 56, 77;
Jones, Jesse H. and, 97, 116–20;
LaSalle Street National Bank and,
19; Lorimer and, 19; McCarthy,
Wilson, and, 93–94; to Middle West
Utilities Company, 49, 56, 77; to
Midland Utilities Company, 53–54;
National Bank of the Republic and,
150; from NCC, 163, 165; Peoples
National Bank and Trust Company
and, 160–63; to Public Service
Company of Northern Illinois,
55–56; RFC and, xv, 94–97, 120,
288, 290; RFC to Bank of America,
121–22, 124–26, 182–83; RFC to
Bowmanville National Bank loans,
156–59; RFC to Dawes bank, 87–88,
121, 141; RFC to First National
Bank of Chicago, 142–43; RFC to
Peoples National Bank and Trust
Company, 160–63; RFC to United
American Trust and Savings Bank,
147–48; RFC unsecured and, 164;
Traylor and, 164–65; unsecured to
Bain, John, 165, 167
Lokken, Roy N., 298
Long, Huey, 128n10
Longworth, Nicholas, 101
Lord, Clifford L., 297
Lorimer, William, 8, *17*, 26, 34, 251;
banking abuses of, 16–17; bribery
and, 16–17; Dawes, Charles G.,
and, 15–16, 18; favoritism and, 18;
fraud and, 18, 21; insider abuse
and, 19–20; phony loans and, 19; as
senator, 16
Louisiana and Arkansas Railroad, 94
Lowden, Frank O., 9, 74, 242
Lucey, Patrick J., 20, 74–75, 242
Lynch, John A., 172n12

M. T. Jones Lumber Company, 99
MacNally, Raymond J., 74
Madison Square State Bank, 144,
148–49, 177n54
mail fraud, 243, 251, 292, 299
Marshall Field and Company,
78–79
Mason, Joseph R., 287–88
Mattingly, B. A., 67
Mayer, Meyer, Austrian, and Platt law
firm, 224
McAdoo, William Gibbs, 102, 257
McAlpin, Sidney, xiv
McCarthy, Joseph, 200
McCarthy, Wilson, 88; Couch and,
94–95; Dawes bank and, 191–92;
granting loans to, 93–94; Jones, Jesse
H. and, 92, 94; new Dawes bank plan
and, 215, 217, 219, 229; personal
fortune of, 92; on RFC board, 91–92,
221
McCraw, Thomas, xix
McCulloch, Charles A., 71
McDonald, Forrest, 10, 55, 63, 292–94;
historical contradictions of, 298–99;
impartiality of questioned, 297–98;
Insull, Samuel, Jr., deals and,
296–97; Insull, Samuel, Sr., as hero
of, 295; on Middle West Utilities
Company insolvency, 295–96
McDonough, J. B., 59
McDougal, James B., 185
McElroy, R. H., Jr., 254
McFadden, Louis T., 95
McIlvaine, Wynett W., 252
McKeage, Everett C., 199–200
McKee, John K., 221
McKinley, William, 15, 26
McLennan, Donald R., 61
Meador, N. Eugene, 116, 118
Mellon, Andrew, 54, 88, 96
Menkin, Edward, 248
Merchant's National Trust and Savings
Bank of Los Angeles, 125

The Merchant of Power: Samuel Insull, Thomas Edison, and the Creation of the Modern Metropolis (Wasik), 292

Merz, G. W., 229–30

Metropolitan Gas and Electric Company, 29, 153

Meyer, Eugene, 88–89, 92, 120; Dawes bank and, 189–92, 194; as RFC chairman, 95, 185–86

Middle West Utilities Company, 8, 27, 31–35; assets of, 70; bankruptcy of, 50–51, 240; control of, 59; five-year debt of, 61; loans to, 49, 56, 77; McDonald on insolvency, 295–96; receivership of, 69–72, 73; shares of, 60; stock collapse of, 73; stockholders of, 72; stock sale of, 50, 52

Midland Mortgage Company, 116

Midland National Bank, 168–70

Midland Utilities Company, 31–32, 66; bankruptcy of, 240; loans to, 53–54

Milam Properties, Inc., 113–14, 118

Milford, W. R., 203–2

Miller, Charles, 99, 221

Miller, William H., 153

Mills, Ogden, 92, 95–96; Dawes bank bailout and, 186, 190, 192, 194

mismanagement: Insull, Martin, 76; Reynolds, Arthur, 256; Reynolds, George, 256

Mississippi Valley Utilities Investment Company, 73

Mitchell, Charles, 63

Mizner Development Corporation, 25

A Monetary History of the United States 1867-1960 (Friedman/Schwartz), 286, 289

Moody, Dan, 103

Moore, Harry R., 143

Morgan, J. P., ix

Morgan Stanley, 276

Morgenthau, Robert M., 271

Mr. Houston, 99

Mueller, Carl A., 156

Munday, Charles B., 17, 20

Munger, Royal F., 115

Munroe, Charles A., 243

Murray, Lawrence O., 18

Nash, Thomas D., 162

National Bank of Commerce, 115–16, 134n70. *See also* Jones bank

National Bank of the Republic, 174n26; branches of, 144; Dawes bank merger and, 143–51, 232; fraud of, 151; loans of, 150; unethical conduct of its officials, 151

National Bank of Woodlawn, 168

National City Bank of New York, 63, 158, 244

National Credit Corporation (NCC), 88–89, 158; loans from, 163, 165

National Electric Light Association, 6, 7

National Industrial Recovery Act, 33

National Public Service Corporation, 49

National Recovery Administration, 75

National Republic Bancorporation, 143–44, 148; chain and, 160–61; insolvency of, 149; shares in, 150

NCC. *See* National Credit Corporation

Nelson, Oscar, 148, 152–54, 245, 248

Networks of Power: Electrification in Western Society 1880-1930 (Hughes), 291–92

New Dawes bank plan: Baruch and, 215–19, 231; Bogue and, 221, 224–27; Brown and, 222; Clarke, Philip, and, 220, 222–24, 230; Couch and, 215, 228–29; Dawes, Henry, and, 221–22; of Dawes, Charles G., and, 214–33; Jones, Jesse H., and, 224–33; McCarthy, Wilson, and, 215, 217, 219, 229; Reynolds, George, and, 232; RFC and, 221–30; Roosevelt, Franklin, and, 215–16; Traylor, Melvin, and, 222, 224, 232; Young and, 213–24

New Deal, 246, 290; disclosures during, xiv–xv; passage of reforms in, 101, 269, 273. *See also* Roosevelt, Franklin
New York and Richmond Gas Company, 30
New York City Clearing House, 88
New York Stock Exchange, 68
New York Times, 95, 96, 97
New York Trust Company, 89
Noel State Bank of Chicago, 74
Norris, George, 91
North Shore Electric Company, 26
Northwestern Gas Light and Coke Company, 25–26

Obama, Barack, xix, 275; campaign contributions and, 277; economic advisors to, 275; election of, 273–74; lobbyists and, xi
Obama, Michelle, xi
O'Connell, William L., 161–62, 248
O'Connor, J. F. T. ("Jefty"), 232, 257
Olson, James, 125, 290
On the Brink (Paulson), 273
O'Shaughnessy, John P., 158
Other People's Money and How the Bankers Use It (Brandeis), xix
Otis, Joseph Edward, 51–52, 58, 62, 64, 67; Dawes bank and, 74, 140–41; on utility bonds, 146–46
Otis and Company, 58
Otte, Hugo, 159–60, 168, 172n12
Owen D. Young: A New Type of Industrial Leader (Tarbell), 213

Pacific Coast Joint Stock Land Bank of San Francisco, 95
Pacific Coast Mortgage Company, 95
Palace Building Company, 112
Panic of 1893, 6, 233
Panic of 1907, 100, 130n30, 233
Paris Peace Conference of 1919, 101
Patman, Wright, 123

Patterson, Mark, xi
Paulson, Henry M., xix, 273
Payne, John Barton, 24
Pecora, Ferdinand, 50, 57, 59
Penney, Edgar B., 247
Penney, Minnie F., 247
Peoples Gas, Light, and Coke Company, 31, 59, 243; rebates to, 74; shares of, 60–61, 76, 78; stock collapse of, 73; survival of, 66–67
Peoples National Bank and Trust Company, 143; closing of, 159–60; fraud and, 163; liquidation of, 256; RFC loans and, 160–63
Peoples State Bank of Maywood, 156
Permanent Subcommittee on Investigations, xi
Pershing, John J., 22
Phillips, Earl D., 156
Phillip State Bank and Trust Company of Chicago, 159
Pinchot, Gifford, 198–99
Platt, Harold L., 292
Pole, John, 35–36, 120, 148, 163; as comptroller of the currency, 150, 157; as friend of Dawes, 120, 151
Pomerene, Atlee, 96–99, 199, 221
Porter, Gilbert E., 85n65
portfolio speculation, 57
Portrait of an American: Charles G. Dawes (Timmons), 285
Prelude to Panic: The Story of the Bank Holiday (Sullivan), 289
Preston, Howard P., 185, 190, 221
Proctor, John L., 157–59, 169
Progressive Era, 16, 297
Progressive Party, 18, 24–25
Prohibition, ix, 101
Prudential State Savings Bank, 143, 177n54
Public Service Company of Northern Illinois, 8, 31; control of, 59; debt of, 72; loans to, 55–56; shares and,

60–61, 76, 78; stock collapse and, 73; survival of, 66–67

Public Service Corporation of New Jersey, 65

Pullman Company, 11

Pure Food Law, xix–xx

Pure Oil Company, 65, 142–44, 254

Quinn, Riordan, Jacobs and Barry law firm, 294

Rainbow's End (Klein), xxiiin18

Rainey, Henry T., 122

Ravenswood National Bank, 168

Reagan, Ronald, 272

Realty Management Company, 109, 111

receivership: Central Republic Bank and Trust Company of Chicago, 72; Coolidge and, 75; Corporation Securities Company and, 72, 74; Dawes, Rufus, and, 75; Dawes bank and, 248–49, 253; Insull, Samuel, Sr., and, 71–75; IUI and, 68, 72, 74; Middle West Utilities Company and, 69–72, 73

Reconstruction Finance Corporation (RFC), x, 36, 73, 116, 123; Bank of America loans and, 121–22, 124–26, 182–83; bank records on, xiii; Bowmanville National Bank loans and, 156–59; Couch on board, 90–92, 221; creation of, 49; Dawes, Charles G., as head of, 3, 47, 87, 90, 92, 290; Dawes, Charles G., lawsuit and, 250–51; Dawes, Charles G., on loan policies, 122–23; Dawes, Charles G., resignation of, 124, 139, 181, 229; Dawes bank bailout and, x, 87–88, 92, 97, 117, 121, 125–26, 140, 141, 182–200, 205; Dawes bank loans and, 87–88, 121, 141; demise of, 255–59; favoritism of, 257–59, 290; First National Bank of Chicago loans and, 142–43; foreign securities of, 205–6; fraud and, 275; Hoover and, 88–90, 95–96, 121, 198–99, 258; insiders and, 87–126; Jones, Jesse H., as head of, xv, 99–120, 249, 253; Jones, Jesse H., defends, 258; Jones, Jesse H., loans and, 116–17, 119–20; Jones, Jesse H., on board, xv, 90–92, 221; Jones, Jesse H., on procedures, 202–203; Jones bank stock purchase and, 119–20, 135n80; loans of, xv, 94–97, 120, 288, 290; McCarthy, Wilson, on board and, 91–92, 221; Meyer as chairman, 95, 185–86; new Dawes bank plan and, 221–30; Peoples National Bank and Trust Company loans and, 160–63; policy on directors, 227; power trust and, 91; Roosevelt, Franklin, and, 226; shut down and, 239–40, 257; United American Trust and Savings Bank loans and, 148–49; unsecured loans and, 164; web of self-interest and, 90–99

Reconstruction Finance Corporation Liquidation Act, 259

Recovering the Past: A Historian's Memoir (McDonald), 296

Reliance Bank and Trust Company, 143, 156

Republican Party, 8, 16, 26, 199; Dawes, Charles G., titan of, 23; progressive wing, 91; split, 18

Reynolds, Arthur, 10, 13, 34, 53–54; at Bank of America, 256–57; mismanagement of, 256

Reynoids, Earle H., 70

Reynolds, George, 10, 13, 34, 53–54; Dawes bank bailout and, 189, 193; mismanagement, 256; NCC and, 89; new Dawes bank plan and, 232

RFC. *See* Reconstruction Finance Corporation

Rice, William March, Jr., 100

Rice Hotel, 100–103, 108–11
Rice Properties, Inc., 108–9, 110
Richberg, Donald R., 75
Ridgely, William Barret, 27, 29
Rife, John H., 21
Robinson, Henry M., 229
Robinson, Joseph T., 90–91, 250
Roosevelt, Franklin, xiv, 50, 91, 101–2, 253; Dawes, Charles G. and, 245–46; new Dawes bank plan and, 215–16; RFC and, 226
Roosevelt, Theodore, 18, 198
Roosevelt-Bankers State Bank, 156
Rosenthal, Maurice A., 109
Rubin, Robert E., xix, 273, 274

Samuels, Helen, 67–68
San Francisco Daily News, 107
Sarbanes-Oxley legislation, xvii, 271, 280n14
Saving Capitalism: The Reconstruction Finance Corporation and the New Deal, 1933-1940 (Olson), 290
Schmidt, John A., 157
Schuyler, Daniel J., 71, 75
Schuyler, Dunbar and Weinfeld law firm, 71–72, 75–76, 153
Schuyler, Weinfeld and Hennessy law firm, 71–72
Schwartz, Anna Jacobson, 286, 289
Securities Act of 1933, xiv–xv
Securities and Exchange Commission, 268, 270, 272
Security-First National Bank of Los Angeles, 229
Seiberling, Francis, 229–30
Senate Committee on Banking and Currency, 48, 257, 269–79
Senate Committee on Interstate Commerce, 258
Shanahan, David E., 168
shares: Commonwealth Edison Company and, 60–61, 76, 78; Corporation Securities Company

and, 53; IUI and, 72; Middle West Utilities Company and, 60; National Republic Bancorporation and, 150; Peoples Gas, Light, and Coke Company and, 60–61, 76, 78; Public Service Company of Northern Illinois and, 60–61, 76, 78. *See also* stockholders; stocks
Shell Petroleum Corporation, 254
Sheppard, Morris, 101
Sherman, Lawrence Y., 11, *12*, 13, 15, 248–49; Dawes, Charles G. friendship with, 21–23; on U.S. budget committee, 22–23
Sherman Antitrust Act, 254
Shurtleff, Edward D., 152–54
Simpson, A. D., 118
Simpson, James, 78
S&L crisis, xi, xvii, 267-68, 272, 274–75, 278
Small, Len, 242
Smiley, Gene, 288–90
Smith, Alfred E., 90, 95, 101, 102
Smith, Ashbel V., 152
Smith, Frank L., 13
Smith, Solomon A., 64
Southern Indiana Railway Company, 28
Southern United Gas Company, 72
South Side Savings Bank and Trust Company, 75, 248
Squire, Andrew, 96
Squire, Sanders and Dempsey law firm, 97
Standard Bank, 159–60
Standard National Bank, 162
Standard Oil Company, 242
State Historical Society, 297–98
Steagall, Henry B., *246*
Stewart, Ashby O., 95
Stilwell, Abner J., 68, 74, 222, 298
Stilwell & Co., 298
stockholders: Central Republic Bank and Trust Company of Chicago and, 246, 249–50, 255; Commonwealth

Edison Company and, 62–63;
Corporation Securities Company
and, 62; Dawes bank and, 34, 247–
48, 298; Dawes Brothers, Inc., and,
250–52; IUI and, 62; Middle West
Utilities Company and, 72
Stockmen's Trust and Savings Bank,
156
stock market crash of 1929, 4, 47,
54–55, 69. *See also* Black Thursday
stocks: City National Bank and, 251;
Commonwealth Edison Company
and, 73; Corporation Securities
Company and, 73; Houston
Properties Corporation and, 111;
IUI and, 52–53, 73, 74; Jones bank
and, 119–20, 135n80; Middle West
Utilities Company and, 50, 52,
73; Peoples Gas, Light, and Coke
Company and, 73; Public Service
Company of Northern Illinois and,
73; Insull, Samuel, Sr., sale of, 52
Stone, Patrick T., 254
Straus, Samuel J. T., 113
Straus and Company, 103–5, 111;
complaints about, 107–8; protective
committees and, 108
Streetman, Sam, 118
Stuart, Harold L., 30, 74; indictment of,
240
Suckow, Elmer A., 158
Sullivan, Lawrence, 289
Summers, Lawrence H., xix, 274
Sun Life Assurance Company, 47
Sunny, Bernard E., 35, 83n45
Swanson, John A., 34, 232, 240-41,
245; reelection campaign of, 155–56
Swedish Match Company, 205
Swope, Gerard, 33–34, 48–49

T. W. House & Company, 100
Taft, William Howard, *13*, 16, 18, 101,
194, 242
Talley, Lynn P., 189–90, 208n25, 221

Tarbell, Ida, 213
TARP. *See* Troubled Assets Relief
Program
Tate, Alfred O., 4
Taylor, Melvin A., 30
Teapot Dome Scandal, 96
Teter, Lucius, 162, 172n12
Thomson-Houston Electric Company,
5, 35
Throop, Allen E., 221
Timmons, Bascom N., 285, 299n1
Tobey, Waldo F., 75, 240
Traylor, Melvin, 34–36, 55, 64, 74,
79; angry depositors and, 184–85;
banker-political boss, 50; Dawes
bank and, 186–87, 189, 200, 205;
Insull, Samuel, Sr., and, 48–51,
77–78; IUI share purchase, 72;
Jones, Jesse H., and, 104, 117, 257;
new Dawes bank plan and, 222, 224,
232; personal fortune, 143; seeking
loans, 164–65; vice-presidency and,
214, 249
trials: fraud and, 152; Insull, Samuel,
Sr., and, 242–43
Troubled Assets Relief Program
(TARP), 273
Truman, Harry, 259
Tumulty, Joseph P., 34

Unemployment Relief Organization, 91
Union Gas and Electric Company, 29,
153
Union Trust Company of Cleveland,
96, 98
United American Trust and Savings
Bank, 144, 160; RFC loans, 147–48
United Gas Improvement Company of
Philadelphia, 65
United Public Service Company of New
Jersey, 72
United Public Utilities Company, 72
University of Chicago Press, 294,
296–97, 301n22

Upham, Cyril B., 289
Utt, John F., 157

Wagner, Edwin L., 153
Waldeck, Herman, 64
Walsh, John R.: Dawes, Charles G. and, 25–28; Dawes bank and, 27–28; imprisonment of, 27; insider abuse and, 27; Insull, Samuel, Sr., and, 26–28; as powerful political player, 26
Walton, Lyman A., 28
Ward, M. M., 166
War Finance Corporation, 88–89, 95, 189
War Industries Board, 33, 95
Warner, Rawleigh, 143, 172n10
Washington Post, 90, 96
Wasik, John F., 292
Waukegan Electric Light Company, 154
Waukegan State Bank, 152–54
Webb, Frank L., 168
Webster, Clarence R., 163
week of hysteria, 154, *155*
Wells Fargo, 276
Western United Gas and Electric Company, 31
Westinghouse Electric and Manufacturing Company, 7–8
We the People (McDonald), 294, 296–98
Wheeler, Burton K., 24, 258
White, Samuel W., 72
Wicker, Elmus, 286–87

Wieboldt, W. A., 150
Wilkerson, James H., 70, 76, 242–43, 251–53
Wilson, Winston P., 183
Wilson, Woodrow, 18, 24, 34, 99–101, 242
Wisconsin Utilities Association, 297-98
Wolf, Charles J., 156
Wolf, Walter, 156
Wood, R. B., 150–51
Woodruff, George, 145, 153, 247
WorldCom financial scandal, xi, xvii, 272; gatekeepers and, xvii–xviii, 270
World Court, 13-14
World War I: credit demands and, 88; land boom and, 9
World War II, 253

Yerby, Dorothy Arnold, 214
Young, Owen, 1, 23, *51*, 186, 228; Chicago World's Fair of 1933 and, 29–31, 233; as Dawes, Charles G. playing card, 30–31, 204, 213–25, 250; insider treatment of, 32–34; Insull, Samuel, Sr., and, 30–33, 48–50, 59, 63–64, 67–68, 79, 83n49; new Dawes bank plan and, 213–24; political power of, 213–14; as "Prince of Friends," 31; profile of, 29–36

Zaharoff, Basil, 241
Zamansky, Jacob H., 271
Zepp, Carl W., 174n26